Charles S. (Charles Seymour) Robinson

Laudes Domini

A Selection of spiritual Songs ancient & modern for use in the Prayer-Meeting

Charles S. (Charles Seymour) Robinson

Laudes Domini

A Selection of spiritual Songs ancient & modern for use in the Prayer-Meeting

ISBN/EAN: 9783337181123

Printed in Europe, USA, Canada, Australia, Japan

Cover: Foto ©Thomas Meinert / pixelio.de

More available books at **www.hansebooks.com**

LAUDES DOMINI

A SELECTION OF
SPIRITUAL SONGS
ANCIENT & MODERN

FOR USE IN THE

PRAYER-MEETING

EDITED BY
CHAS. S. ROBINSON, D. D., LL. D.

NEW YORK
THE CENTURY CO.

THE books of the Laudes Domini Series are now offered to the Christian public for use in all the departments of religious work and devotion: I. Laudes Domini for the Church and the Choir; II. Laudes Domini abridged for Chapels and smaller Churches, for High Schools, Colleges, and Seminaries; III. Laudes Domini for the Prayer-Meeting; IV. Laudes Domini for the Sunday School. It is believed that the use of such a series of Manuals in the singing of the people, young and old together, will at once elevate the taste and increase the interest of all.

COPYRIGHT, 1884, BY THE CENTURY CO.

COPYRIGHT, 1887, BY THE CENTURY CO.

COPYRIGHT, 1888, BY THE CENTURY CO.

COPYRIGHT, 1890, BY THE CENTURY CO.

SPECIAL COPYRIGHT NOTICE.

The Publishers deem it necessary to call attention to the fact that in addition to the many tunes, musical arrangements, hymns and adaptations in this volume owned and copyrighted by them, many others are used by the permission of other publishers and owners of the copyrights. Among these are Nos. 62, 280, 286, 298, 299, 300, 318, 341, 384, 442, 448, by Drs. Bradbury, Lowry and Doane, belonging to Messrs. Biglow & Main. All rights of republication are reserved, and will be defended by the owners of the copyrights.

MUSIC IN PRAYER-MEETINGS: PREFACE.

ONE reason why the music in many prayer-meetings gives so little assistance in the worship, is found in the worn-out familiarity of the hymns and tunes employed. There is no growth in the exercise. What is wanted is a wider range and a fresher adaptation. But the prayer-meetings are destroyed the moment one undertakes to make singing-classes of them; an instructor is given to the Sunday-school, and the choir lead in the sanctuary, but help must come from outside in this case. No adequate chance for increase is offered, unless the experiences of Sabbath success can be taken into the week-day monotony.

Then, on the other hand, one reason why the music on the Lord's Day has often so feeble a force, is found in its exclusiveness as a thing of high art. It remains too far out of reach of the congregation. What is wanted is a common source of instruction; then the same tunes being used, and so being taught and becoming familiar, and the same hymns being learned and becoming usable, the Sunday-school and the choir will unite their wonderful help in rendering the prayer-meetings welcome by a new ring of reality in the praises of the Lord Christ.

Both of these ends will, therefore, be best secured by the constant use of the same manual for all the services. Then the skill of trained singers in the sanctuary will tell on the social meetings; and the painstaking drill of the Sabbath-school will give aid; and the education of the whole people will react powerfully upon the worship everywhere; and work will be delightful when it is inspirited by rhythm like that of singing sailors on the sea.

CHARLES SEYMOUR ROBINSON.

New York: 57 East Fifty-fourth Street.
    June 1, 1890.

ORDER OF ARRANGEMENT.

	HYMN.
MORNING WORSHIP	1— 7
THE LORD'S DAY	8— 14
GENERAL PRAISE	15— 30
PRAYER AND INVOCATION	31— 65
CLOSE OF SERVICE	30—102
THE HOLY SCRIPTURES	103—114
GOD: THE ALMIGHTY FATHER	115—136

THE LORD JESUS CHRIST:—

INCARNATION AND BIRTH	137—146
LIFE AND CHARACTER	147—159
SUFFERINGS AND DEATH	160—170
RESURRECTION AND REIGN	171—180
EXALTATION AND OFFICES	181—184
COMING AGAIN	185—199

THE HOLY SPIRIT	200—219

THE GOSPEL ATONEMENT:—

NEEDED; MAN'S LOST STATE	220—229
PROVIDED; PLAN OF SALVATION	230—244
OFFERED; INVITATIONS	245—257
ACCEPTED; REPENTANCE	258—288

THE CHRISTIAN LIFE:—

	HYMN.
CONFLICT WITH SIN	289—323
COURAGE AND CHEER	324—373
COMMUNION WITH CHRIST	374—417
GRACES OF THE SPIRIT	418—429
PRIVILEGES OF BELIEVERS	430—449
DISCIPLINE AND SORROW	450—458
ACTIVITY AND ZEAL	459—484

THE CHURCH OF GOD:—

CHRISTIAN FELLOWSHIP	485—490
THE SUNDAY-SCHOOL	491—497
THE LORD'S SUPPER	498—512
MISSIONS AND GROWTH	513—537

THE CHRISTIAN'S DEATH	538—548
THE GENERAL JUDGMENT	549—552
THE REST OF HEAVEN	553—572
MISCELLANEOUS	573—579

INDEXES:—

OF TUNES	235
OF SUBJECTS	236
OF FIRST LINES	238

LAUDES DOMINI

1 *Praise to Christ.*
WHEN morning gilds the skies,
My heart awaking cries,
  May Jesus Christ be praised:
Alike at work and prayer,
To Jesus I repair;
  May Jesus Christ be praised.

2 To thee, O God, above,
I cry with glowing love,
  May Jesus Christ be praised:
This song of sacred joy,
It never seems to cloy:
  May Jesus Christ be praised.

3 Does sadness fill my mind,
A solace here I find;
  May Jesus Christ be praised:
Or fades my earthly bliss,
My comfort still is this:
  May Jesus Christ be praised.

4 When evil thoughts molest,
With this I shield my breast:
  May Jesus Christ be praised:
The powers of darkness fear,
When this sweet chant I hear:
  May Jesus Christ be praised.

5 When sleep her balm denies,
My silent spirit sighs,
  May Jesus Christ be praised:
The night becomes as day,
When from the heart we say,
  May Jesus Christ be praised.

6 Be this, while life is mine,
My canticle divine,
  May Jesus Christ be praised:
Be this the eternal song,
Through all the ages long:
  May Jesus Christ be praised.
                E. Caswall, tr.

MORNING WORSHIP.

NICAEA. P. M.   J. B. Dykes.

2
The triune God.

HOLY, holy, holy, Lord God Almighty!
  Early in the morning our song shall rise to thee;
Holy, holy, holy, merciful and mighty,
  God in three persons, blessèd Trinity!

2 Holy, holy, holy! all the saints adore thee,
  Casting down their golden crowns around the glassy sea;
Cherubim and seraphim falling down before thee,
  Which wert and art and evermore shalt be.

3 Holy, holy, holy! though the darkness hide thee,
  Though the eye of sinful man thy glory may not see;
Only thou art holy; there is none beside thee,
  Perfect in power, in love and purity.

4 Holy, holy, holy! Lord God Almighty!
  All thy works shall praise thy name, in earth and sky and sea;
Holy, holy, holy, merciful and mighty;
  God in three persons, blessèd Trinity!
Reginald Heber.

HALLE. 7s, 6l.   Arr. by T. Hastings.

3
The Day-Star.

CHRIST, whose glory fills the skies,
  Christ, the true, the only light,
Sun of Righteousness, arise,
  Triumph o'er the shades of night;
Day-spring from on high, be near,
Day-star in my heart appear.

2 Dark and cheerless is the morn,
  If thy light is hid from me;
Joyless is the day's return,
  Till thy mercy's beams I see;
Till they inward light impart,
Warmth and gladness to my heart.

3 Visit, then, this soul of mine,
  Pierce the gloom of sin and grief;
Fill me, radiant Sun divine!
  Scatter all my unbelief;
More and more thyself display,
Shining to the perfect day.
Charles Wesley.

MORNING WORSHIP.

WARWICK. C. M.   S. STANLEY.

Lord! in the morn-ing thou shalt hear My voice as-cend-ing high; To thee will I di-rect my prayer, To thee lift up mine eye:—

4   *Psalm 5.*

Lord! in the morning thou shalt hear
  My voice ascending high;
To thee will I direct my prayer,
  To thee lift up mine eye:—

2 Up to the hills, where Christ has gone
  To plead for all his saints,
Presenting at his Father's throne,
  Our songs and our complaints.

3 Thou art a God, before whose sight,
  The wicked shall not stand;

Sinners shall ne'er be thy delight,
  Nor dwell at thy right hand.

4 But to thy house will I resort,
  To taste thy mercies there;
I will frequent thy holy court,
  And worship in thy fear.

5 Oh, may thy Spirit guide my feet,
  In ways of righteousness;
Make every path of duty straight,
  And plain before my face.
                 Isaac Watts.

MEAR. C. M.   A. WILLIAMS.

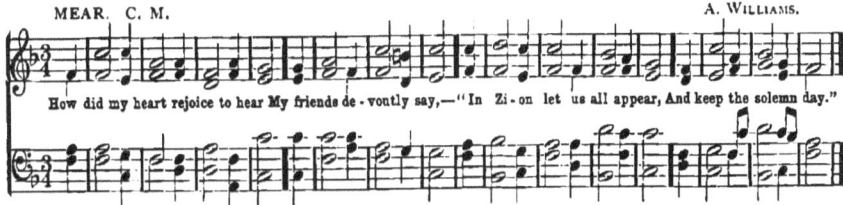

How did my heart rejoice to hear My friends de-voutly say,—"In Zi-on let us all appear, And keep the solemn day."

5   *Psalm 122.*

How DID my heart rejoice to hear
  My friends devoutly say,—
"In Zion let us all appear,
  And keep the solemn day."

2 I love her gates, I love the road;
  The Church, adorned with grace,
Stands like a palace built for God,
  To show his milder face.

3 Up to her courts, with joys unknown,
  The holy tribes repair;

The Son of David holds his throne,
  And sits in judgment there.

4 Peace be within this sacred place,
  And joy a constant guest;
With holy gifts and heavenly grace,
  Be her attendants blest.

5 My soul shall pray for Zion still,
  While life or breath remains;
There my best friends, my kindred dwell,
  There God, my Saviour reigns.
                 Isaac Watts.

MORNING WORSHIP.

LOWRY. L. M.   G. F. Root.

A-wake, my soul, and with the sun Thy dai-ly stage of du-ty run;
Shake off dull sloth, and joy-ful rise To pay thy morn-ing sac-ri-fice.

6   *Morning.*

Awake, my soul, and with the sun
Thy daily stage of duty run;
Shake off dull sloth, and joyful rise
To pay thy morning sacrifice.

2 Awake, lift up thyself, my heart,
And with the angels bear thy part,
Who all night long unwearied sing
High praises to the eternal King.

3 Glory to thee, who safe hast kept,
And hast refreshed me when I slept;
Grant, Lord, when I from death shall wake,
I may of endless life partake.

4 Lord, I my vows to thee renew:
Scatter my sins as morning dew;
Guard my first springs of thought and will,
And with thyself my Spirit fill.

5 Direct, control, suggest, this day,
All I design, or do or say;
That all my powers, with all their might,
In thy sole glory may unite.
                                 Thomas Ken.

7   *Psalm 92.*

Sweet is the work, my God, my King!
To praise thy name, give thanks, and sing;
To show thy love by morning light,
And talk of all thy truth at night.

2 Sweet is the day of sacred rest;
No mortal cares shall seize my breast;
Oh! may my heart in tune be found,
Like David's harp of solemn sound!

3 My heart shall triumph in my Lord,
And bless his works, and bless his word;
Thy works of grace, how bright they shine!
How deep thy counsels! how divine!

4 Lord! I shall share a glorious part,
When grace hath well refined my heart,
And fresh supplies of joy are shed,
Like holy oil to cheer my head.

5 Then shall I see, and hear, and know
All I desired or wished below;
And every power find sweet employ,
In that eternal world of joy.
                                 Isaac Watts.

CANONBURY. L. M.   Arr. fr. Schumann.

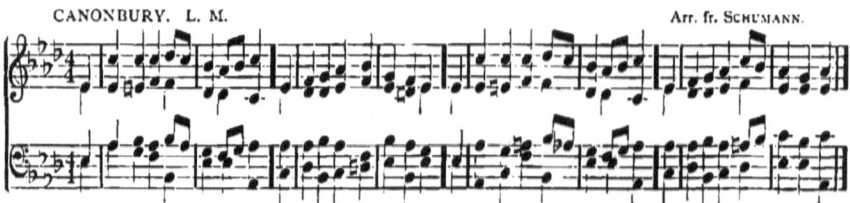

THE LORD'S DAY.

MIGDOL. L. M.   LOWELL MASON.

How pleasant, how di-vine-ly fair, O Lord of hosts! thy dwellings are!
With long de-sire my spir-it faints, To meet th'as-sem-blies of thy saints.

8   *Psalm 84.*

How PLEASANT, how divinely fair,
O Lord of hosts! thy dwellings are!
With long desire my Spirit faints,
To meet the assemblies of thy saints.

2 My flesh would rest in thine abode,
My panting heart cries out for God;
My God! my King! why should I be
So far from all my joys, and thee?

3 Blest are the saints who sit on high,
Around thy throne of majesty;
Thy brightest glories shine above,
And all their work is praise and love.

4 Blest are the souls who find a place
Within the temple of thy grace;
There they behold thy gentler rays,
And seek thy face, and learn thy praise.

5 Cheerful they walk with growing strength,
Till all shall meet in heaven at length;
Till all before thy face appear,
And join in nobler worship there.
Isaac Watts.

9   *Each day's Duties.*

NEW every morning is the love
Our wakening and uprising prove;
Through sleep and darkness safely brought,
Restored to life, and power, and thought.

2 New mercies, each returning day,
Hover around us while we pray;
New perils past, new sins forgiven,
New thoughts of God, new hopes of heaven.

3 If, on our daily course, our mind
Be set to hallow all we find,
New treasures still, of countless price,
God will provide for sacrifice.

4 The trivial round, the common task,
Will furnish all we need to ask,
Room to deny ourselves, a road
To bring us daily nearer God.

5 Only, O Lord! in thy dear love
Fit us for perfect rest above;
And help us, this and every day,
To live more nearly as we pray.
John Keble.

10   *"A nobler Rest."*

THINE earthly Sabbaths, Lord, we love,
But there's a nobler rest above;
To that our longing souls aspire,
With cheerful hope and strong desire.

2 No more fatigue, no more distress,
Nor sin nor death shall reach the place;
No groans shall mingle with the songs
That warble from immortal tongues.

3 No rude alarms of raging foes,
No cares to break the long repose,
No midnight shade, no clouded sun,
But sacred, high, eternal noon.

4 O long-expected day, begin!
Dawn on these realms of woe and sin;
Fain would we leave this weary road,
And sleep in death to rest with God.
Philip Doddridge.

THE LORD'S DAY.

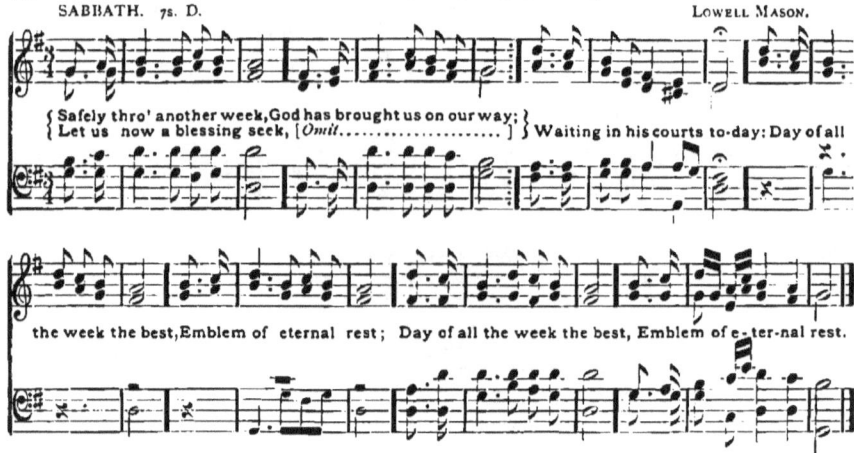

SABBATH. 7s. D. — LOWELL MASON.

Safely thro' another week, God has brought us on our way; Let us now a blessing seek, [Omit......] Waiting in his courts to-day: Day of all the week the best, Emblem of eternal rest; Day of all the week the best, Emblem of eternal rest.

11 *Sabbath Morning.*

SAFELY through another week,
  God has brought us on our way;
Let us now a blessing seek,
  Waiting in his courts to-day:
Day of all the week the best,
Emblem of eternal rest.

2 While we seek supplies of grace,
  Through the dear Redeemer's name;
Show thy reconciling face,—
  Take away our sin and shame;
From our worldly cares set free,—
May we rest this day in thee.

3 Here we come thy name to praise;
  Let us feel thy presence near;
May thy glory meet our eyes,
  While we in thy house appear:
Here afford us, Lord, a taste
Of our everlasting feast.

4 May thy gospel's joyful sound
  Conquer sinners, comfort saints;
Make the fruits of grace abound,
  Bring relief for all complaints:
Thus let all our Sabbaths prove,
Till we rest in thee above.
John Newton.

LISBON. S. M. — D. READ.

Welcome, sweet day of rest, That saw the Lord a-rise! Welcome to this re-viv-ing breast, And these rejoic-ing eyes!

12 *Psalm 84.*

WELCOME, sweet day of rest,
  That saw the Lord arise!
Welcome to this reviving breast,
  And these rejoicing eyes!

2 The King himself comes near,
  And feasts his saints to-day;
Here may we sit and see him here,
  And love, and praise, and pray.

3 One day, amid the place
  Where my dear Lord hath been,
Is sweeter than ten thousand days
  Within the tents of sin.

4 My willing soul would stay
  In such a frame as this,
And sit and sing herself away
  To everlasting bliss.
Isaac Watts.

THE LORD'S DAY.

13 *"Day of Rest."*
O DAY of rest and gladness,
 O day of joy and light,
O balm of care and sadness,
 Most beautiful, most bright;
On thee, the high and lowly,
 Bending before the throne,
Sing, Holy, Holy, Holy,
 To the Great Three in One.

2 To-day on weary nations
 The heavenly manna falls;
To holy convocations
 The silver trumpet calls,
Where gospel light is glowing
 With pure and radiant beams,
And living water flowing
 With soul-refreshing streams.

3 New graces ever gaining
 From this our day of rest,
We reach the rest remaining
 To spirits of the blest.
To Holy Ghost be praises,
 To Father and to Son;
The Church her voice upraises
 To thee, blest Three in One.
 C. Wordsworth.

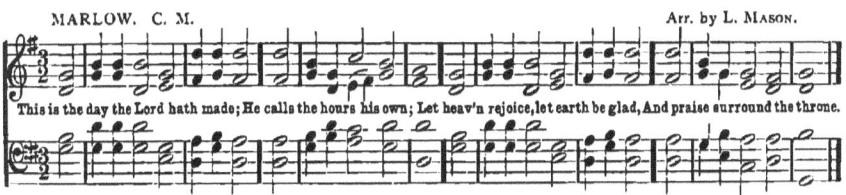

14 *Psalm 118.*
THIS is the day the Lord hath made;
 He calls the hours his own;
Let heaven rejoice, let earth be glad,
 And praise surround the throne.

2 To-day he rose, and left the dead,
 And Satan's empire fell;
To-day the saints his triumph spread,
 And all his wonders tell.

3 Hosanna to the anointed King,
 To David's only Son;
Help us, O Lord; descend, and bring
 Salvation from thy throne.

4 Blest be the Lord who comes to men
 With messages of grace;
Who comes, in God his Father's name,
 To save our sinful race.

5 Hosanna in the highest strains
 The church on earth can raise;
The highest heavens, in which he reigns,
 Shall give him nobler praise.
 Isaac Watts.

GENERAL PRAISE.

OLD HUNDRED. L. M.   G. FRANC.

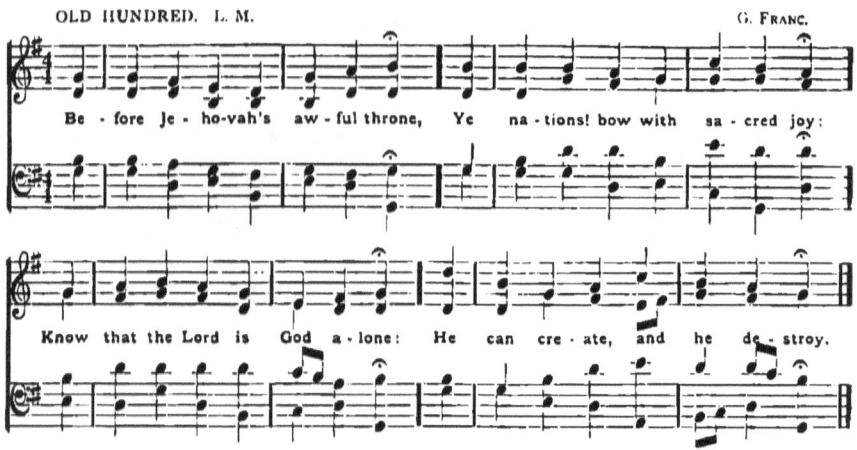

Be - fore Je - ho-vah's aw - ful throne, Ye na - tions! bow with sa - cred joy:
Know that the Lord is God a - lone: He can cre - ate, and he de - stroy.

15   *Psalm 100.*
BEFORE Jehovah's awful throne,
  Ye nations! bow with sacred joy:
Know that the Lord is God alone:
  He can create, and he destroy.

2 His sovereign power, without our aid,
  Made us of clay, and formed us men;
And when, like wandering sheep, we strayed,
  He brought us to his fold again.

3 We are his people, we his care,—
  Our souls, and all our mortal frame:
What lasting honors shall we rear,
  Almighty Maker! to thy name?

4 We'll crowd thy gates with thankful songs,
  High as the heavens our voices raise;
And earth, with her ten thousand tongues,
  Shall fill thy courts with sounding praise.

5 Wide as the world is thy command,
  Vast as eternity, thy love;
Firm as a rock thy truth must stand,
  When rolling years shall cease to move.
Isaac Watts.

16   *Psalm 100.*
ALL people that on earth do dwell,
  Sing to the Lord with cheerful voice:
Him serve with mirth, his praise forth tell,
  Come ye before him and rejoice.

2 Know that the Lord is God indeed;
  Without our aid he did us make:
We are his flock, he doth us feed,
  And for his sheep he doth us take.

3 Oh, enter then his gates with praise,
  Approach with joy his courts unto:
Praise, laud, and bless his name always,
  For it is seemly so to do.

4 For why? the Lord our God is good,
  His mercy is for ever sure;
His truth at all times firmly stood,
  And shall from age to age endure.
William Kethe.

17   *Doxology.*
PRAISE God, from whom all blessings flow;
Praise him, all creatures here below;
Praise him above, ye heavenly host;
Praise Father, Son, and Holy Ghost.
Thomas Ken.

18   *Doxology.*
TO GOD the Father, God the Son,
And God the Spirit, Three in One,
Be honor, praise, and glory given,
By all on earth, and all in heaven.
Isaac Watts.

19   *Psalm 117.*
FROM all that dwell below the skies,
  Let the Creator's praise arise:
Let the Redeemer's name be sung,
  Through every land, by every tongue.

2 Eternal are thy mercies, Lord!
  Eternal truth attends thy word:
Thy praise shall sound from shore to shore,
  Till sun shall rise and set no more.
Isaac Watts.

GENERAL PRAISE.

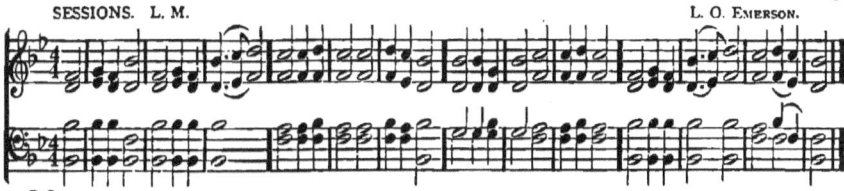

20 *Psalm 65.*

Praise, Lord, for thee in Zion waits;
Prayer shall besiege thy temple gates;
All flesh shall to thy throne repair,
And find, through Christ, salvation there.

2 How blest thy saints! how safely led!
How surely kept! how richly fed!
Saviour of all in earth and sea,
How happy they who rest in thee!

3 Thy hand sets fast the mighty hills,
Thy voice the troubled ocean stills;
Evening and morning hymn thy praise,
And earth thy bounty wide displays.

4 The year is with thy goodness crowned;
Thy clouds drop wealth the world around;
Through thee the deserts laugh and sing,
And nature smiles and owns her King.

5 Lord, on our souls thy Spirit pour;
The moral waste within restore;
Oh, let thy love our spring-tide be,
And make us all bear fruit to thee.
Henry F. Lyte.

21 *Psalm 146.*

I'll praise my Maker with my breath,
And, when my voice is lost in death,
  Praise shall employ my nobler powers:
My days of praise shall ne'er be past,
While life, and thought, and being last,
  Or immortality endures.

2 Happy the man, whose hopes rely
On Israel's God;—he made the sky,
  And earth, and seas, with all their train:
His truth for ever stands secure;
He saves the oppressed, he feeds the poor;
  And none shall find his promise vain.

3 He loves his saints—he knows them well,
But turns the wicked down to hell:
  Thy God, O Zion! ever reigns;
Let every tongue, let every age,
In this exalted work engage:
  Praise him in everlasting strains.

4 I'll praise him while he lends me breath,
And, when my voice is lost in death,
  Praise shall employ my nobler powers:
My days of praise shall ne'er be past,
While life, and thought, and being last,
  Or immortality endures.
Isaac Watts.

GENERAL PRAISE.

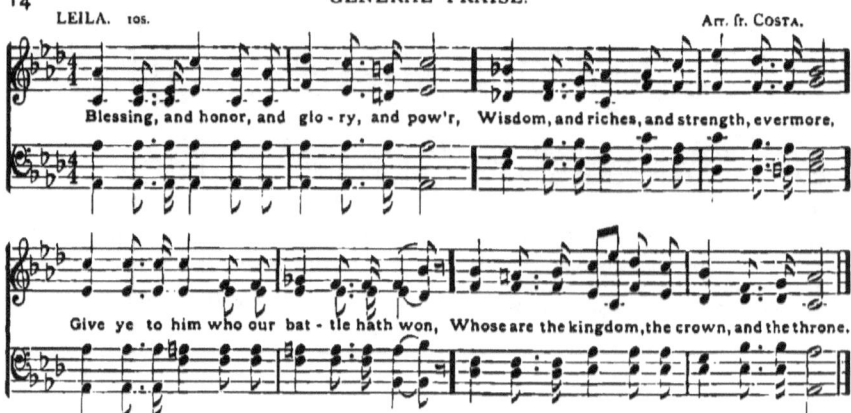

22   *Glory to the Lamb.*

BLESSING, and honor, and glory, and power,
Wisdom, and riches, and strength, evermore,
Give ye to him who our battle hath won,
Whose are the kingdom, the crown, and
   the throne.

2 Dwelleth the light of the glory with him,
Light of a glory that cannot grow dim,
Light in its silence and beauty and calm,
Light in its gladness and brightness and
   balm.

3 Ever ascendeth the song and the joy,
Ever descendeth the love from on high,

Blessing, and honor, and glory, and praise,
This is the theme of the hymns that we
   raise.

4 Life of all life, and true Light of all light,
Star of the dawning, unchangingly bright,
Sun of the Salem whose lamp is the Lamb,
Theme of the ever-new, ever-glad psalm!

5 Give we the glory and praise to the Lamb,
Take we the robe and the harp and the
   palm,
Sing we the song of the Lamb that was slain,
Dying in weakness, but rising to reign.
Horatius Bonar.

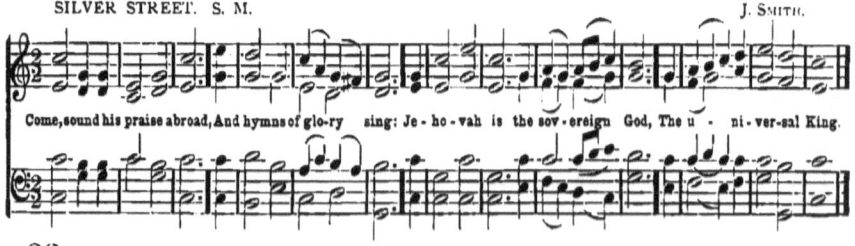

23   *Psalm 95.*

COME, sound his praise abroad,
   And hymns of glory sing:
Jehovah is the sovereign God,
   The universal King.

2 He formed the deeps unknown;
   He gave the seas their bound;
The watery worlds are all his own,
   And all the solid ground.

3 Come, worship at his throne,
   Come, bow before the Lord:
We are his work, and not our own,
   He formed us by his word.

4 To-day attend his voice,
   Nor dare provoke his rod;
Come, like the people of his choice,
   And own our gracious God.
Isaac Watts.

GENERAL PRAISE.

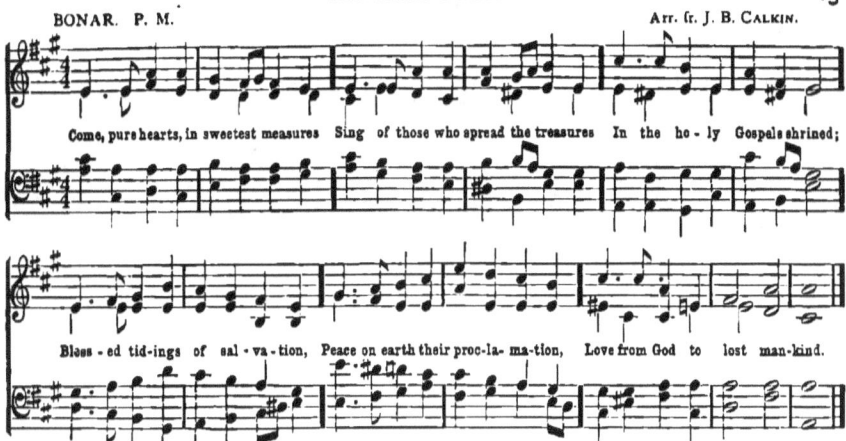

24 *Wells of Salvation.*

COME, pure hearts, in sweetest measures
Sing of those who spread the treasures
  In the holy Gospels shrined;
Blessèd tidings of salvation,
Peace on earth their proclamation,
  Love from God to lost mankind.

2 See the rivers four that gladden
With their streams the better Eden
  Planted by our Lord most dear;
Christ the fountain, these the waters;
Drink, O Zion's sons and daughters,
  Drink and find salvation here.

3 Oh, that we, thy truth confessing,
And thy holy word possessing,
  Jesus, may thy love adore;
Unto thee our voices raising,
Thee with all thy ransomed praising,
  Ever and for evermore.
                            R. Campbell, tr.

25 *"Deliver us from evil."*

FATHER, in high heaven dwelling,
May our evening song be telling
  Of thy mercy large and free:
Through the day thy love hath fed us,
Through the day thy care hath led us,
  With divinest charity.

2 This day's sins, oh, pardon, Saviour!
Evil thoughts, perverse behavior,
  Envy, pride, and vanity;
From all evil us deliver;
Save us now, and save us ever,
  O thou Lamb of Calvary!

3 Whilst the night-dews are distilling,
Holy Ghost, each heart be filling
  With thine own serenity;
Softly let our eyes be closing,
Loving souls on thee reposing,
  Ever-blessèd Trinity.
                            George Rawson.

26 *Evening Song.*

UPWARD where the stars are burning,
Silent, silent in their turning,
  Round the never changing pole;
Upward where the sky is brightest,
Upward where the blue is lightest,—
  Lift I now my longing soul.

2 Far beyond the arch of gladness,
Far beyond these clouds of sadness,
  Are the many mansions fair:
Far from pain and sin and folly,
In that palace of the holy—
  I would find my mansion there.

3 Where the Lamb on high is seated,
By ten thousand voices greeted:
  Lord of lords, and King of kings!
Son of man, they crown, they crown him,
Son of God, they own, they own him,
  With his name the palace rings.

4 Blessing, honor, without measure,
Heavenly riches, earthly treasure,
  Lay we at his blessèd feet:
Poor the praise that now we render,
Loud shall be our voices yonder,
  When before his throne we meet.
                            Horatius Bonar.

GENERAL PRAISE.

27 *"Immanuel's Ground."*

Come, we who love the Lord,
  And let our joys be known;
Join in a song of sweet accord,
  And thus surround the throne.

2 Let those refuse to sing
  Who never knew our God;
But children of the heavenly King
  May speak their joys abroad.

3 The men of grace have found
  Glory begun below;
Celestial fruits on earthly ground
  From faith and hope may grow.

4 The hill of Zion yields
  A thousand sacred sweets
Before we reach the heavenly fields,
  Or walk the golden streets.

5 Then let our songs abound,
  And every tear be dry;
We're marching through Immanuel's ground
  To fairer worlds on high.
  Isaac Watts.

28 *"Worthy the Lamb."*

Sing we the song of those who stand
  Around the eternal throne,
Of every kindred, clime, and land,
  A multitude unknown.

2 Life's poor distinctions vanish here:
  To-day the young, the old,
Our Saviour and his flock appear
  One Shepherd and one fold.

3 Toil, trial, sufferings still await
  On earth the pilgrim throng;
Yet learn we in our low estate
  The Church Triumphant's song.

4 "Worthy the Lamb for sinners slain,"—
  Cry the redeemed above;
"Blessing and honor to obtain,
  And everlasting love!"

5 "Worthy the Lamb," on earth we sing,
  "Who died our souls to save!
Henceforth, O Death! where is thy sting?
  Thy victory, O Grave!"
  James Montgomery.

GENERAL PRAISE.

ST. THOMAS. S. M. — WILLIAM TANSUR.

How charming is the place Where my Re-deem-er, God, Unvails the beauty of his face, And sheds his love abroad!

29 *The Sanctuary.*
How CHARMING is the place
  Where my Redeemer, God,
Unvails the beauty of his face,
  And sheds his love abroad!

2 Not the fair palaces,
  To which the great resort,
Are once to be compared with this,
  Where Jesus holds his court.

3 Here on the mercy-seat,
  With radiant glory crowned,
Our joyful eyes behold him sit
  And smile on all around.

4 Give me, O Lord, a place
  Within thy blest abode,
Among the children of thy grace,
  The servants of my God.
    Samuel Stennett.

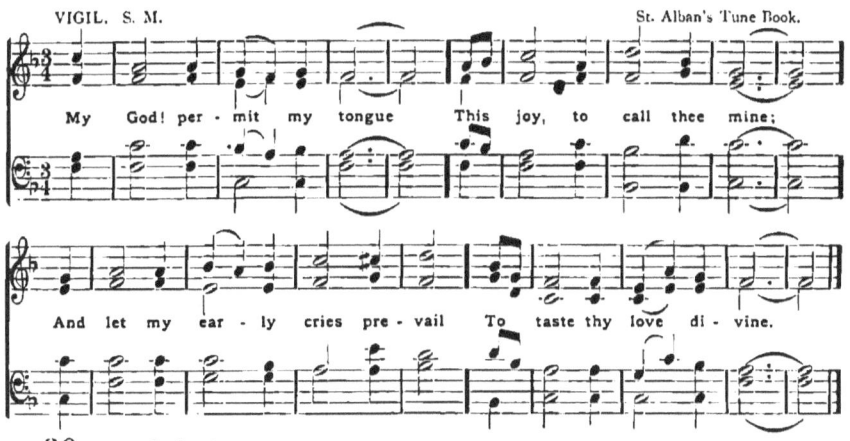

VIGIL. S. M. — St. Alban's Tune Book.

My God! per-mit my tongue This joy, to call thee mine; And let my ear-ly cries pre-vail To taste thy love di-vine.

30 *Psalm 63.*
My God! permit my tongue
  This joy, to call thee mine;
And let my early cries prevail
  To taste thy love divine.

2 My thirsty fainting soul
  Thy mercy doth implore;
Not travelers, in desert lands,
  Can pant for water more.

3 For life, without thy love,
  No relish can afford;
No joy can be compared to this,
  To serve and please the Lord.

4 In wakeful hours at night,
  I call my God to mind;
I think how wise thy counsels are,
  And all thy dealings kind.

5 Since thou hast been my help,
  To thee my spirit flies;
And, on thy watchful providence,
  My cheerful hope relies.

6 The shadow of thy wings
  My soul in safety keeps;
I follow where my Father leads,
  And he supports my steps.
    Isaac Watts.

2 P

PRAYER AND INVOCATION.

WOODSTOCK. C. M. — D. DUTTON.

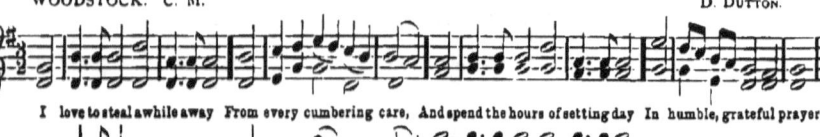

31 *Retirement.*

I love to steal awhile away
  From every cumbering care,
And spend the hours of setting day
  In humble, grateful prayer.

2 I love in solitude to shed
  The penitential tear,
And all his promises to plead,
  Where none but God can hear.

3 I love to think on mercies past,
  And future good implore,
And all my cares and sorrows cast
  On him whom I adore.

4 I love by faith to take a view
  Of brighter scenes in heaven;
The prospect doth my strength renew,
  While here by tempests driven.

5 Thus, when life's toilsome day is o'er,
  May its departing ray
Be calm as this impressive hour,
  And lead to endless day.
                      Mrs. Phoebe H. Brown.

SOUTHPORT. C. M. — GEO. KINGSLEY.

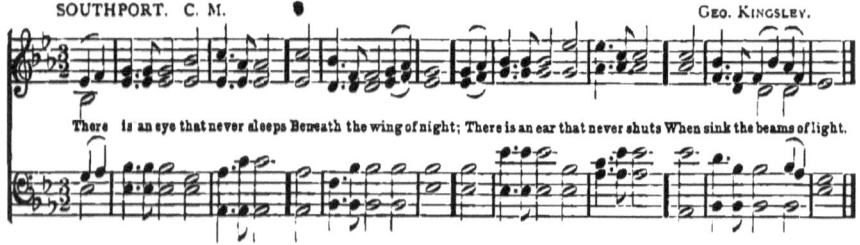

32 *Prayer has power.*

THERE is an eye that never sleeps
  Beneath the wing of night;
There is an ear that never shuts
  When sink the beams of light.

2 There is an arm that never tires,
  When human strength gives way;
There is a love that never fails,
  When earthly loves decay.

3 That eye is fixed on seraph throngs;
  That arm upholds the sky;
That ear is filled with angel songs;
  That love is throned on high.

4 But there's a power which man can wield
  When mortal aid is vain,
That eye, that arm, that love to reach,
  That listening ear to gain.

5 That power is prayer, which soars on high,
  Through Jesus, to the throne;
And moves the hand which moves the world,
  To bring salvation down!
                      John A. Wallace.

33 *"Two or three."*

WHEREVER two or three may meet,
  To worship in thy name,
Bending beneath thy mercy-seat,
  This promise they may claim:—

2 Jesus in love will condescend
  To bless the hallowed place;
The Saviour will himself attend,
  And show his smiling face.

3 How bright the assurance! gracious Lord,
  Fountain of peace and love,
Fulfill to us thy precious word,
  Thy loving-kindness prove.
                      Thomas Hastings.

PRAYER AND INVOCATION.

34   *"Come, Lord."*

Come, thou Desire of all thy saints!
  Our humble strains attend,
While with our praises and complaints,
  Low at thy feet we bend.

2 How should our songs, like those above,
  With warm devotion rise!
How should our souls, on wings of love,
  Mount upward to the skies!

3 Come, Lord! thy love alone can raise
  In us the heavenly flame;
Then shall our lips resound thy praise,
  Our hearts adore thy name.

4 Dear Saviour, let thy glory shine,
  And fill thy dwellings here,
Till life, and love, and joy divine
  A heaven on earth appear.
Anne Steele.

35   *Sincerity.*

Lord! when we bend before thy throne,
  And our confessions pour,
Oh, may we feel the sins we own,
  And hate what we deplore.

2 Our contrite spirits pitying see;
  True penitence impart:
And let a healing ray from thee
  Beam hope on every heart.

3 When we disclose our wants in prayer,
  May we our wills resign;
Nor let a thought our bosom share,
  Which is not wholly thine.

4 Let faith each meek petition fill,
  And waft it to the skies;
And teach our heart 't is goodness still
  That grants it or denies.
Jos. Dacre Carlyle.

PRAYER AND INVOCATION.

FARRANT. C. M.   R. FARRANT.

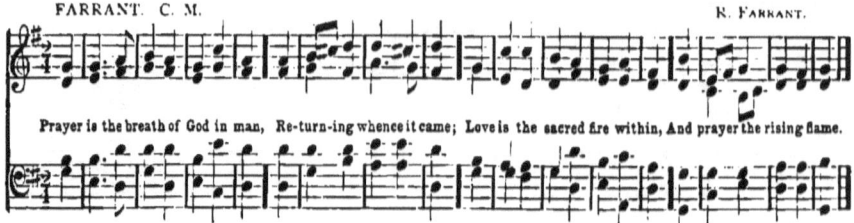

36   *"The sacred fire."*
PRAYER is the breath of God in man,
  Returning whence it came;
Love is the sacred fire within,
  And prayer the rising flame.

2 It gives the burdened spirit ease,
  And soothes the troubled breast;
Yields comfort to the mourning soul,
  And to the weary rest.

3 When God inclines the heart to pray,
  He hath an ear to hear;
To him there's music in a sigh,
  And beauty in a tear.

4 The humble suppliant cannot fail
  To have his wants supplied,
Since he for sinners intercedes,
  Who once for sinners died.
                Benjamin Beddome.

37   *Retirement.*
FAR from the world, O Lord, I flee,
  From strife and tumult far;
From scenes where Satan wages still
  His most successful war.

2 The calm retreat, the silent shade,
  With prayer and praise agree;
And seem by thy great bounty made
  For those who follow thee.

3 There, if thy Spirit touch the soul,
  And grace her mean abode;
Oh! with what peace, and joy, and love,
  She then communes with God.

4 Author and Guardian of my life!
  Sweet Source of light divine,
And—all harmonious names in one—
  My Saviour!—thou art mine!
                William Cowper.

BYEFIELD. C. M.   THOS. HASTINGS.

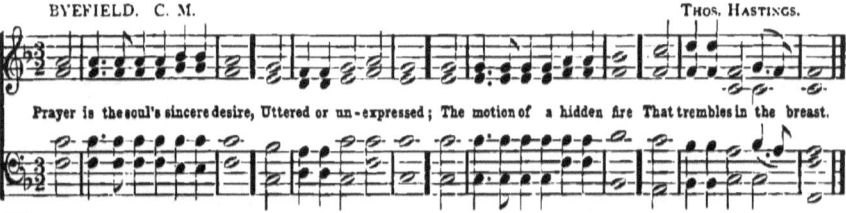

38   *"Behold he prays."*
PRAYER is the soul's sincere desire,
  Uttered or unexpressed;
The motion of a hidden fire
  That trembles in the breast.

2 Prayer is the burden of a sigh,
  The falling of a tear,
The upward glancing of an eye,
  When none but God is near.

3 Prayer is the simplest form of speech
  That infant lips can try;
Prayer the sublimest strains that reach
  The Majesty on high.

4 Prayer is the Christian's vital breath,
  The Christian's native air:
His watchword at the gates of death—
  He enters heaven with prayer.

5 Prayer is the contrite sinner's voice,
  Returning from his ways;
While angels in their songs rejoice,
  And cry—"Behold he prays!"

6 O thou, by whom we come to God—
  The Life, the Truth, the Way;
The path of prayer thyself hast trod;
  Lord! teach us how to pray.
                James Montgomery.

PRAYER AND INVOCATION.

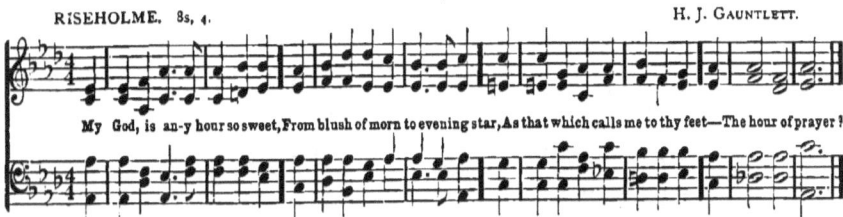

39 *The hour of prayer.*

My God, is any hour so sweet,
From blush of morn to evening star,
As that which calls me to thy feet—
The hour of prayer?

2 Then is my strength by thee renewed;
Then are my sins by thee forgiven;
Then dost thou cheer my solitude,
With hopes of heaven.

3 No words can tell what sweet relief
Here for my every want I find:
What strength for warfare, balm for grief,
What peace of mind!

4 Hushed is each doubt, gone every fear;
My spirit seems in heaven to stay;
And ev'n the penitential tear
Is wiped away.

5 Lord, till I reach yon blissful shore,
No privilege so dear shall be
As thus my inmost soul to pour
In prayer to thee.
Charlotte Elliott.

40 *Evening psalm.*

THREE in One, and One in Three,
Ruler of the earth and sea,
Hear us, while we lift to thee
  Holy chant and psalm.

2 Light of lights; with morning, shine;
Lift on us thy light divine;
And let charity benign
  Breathe on us her balm.

3 Light of lights; when falls the even,
Let it close on sin forgiven;
Fold us in the peace of heaven,
  Shed a vesper calm.

4 Three in One, and One in Three,
Darkling here we worship thee;
With the saints hereafter we
  Hope to bear the palm.
Gilbert Rorison.

41 *Jesus, have mercy.*

LORD of mercy and of might,
Of mankind the life and light,
Maker, Teacher, Infinite;
  Jesus, hear and save!

2 Strong Creator, Saviour mild,
Humbled to a mortal child,
Captive, beaten, bound, reviled;
  Jesus, hear and save!

3 Throned above celestial things,
Borne aloft on angels' wings,
Lord of lords, and King of kings,
  Jesus, hear and save!

4 Soon to come to earth again,
Judge of angels and of men,
Hear us now, and hear us then,
  Jesus, hear and save!
Reginald Heber.

PRAYER AND INVOCATION.

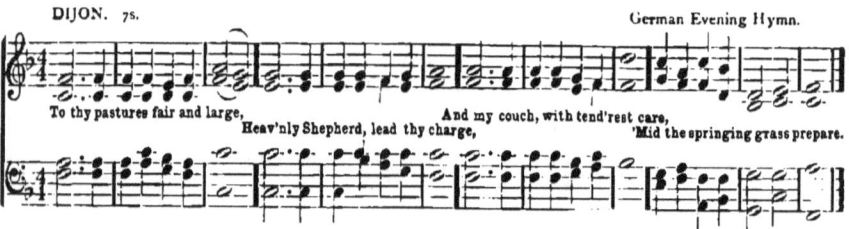

DIJON. 7s.   German Evening Hymn.

42   *Psalm 23.*
To THY pastures fair and large,
 Heavenly Shepherd, lead thy charge,
And my couch, with tenderest care,
 'Mid the springing grass prepare.

2 When I faint with summer's heat,
 Thou shalt guide my weary feet
To the streams that, still and slow,
 Through the verdant meadows flow.

3 Safe the dreary vale I tread,
 By the shades of death o'erspread,
With thy rod and staff supplied,
 This my guard—and that my guide.

4 Constant to my latest end,
 Thou my footsteps shalt attend;
And shalt bid thy hallowed dome
 Yield me an eternal home.
                James Merrick.

43   *Quiet communion.*
STEALING from the world away,
 We are come to seek thy face;
Kindly meet us, Lord, we pray,
 Grant us thy reviving grace.

2 Yonder stars that gild the sky
 Shine but with a borrowed light;
We, unless thy light be nigh,
 Wander, wrapt in gloomy night.

3 Sun of Righteousness! dispel
 All our darkness, doubts, and fears;
May thy light within us dwell,
 Till eternal day appears.

4 Warm our hearts in prayer and praise,
 Lift our every thought above;
Hear the grateful songs we raise,
 Fill us with thy perfect love.
                Ray Palmer.

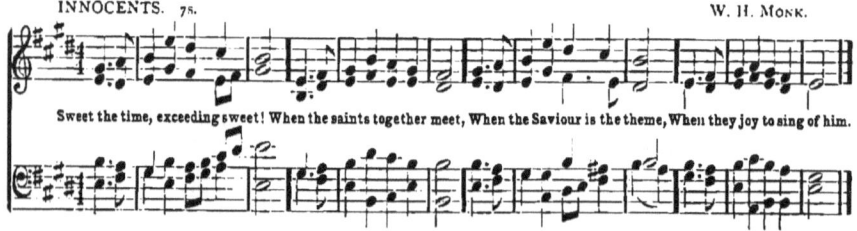

INNOCENTS. 7s.   W. H. MONK.

44   *Redeeming Love.*
SWEET the time, exceeding sweet!
When the saints together meet,
When the Saviour is the theme,
When they joy to sing of him.

2 Sing we then eternal love,
Such as did the Father move:
He beheld the world undone,
Loved the world, and gave his Son.

3 Sing the Son's amazing love;
How he left the realms above,
Took our nature and our place,
Lived and died to save our race.

4 Sing we, too, the Spirit's love;
With our stubborn hearts he strove,
Filled our minds with grief and fear,
Brought the precious Saviour near.

5 Sweet the place, exceeding sweet,
Where the saints in glory meet;
Where the Saviour's still the theme,
Where they see and sing of him.
                George Burder.

PRAYER AND INVOCATION.

HENDON. 7s. C. MALAN.

Lord, we come be-fore thee now, At thy feet we humbly bow; Oh, do not our suit dis-dain! Shall we seek thee, Lord, in vain? Shall we seek thee, Lord, in vain?

45 *"Thy face we seek."*

LORD, we come before thee now,
At thy feet we humbly bow;
Oh, do not our suit disdain!
Shall we seek thee, Lord, in vain?

2 Lord, on thee our souls depend,
In compassion now descend;
Fill our hearts with thy rich grace,
Tune our lips to sing thy praise.

3 In thine own appointed way,
Now we seek thee; here we stay;
Lord, we know not how to go,
Till a blessing thou bestow.

4 Comfort those who weep and mourn;
Let the time of joy return;
Those that are cast down lift up;
Make them strong in faith and hope.

5 Grant that all may seek and find
Thee a God supremely kind;
Heal the sick; the captive free;
Let us all rejoice in thee.
William Hammond.

46 *God everywhere.*

THEY who seek the throne of grace
Find that throne in every place;
If we live a life of prayer,
God is present everywhere.

2 In our sickness and our health,
In our want, or in our wealth,
If we look to God in prayer,
God is present everywhere.

3 When our earthly comforts fail,
When the foes of life prevail,
'Tis the time for earnest prayer;
God is present everywhere.

4 Then, my soul, in every strait,
To thy Father come, and wait;
He will answer every prayer:
God is present everywhere.
Oliver Holden, alt.

47 *A prayer in need.*

COME, my soul, thy suit prepare,
Jesus loves to answer prayer;
He himself has bid thee pray,
Therefore will not say thee nay.

2 With my burden I begin:—
Lord! remove this load of sin;
Let thy blood, for sinners spilt,
Set my conscience free from guilt.

3 Lord! I come to thee for rest;
Take posession of my breast:
There, thy blood-bought right maintain,
And, without a rival, reign.

4 While I am a pilgrim here,
Let thy love my spirit cheer;
As my Guide, my Guard, my Friend,
Lead me to my journey's end.

5 Show me what I have to do,
Every hour my strength renew;
Let me live a life of faith,
Let me die thy people's death.
John Newton.

PRAYER AND INVOCATION.

RETREAT. L. M. — Thos. Hastings.

48 *The mercy seat.*

From every stormy wind that blows,
From every swelling tide of woes,
There is a calm, a sure retreat;
'T is found beneath the mercy-seat.

2 There is a place where Jesus sheds
The oil of gladness on our heads,—
A place than all besides more sweet;
It is the blood-bought mercy-seat.

3 There is a scene where spirits blend,
Where friend holds fellowship with friend;
Though sundered far, by faith they meet,
Around one common mercy-seat.

4 There, there, on eagle wings we soar,
And sense and sin molest no more,
And heaven comes down our souls to greet,
And glory crowns the mercy-seat!

5 Oh! let my hand forget her skill,
My tongue be silent, cold, and still,
This throbbing heart forget to beat,
If I forget the mercy-seat.

Hugh Stowell.

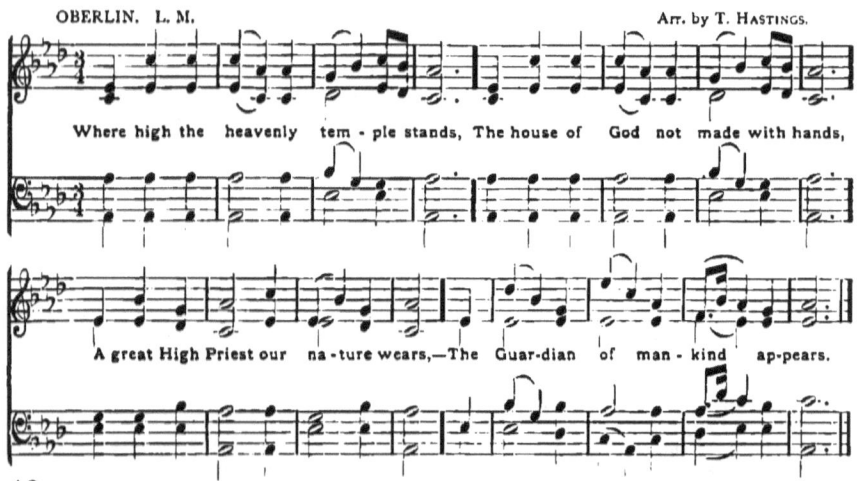

OBERLIN. L. M. — Arr. by T. Hastings.

Where high the heavenly tem-ple stands, The house of God not made with hands,
A great High Priest our na-ture wears,—The Guar-dian of man-kind ap-pears.

49 *"The evil hour."*

Where high the heavenly temple stands,
The house of God not made with hands,
A great High Priest our nature wears,—
The Guardian of mankind appears.

2 Though now ascended up on high,
He bends on earth a brother's eye;
Partaker of the human name,
He knows the frailty of our frame.

3 Our Fellow-sufferer yet retains
A fellow-feeling of our pains;
And still remembers, in the skies,
His tears, his agonies, and cries.

4 In every pang that rends the heart,
The Man of Sorrows had a part;
He sympathizes with our grief,
And to the sufferer sends relief.

5 With boldness, therefore, at the throne,
Let us make all our sorrows known;
And ask the aid of heavenly power,
To help us in the evil hour.

Michael Bruce.

PRAYER AND INVOCATION.

SHIRLAND. S. M. S Stanley

Our heav'nly Father calls, And Christ invites us near; With both, our friendship shall be sweet, And our com-mun-ion dear.

50 *"God pities."*
Our heavenly Father calls,
  And Christ invites us near;
With both, our friendship shall be sweet,
  And our communion dear.

2 God pities all our griefs:
  He pardons every day;
Almighty to protect our souls,
  And wise to guide our way.

3 How large his bounties are!
  What various stores of good,
Diffused from our Redeemer's hand,
  And purchased with his blood!

4 Jesus, our living Head,
  We bless thy faithful care;
Our Advocate before the throne,
  And our Forerunner there.

5 Here fix, my roving heart!
  Here wait, my warmest love!
Till the communion be complete,
  In nobler scenes above.
  Philip Doddridge.

51 *"The throne of grace."*
Behold the throne of grace!
  The promise calls me near;
There Jesus shows a smiling face,
  And waits to answer prayer.

2 That rich atoning blood,
  Which sprinkled round I see,
Provides for those who come to God
  An all-prevailing plea.

3 My soul! ask what thou wilt;
  Thou canst not be too bold:
Since his own blood for thee he spilt,
  What else can he withhold?

4 Thine image, Lord, bestow,
  Thy presence and thy love;
I ask to serve thee here below,
  And reign with thee above.

5 Teach me to live by faith;
  Conform my will to thine:
Let me victorious be in death,
  And then in glory shine.
  John Newton.

LANGTON. S. M. Arr. by C. Streetfield.

Jesus, who knows full well The heart of ev-ery saint, Invites us all our grief to tell, To pray and never faint.

52 *Importunity.*
Jesus, who knows full well
  The heart of every saint,
Invites us all our grief to tell,
  To pray and never faint.

2 He bows his gracious ear,—
  We never plead in vain;
Then let us wait till he appear,
  And pray, and pray again.

3 Jesus, the Lord, will hear
  His chosen when they cry;
Yes, though he may a while forbear,
  He'll help them from on high.

4 Then let us earnest cry,
  And never faint in prayer;
He sees, he hears, and, from on high,
  Will make our cause his care.
  John Newton.

PRAYER AND INVOCATION.

53 *Humility.*
While we lowly bow before thee,
 Wilt thou, gracious Saviour, hear?
We are poor and needy sinners,
 Full of doubt and full of fear;
  Gracious Saviour,
 Make us humble and sincere.

2 Fill us with thy Holy Spirit;
 Sanctify us by thy grace;
Oh, incline us more to love thee,
 And in dust our souls abase.
  Hear us, Saviour,
 And unvail thy glorious face.

3 None in vain did ever ask thee
 For the Spirit of thy love;
Hear us, then, dear Saviour, hear us;
 Grant an answer from above;
  Blessèd Saviour,
 Hear and answer from above.
   D. C. Colesworthy.

54 *"Send blessing."*
Saviour, send a blessing to us,
 Send a blessing from above;
All thy truth and mercy show us,
 Be thou here in power and love;
  Grant thy presence,
 Be it ours thy grace to prove.

2 Nothing have we, Lord, without thee,
 But thy promise is our stay;
And thy people must not doubt thee;
 Saviour, now thy power display;
  And let gladness
 Fill thy people's hearts to-day.
   Thomas Kelly.

55 *"Father, hear us!"*
God Almighty and All-seeing!
 Holy One, in whom we all
Live, and move, and have our being,
 Hear us when on thee we call;
  Father, hear us,
 As before thy throne we fall.

2 Of all good art thou the Giver;
 Weak and wandering ones are we;
Then for ever, yea, for ever,
 In thy presence would we be;
  Oh, be near us,
 That we wander not from thee.
   F. S. Pierpont.

56 *Glory to God!*
Glory be to God the Father,
 Glory be to God the Son,
Glory be to God the Spirit,
 Great Jehovah, Three in One:
  Glory, glory,
 While eternal ages run!

2 Glory be to him who loved us,
 Washed us from each spot and stain;
Glory be to him who bought us,
 Made us kings with him to reign:
  Glory, glory,
 To the Lamb that once was slain!

3 Glory, blessing, praise eternal!
 Thus the choir of angels sings;
Honor, riches, power, dominion!
 Thus its praise creation brings:
  Glory, glory,
 Glory to the King of kings.
   Horatius Bonar.

PRAYER AND INVOCATION.

57 *"Let thy servants hear."*

In thy name, O Lord! assembling,
  We, thy people, now draw near;
Teach us to rejoice with trembling;
  Speak, and let thy servants hear,—
    Hear with meekness,—
Hear thy word with godly fear.

2 While our days on earth are lengthened,
  May we give them, Lord! to thee;
Cheered by hope, and daily strengthened,
  May we run, nor weary be,
    Till thy glory
Without clouds in heaven we see.

3 There, in worship purer, sweeter,
  Thee thy people shall adore;
Tasting of enjoyment greater
  Than they could conceive before;
    Full enjoyment,
Full, unmixed, and evermore.
Thomas Kelly.

58 *"Bless the seed."*

Come, thou soul-transforming Spirit,
  Bless the sower and the seed;
Let each heart thy grace inherit;
  Raise the weak, the hungry feed!
    From the gospel
Now supply thy people's need.

2 Oh, may all enjoy the blessing
  Which thy word 's designed to give;
Let us all, thy love possessing,
  Joyfully the truth receive;
    And for ever
To thy praise and glory live.
Jonathan Evans.

59 *God's presence.*

God is in his holy temple;
  All the earth keep silence here;
Worship him in truth and spirit;
  Reverence him with godly fear;
    Holy, holy
Lord of hosts, our God, appear!

2 God in Christ reveals his presence,
  Throned upon the mercy-seat;
Saints, rejoice, and sinners, tremble;
  Each prepare his God to meet;
    Lowly, lowly
Bow, adoring, at his feet.
James Montgomery.

60 *Continued meetings.*

Welcome, days of solemn meeting;
  Welcome, days of praise and prayer;
Far from earthly scenes retreating,
  In your blessings we would share;
    Sacred seasons,
In your blessings we would share.

2 Be thou near us, blessèd Saviour,
  Still at morn and eve the same;
Give us faith that cannot waver;
  Kindle in us heaven's own flame;
    Blessèd Saviour,
Kindle in us heaven's own flame.

3 When the fervent heart is glowing,
  Holy Spirit, hear that prayer:
When the song of praise is flowing,
  Let that song thine impress bear;
    Holy Spirit,
Let that song thine impress bear.
S. F. Smith.

PRAYER AND INVOCATION.

HORTON. 7s.   Arr. fr. Wartensee.

Lord! I cannot let thee go, Till a blessing thou bestow; Do not turn away thy face, Mine's an urgent, pressing case.

61   *Gen. 32: 26.*

Lord! I cannot let thee go,
Till a blessing thou bestow;
Do not turn away thy face,
Mine's an urgent, pressing case.

2 Once a sinner, near despair,
Sought thy mercy-seat by prayer;
Mercy heard and set him free—
Lord! that mercy came to me.

3 Many days have passed since then,
Many changes I have seen;
Yet have been upheld till now,
Who could hold me up but thou?

4 Thou hast helped in every need—
This emboldens me to plead;
After so much mercy past,
Canst thou let me sink at last?

5 No—I must maintain my hold;
'T is thy goodness makes me bold;
I can no denial take,
Since I plead for Jesus' sake.
John Newton.

SWEET HOUR. L. M. D.   W. B. Bradbury.

{Sweet hour of prayer! sweet hour of prayer! That calls me from a world of care,}
{And bids me, at my Father's throne, Make all my wants and (*Omit*........)} wish-es known:
D.C.—And oft es-caped the tempter's snare, By thy re-turn, sweet (*Omit*........) hour of prayer.

In sea-sons of dis-tress and grief, My soul has oft-en found re-lief,

62   *"Sweet hour."*

Sweet hour of prayer! sweet hour of prayer!
That calls me from a world of care,
And bids me, at my Father's throne,
Make all my wants and wishes known:
In seasons of distress and grief,
My soul has often found relief,
And oft escaped the tempter's snare,
By thy return, sweet hour of prayer!

2 Sweet hour of prayer! sweet hour of prayer!
Thy wings shall my petition bear
To him, whose truth and faithfulness
Engage the waiting soul to bless:
And, since he bids me seek his face,
Believe his word, and trust his grace,
I'll cast on him my every care,
And wait for thee, sweet hour of prayer!
W. W. Walford.

PRAYER AND INVOCATION.

DIX. 7s, 6l.   Arr. by W. H. Monk.

{ Ho-ly, ho-ly, ho-ly Lord, God of hosts, e-ternal King, } { By the heav'ns and earth adored; Angels and archangels sing, } Chanting ev-er-last-ing-ly To the blessed Trin-i-ty.

63 *"The blessed Trinity."*

Holy, holy, holy Lord,
God of hosts, eternal King,
By the heavens and earth adored;
Angels and archangels sing,
Chanting everlastingly
To the blessèd Trinity.

2 Thousands, tens of thousands, stand,
Spirits blest, before the throne,
Speeding thence at thy command,
And, when thy commands are done,
Singing everlastingly
To the blessèd Trinity.

3 Cherubim and seraphim
Vail their faces with their wings;
Eyes of angels are too dim
To behold the King of kings,
While they sing eternally
To the blessèd Trinity.

4 Thee apostles, prophets thee,
Thee the noble martyr band,
Praise with solemn jubilee,
Thee, the church in every land;
Singing everlastingly
To the blessèd Trinity.

5 Hallelujah! Lord, to thee,
Father, Son, and Holy Ghost;
Godhead one, and Persons three;
Join us with the heavenly host,
Singing everlastingly
To the blessèd Trinity.
C. Wordsworth.

64 *Nature's King.*

Oh, give thanks to him who made
Morning light and evening shade;
Source and giver of all good,
Nightly sleep and daily food;
Quickener of our wearied powers;
Guard of our unconscious hours.

2 Oh, give thanks to nature's King,
Who made every breathing thing:
His, our warm and sentient frame,
His, the mind's immortal flame.
Oh, how close the ties that bind
Spirits to the Eternal Mind!

3 Oh, give thanks with heart and lip,
For we are his workmanship;
And all creatures are his care:
Not a bird that cleaves the air
Falls unnoticed; but who can
Speak the Father's love to man?

4 Oh, give thanks to him who came
In a mortal, suffering frame—
Temple of the Deity—
Came, for rebel man to die;
In the path himself hath trod,
Leading back his saints to God.
Josiah Conder.

65 *The Babe of Bethlehem.*

As with gladness men of old
Did the guiding star behold,
As with joy they hailed its light,
Leading onward, beaming bright;
So, most gracious Lord, may we
Evermore be led to thee.

2 As with joyful steps they sped,
Saviour, to thy manger bed,
There to bend the knee before
Thee whom heaven and earth adore;
So may we with willing feet
Ever seek the mercy-seat.

3 As they offered gifts most rare
At thy cradle rude and bare,
So may we with holy joy,
Pure and free from sin's alloy,
All our costliest treasures bring,
Christ, to thee our heavenly King.

4 Holy Jesus, every day
Keep us in the narrow way;
And, when earthly things are past,
Bring our ransomed souls at last
Where they need no star to guide,
Where no clouds thy glory hide.
William C. Dix.

CLOSE OF SERVICE.

HURSLEY. L. M.   Arr. by W. H. Monk.

[music]

66   *"Sun of my soul!"*
Sun of my soul! thou Saviour dear,
It is not night if thou be near:
Oh, may no earth-born cloud arise
To hide thee from thy servant's eyes!

2 When soft the dews of kindly sleep
My weary eyelids gently steep,
Be my last thought—how sweet to rest
For ever on my Saviour's breast!

3 Abide with me from morn till eve,
For without thee I cannot live;
Abide with me when night is nigh,
For without thee I dare not die.

4 Be near to bless me when I wake,
Ere through the world my way I take,
Abide with me till in thy love
I lose myself in heaven above.
John Keble.

67   *Evening Shadows.*
Again, as evening's shadow falls,
We gather in these hallowed walls;
And evening hymn and evening prayer
Rise mingling on the holy air.

2 May struggling hearts, that seek release,
Here find the rest of God's own peace;
And, strengthened here by hymn and prayer,
Lay down the burden and the care.

3 O God our Light, to thee we bow:
Within all shadows standest thou:
Give deeper calm than night can bring,
Give sweeter songs than life can sing.

4 Life's tumult we must meet again
We cannot at the shrine remain;
But in the spirit's secret cell,
May hymn and prayer for ever dwell.
Samuel Longfellow.

EVENING HYMN. L. M.   T. Tallis.

[music]

68   *Evening song.*
Glory to thee, my God, this night,
For all the blessings of the light;
Keep me, oh, keep me, King of kings!
Beneath thine own almighty wings.

2 Forgive me, Lord, for thy dear Son,
The ill which I this day have done;
That with the world, myself, and thee,
I, ere I sleep, at peace may be.

3 Teach me to live, that I may dread
The grave as little as my bed:
Teach me to die, that so I may
Rise glorious at the judgment-day.

4 Oh, let my soul on thee repose,
And may sweet sleep mine eyelids close!
Sleep, which shall me more vigorous make,
To serve my God when I awake.

5 Praise God, from whom all blessings flow;
Praise him, all creatures here below;
Praise him above, ye heavenly host;
Praise Father, Son, and Holy Ghost!
Thomas Ken.

CLOSE OF SERVICE.

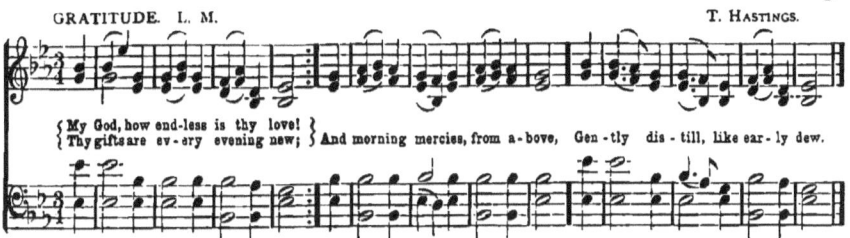

GRATITUDE. L. M.   T. Hastings.

My God, how end-less is thy love! Thy gifts are ev-ery evening new; And morning mercies, from a-bove, Gen-tly dis-till, like ear-ly dew.

69   *"Perpetual blessings."*

My God, how endless is thy love!
  Thy gifts are every evening new;
And morning mercies, from above,
  Gently distill, like early dew.

2 Thou spread'st the curtains of the night,
  Great Guardian of my sleeping hours;
Thy sovereign word restores the light,
  And quickens all my drowsy powers.

3 I yield my powers to thy command;
  To thee I consecrate my days;
Perpetual blessings from thy hand
  Demand perpetual songs of praise.
                  Isaac Watts.

70   *Benediction.*

The peace which God alone reveals,
  And by his word of grace imparts,
Which only the believer feels,
  Direct, and keep, and cheer our hearts!

2 And may the holy Three in One,
  The Father, Word, and Comforter,
Pour an abundant blessing down
  On every soul assembled here!

3 Praise God, from whom all blessings flow:
  Praise him, all creatures here below;
Praise him above, ye heavenly host!
  Praise Father, Son, and Holy Ghost.
                  John Newton.

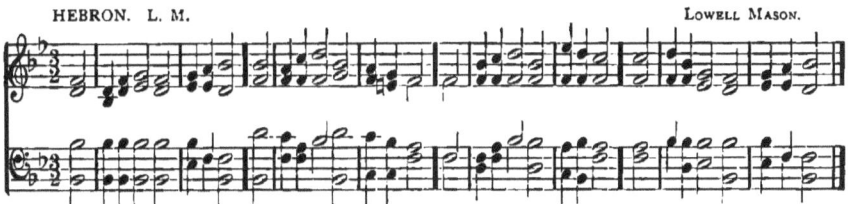

HEBRON. L. M.   Lowell Mason.

71   *Evening.*

Thus far the Lord has led me on;
  Thus far his power prolongs my days;
And every evening shall make known
  Some fresh memorial of his grace.

2 Much of my time has run to waste,
  And I, perhaps, am near my home,
But he forgives my follies past,
  And gives me strength for days to come.

3 I lay my body down to sleep;
  Peace is the pillow for my head;
While well-appointed angels keep
  Their watchful stations round my bed.

4 Thus when the night of death shall come,
  My flesh shall rest beneath the ground,
And wait thy voice to break my tomb,
  With sweet salvation in the sound.
                  Isaac Watts.

72   *Dismissal.*

Dismiss us with thy blessing, Lord!
  Help us to feed upon thy word;
All that has been amiss, forgive,
  And let thy truth within us live.

2 Though we are guilty, thou art good;
  Wash all our works in Jesus' blood;
Give every burdened soul release,
  And bid us all depart in peace.
                  Joseph Hart.

CLOSE OF SERVICE.

73 *"He careth."*
How GENTLE God's commands!
 How kind his precepts are!
Come, cast your burdens on the Lord,
 And trust his constant care.

2 Beneath his watchful eye
 His saints securely dwell;
That hand which bears creation up
 Shall guard his children well.

3 Why should this anxious load
 Press down your weary mind?
Haste to your heavenly Father's throne,
 And sweet refreshment find.

4 His goodness stands approved,
 Unchanged from day to day:
I'll drop my burden at his feet,
 And bear a song away.
Philip Doddridge.

74 *"Still with thee."*
STILL, still with thee, my God,
 I would desire to be:
By day, by night, at home, abroad,
 I would be still with thee.

2 With thee, when dawn comes in,
 And calls me back to care,
Each day returning to begin
 With thee, my God, in prayer.

3 With thee, when day is done,
 And evening calms the mind;
The setting, as the rising, sun
 With thee my heart would find.

4 With thee, in thee, by faith
 Abiding I would be;
By day, by night, in life, in death,
 I would be still with thee.
James D. Burns.

75 *"Abide with us"*
THE day, O Lord, is spent;
 Abide with us, and rest;
Our hearts' desires are fully bent
 On making thee our guest.

2 We have not reached that land,
 That happy land, as yet,
Where holy angels round thee stand,
 Whose sun can never set.

3 Our sun is sinking now,
 Our day is almost o'er;
O Sun of Righteousness, do thou
 Shine on us evermore!

4 The grace of Christ our Lord,
 The Father's boundless love,
The Spirit's blest communion, too,
 Be with us from above.
John M. Neale.

CLOSE OF SERVICE.

SCHUMANN. S. M.   R. Schumann.

Once more, before we part, Oh, bless the Saviour's name! Let every tongue and every heart Adore and praise the same.

76   *At Dismission.*

ONCE more, before we part,
  Oh, bless the Saviour's name!
Let every tongue and every heart
  Adore and praise the same.

2 Lord, in thy grace we came,
  That blessing still impart;
We met in Jesus' sacred name,
  In Jesus' name we part.

3 Still on thy holy word
  Help us to feed, and grow,
Still to go on to know the Lord,
  And practice what we know.

4 Now, Lord, before we part,
  Help us to bless thy name:
Let every tongue and every heart
  Adore and praise the same.
                    Joseph Hart.

77   *Evening.*

THE swift declining day,
  How fast its moments fly!
While evening's broad and gloomy shade
  Gains on the western sky.

2 Ye mortals, mark its pace,
  And use the hours of light;
And know, its Maker can command
  At once eternal night.

3 Give glory to the Lord,
  Who rules the whirling sphere;
Submissive at his footstool bow,
  And seek salvation there.

4 Then shall new lustre break
  Through death's impending gloom,
And lead you to unchanging light,
  In your celestial home.
                    Philip Doddridge.

EVENING. S. M.   A. Chapin.

The day is past and gone, The evening shades appear; Oh, may we all remember well The night of death draws near!

78   *Home Hymn.*

THE day is past and gone,
  The evening shades appear;
Oh, may we all remember well
  The night of death draws near!

2 We lay our garments by,
  Upon our beds to rest;
So death will soon disrobe us all
  Of what we here possessed.

3 Lord, keep us safe this night,
  Secure from all our fears;

3 P

May angels guard us while we sleep,
  Till morning light appears.

4 And when we early rise,
  And view the unwearied sun,
May we set out to win the prize,
  And after glory run.

5 And when our days are past,
  And we from time remove,
Oh, may we in thy bosom rest,
  The bosom of thy love!
                    John Leland.

CLOSE OF SERVICE.

EVENTIDE. 10s.   W. H. MONK.

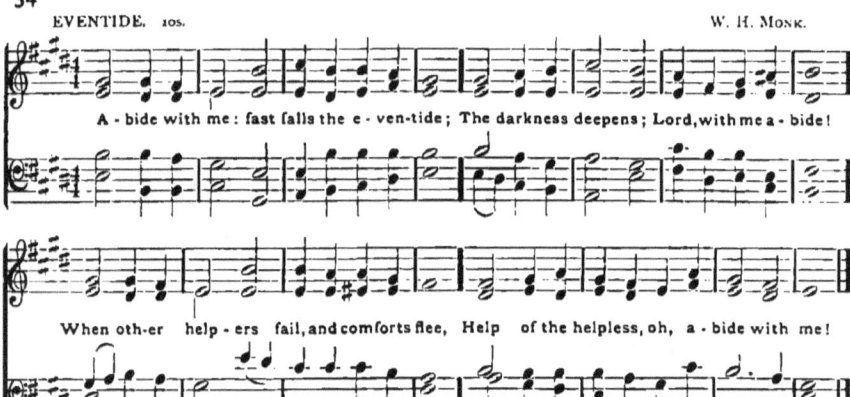

A-bide with me: fast falls the e-ven-tide; The darkness deepens; Lord, with me a-bide!

When oth-er help-ers fail, and comforts flee, Help of the helpless, oh, a-bide with me!

79   *Evening of the Day.*

ABIDE with me: fast falls the eventide;
The darkness deepens; Lord, with me abide!
When other helpers fail, and comforts flee,
Help of the helpless, oh, abide with me!

2 Not a brief glance I beg, a passing word,
But as thou dwell'st with thy disciples, Lord,
Familiar, condescending, patient, free,
Come, not to sojourn, but abide with me.

3 I need thy presence every passing hour:
What but thy grace can foil the tempter's power?
Who like thyself my guide and stay can be?
Thro' cloud and sunshine, oh, abide with me!
                                Henry F. Lyte.

80   *Evening of Life.*

SWIFT to its close ebbs out life's little day;
Earth's joys grow dim, its glories pass away:
Change and decay in all around I see;
O thou, who changest not, abide with me!

2 Come not in terrors, as the King of kings;
But kind and good, with healing in thy wings,
Tears for all woes, a heart for every plea;
Come, Friend of sinners, and abide with me.

3 I fear no foe, with thee at hand to bless,
Ills have no weight, and tears no bitterness:
Where is Death's sting? where, Grave, thy victory?
I triumph still, if thou abide with me.

4 Hold thou thy cross before my closing eyes;
Shine through the gloom, and point me to the skies;
Heaven's morning breaks, and earth's vain shadows flee:
In life, in death, O Lord, abide with me!
                               Henry F. Lyte.

81   *"A word of Blessing."*

O LORD, who by thy presence hast made light
The heat and burden of the toilsome day,
Be with us also in the silent night,
Be with us when the daylight fades away.

2 Oh, speak a word of blessing, gracious Lord!
Thy blessing is endued with soothing power;
On human hearts worn out with toil, thy word
Falls soft and gentle as the evening shower.

3 Come then, O Lord, and deign to be our guest,
After the day's confusion, toil, and din;
Oh, come to bring us peace, and joy, and rest,
To give salvation, and to pardon sin!

4 Bind up the wounds, assuage the aching smart
Left in each bosom from the day just past,
And let us on a Father's loving heart
Forget our griefs, and find sweet rest at last.
                              Richard Massie, tr.

CLOSE OF SERVICE.

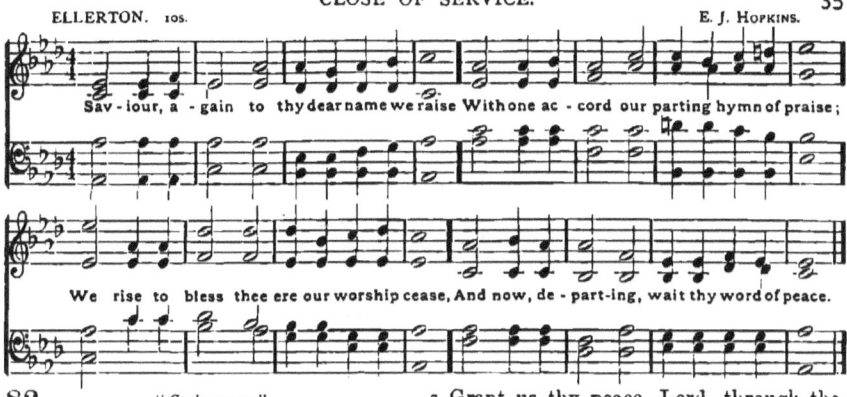

ELLERTON. 10s.   E. J. HOPKINS.

Sav-iour, a-gain to thy dear name we raise With one ac-cord our parting hymn of praise;
We rise to bless thee ere our worship cease, And now, de-part-ing, wait thy word of peace.

82   *"Go in peace."*

SAVIOUR, again to thy dear name we raise
With one accord our parting hymn of praise;
We rise to bless thee ere our worship cease,
And now, departing, wait thy word of peace.

2 Grant us thy peace upon our homeward way;
With thee began, with thee shall end the day;
Guard thou the lips from sin, the hearts from shame,
That in this house have called upon thy name.

3 Grant us thy peace, Lord, through the coming night;
Turn thou for us its darkness into light;
From harm and danger keep thy children free,
For dark and light are both alike to thee.

4 Grant us thy peace throughout our earthly life,
Our balm in sorrow, and our stay in strife;
Then, when thy voice shall bid our conflict cease,
Call us, O Lord, to thine eternal peace.
John Ellerton.

HENLEY. 11s, 10s.   LOWELL MASON.   D. S.

Father! in thy mysterious presence kneeling, Fain would our souls feel all thy kindling love; For we are weak, and need some deep
D. S.—Of trust, and strength, and calmness from above.   [revealing

83   *"Trust, strength, calmness."*

FATHER! in thy mysterious presence kneeling,
   Fain would our souls feel all thy kindling love;
For we are weak, and need some deep revealing
   Of trust, and strength, and calmness from above.

2 Lord! we have wandered forth through doubt and sorrow,
   And thou hast made each step an onward one;
And we will ever trust each unknown morrow;
   Thou wilt sustain us till its work is done.

3 In the heart's depths, a peace serene and holy
   Abides; and, when pain seems to have her will,
Or we despair, oh! may that peace rise slowly,
   Stronger than agony, and we be still.

4 Now, Father! now in thy dear presence kneeling,
   Our spirits yearn to feel thy kindling love;
Now make us strong; we need thy deep revealing
   Of trust, and strength, and calmness from above.
Samuel Johnson.

CLOSE OF SERVICE.

SEYMOUR. 7s. Arr. fr. Von Weber.

Soft-ly now the light of day Fades up-on my sight a-way;
Free from care, from la-bor free, Lord, I would com-mune with thee.

84 *Evening.*

SOFTLY now the light of day
Fades upon my sight away;
Free from care, from labor free,
Lord, I would commune with thee.

2 Thou, whose all-pervading eye
Naught escapes without, within,
Pardon each infirmity,
Open fault, and secret sin.

3 Soon, for me, the light of day
Shall for ever pass away;
Then, from sin and sorrow free,
Take me, Lord, to dwell with thee.

4 Thou who, sinless, yet hast known
All of man's infirmity;
Then from thine eternal throne,
Jesus, look with pitying eye.
G. W. Doane.

85 *Sabbath Evening.*

FOR the mercies of the day,
For this rest upon our way,
Thanks to thee alone be given,
Lord of earth and King of heaven!

2 Cold our services have been,
Mingled every prayer with sin:
But thou canst and wilt forgive;
By thy grace alone we live.

3 While this thorny path we tread,
May thy love our footsteps lead;
When our journey here is past,
May we rest with thee at last.

4 Let these earthly Sabbaths prove
Fortastes of our joys above;
While their steps thy children bend
To the rest which knows no end.
O. P., 1836.

BEMINSTER. 7s. BRISTOL COLLECTION.

Now may he who from the dead Brought the Shepherd of the sheep, Jesus Christ, our King and Head, All our souls in safety keep.

86 *Closing Benediction.*

Now MAY he who from the dead
Brought the Shepherd of the sheep,
Jesus Christ, our King and Head,
All our souls in safety keep.

2 May he teach us to fulfill
What is pleasing in his sight;
Perfect us in all his will,
And preserve us day and night.
John Newton.

87 *Doxology.*

PRAISE the God of our salvation;
Praise the Father's boundless love;
Praise the Lamb, our expiation;
Praise the Spirit from above:—

2 Author of the new creation,
Him by whom our spirits live;—
Undivided adoration
To the one Jehovah give!
Josiah Conder.

CLOSE OF SERVICE.

EVENING PRAISE. P. M.   W. F. SHERWIN.

Day is dy-ing in the West; Heav'n is touch-ing earth with rest: Wait and wor-ship while the night

Sets her even-ing lamps a-light Thro' all the sky. Ho-ly, ho-ly, ho-ly, Lord God of Hosts!

Heav'n and earth are full of thee! Heav'n and earth are prais-ing thee, O Lord most high!

88   *"Day is dying."*
Day is dying in the West;
Heaven is touching earth with rest:
Wait and worship while the night
Sets her evening lamps alight
  Through all the sky.—CHO.

2 Lord of life, beneath the dome
Of the universe, thy home,
Gather us who seek thy face
To the fold of thy embrace,
  For thou art nigh.—CHO.
Mary A. Lathbury.

HOLLEY. 7s.   GEO. HEWS.

89   *Separation.*
For a season called to part,
  Let us now ourselves commend
To the gracious eye and heart
  Of our ever-present Friend.

2 Jesus, hear our humble prayer;
  Tender Shepherd of thy sheep!
Let thy mercy and thy care
  All our souls in safety keep.

3 In thy strength may we be strong;
  Sweeten every cross and pain:
Give us, if we live, ere long
  Here to meet in peace again.
                  John Newton.

90   *Hymn at Parting.*
THOU, from whom we never part,
  Thou, whose love is everywhere,
Thou, who seest every heart,
  Listen to our evening prayer.

2 Father, fill our hearts with love,
  Love unfailing, full and free;
Love that no alarm can move,
  Love that ever rests on thee.

3 Heavenly Father! through the night
  Keep us safe from every ill;
Cheerful as the morning light,
  May we wake to do thy will.
                  Eliza Lee Follen.

CLOSE OF SERVICE.

VESPER HYMN. 8s, 7s. D. Arr. by L. Mason.

Saviour, breathe an evening blessing, Ere re-pose our spir-its seal;
Sin and want we come confess-ing; Thou canst save, and thou canst heal.
Tho' destruction walk around us, Tho' the ar-row near us fly, Angel guards from thee surround us, We are safe if thou art nigh.

91 *Evening blessing.*

Saviour, breathe an evening blessing,
  Ere repose our spirits seal;
Sin and want we come confessing;
  Thou canst save, and thou canst heal.
Though destruction walk around us,
  Though the arrow near us fly,
Angel guards from thee surround us,
  We are safe if thou art nigh.

2 Though the night be dark and dreary,
  Darkness cannot hide from thee;
Thou art he who, never weary,
  Watcheth where thy people be.
Should swift death this night o'ertake us,
  And our couch become our tomb,
May the morn in heaven awake us,
  Clad in light and deathless bloom.
  James Edmeston.

92 *The Pilgrim.*

Gently, Lord, oh, gently lead us,
  Through this lonely vale of tears;
Through the changes thou 'st decreed us,
  Till our last great change appears.
When temptation's darts assail us,
  When in devious paths we stray,
Let thy goodness never fail us,
  Lead us in thy perfect way.

2 In the hour of pain and anguish,
  In the hour when death draws near,
Suffer not our hearts to languish,
  Suffer not our souls to fear.
And when mortal life is ended,
  Bid us in thine arms to rest,
Till, by angel bands attended,
  We awake among the blest.
  Thomas Hastings.

STOCKWELL. 8s, 7s. D. E. Jones.

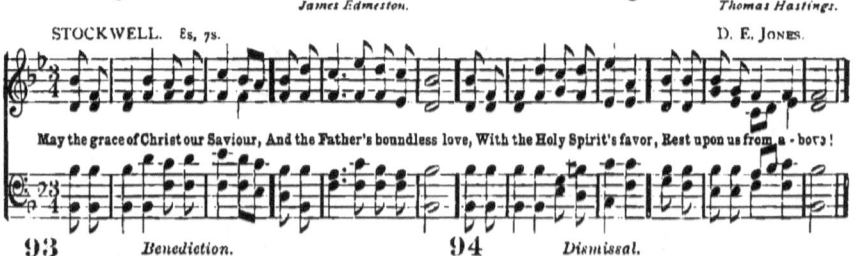

May the grace of Christ our Saviour, And the Father's boundless love, With the Holy Spirit's favor, Rest upon us from a-bove!

93 *Benediction.*

May the grace of Christ our Saviour,
  And the Father's boundless love,
With the Holy Spirit's favor,
  Rest upon us from above!

2 Thus may we abide in union
  With each other and the Lord,
And possess, in sweet communion,
  Joys which earth cannot afford.
  John Newton.

94 *Dismissal.*

Lord, dismiss us with thy blessing;
  Bid us now depart in peace;
Still on heavenly manna feeding,
  Let our faith and love increase.

2 Fill each breast with consolation;
  Up to thee our hearts we raise;
When we reach our blissful station,
  Then we 'll give thee nobler praise.
  Robert Hawker.

CLOSE OF SERVICE.

95 *Dismissal.*
Lord, dismiss us with thy blessing,
  Fill our hearts with joy and peace;
Let us each, thy love possessing,
  Triumph in redeeming grace;
    Oh, refresh us,
  Traveling through this wilderness.

2 Thanks we give, and adoration,
  For thy gospel's joyful sound,
May the fruits of thy salvation
  In our hearts and lives abound;
    May thy presence
  With us evermore be found.

3 So, whene'er the signal 's given,
  Us from earth to call away;
Borne on angels' wings to heaven,
  Glad to leave our cumbrous clay,
    May we, ready,
  Rise and reign in endless day.
                    John Fawcett.

96 *"Keep us safe."*
God of our salvation! hear us;
  Bless, oh, bless us, ere we go;
When we join the world, be near us,
  Lest we cold and careless grow.
    Saviour! keep us;
  Keep us safe from every foe.

2 As our steps are drawing nearer
  To our everlasting home,
May our view of heaven grow clearer,
  Hope more bright of joys to come;
    And, when dying,
  May thy presence cheer the gloom.
                    Thomas Kelly.

97 *"By Galilee."*
Break thou the bread of life,
  Dear Lord, to me,
As thou didst break the loaves
  Beside the sea;
Beyond the sacred page
  I seek thee, Lord;
My spirit pants for thee,
  O living Word!

2 Bless thou the truth, dear Lord,
  To me—to me—
As thou didst bless the bread
  By Galilee;
Then shall all bondage cease,
  All fetters fall;
And I shall find my peace,
  My All-in-All!
                    Mary A. Lathbury.

CLOSE OF SERVICE.

98 *Evening Prayer.*

HEAR my prayer, O heavenly Father,
  Ere I lay me down to sleep:
Bid thine angels, pure and holy,
  Round my bed their vigil keep.

2 Great my sins are, but thy mercy
  Far outweighs them every one;
Down before thy cross I cast them,
  Trusting in thy help alone.

3 Keep me, through this night of peril,
  Underneath its boundless shade;
Take me to thy rest, I pray thee,
  When my pilgrimage is made.

4 None shall measure out thy patience
  By the span of human thought;
None shall bound the tender mercies
  Which thy holy Son has brought.

5 Pardon all my past transgressions;
  Give me strength for days to come;
Guide and guard me with thy blessing,
  Till thine angels bid me home.
        Harriet Parr.

99 *"Turn us, O Lord!"*

HEAVENLY Father, grant thy blessing
  On the teaching of this day;
That our hearts, thy fear possessing,
  May from sin be turned away.

2 Have we wandered? oh, forgive us;
  Have we wished from truth to rove?
Turn, oh, turn us, and receive us,
  And incline us thee to love.
        Anon., 1835.

100 *"Thou hearest."*

LORD! in love and mercy save us,
  For our trust is all in thee:
In that cleansing fountain lave us,
  Which alone can make us free!

2 Weary, life's rough billows breasting,
  Through the long lone dismal night,
Grant that calmly, on thee resting,
  We may wait for morning light.

3 Lord! we pray, and know thou hearest,
  For thy promises are true:
Grant the heart-wish that is dearest;
  He who knows can also do!
        A. J. Symington.

101 *Blessing sought.*

GRACIOUS Saviour, thus before thee
  With our varied want and care;
For a blessing we implore thee,
  Listen to our evening prayer!

2 By thy favor safely living,
  With a grateful heart we raise
Songs of jubilant thanksgiving;
  Listen to our evening praise.

3 Through the day, Lord, thou hast given
  Strength sufficient for our need;
Cheered us with sweet hopes of heaven,
  Helped and comforted indeed.

4 Lord, we thank thee, and adore thee,
  For the solace of thy love;
And rejoicing thus before thee,
  Wait thy blessing from above!
        Henry Bateman.

CLOSE OF SERVICE.

102 *Rom. 16 : 20.*

GOD be with you till we meet again,
By his counsels guide, uphold you,
With his sheep securely fold you,
God be with you till we meet again.

CHO.—Till we meet, till we meet,
Till we meet at Jesus' feet;
Till we meet, till we meet,
God be with you till we meet again.

2 God be with you till we meet again.
'Neath his wings protecting hide you;
Daily manna still provide you,
God be with you till we meet again.

3 God be with you till we meet again,
When life's perils thick confound you;
Put his arms unfailing round you,
God be with you till we meet again.

4 God be with you till we meet again;
Keep love's banner floating o'er you;
Smite death's threatening wave before you,
God be with you till we meet again.

J. E. Rankin.

THE SCRIPTURES.

SOUTHWELL. C. M.   H. S. Irons.

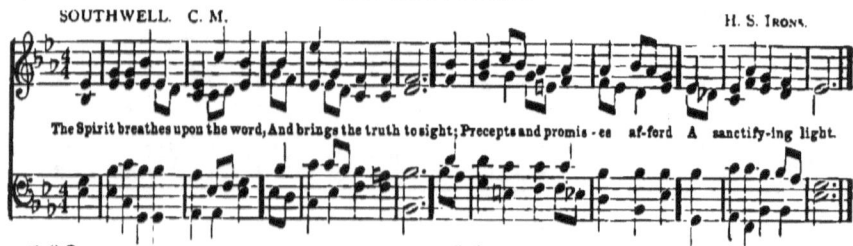

103 *Psalm 119.*
The Spirit breathes upon the word,
  And brings the truth to sight;
Precepts and promises afford
  A sanctifying light.

2 A glory gilds the sacred page,
  Majestic, like the sun;
It gives a light to every age;—
  It gives, but borrows none.

3 The hand, that gave it, still supplies
  The gracious light and heat;
Its truths upon the nations rise,—
  They rise, but never set.

4 Let everlasting thanks be thine,
  For such a bright display,
As makes a world of darkness shine
  With beams of heavenly day.

5 My soul rejoices to pursue
  The steps of him I love,
Till glory breaks upon my view,
  In brighter worlds above.
          William Cowper.

104 *Psalm 119.*
How shall the young secure their hearts,
  And guard their lives from sin?
Thy word the choicest rules imparts
  To keep the conscience clean.

2 When once it enters to the mind,
  It spreads such light abroad;
The meanest souls instruction find,
  And raise their thoughts to God.

3 'T is like the sun, a heavenly light,
  That guides us all the day;
And, through the dangers of the night,
  A lamp to lead our way.

4 Thy precepts make me truly wise;
  I hate the sinner's road;
I hate my own vain thoughts that rise,
  But love thy law, my God!

5 Thy word is everlasting truth;
  How pure is every page!
That holy book shall guide our youth,
  And well support our age.
          Isaac Watts.

KNOX. C. M.   Fr. Temple Melodies.

105 *Psalm 119.*
How precious is the book divine,
  By inspiration given!
Bright as a lamp its doctrines shine,
  To guide our souls to heaven.

2 O'er all the strait and narrow way
  Its radiant beams are cast;
A light whose never weary ray
  Grows brightest at the last.

3 It sweetly cheers our drooping hearts,
  In this dark vale of tears;
Life, light, and joy, it still imparts,
  And quells our rising fears.

4 This lamp, through all the tedious night
  Of life, shall guide our way,
Till we behold a clearer light
  Of an eternal day.
          John Fawcett.

THE SCRIPTURES.

CHIMES. C. M.   LOWELL MASON.

Fa-ther of mercies! in thy word What end-less glo-ry shines! For ev-er be thy name adored, For these ce-les-tial lines.

106   *"Endless glory."*
FATHER of mercies! in thy word
What endless glory shines!
For ever be thy name adored,
For these celestial lines.

2 Here, the fair tree of knowledge grows,
And yields a free repast;
Sublimer sweets than nature knows
Invite the longing taste.

3 Here, the Redeemer's welcome voice
Spreads heavenly peace around;
And life and everlasting joys
Attend the blissful sound.

4 Oh, may these heavenly pages be
My ever dear delight;
And still new beauties may I see,
And still increasing light.

5 Divine Instructor, gracious Lord!
Be thou for ever near;
Teach me to love thy sacred word,
And view my Saviour there.
Anne Steele.

107   *Psalm 119.*
OH, how I love thy holy law!
'T is daily my delight;
And thence my meditations draw
Divine advice by night.

2 How doth thy word my heart engage!
How well employ my tongue!
And in my tiresome pilgrimage
Yields me a heavenly song.

3 Am I a stranger, or at home,
'T is my perpetual feast:
Not honey dropping from the comb,
So much allures the taste.

4 No treasures so enrich the mind,
Nor shall thy word be sold
For loads of silver well-refined,
Nor heaps of choicest gold.

5 When nature sinks, and spirits droop,
Thy promises of grace
Are pillars to support my hope,
And there I write thy praise.
Isaac Watts.

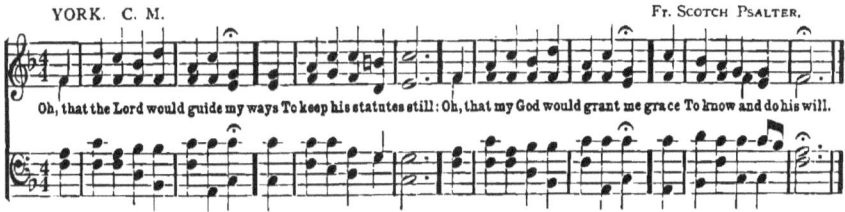

YORK. C. M.   FT. SCOTCH PSALTER.

Oh, that the Lord would guide my ways To keep his statutes still: Oh, that my God would grant me grace To know and do his will.

108   *Psalm 119.*
OH, that the Lord would guide my ways
To keep his statutes still:
Oh, that my God would grant me grace
To know and do his will.

2 Oh, send thy Spirit down, to write
Thy law upon my heart;
Nor let my tongue indulge deceit,
Or act the liar's part.

3 Order my footsteps by thy word,
And make my heart sincere;
Let sin have no dominion, Lord!
But keep my conscience clear.

4 Make me to walk in thy commands—
'T is a delightful road;
Nor let my head, or heart, or hands,
Offend against my God.
Isaac Watts.

THE SCRIPTURES.

CLYDE. 8s, 4. Arr. by EMMELAR.

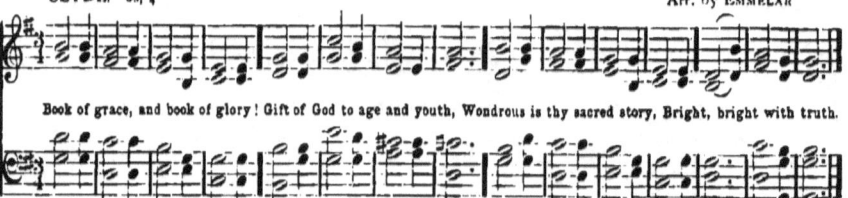

Book of grace, and book of glory! Gift of God to age and youth, Wondrous is thy sacred story, Bright, bright with truth.

109 *Gift of God.*

Book of grace, and book of glory!
　Gift of God to age and youth,
Wondrous is thy sacred story,
　Bright, bright with truth.

2 Book of love! in accents tender
　Speaking unto such as we;
May it lead us, Lord, to render
　All, all to thee.

3 Book of hope! the spirit, sighing,
　Sweetest comfort finds in thee,
As it hears the Saviour crying,
　"Come, come to me!"

4 Book of life! when we, reposing,
　Bid farewell to friends we love,
Give us, for the life then closing,
　Life, life above.
　　　　　　　　　Anon.

UXBRIDGE. L. M. LOWELL MASON.

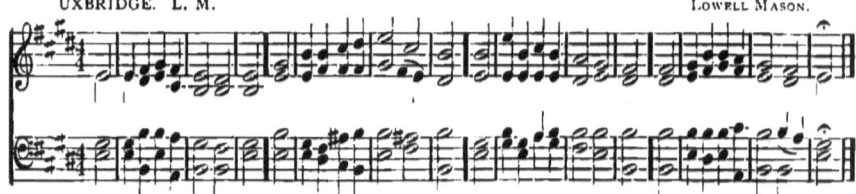

110 *Psalm 19.*

THE heavens declare thy glory, Lord!
　In every star thy wisdom shines;
But, when our eyes behold thy word,
　We read thy name in fairer lines.

2 The rolling sun, the changing light,
　And nights and days thy power confess;
But the blest volume thou hast writ
　Reveals thy justice and thy grace.

3 Sun, moon, and stars convey thy praise
　Round the whole earth, and never stand;
So, when thy truth began its race,
　It touched and glanced on every land.

4 Nor shall thy spreading gospel rest,
　Till through the world thy truth has run,
Till Christ has all the nations blessed,
　That see the light, or feel the sun.
　　　　　　　　　Isaac Watts.

111 *Psalm 19.*

GREAT Sun of Righteousness, arise!
　Oh, bless the world with heavenly light!
Thy gospel makes the simple wise:
　Thy laws are pure, thy judgments right.

2 Thy noblest wonders here we view,
　In souls renewed and sins forgiven:—
Lord, cleanse my sins, my soul renew,
　And make thy word my guide to heaven.
　　　　　　　　　Isaac Watts.

112 *Psalm 19.*

ALMIGHTY Lord, the sun shall fail,
The moon forget her nightly tale,
And deepest silence hush on high,
The radiant chorus of the sky;—

2 But fixed for everlasting years,
Unmoved, amid the wreck of spheres,
Thy word shall shine in cloudless day,
When heaven and earth have passed away.
　　　　　　　　　Robert Grant.

DAY OF REST. 7s, 6s. D. J. W. Elliott.

The heavens declare his glo - ry, Their Mak - er's skill the skies; Each day repeats the
sto - ry, And night to night re - plies. Their si - lent proc - la - ma - tion
Voices in Unison.
In Harmony.
Throughout the earth is heard; The rec - ord of cre - a - tion, The page of nature's word.

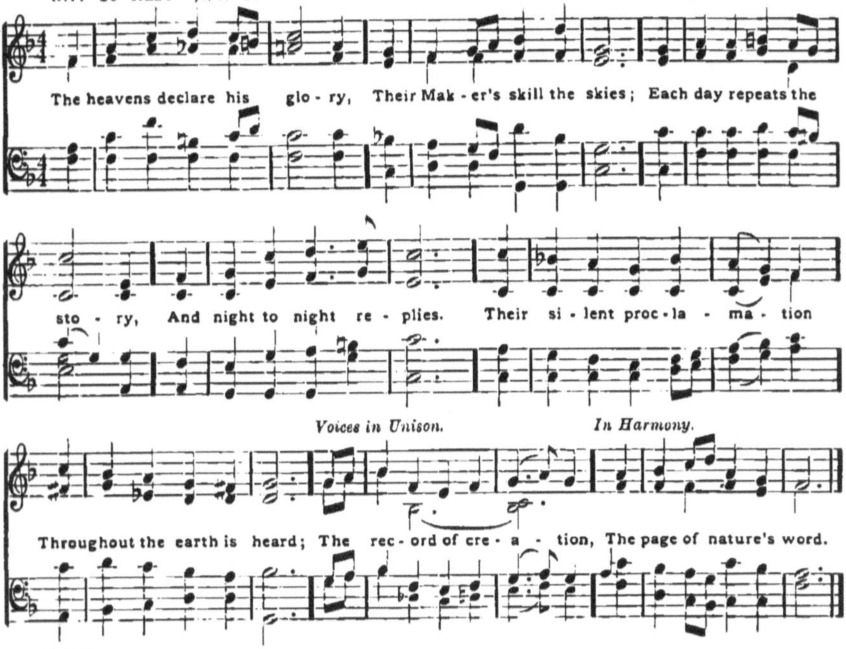

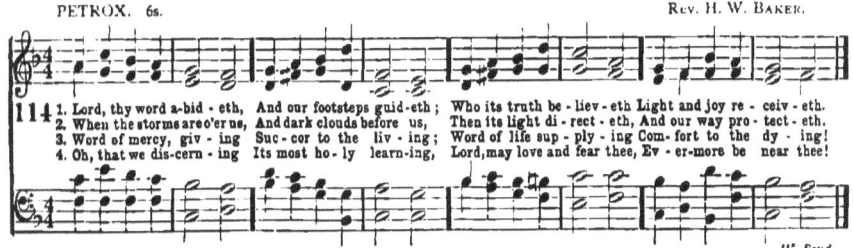

113 *Psalm 19.*

THE heavens declare his glory,
  Their Maker's skill the skies;
Each day repeats the story,
  And night to night replies.
Their silent proclamation
  Throughout the earth is heard;
The record of creation,
  The page of nature's word.

2 So pure, so soul-restoring,
  Is truth's diviner ray;
A brighter radiance pouring
  Than all the pomp of day:
The wanderer surely guiding,
  It makes the simple wise;
And, evermore abiding,
  Unfailing joy supplies.

3 Thy word is richer treasure
  Than lurks within the mine;
And daintiest fare less pleasure
  Yields than this food divine.
How wise each kind monition!
  Led by thy counsels, Lord,
How safe the saints' condition,
  How great is their reward!

J. Conder.

PETROX. 6s. Rev. H. W. Baker.

114
1. Lord, thy word a-bid - eth, And our footsteps guid-eth; Who its truth be - liev - eth Light and joy re - ceiv - eth.
2. When the storms are o'er us, And dark clouds before us, Then its light di - rect - eth, And our way pro - tect - eth.
3. Word of mercy, giv - ing Suc - cor to the liv - ing; Word of life sup - ply - ing Com - fort to the dy - ing!
4. Oh, that we dis-cern - ing Its most ho - ly learn-ing, Lord, may love and fear thee, Ev - er-more be near thee!

W. Boyd.

GOD:—THE FATHER.

ST. ANN'S. C. M. — W. Croft.

Keep si-lence, all created things! And wait your Maker's nod; My soul stands trembling, while she sings The honors of her God.

115 *Providence.*

Keep silence, all created things!
　And wait your Maker's nod;
My soul stands trembling, while she sings
　The honors of her God.

2 Life, death, and hell, and worlds unknown,
　Hang on his firm decree;
He sits on no precarious throne,
　Nor borrows leave to be.

3 His providence unfolds the book,
　And makes his counsels shine;
Each opening leaf, and every stroke,
　Fulfills some deep design.

4 My God! I would not long to see
　My fate with curious eyes—
What gloomy lines are writ for me,
　Or what bright scenes may rise.

5 In thy fair book of life and grace,
　Oh, may I find my name
Recorded in some humble place,
　Beneath my Lord, the Lamb.
　　　　　　　　　Isaac Watts.

116 *Providence.*

God moves in a mysterious way
　His wonders to perform;
He plants his footsteps in the sea,
　And rides upon the storm.

2 Ye fearful saints, fresh courage take!
　The clouds ye so much dread,
Are big with mercy, and will break
　In blessings on your head.

3 Judge not the Lord by feeble sense,
　But trust him for his grace;
Behind a frowning providence
　He hides a smiling face.

4 His purposes will ripen fast,
　Unfolding every hour;
The bud may have a bitter taste,
　But sweet will be the flower.

5 Blind unbelief is sure to err,
　And scan his work in vain;
God is his own interpreter,
　And he will make it plain.
　　　　　　　　William Cowper.

MANOAH. C. M. — Arr. fr. Rossini.

Begin, my tongue, some heav'nly theme, And speak some boundless thing; The mighty works or mightier name Of our eternal King.

117 *Faithfulness.*

Begin, my tongue, some heavenly theme,
　And speak some boundless thing;
The mighty works or mightier name
　Of our eternal King.

2 Tell of his wondrous faithfulness,
　And sound his power abroad;
Sing the sweet promise of his grace,
　And the performing God.

3 His very word of grace is strong,
　As that which built the skies;
The voice that rolls the stars along,
　Speaks all the promises.

4 Oh, might I hear thy heavenly tongue
　But whisper, "Thou art mine!"
Those gentle words should raise my song
　To notes almost divine.
　　　　　　　　　Isaac Watts.

ATTRIBUTES.

118 [Tune—St. Ann's.]

The Lord, our God, is full of might,
  The winds obey his will;
He speaks,—and, in his heavenly height,
  The rolling sun stands still.

2 Rebel, ye waves, and o'er the land
  With threatening aspect roar;
The Lord uplifts his awful hand,
  And chains you to the shore.

3 Howl, winds of night, your force combine;
  Without his high behest,
Ye shall not, in the mountain pine,
  Disturb the sparrow's nest.

4 His voice sublime is heard afar,
  In distant peals it dies;
He yokes the whirlwind to his car,
  And sweeps the howling skies.

5 Ye nations, bend—in reverence bend;
  Ye monarchs, wait his nod,
And bid the choral song ascend
  To celebrate your God.
  Henry Kirke White.

CAROLYN. 7s, 6s. D. Arr. by Emmelar.

O God, the Rock of Ages, Who evermore hast been, What time the tempest rages, Our dwelling-place serene; Before thy first creations, O Lord, the same as now, To endless generations, The Everlasting thou!

119 *Everlasting.—Ps. 90.*

O God, the Rock of Ages,
  Who evermore hast been,
What time the tempest rages,
  Our dwelling-place serene:
Before thy first creations,
  O Lord, the same as now,
To endless generations,
  The Everlasting thou!

2 Our years are like the shadows
  On sunny hills that lie,
Or grasses in the meadows
  That blossom but to die:
A sleep, a dream, a story,
  By strangers quickly told,
An unremaining glory
  Of things that soon are old.

3 O thou who canst not slumber,
  Whose light grows never pale,
Teach us aright to number
  Our years before they fail!
On us thy mercy lighten,
  On us thy goodness rest,
And let thy Spirit brighten
  The hearts thyself hast blessed!
  E. H. Bickersteth.

120 *Providence.*

WHILE thee I seek, protecting Power!
  Be my vain wishes stilled;
And may this consecrated hour
  With better hopes be filled;
Thy love the power of thought bestowed,
  To thee my thoughts would soar:
Thy mercy o'er my life has flowed;
  That mercy I adore.

2 In each event of life how clear
  Thy ruling hand I see!
Each blessing to my soul more dear
  Because conferred by thee.
In every joy that crowns my days,
  In every pain I bear,
My heart shall find delight in praise
  Or seek relief in prayer.

3 When gladness wings my favored hour,
  Thy love my thoughts shall fill;
Resigned, when storms of sorrow lower,
  My soul shall meet thy will.

My lifted eye, without a tear,
  The gathering storm shall see;
My steadfast heart shall know no fear;
  That heart will rest on thee.
Helen M. Williams.

121 *Psalm 116.*

WHAT shall I render to my God,
  For all his kindness shown?
My feet shall visit thine abode,
  My songs address thy throne.

2 Among the saints that fill thine house,
  My offering shall be paid;
There shall my zeal perform the vows,
  My soul in anguish made.

3 How much is mercy thy delight,
  Thou ever blessèd God!
How dear thy servants in thy sight!
  How precious is their blood!

4 How happy all thy servants are!
  How great thy grace to me!
My life, which thou hast made thy care,
  Lord, I devote to thee.
Isaac Watts.

ATTRIBUTES.

122 *Continued help.*

When all thy mercies, O my God!
 My rising soul surveys,
Transported with the view, I'm lost
 In wonder, love, and praise.

2 Unnumbered comforts, to my soul,
 Thy tender care bestowed,
Before my infant heart conceived
 From whom those comforts flowed.

3 When, in the slippery paths of youth,
 With heedless steps, I ran,
Thine arm, unseen, conveyed me safe,
 And led me up to man.

4 Ten thousand, thousand precious gifts
 My daily thanks employ;
Nor is the least a cheerful heart,
 That tastes those gifts with joy.

5 Through every period of my life,
 Thy goodness I'll pursue;
And after death, in distant worlds,
 The glorious theme renew.

6 Through all eternity, to thee
 A joyful song I'll raise:
For, oh, eternity's too short
 To utter all thy praise!
 Joseph Addison.

123 *Psalm 90.*

Our God, our help in ages past,
 Our hope for years to come;
Our shelter from the stormy blast,
 And our eternal home!
Under the shadow of thy throne
 Thy saints have dwelt secure;
Sufficient is thine arm alone,
 And our defence is sure.

2 Before the hills in order stood,
 Or earth received her frame,
From everlasting thou art God
 To endless years the same.
A thousand ages, in thy sight,
 Are like an evening gone;
Short as the watch that ends the night,
 Before the rising sun.

3 Time, like an ever-rolling stream
 Bears all its sons away;
They fly, forgotten, as a dream
 Dies at the opening day.
Our God, our help in ages past,
 Our hope for years to come,
Be thou our guard while troubles last,
 And our eternal home.
 Isaac Watts.

CORINTH. C. M.   Lowell Mason.

My God, how wonderful thou art, Thy majesty how bright! How glorious is thy mercy-seat, In depths of burning light!

124 *"Herein is Love."*

My God, how wonderful thou art,
 Thy majesty how bright!
How glorious is thy mercy-seat,
 In depths of burning light!

2 How dread are thine eternal years,
 O everlasting Lord!
By prostrate spirits day and night
 Incessantly adored.

3 Oh, how I fear thee, living God,
 With deepest, tenderest fears,
And worship thee with trembling hope,
 And penitential tears.

4 Yet I may love thee too, O Lord,
 Almighty as thou art,
For thou hast stooped to ask of me
 The love of my poor heart.

5 No earthly father loves like thee,
 No mother half so mild
Bears and forbears, as thou hast done
 With me, thy sinful child.

6 My God, how wonderful thou art,
 Thou everlasting Friend!
On thee I stay my trusting heart,
 Till faith in vision end.
 Frederick W. Faber.

GOD:—THE FATHER.

125 *My Father.*

O GOD, thy power is wonderful,
　Thy glory passing bright;
Thy wisdom, with its deep on deep,
　A rapture to the sight.
I see thee in the eternal years
　In glory all alone,
Ere round thine uncreated fires
　Created light had shone.

2 I see thee walk in Eden's shade,
　I see thee all through time;
Thy patience and compassion seem
　New attributes sublime.
I see thee when the doom is o'er,
　And outworn time is done,
Still, still incomprehensible,
　O God, yet not alone.

3 Angelic spirits, countless souls,
　Of thee have drunk their fill;
And to eternity will drink
　Thy joy and glory still.
O little heart of mine! shall pain
　Or sorrow make thee moan,
When all this God is all for thee,
　A Father all thine own?
　　　　　　Frederick W. Faber.

126 *Perfections.*

I SING the almighty power of God,
　That made the mountains rise,
That spread the flowing seas abroad,
　And built the lofty skies.
I sing the wisdom that ordained
　The sun to rule the day;
The moon shines full at his command,
　And all the stars obey.

2 I sing the goodness of the Lord,
　That filled the earth with food;
He formed the creatures with his word,
　And then pronounced them good.
Lord! how thy wonders are displayed
　Where'er I turn mine eye!
If I survey the ground I tread,
　Or gaze upon the sky!

3 There's not a plant or flower below
　But makes thy glories known;
And clouds arise, and tempests blow,
　By order from thy throne.
Creatures that borrow life from thee
　Are subject to thy care;
There's not a place where we can flee,
　But God is present there.
　　　　　　Isaac Watts.

ATTRIBUTES.

127 [Tune—Noel.]
My Shepherd will supply my need,
  Jehovah is his name;
In pastures fresh he makes me feed,
  Beside the living stream.
He brings my wandering spirit back,
  When I forsake his ways;
And leads me, for his mercy's sake,
  In paths of truth and grace.

2 When I walk through the shades of death,
  Thy presence is my stay;
A word of thy supporting breath,
  Drives all my fears away.
Thy hand, in sight of all my foes,
  Doth still my table spread;
My cup with blessings overflows,
  Thine oil anoints my head.

3 The sure provisions of my God
  Attend me all my days;
Oh, may thy house be mine abode,
  And all my works be praise:
There would I find a settled rest,
  While others go and come,—
No more a stranger, or a guest,
  But like a child at home.
                              Isaac Watts.

128 [Tune—Noel.]
Father! how wide thy glory shines!
  How high thy wonders rise!
Known through the earth by thousand signs,
  By thousand through the skies.

2 Those mighty orbs proclaim thy power,
  Their motions speak thy skill;
And on the wings of every hour,
  We read thy patience still.

3 But, when we view thy strange design
  To save rebellious worms,
Where vengeance and compassion join
  In their divinest forms,—

4 Here the whole Deity is known;
  Nor dares a creature guess
Which of the glories brightest shone,
  The justice, or the grace.

5 Now the full glories of the Lamb
  Adorn the heavenly plains;
Bright seraphs learn Immanuel's name,
  And try their choicest strains.

6 Oh, may I bear some humble part,
  In that immortal song;
Wonder and joy shall tune my heart,
  And love command my tongue.
                              Isaac Watts.

ITALIAN HYMN. 6s, 4s.

Come, thou Almighty King,
  Help us thy name to sing,
Help us to praise: Father! all-glorious,
O'er all vic-to-rious, Come, and reign over us, Ancient of Days!

129 "*One in Three.*"
Come, thou Almighty King,
Help us thy name to sing,
  Help us to praise:
Father! all-glorious,
O'er all victorious,
Come, and reign over us,
  Ancient of Days!

2 Come, thou incarnate Word,
Gird on thy mighty sword;
  Our prayer attend;
Come, and thy people bless,
And give thy word success,
Spirit of holiness!
  On us descend.

3 Come, holy Comforter!
Thy sacred witness bear,
  In this glad hour:
Thou, who almighty art,
Now rule in every heart,
And ne'er from us depart,
  Spirit of power!

4 To the great One in Three,
The highest praises be,
  Hence evermore!
His sovereign majesty
May we in glory see,
And to eternity
  Love and adore.
                              Charles Wesley.

GOD: THE FATHER.

LAUD. C. M.   J. B. DYKES.

O God! we praise thee, and confess That thou the only Lord
And everlasting Father art, By all the earth adored.

130   *"Te Deum."*

O God! we praise thee, and confess
  That thou the only Lord
And everlasting Father art,
  By all the earth adored.

2 To thee all angels cry aloud;
  To thee the powers on high,
Both cherubim and seraphim,
  Continually do cry:—

3 O holy, holy, holy Lord,
  Whom heavenly hosts obey,
The world is with the glory filled
  Of thy majestic sway!

4 The apostles' glorious company,
  And prophets crowned with light,
With all the martyrs' noble host,
  Thy constant praise recite.

5 The holy church throughout the world,
  O Lord, confesses thee,
That thou the eternal Father art,
  Of boundless majesty.
N. Tate, tr.

DOWNS. C. M.   LOWELL MASON.

Come, ye that know and fear the Lord, And raise your tho'ts above: Let every heart and voice accord, To sing that "God is love."

131   *Love.*

COME, ye that know and fear the Lord,
  And raise your thoughts above:
Let every heart and voice accord,
  To sing that "God is love."

2 This precious truth his word declares,
  And all his mercies prove;
Jesus, the gift of gifts, appears,
  To show that "God is love."

3 Behold his patience, bearing long
  With those who from him rove;
Till mighty grace their hearts subdues,
  To teach them—"God is love."

4 Oh, may we all, while here below,
  This best of blessings prove;
Till warmer hearts, in brighter worlds,
  Proclaim that "God is love."
George Burder.

ATTRIBUTES.

ERIE. 8s, 7s. D.   C. C. CONVERSE.

132   *God's Welcome.*

There's a wideness in God's mercy,
  Like the wideness of the sea:
There's a kindness in his justice,
  Which is more than liberty.
There is welcome for the sinner,
  And more graces for the good;
There is mercy with the Saviour;
  There is healing in his blood.

2 There is no place where earth's sorrows
  Are more felt than up in heaven;
There is no place where earth's failings
  Have such kindly judgment given.
There is plentiful redemption
  In the blood that has been shed;
There is joy for all the members
  In the sorrows of the Head.

3 For the love of God is broader
  Than the measure of man's mind;
And the heart of the Eternal
  Is most wonderfully kind.
If our love were but more simple,
  We should take him at his word;
And our lives would be all sunshine
  In the sweetness of our Lord.
              Frederick W. Faber.

DUNDEE. C. M.   G. FRANC.

133   *Eternity.*

Great God! how infinite art thou!
  What worthless worms are we!
Let the whole race of creatures bow,
  And pay their praise to thee.

2 Thy throne eternal ages stood,
  Ere seas or stars were made:
Thou art the ever-living God,
  Were all the nations dead.

3 Eternity, with all its years,
  Stands present in thy view;
To thee there's nothing old appears—
  Great God! there's nothing new.

4 Our lives through various scenes are drawn,
  And vexed with trifling cares;
While thine eternal thought moves on
  Thine undisturbed affairs.

5 Great God! how infinite art thou!
  What worthless worms are we!
Let the whole race of creatures bow,
  And pay their praise to thee.
              Isaac Watts.

GOD:—THE FATHER.

LOUVAN. L. M. — V. C. Taylor

134 *Omnipresence.*

Lord of all being; throned afar,
Thy glory flames from sun and star;
Centre and soul of every sphere,
Yet to each loving heart how near!

2 Sun of our life, thy quickening ray
Sheds on our path the glow of day;
Star of our hope, thy softened light
Cheers the long watches of the night.

3 Our midnight is thy smile withdrawn;
Our noontide is thy gracious dawn;
Our rainbow arch thy mercy's sign;
All, save the clouds of sin, are thine!

4 Lord of all life, below, above,
Whose light is truth, whose warmth is love,
Before thy ever-blazing throne
We ask no lustre of our own.

5 Grant us thy truth to make us free,
And kindling hearts that burn for thee,
Till all thy living altars claim
One holy light, one heavenly flame!
Oliver Wendell Holmes.

135 *Providence.*

Lord, how mysterious are thy ways!
How blind are we, how mean our praise!
Thy steps no mortal eyes explore;
'T is ours to wonder and adore.

2 Great God! I do not ask to see
What in futurity shall be;
Let light and bliss attend my days,
And then my future hours be praise.

3 Are darkness and distress my share?
Give me to trust thy guardian care;
Enough for me, if love divine
At length through every cloud shall shine.

4 Yet this my soul desires to know,
Be this my only wish below;
That Christ is mine!—this great request,
Grant, bounteous God, and I am blest.
Anne Steele.

136 *Sovereignty.*

Lord, my weak thought in vain would climb
 To search the starry vault profound;
In vain would wing her flight sublime,
 To find creation's outmost bound.

2 But weaker yet that thought must prove
 To search thy great eternal plan,—
Thy sovereign counsels, born of love
 Long ages ere the world began.

3 When my dim reason would demand
 Why that, or this, thou dost ordain,
By some vast deep I seem to stand,
 Whose secrets I must ask in vain.

4 When doubts disturb my troubled breast,
 And all is dark as night to me,
Here, as on solid rock, I rest;
 That so it seemeth good to thee.

5 Be this my joy, that evermore
 Thou rulest all things at thy will;
Thy sovereign wisdom I adore,
 And calmly, sweetly, trust thee still.
Ray Palmer.

THE LORD JESUS CHRIST.

IRBY. 8s, 7s, 7s. H. J. GAUNTLETT.

Once in roy-al David's cit-y Stood a low-ly cat-tle shed, Where a moth-er laid her Ba-by, In a manger for his bed: Ma-ry was that mother mild, Je-sus Christ her lit-tle child.

137 *"The child Jesus."*

Once in royal David's city
　Stood a lowly cattle shed,
Where a mother laid her Baby,
　In a manger for his bed:
Mary was that mother mild,
Jesus Christ her little child.

2 He came down to earth from heaven
　Who is God and Lord of all,
And his shelter was a stable,
　And his cradle was a stall;
With the lowly, poor, and mean,
Lived on earth our Saviour then.

3 And, through all his wondrous childhood,
　He would honor and obey,
Love, and watch the lowly maiden
　In whose gentle arms he lay:
Christian children all must be
Mild, obedient, good as he.

4 Oh, our eyes at last shall see him,
　Through his own redeeming love,
For that child so dear and gentle
　Is our God in heaven above;
And he leads his children on
To the place where he is gone.

5 Not in that poor lowly stable,
　With the oxen standing by,
We shall see him; but in heaven,
　Set at God's right hand on high;
When like stars his children crowned
All in white shall wait around.
　　　　　　Mrs. C. F. Alexander.

138 *"Friend of Sinners."*

One there is above all others,
　Well deserves the name of Friend;
His is love beyond a brother's,
　Costly, free, and knows no end:
They who once his kindness prove
Find it everlasting love.

2 Which of all our friends, to save us,
　Could or would have shed his blood?
But our Jesus died to have us
　Reconciled in him to God:
This was boundless love indeed!
Jesus is a friend in need.

3 When he lived on earth abased,
　"Friend of sinners" was his name;
Now above all glories raiséd,
　He rejoices in the same;
Still he calls them brethren, friends,
And to all their wants attends.

4 Could we bear from one another
　What he daily bears from us?
Yet this glorious Friend and Brother
　Loves us though we treat him thus:
Though for good we render ill,
He accounts us brethren still.

5 Oh, for grace our hearts to soften!
　Teach us, Lord, at length to love;
We, alas! forget too often
　What a Friend we have above:
But when home our souls are brought,
We will love thee as we ought.
　　　　　　John Newton.

THE LORD JESUS CHRIST.

CAROL C. M. D.   R. S. Willis.

139   *The Angels' Song.*

It came upon the midnight clear,
  That glorious song of old,
From angels bending near the earth,
  To touch their harps of gold;
"Peace to the earth, good-will to men,
  From heaven's all-gracious King:"
The earth in solemn stillness lay,
  To hear the angels sing.

2 Still through the cloven skies they come,
  With peaceful wings unfurled;
And still celestial music floats
  O'er all the weary world;
Above its sad and lowly plains
  They bend on heavenly wing,
And ever o'er its Babel sounds,
  The blessèd angels sing.

3 O ye, beneath life's crushing load,
  Whose forms are bending low,
Who toil along the climbing way,
  With painful steps and slow;—
Look up! for glad and golden hours
  Come swiftly on the wing;
Oh, rest beside the weary road,
  And hear the angels sing!

4 For lo! the days are hastening on,
  By prophet-bards foretold,
When with the ever-circling years
  Comes round the age of gold!
When peace shall over all the earth
  Its final splendors fling,
And the whole world send back the song
  Which now the angels sing!

Edwin H. Sears.

CHRISTMAS. C. M.   Arr. fr. Händel.

INCARNATION AND BIRTH.

NOEL. C. M. D.   Arr. by A. S. Sullivan.

While shepherds watched their flocks by night, All seated on the ground; The angel of the Lord came down, And glory shone around. "Fear not," said he,—for mighty dread Had seized their troubled mind,—"Glad tidings of great joy I bring, To you and all mankind.

140   *Bethlehem Song.*

WHILE shepherds watched their flocks by
  All seated on the ground; [night,
The angel of the Lord came down,
  And glory shone around.
"Fear not," said he,—for mighty dread
  Had seized their troubled mind,—
"Glad tidings of great joy I bring,
  To you and all mankind.

2 "To you, in David's town this day,
  Is born of David's line,
The Saviour, who is Christ, the Lord,
  And this shall be the sign;—
The heavenly babe you there shall find
  To human view displayed,
All meanly wrapped in swathing bands,
  And in a manger laid."

3 Thus spake the seraph—and forthwith
  Appeared a shining throng
Of angels, praising God, who thus
  Addressed their joyful song:—
"All glory be to God on high,
  And to the earth be peace;
Good-will henceforth from heaven to men
  Begin, and never cease!"
                    Nahum Tate.

141   *Angels' music.*

CALM on the listening ear of night,
  Come heaven's melodious strains,
Where wild Judea stretches far
  Her silver-mantled plains.
Celestial choirs, from courts above,
  Shed sacred glories there,
And angels, with their sparkling lyres,
  Make music on the air.

2 The answering hills of Palestine
  Send back the glad reply,
And greet from all their holy heights
  The Dayspring from on high;
O'er the blue depths of Galilee
  There comes a holier calm;
And Sharon waves in solemn praise
  Her silent groves of palm.

3 "Glory to God!" the lofty strain
  The realms of ether fills;
How sweeps the song of solemn joy
  O'er Judah's sacred hills!
"Glory to God!" the sounding skies
  Loud with their anthems ring:
"Peace on the earth; good-will to men,
  From heaven's eternal King."
                    Edwin H. Sears.

THE LORD JESUS CHRIST.

HERALD ANGELS. 7s. D.   Arr. fr. MENDELSSOHN.

142   *The Nativity.*

HARK! the herald angels sing
"Glory to the new-born King;
Peace on earth, and mercy mild,
God and sinners reconciled!"
Joyful, all ye nations, rise,
Join the triumph of the skies;
With the angelic host proclaim,
Christ is born in Bethlehem!

2 Christ, by highest heaven adored;
Christ, the everlasting Lord;
Late in time behold him come,
Offspring of the Virgin's womb:
Vailed in flesh the Godhead see;
Hail the incarnate Deity,
Pleased as man with men to dwell;
Jesus, our Immanuel!

3 Hail! the heaven-born Prince of Peace!
Hail the Sun of Righteousness!
Light and life to all he brings,
Risen with healing in his wings:
Mild he lays his glory by,
Born that man no more may die:
Born to raise the sons of earth,
Born to give them second birth.
Charles Wesley.

143   *"The Christ of God."*

HE has come! the Christ of God
Left for us his glad abode;
Stooping from his throne of bliss,
To this darksome wilderness.
He has come! the Prince of Peace;
Come to bid our sorrows cease;
Come to scatter with his light
All the shadows of our night.

2 He the mighty King has come!
Making this poor earth his home;
Come to bear our sin's sad load;
Son of David, Son of God!
He has come, whose name of grace
Speaks deliverance to our race;
Left for us his glad abode;
Son of Mary, Son of God!

3 Unto us a child is born!
Ne'er has earth beheld a morn,
Among all the morns of time,
Half so glorious in its prime.
Unto us a Son is given!
He has come from God's own heaven,
Bringing with him from above
Holy peace and holy love.
Horatius Bonar.

INCARNATION AND BIRTH.

ANTIOCH. C. M.   Arr. by L. Mason.

144   *Psalm 98.*

Joy to the world; the Lord is come!
  Let earth receive her King;
Let every heart prepare him room,
  And heaven and nature sing.

2 Joy to the earth; the Saviour reigns;
  Let men their songs employ;
While fields and floods, rocks, hills, and plains,
  Repeat the sounding joy.

3 No more let sins and sorrows grow,
  Nor thorns infest the ground;
He comes to make his blessings flow
  Far as the curse is found.

4 He rules the world with truth and grace,
  And makes the nations prove
The glories of his righteousness,
  And wonders of his love.
                    Isaac Watts.

---

145   7s. D.   *"All hail the morn!"*

Hail the night, all hail the morn,
When the Prince of Peace was born!
When, amid the wakeful fold,
Tidings good the angels told.
Now our solemn chant we raise
Duly to the Saviour's praise;
Now with carol hymns we bless
Christ the Lord, our righteousness.

2 While resounds the joyful cry,
"Glory be to God on high,
Peace on earth, good-will to men!"
Gladly we respond, "Amen!"
Thus we greet this holy day,
Pouring forth our festive lay;
Thus we tell, with saintly mirth,
Of Immanuel's wondrous birth.
                    Anon., 1857.

146   7s. D.   *Immanuel.*

God with us! oh, glorious name!
Let it shine in endless fame;
God and man in Christ unite;
Oh, mysterious depth and height!
God with us! the eternal Son
Took our soul, our flesh, and bone;
Now, ye saints, his grace admire,
Swell the song with holy fire.

2 God with us! but tainted not
With the first transgressor's blot;
Yet did he our sins sustain,
Bear the guilt, the curse, the pain.
God with us! oh, wondrous grace!
Let us see him face to face;
That we may Immanuel sing,
As we ought, our God and King!
                    Sarah Slinn.

147 *The name "Jesus."*

The Saviour! oh, what endless charms
  Dwell in the blissful sound!
Its influence every fear disarms,
  And spreads sweet comfort round.
The almighty Former of the skies
  Stooped to our vile abode;
While angels viewed with wondering eyes
  And hailed the incarnate God.

2 Oh, the rich depths of love divine!
  Of bliss a boundless store!
Dear Saviour, let me call thee mine;
  I cannot wish for more.
On thee alone my hope relies,
  Beneath thy cross I fall;
My Lord, my Life, my Sacrifice,
  My Saviour, and my All!
Anne Steele.

148 *Jesus' Words.*

I heard the voice of Jesus say,—
  "Come unto me and rest;
Lay down, thou weary one, lay down
  Thy head upon my breast!"
I came to Jesus as I was,
  Weary, and worn, and sad,
I found in him a resting-place,
  And he hath made me glad.

2 I heard the voice of Jesus say,—
  "Behold I freely give
The living water; thirsty one,
  Stoop down, and drink, and live!"
I came to Jesus, and I drank
  Of that life-giving stream;
My thirst was quenched, my soul revived,
  And now I live in him.

3 I heard the voice of Jesus say,—
  "I am this dark world's light;
Look unto me, thy morn shall rise
  And all thy day be bright!"
I looked to Jesus, and I found
  In him my Star, my Sun;
And in that light of life I'll walk,
  Till all my journey's done.
Horatius Bonar.

149 *"His free ways."*

Oh, see how Jesus trusts himself
  Unto our childish love!
As though by his free ways with us
  Our earnestness to prove.
His sacred name a common word
  On earth he loves to hear;
There is no majesty in him
  Which love may not come near.

2 The light of love is round his feet,
  His paths are never dim;
And he comes nigh to us when we
  Dare not come nigh to him.
Let us be simple with him then,
  Not backward, stiff, nor cold,
As though our Bethlehem could be
  What Sinai was of old.
F. W. Faber.

LIFE AND CHARACTER.

150 *"Altogether Lovely."*

MAJESTIC sweetness sits enthroned
Upon the Saviour's brow;
His head with radiant glories crowned,
His lips with grace o'erflow.

2 No mortal can with him compare,
Among the sons of men;
Fairer is he than all the fair
That fill the heavenly train.

3 He saw me plunged in deep distress,
He flew to my relief;
For me he bore the shameful cross,
And carried all my grief.

4 To him I owe my life and breath,
And all the joys I have;
He makes me triumph over death,
He saves me from the grave.

5 To heaven, the place of his abode,
He brings my weary feet;
Shows me the glories of my God,
And makes my joy complete.

6 Since from his bounty I receive
Such proofs of love divine,
Had I a thousand hearts to give,
Lord! they should all be thine.
Samuel Stennett.

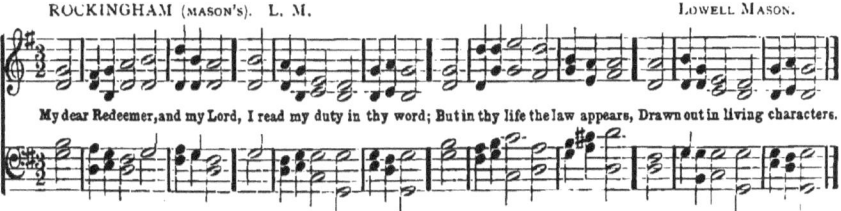

151 *The Divine Pattern.*

MY dear Redeemer, and my Lord,
I read my duty in thy word;
But in thy life the law appears,
Drawn out in living characters.

2 Such was thy truth and such thy zeal,
Such deference to thy Father's will,
Such love, and meekness so divine,
I would transcribe and make them mine.

3 Cold mountains and the midnight air
Witnessed the fervor of thy prayer;
The desert thy temptations knew,
Thy conflict and thy victory too.

4 Be thou my pattern; make me bear
More of thy gracious image here;
Then God, the Judge, shall own my name
Among the followers of the Lamb.
Isaac Watts.

THE LORD JESUS CHRIST.

SESSIONS. L. M.   L. O. EMERSON.

How sweetly flowed the gos-pel sound From lips of gen-tle-ness and grace,
When listening thousands gathered round, And joy and glad-ness filled the place!

152 *The Great Teacher.*
How SWEETLY flowed the gospel sound
  From lips of gentleness and grace,
When listening thousands gathered round,
  And joy and gladness filled the place!

2 From heaven he came, of heaven he spoke,
  To heaven he led his followers' way;
Dark clouds of gloomy night he broke,
  Unvailing an immortal day.

3 "Come, wanderers, to my Father's home,
  Come, all ye weary ones, and rest:"
Yes, sacred Teacher, we will come,
  Obey thee, love thee, and be blest!

4 Decay then, tenements of dust;
  Pillars of earthly pride, decay:
A nobler mansion waits the just,
  And Jesus has prepared the way.
                         John Bowring.

153 *"Holy, harmless."*
How BEAUTEOUS were the marks divine,
That in thy meekness used to shine,
That lit thy lonely pathway, trod
In wondrous love, O Son of God!

2 Oh, who like thee, so calm, so bright,
So pure, so made to live in light?
Oh, who like thee did ever go
So patient through a world of woe?

3 Oh, who like thee so humbly bore
The scorn, the scoffs of men, before?
So meek, forgiving, godlike, high,
So glorious in humility?

4 Even death, which sets the prisoner free,
Was pang, and scoff, and scorn to thee;
Yet love through all thy torture glowed,
And mercy with thy life-blood flowed.

5 Oh, in thy light be mine to go,
Illuming all my way of woe!
And give me ever on the road
To trace thy footsteps, Son of God.
                         Arthur C. Coxe.

154 *"He healed them."*
WHEN, like a stranger on our sphere,
The lowly Jesus wandered here,
Where'er he went, affliction fled,
And sickness reared her fainting head.

2 The eye that rolled in irksome night,
Beheld his face—for God is light;
The opening ear, the loosened tongue,
His precepts heard, his praises sung.

3 With bounding steps the halt and lame,
To hail their great Deliverer came;
O'er the cold grave he bowed his head,
He spake the word, and raised the dead.

4 Despairing madness, dark and wild,
In his inspiring presence smiled;
The storm of horror ceased to roll,
And reason lightened through the soul.

5 Through paths of loving-kindness led,
Where Jesus triumphed we would tread;
To all, with willing hands dispense
The gifts of our benevolence.
                         James Montgomery.

LIFE AND CHARACTER.

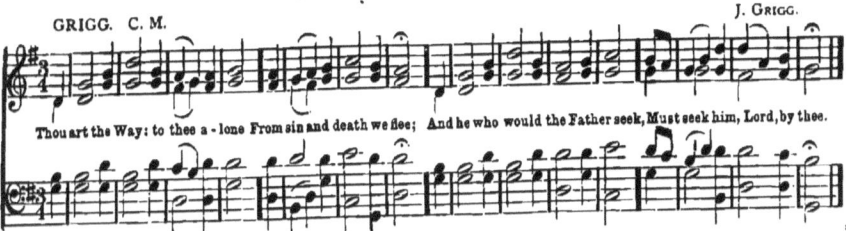

GRIGG. C. M.   J. GRIGG.

Thou art the Way: to thee alone From sin and death we flee; And he who would the Father seek, Must seek him, Lord, by thee.

155 *"Way, Truth, and Life."*

Thou art the Way: to thee alone
  From sin and death we flee;
And he who would the Father seek,
  Must seek him, Lord, by thee.

2 Thou art the Truth: thy word alone
  True wisdom can impart;
Thou only canst inform the mind,
  And purify the heart.

3 Thou art the Life: the rending tomb
  Proclaims thy conquering arm;
And those who put their trust in thee
  Nor death nor hell shall harm.

4 Thou art the Way, the Truth, the Life:
  Grant us that Way to know;
That Truth to keep, that Life to win,
  Whose joys eternal flow.
George W. Doane.

HELENA. C. M.   W. B. BRADBURY.

Lord, as to thy dear cross we flee, And pray to be for-given, So let thy life our pattern be, And form our souls for heaven.

156 *Pattern of Forgiveness.*

Lord, as to thy dear cross we flee,
  And pray to be forgiven,
So let thy life our pattern be,
  And form our souls for heaven.

2 Help us, through good report and ill,
  Our daily cross to bear;
Like thee, to do our Father's will,
  Our brother's griefs to share.

3 Let grace our selfishness expel,
  Our earthliness refine;
And kindness in our bosoms dwell
  As free and true as thine.

4 If joy shall at thy bidding fly,
  And grief's dark day come on,
We, in our turn, would meekly cry,
  "Father, thy will be done!"

5 Kept peaceful in the midst of strife,
  Forgiving and forgiven,
Oh, may we lead the pilgrim's life,
  And follow thee to heaven!
John H. Gurney.

157 *"Shall we forget."*

Jesus! thy love shall we forget,
  And never bring to mind
The grace that paid our hopeless debt,
  And bade us pardon find?

2 Shall we thy life of grief forget,
  Thy fasting and thy prayer;
Thy locks with mountain vapors wet,
  To save us from despair?

3 Gethsemane can we forget—
  Thy struggling agony
When night lay dark on Olivet,
  And none to watch with thee?

4 Our sorrows and our sins were laid
  On thee, alone on thee;
Thy precious blood our ransom paid—
  Thine all the glory be!

5 Life's brightest joys we may forget—
  Our kindred cease to love;
But he who paid our hopeless debt,
  Our constancy shall prove.
William Mitchell.

THE LORD JESUS CHRIST.

SERENITY. C. M.   Arr. fr. W. V. WALLACE.

We may not climb the heavenly steeps To bring the Lord Christ down; In vain we search the lowest deeps, For him no depths can drown.

158   *The true Test.*

WE may not climb the heavenly steeps
  To bring the Lord Christ down;
In vain we search the lowest deeps,
  For him no depths can drown.

2 But warm, sweet, tender, even yet
  A present help is he;
And faith has yet its Olivet,
  And love its Galilee.

3 The healing of the seamless dress
  Is by our beds of pain;
We touch him in life's throng and press,
  And we are whole again.

4 Through him the first fond prayers are said
  Our lips of childhood frame;
The last low whispers of our dead
  Are burdened with his name.

5 O Lord and Master of us all,
  Whate'er our name or sign,
We own thy sway, we hear thy call,
  We test our lives by thine!

John G. Whittier.

ARIEL. C. P. M.   LOWELL MASON.

Oh, could I speak the matchless worth, Oh, could I sound the glories forth Which in my Saviour shine! I'd soar, and touch the heavenly strings, And vie with Gabriel while he sings In notes almost di-vine, In notes al-most di-vine.

159   *"He is precious."*

OH, could I speak the matchless worth
Oh, could I sound the glories forth,
  Which in my Saviour shine!
I'd soar, and touch the heavenly strings,
And vie with Gabriel while he sings
  In notes almost divine.

2 I'd sing the precious blood he spilt,
My ransom from the dreadful guilt
  Of sin and wrath divine!
I'd sing his glorious righteousness,
In which all-perfect heavenly dress
  My soul shall ever shine.

3 I'd sing the characters he bears,
And all the forms of love he wears,
  Exalted on his throne:
In loftiest songs of sweetest praise,
I would to everlasting days
  Make all his glories known.

4 Well—the delightful day will come,
When my dear Lord will bring me home,
  And I shall see his face:
Then with my Saviour, Brother, Friend,
A blest eternity I'll spend,
  Triumphant in his grace.

Samuel Medley.

SUFFERINGS AND DEATH.

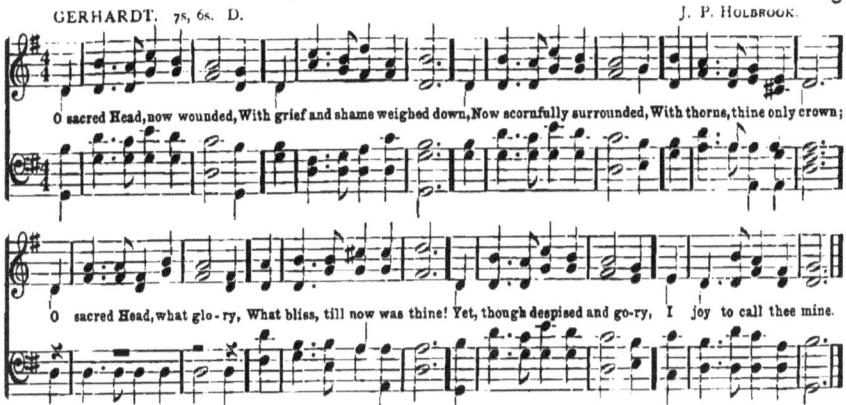

160 *At the Cross.*

O sacred Head, now wounded,
 With grief and shame weighed down,
Now scornfully surrounded,
 With thorns, thine only crown;
O sacred Head, what glory,
 What bliss, till now was thine!
Yet, though despised and gory,
 I joy to call thee mine.

2 What thou, my Lord, hast suffered
 Was all for sinners' gain:
Mine, mine was the transgression,
 But thine the deadly pain;
Lo, here I fall, my Saviour!
 'Tis I deserved thy place;
Look on me with thy favor,
 Vouchsafe to me thy grace.

3 What language shall I borrow,
 To thank thee, dearest Friend,
For this, thy dying sorrow,
 Thy pity without end?
Lord, make me thine for ever,
 Nor let me faithless prove;
Oh, let me never, never,
 Abuse such dying love.

J. W. Alexander, tr.

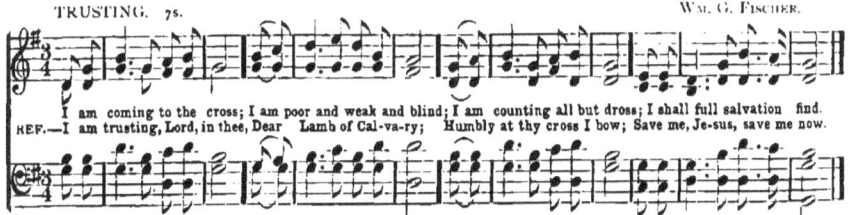

161 *"Cleanseth from all sin."*

I am coming to the cross;
 I am poor and weak and blind;
I am counting all but dross;
 I shall full salvation find.
Ref.—I am trusting, Lord, in thee,
  Dear Lamb of Calvary;
  Humbly at thy cross I bow;
  Save me, Jesus, save me now.

2 Long my heart has sighed for thee;
 Long has evil dwelt within;
Jesus sweetly speaks to me,
 I will cleanse you from all sin.—Ref.

3 Here I give my all to thee,—
 Friends and time and earthly store;
Soul and body thine to be—
 Wholly thine for ever more.—Ref.

4 In the promises I trust;
 Now I feel the blood applied;
I am prostrate in the dust;
 I with Christ am crucified.—Ref.

W. M. Donald.

THE LORD JESUS CHRIST.

MANOAH. C. M.   Arr. fr. ROSSINI.

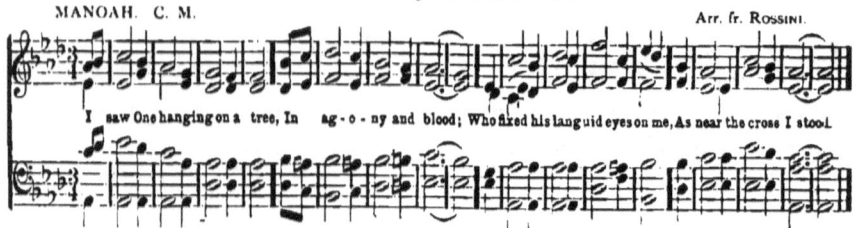

I saw One hanging on a tree, In ag-o-ny and blood; Who fixed his languid eyes on me, As near the cross I stood.

162   *The two Looks.*
I saw One hanging on a tree,
  In agony and blood;
Who fixed his languid eyes on me,
  As near the cross I stood.

2 Sure, never, till my latest breath,
  Can I forget that look:
It seemed to charge me with his death,
  Though not a word he spoke.

3 Alas! I knew not what I did,—
  But now my tears are vain;
Where shall my trembling soul be hid,
  For I the Lord have slain!

4 A second look he gave, that said,
  "I freely all forgive;
This blood is for thy ransom paid;
  I die that thou may'st live."

5 Thus while his death my sin displays
  In all its blackest hue,
Such is the mystery of grace,
  It seals my pardon too!
               John Newton.

163   *"O Christ of God!"*
O Jesus, sweet the tears I shed,
  While at thy cross I kneel,
Gaze on thy wounded, fainting head,
  And all thy sorrows feel.

2 My heart dissolves to see thee bleed,
  This heart so hard before;
I hear thee for the guilty plead,
  And grief o'erflows the more.

3 I know this cleansing blood of thine
  Was shed, dear Lord, for me;
For me, for all,—oh, grace divine!—
  Who look by faith on thee.

4 O Christ of God, O spotless Lamb,
  By love my soul is drawn;
Henceforth, for ever, thine I am;
  Here life and peace are born.

5 In patient hope, the cross I'll bear,
  Thine arm shall be my stay;
And thou, enthroned, my soul shalt spare,
  On thy great judgment-day.
               Ray Palmer.

HOLY TRINITY. C. M.   J. BARNBY.

How condescending and how kind Was God's eternal Son! Our misery reach'd his heav'nly mind, And pity brought him down.

164   *"He remembers Calvary."*
How condescending and how kind
  Was God's eternal Son!
Our misery reached his heavenly mind,
  And pity brought him down.

2 He sunk beneath our heavy woes,
  To raise us to his throne;
There's ne'er a gift his hand bestows,
  But cost his heart a groan.

3 This was compassion, like a God,
  That when the Saviour knew
The price of pardon was his blood,
  His pity ne'er withdrew.

4 Now, though he reigns exalted high,
  His love is still as great;
Well he remembers Calvary,
  Nor let his saints forget.
               Isaac Watts.

SUFFERINGS AND DEATH. 67

AVON. C. M.   HUGH WILSON.

A-las! and did my Saviour bleed, And did my Sovereign die? Would he devote that sacred head For such a worm as I?

165   *"Grace unknown."*

ALAS! and did my Saviour bleed,
And did my Sovereign die?
Would he devote that sacred head
For such a worm as I?

2 Was it for crimes that I had done
He groaned upon the tree?
Amazing pity! grace unknown!
And love beyond degree!

3 Well might the sun in darkness hide,
And shut his glories in,
When Christ, the great Creator, died
For man, the creature's sin.

4 Thus might I hide my blushing face
While his dear cross appears;
Dissolve my heart in thankfulness,
And melt my eyes to tears.

5 But drops of grief can ne'er repay
The debt of love I owe;
Here, Lord, I give myself away,
'Tis all that I can do.
Isaac Watts.

COMMUNION. C. M.   S. JENKS.

Oh, if my soul were formed for woe, How would I vent my sighs!
Re - pent - ance should like riv - ers flow From both my stream-ing eyes.

166   *Suffered for sin.*

OH, if my soul were formed for woe,
How would I vent my sighs!
Repentance should like rivers flow
From both my streaming eyes.

2 'Twas for my sins my dearest Lord
Hung on the cursèd tree,
And groaned away a dying life
For thee, my soul! for thee.

3 Oh, how I hate these lusts of mine
That crucified my Lord;
Those sins that pierced and nailed his flesh
Fast to the fatal wood!

4 Yes, my Redeemer— they shall die;
My heart has so decreed;
Nor will I spare the guilty things
That made my Saviour bleed.

5 While with a melting, broken heart,
My murdered Lord I view,
I'll raise revenge against my sins,
And slay the murderers too.
Isaac Watts.

SUFFERINGS AND DEATH.

HAMBURG. L. M.   Arr. by L. Mason.

169 *"The wondrous Cross."*

When I survey the wondrous cross,
 On which the Prince of glory died,
My richest gain I count but loss,
 And pour contempt on all my pride.

2 Forbid it, Lord! that I should boast,
 Save in the death of Christ, my God;
All the vain things that charm me most
 I sacrifice them to his blood.

3 See, from his head, his hands, his feet,
 Sorrow and love flow mingled down;
Did e'er such love and sorrow meet,
 Or thorns compose so rich a crown?

4 His dying crimson, like a robe,
 Spreads o'er his body on the tree;
Then I am dead to all the globe,
 And all the globe is dead to me.

5 Were the whole realm of nature mine,
 That were a present far too small;
Love so amazing, so divine,
 Demands my soul, my life, my all.
Isaac Watts.

CRUX CHRISTI. 7s, 6s. D.   A. H. Mann.

170 *"Man of Sorrows."*

O Jesus, "Man of Sorrows,"
 Sole Son of God, the King!
What language shall I borrow
 Thy boundless love to sing?
No mortal words can measure
 The burdens thou didst take,
Accepting pain as pleasure,
 All for my sinful sake.

2 By thine own kin neglected—
 By trusted ones denied—
By bitter foes rejected,
 Thorn-crowned, and crucified
Earth's hatred and affliction
 In patience thou didst bear,
Returning benediction
 For cross and nail and spear.

3 Had ever love such proving!
 Was ever love so priced!
Ah, what is all my loving
 Compared with thine, O Christ!
'T is scarcely worth the gaining—
 This paltry heart of mine;
And yet for its obtaining
 Thou paid'st a price divine.
George S. Dwight.

THE LORD JESUS CHRIST.

DUKE STREET. L. M.   J. Hatton.

Now to the Lord, who makes us know The wonders of his dying love,
Be humble honors paid below, And strains of nobler praise above.

171   *The atoning Priest.*

Now to the Lord, who makes us know
The wonders of his dying love,
Be humble honors paid below,
And strains of nobler praise above.

2 'T was he who cleansed our foulest sins,
And washed us in his precious blood;
'T is he who makes us priests and kings,
And brings us rebels near to God.

3 To Jesus, our atoning Priest,
To Jesus, our eternal King,
Be everlasting power confessed!
Let every tongue his glory sing.

4 Behold! on flying clouds he comes,
And every eye shall see him move;
Though with our sins we pierced him once,
He now displays his pardoning love.

5 The unbelieving world shall wail,
While we rejoice to see the day;
Come, Lord! nor let thy promise fail,
Nor let thy chariot long delay.
Isaac Watts.

172   *"The Song of Songs."*

Come, let us sing the song of songs,—
The saints in heaven began the strain—
The homage which to Christ belongs:
"Worthy the Lamb, for he was slain!"

2 Slain to redeem us by his blood,
To cleanse from every sinful stain,
And make us kings and priests to God—
"Worthy the Lamb, for he was slain!"

3 To him, enthroned by filial right,
All power in heaven and earth proclaim,
Honor, and majesty, and might:
"Worthy the Lamb, for he was slain!"

4 Long as we live, and when we die,
And while in heaven with him we reign:
This song, our song of songs shall be:
"Worthy the Lamb, for he was slain!"
James Montgomery.

173   *"King, Creator, Lord."*

O Christ! our King, Creator, Lord!
Saviour of all who trust thy word!
To them who seek thee ever near,
Now to our praises bend thine ear.

2 In thy dear cross a grace is found,—
It flows from every streaming wound,—
Whose power our inbred sin controls,
Breaks the firm bond, and frees our souls.

3 Thou didst create the stars of night;
Yet thou hast vailed in flesh thy light,
Hast deigned a mortal form to wear,
A mortal's painful lot to bear.

4 When thou didst hang upon the tree,
The quaking earth acknowledged thee;
When thou didst there yield up thy breath,
The world grew dark as shades of death.

5 Now in the Father's glory high,
Great Conqueror! never more to die,
Us by thy mighty power defend,
And reign through ages without end.
Ray Palmer, tr.

RESURRECTION AND REIGN.

ROTHWELL. L. M.   Arr. by L. Mason.

He lives! the great Redeemer lives! What joy the blest assurance gives! And now, before his Father, God, Pleads the full merits of his blood, Pleads the full merits of his blood.

174   *Christ, our Advocate.*
He lives! the great Redeemer lives!
What joy the blest assurance gives!
And now, before his Father, God,
Pleads the full merits of his blood.

2 Repeated crimes awake our fears,
And justice armed with frowns appears;
But in the Saviour's lovely face
Sweet mercy smiles, and all is peace.

3 In every dark, distressful hour,
When sin and Satan join their power,
Let this dear hope repel the dart,
That Jesus bears us on his heart.

4 Great Advocate, almighty Friend!
On him our humble hopes depend,
Our cause can never, never fail,
For Jesus pleads, and must prevail.
                              Anne Steele.

175   *"Behold the Way!"*
Jesus, my All, to heaven is gone,
He whom I fix my hopes upon;
His track I see, and I'll pursue
The narrow way till him I view.

2 The way the holy prophets went,
The road that leads from banishment,
The King's highway of holiness,
I'll go for all his paths are peace.

3 This is the way I long had sought,
And mourned because I found it not;
My grief, my burden, long had been
Because I could not cease from sin.

4 The more I strove against its power,
I sinned and stumbled but the more;
Till late I heard my Saviour say,
"Come hither, soul, I am the Way!"

5 Lo! glad I come; and thou, dear Lamb,
Shalt take me to thee as I am,
Nothing but sin I thee can give;
Nothing but love shall I receive.

6 Then will I tell, to sinners round,
What a dear Saviour I have found;
I'll point to thy redeeming blood,
And say, "Behold the way to God!"
                           John Cennick.

176   *Atonement made.*
Now to the power of God supreme
Be everlasting honors given;
He saves from hell,—we bless his name,—
He guides our wandering feet to heaven.

2 'T was his own purpose that began
To rescue rebels doomed to die:
He gave us grace in Christ, his Son,
Before he spread the starry sky.

3 Jesus, the Lord, appears at last,
And makes his Father's counsels known;
Declares the great transactions past,
And brings immortal blessings down.

4 He dies; and in that dreadful night
Doth all the powers of hell destroy;
Rising, he brings our heaven to light,
And takes possession of the joy.
                            Isaac Watts.

RESURRECTION AND REIGN.

HARWELL. 8s, 7s. D.   LOWELL MASON.

177   *"Jesus reigns."*

Hark! ten thousand harps and voices
  Sound the note of praise above;
Jesus reigns, and heaven rejoices;
  Jesus reigns, the God of love:
See, he sits on yonder throne;
Jesus rules the world alone.

2 King of glory! reign for ever—
  Thine an everlasting crown;
Nothing, from thy love, shall sever
  Those whom thou hast made thine own;—
Happy objects of thy grace,
Destined to behold thy face.

3 Saviour! hasten thine appearing;
  Bring, oh, bring the glorious day,
When, the awful summons hearing,
  Heaven and earth shall pass away;—
Then, with golden harps, we 'll sing,—
"Glory, glory to our King!"
                                 Thomas Kelly.

178   *We live in Him.*

See, the Conqueror mounts in triumph!
  See the King in royal state,
Riding on the clouds, his chariot,
  To his heavenly palace gate!
Hark! the choirs of angel voices
Joyful hallelujahs sing,
And the portals high are lifted
  To receive their heavenly King.

2 Who is this that comes in glory,
  With the trump of jubilee?
Lord of battles, God of armies,
  He has gained the victory;
He, who on the cross did suffer,
He, who from the grave arose,
He has vanquished sin and Satan,
He by death has spoiled his foes.

3 Thou hast raised our human nature,
  On the clouds to God's right hand;
There we sit in heavenly places,
  There with thee in glory stand;
Jesus reigns, adored by angels,
Man with God is on the throne;
Mighty Lord! in thine ascension,
  We by faith behold our own.

4 Lift us up from earth to heaven,
  Give us wings of faith and love,
Gales of holy aspirations,
  Wafting us to realms above;
That, with hearts and minds uplifted,
We with Christ our Lord may dwell,
Where he sits enthroned in glory,
  In the heavenly citadel.

5 So at last, when he appeareth,
  We from out our graves may spring,
With our youth renewed like eagles',
  Flocking round our heavenly King,
Caught up on the clouds of heaven,
And may meet him in the air—
Rise to realms where he is reigning,
  And may reign for ever there.
                                 C. Wordsworth.

RESURRECTION AND REIGN.

AUTUMN. 8s, 7s. D.   Arr. by G. F. Root.

Mighty God! while angels bless thee, May a mortal lisp thy name? Lord of men, as well as an-gels!
D. S.—Sounded thro' the wide creation—

Thou art every creature's theme: Lord of ev - 'ry land and nation! Ancient of e-ternal days!
Be thy just and awful praise.

179   *Christ is God.*

MIGHTY God! while angels bless thee,
  May a mortal lisp thy name?
Lord of men, as well as angels!
  Thou art every creature's theme:
Lord of every land and nation!
  Ancient of eternal days!
Sounded through the wide creation—
  Be thy just and awful praise.

2 For the grandeur of thy nature,—
  Grand, beyond a seraph's thought;
For the wonders of creation,
  Works with skill and kindness wrought;
For thy providence, that governs
  Through thine empire's wide domain,
Wings an angel, guides a sparrow;—
  Blessèd be thy gentle reign.

3 For thy rich, thy free redemption,
  Bright, though vailed in darkness long,
Thought is poor, and poor expression;
  Who can sing that wondrous song?
Brightness of the Father's glory!
  Shall thy praise unuttered lie?
Break, my tongue! such guilty silence,
  Sing the Lord who came to die:—

4 From the highest throne of glory,
  To the cross of deepest woe,
Came to ransom guilty captives!—
  Flow, my praise! for ever flow:

Re-ascend, immortal Saviour!
  Leave thy footstool, take thy throne;
Thence return and reign for ever;—
  Be the kingdom all thine own!
Robert Robinson.

180   *"Lo, Jehovah!"*

CROWN his head with endless blessing,
  Who, in God the Father's name,
With compassions never ceasing,
  Comes salvation to proclaim.
Hail, ye saints, who know his favor,
  Who within his gates are found;
Hail, ye saints, the exalted Saviour,
  Let his courts with praise resound.

2 Lo, Jehovah, we adore thee;
  Thee our Saviour! thee our God!
From his throne his beams of glory
  Shine through all the world abroad.
In his word his light arises,
  Brightest beams of truth and grace;
Bind, oh, bind your sacrifices,
  In his courts your offerings place.

3 Jesus, thee our Saviour hailing,
  Thee our God in praise we own;
Highest honors, never failing,
  Rise eternal round thy throne;
Now, ye saints, his power confessing,
  In your grateful strains adore;
For his mercy, never ceasing,
  Flows, and flows for evermore.
William Goode.

THE LORD JESUS CHRIST.

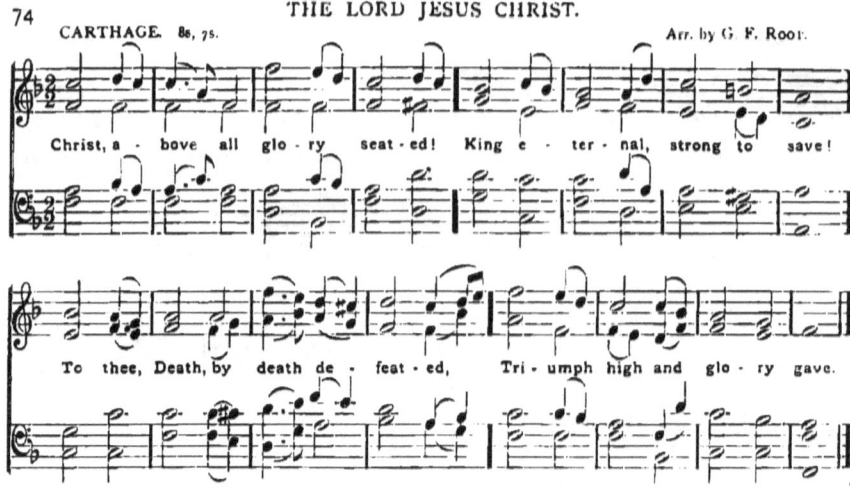

CARTHAGE. 8s, 7s. Arr. by G. F. Root.

Christ, above all glory seated! King eternal, strong to save!
To thee, Death, by death defeated, Triumph high and glory gave.

181 *Christ in Heaven.*

CHRIST, above all glory seated!
  King eternal, strong to save!
To thee, Death, by death defeated,
  Triumph high and glory gave.

2 Thou art gone where now is given
  What no mortal might could gain,
On the eternal throne of heaven,
  In thy Father's power to reign.

3 There thy kingdoms all adore thee,
  Heaven above and earth below,
While the depths of hell before thee,
  Trembling and defeated bow.

4 We, O Lord! with hearts adoring,
  Follow thee above the sky;
Hear our prayers thy grace imploring,
  Lift our souls to thee on high.

5 So when thou again in glory
  On the clouds of heaven shalt shine,
We thy flock shall stand before thee,
  Owned for evermore as thine.

J. R. Woodford, tr.

AZMON. C. M. Arr. by L. Mason.

182 *"Worthy the Lamb."*

COME, let us join our cheerful songs
  With angels round the throne;
Ten thousand thousand are their tongues,
  But all their joys are one.

2 "Worthy the Lamb that died," they cry,
  "To be exalted thus!"
"Worthy the Lamb!" our lips reply,
  "For he was slain for us."

3 Jesus is worthy to receive
  Honor and power divine;
And blessings more than we can give,
  Be, Lord, for ever thine!

4 Let all that dwell above the sky,
  And air, and earth, and seas,
Conspire to lift thy glories high,
  And speak thine endless praise.

5 The whole creation join in one
  To bless the sacred name
Of him who sits upon the throne,
  And to adore the Lamb!

Isaac Watts.

EXALTATION AND OFFICES.

CORONATION. C. M.   O. HOLDEN.

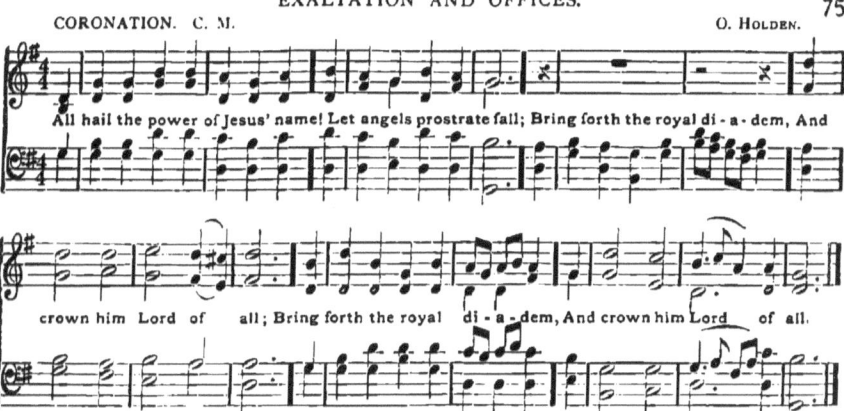

183   *"Lord of all."*

ALL hail the power of Jesus' name!
Let angels prostrate fall;
Bring forth the royal diadem,
And crown him Lord of all.

2 Crown him, ye martyrs of our God,
Who from his altar call;
Extol the stem of Jesse's rod,
And crown him Lord of all.

3 Ye chosen seed of Israel's race,
Ye ransomed from the fall;
Hail him, who saves you by his grace,
And crown him Lord of all.

4 Sinners, whose love can ne'er forget
The wormwood and the gall;
Go, spread your trophies at his feet,
And crown him Lord of all.

5 Let every kindred, every tribe,
On this terrestrial ball,
To him all majesty ascribe,
And crown him Lord of all.

6 Oh, that with yonder sacred throng,
We at his feet may fall;
We'll join the everlasting song
And crown him Lord of all.
Richard Perronet.

VICTORY. 8s, 7s, 4s.   H. H. BEADLE.

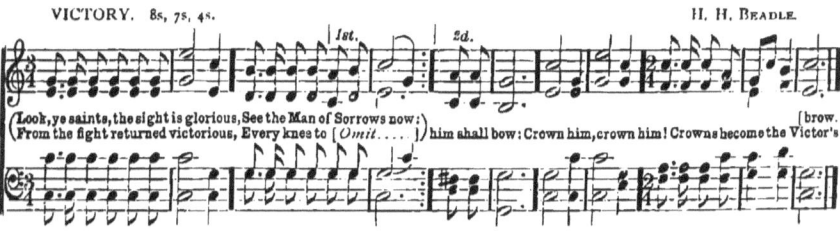

184   *"King of kings."*

LOOK, ye saints, the sight is glorious,
See the Man of Sorrows now:
From the fight returned victorious,
Every knee to him shall bow:
   Crown him, crown him!
Crowns become the Victor's brow.

2 Crown the Saviour, angels, crown him;
Rich the trophies Jesus brings;
In the seat of power enthrone him;
While the vault of heaven rings:
   Crown him, crown him;
Crown the Saviour "King of kings."

3 Hark, those bursts of acclamation!
Hark, those loud triumphant chords!
Jesus takes the highest station;
Oh, what joy the sight affords:
   Crown him, crown him;
"King of kings and Lord of lords."
Thomas Kelly.

THE LORD JESUS CHRIST.

MERIBAH. C. P. M. — LOWELL MASON

When thou, my righteous Judge, shalt come To take thy ransomed people home, Shall I among them stand? {Shall such a worthless worm as I, Who sometimes am afraid to die,} Be found at thy right hand?

185 *The Tribunal.*

WHEN thou, my righteous Judge, shalt come
To take thy ransomed people home,
  Shall I among them stand?
Shall such a worthless worm as I,
Who sometimes am afraid to die,
  Be found at thy right hand?

2 I love to meet thy people now,
Before thy feet with them to bow,
  Though vilest of them all;
But, can I bear the piercing thought,
What if my name should be left out,
  When thou for them shalt call?

3 O Lord, prevent it by thy grace,
Be thou my only hiding-place,
  In this the accepted day;
Thy pardoning voice, oh, let me hear,
To still my unbelieving fear,
  Nor let me fall, I pray.

4 Among thy saints let me be found,
Whene'er the archangel's trump shall sound,
  To see thy smiling face;
Then loudest of the throng I'll sing,
While heaven's resounding mansions ring
  With shouts of sovereign grace.
Lady Huntington.

---

186 7s, 6s. D. *Isaiah 52: 1.*

AWAKE, awake, O Zion,
  Put on thy strength divine,
Thy garments bright in beauty,
  The bridal dress be thine:
Jerusalem the holy,
  To purity restored;
Meek Bride all fair and lowly,
  Go forth to meet thy Lord.

2 From henceforth pure and spotless,
  All glorious within,
Prepared to meet the Bridegroom,
  And cleansed from every sin;
With love and wonder smitten,
  And bowed in guileless shame,
Upon thy heart be written
  The new mysterious name.

3 The Lamb who bore our sorrows,
  Comes down to earth again;
No sufferer now, but victor,
  For evermore to reign:
To reign in every nation,
  To rule in every zone,
Oh, world-wide coronation,
  In every heart a throne.

4 Awake, awake, O Zion,
  Thy bridal day draws nigh,
The day of signs and wonders,
  And marvels from on high.
The sun uprises slowly,
  But keep thy watch and ward:
Fair Bride, all pure and lowly,
  Go forth to meet thy Lord.
Benjamin Gough.

COMING AGAIN.

CHENIES. 7s, 6s. D.   T. R. MATTHEWS.

187 *"Your lamps trimmed."*
REJOICE, rejoice, believers!
And let your lights appear;
The shades of eve are thickening,
And darker night is near;
The Bridegroom is advancing;
Each hour he draws more nigh;
Up! watch and pray, nor slumber;
At midnight comes the cry.

2 See that your lamps are burning,
Your vessels filled with oil;
Wait calmly your deliverance
From earthly pain and toil;
The watchers on the mountains
Proclaim the Bridegroom near;
Go, meet him, as he cometh,
With hallelujahs clear.

3 Our hope and expectation,
O Jesus, now appear!
Arise, thou sun so looked-for,
O'er this benighted sphere!
With hearts and hands uplifted,
We plead, O Lord, to see
The day of our redemption,
And ever be with thee.
Jane Borthwick, tr.

188 *The Lamb's Bridal.*
THE marriage feast is ready,
The marriage of the Lamb,
He calls the faithful children
Of faithful Abraham:
Now from the golden portals
The sounds of triumph ring;
The triumph of the Victor,
The marriage of the King.

2 Nor sigh nor sorrow enter
Where Jesus leads them in;
Nor death may cross the threshold,
Nor pain, nor fear, nor sin:
Now shades of night and darkness
Are past and fled away,
Before the radiant brightness
Of everlasting day.

3 No tear-drops stain that threshold,
No weeping eyes are there;
For God hath wiped all tear-drops,
And God hath stilled all care:
The sunlight of the Presence,
The bright Shechinah-flame,
Lights up the bridal banquet
Of God and of the Lamb.
Gerard Moultrie.

THE LORD JESUS CHRIST.

FORMOSA. 8s, 7s. D.   A. S. SULLIVAN

He is com-ing, he is coming, Not as once he came be-fore, Wailing in-fant, born in weakness On a low-ly sta-ble floor: But up-on his cloud of glo-ry, In the crim-son-tint-ed sky, Where we see the golden sun-rise In the ro-sy distance lie.

189   *The Judgment.*

He is coming, he is coming,
  Not as once he came before,
Wailing infant, born in weakness
  On a lowly stable floor:
But upon his cloud of glory,
  In the crimson-tinted sky,
Where we see the golden sunrise
  In the rosy distance lie.

2 He is coming, he is coming,
  Not in pain, and shame, and woe,
With the thorn-crown on his forehead,
  And the blood-drops trickling slow;
But with diadem upon him,
  And the sceptre in his hand,
And the dead all ranged before him,
  Raised from death, hell, sea, and land.

3 He is coming, he is coming,
  Not as once he wandered through
All the hostile land of Judah,
  With his followers poor and few:
But with all the holy angels
  Waiting round his judgment-seat,
And the chosen twelve apostles
  Sitting crownèd at his feet.

4 He is coming, he is coming:
  Let his lowly first estate,
And his tender love, so teach us
  That in faith and hope we wait,
Till in glory eastward burning,
  Our redemption draweth near;
And we see the sign in heaven
  Of our Judge and Saviour dear.
      Mrs. C. F. Alexander.

190   *"Desire of the Nations."*

Come, thou long-expected Jesus,
  Born to set thy people free;
From our fears and sins release us,
  Let us find our rest in thee:
Israel's Strength and Consolation,
  Hope of all the saints thou art;
Dear Desire of every nation,
  Joy of every longing heart.

2 Born, thy people to deliver;
  Born a child, and yet a King;
Born to reign in us for ever,
  Now thy precious kingdom bring:
By thine own eternal Spirit,
  Rule in all our hearts alone;
By thine all-sufficient merit,
  Raise us to thy glorious throne.
      Charles Wesley.

COMING AGAIN.

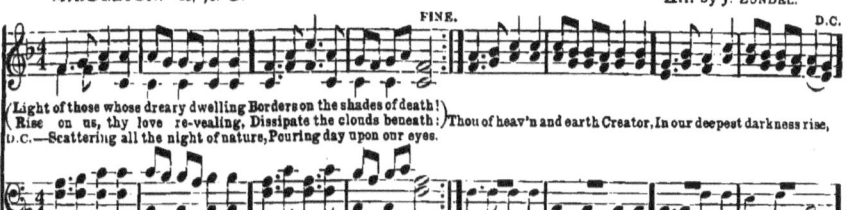

MIDDLETON. 8s, 7s. D.   Arr. by J. ZUNDEL.

191   *The Prince of Peace.*

LIGHT of those whose dreary dwelling
  Borders on the shades of death!
Rise on us, thy love revealing,
  Dissipate the clouds beneath:
Thou of heaven and earth Creator,
  In our deepest darkness rise,—
Scattering all the night of nature,
  Pouring day upon our eyes.

2 Still we wait for thine appearing;
  Life and joy thy beams impart,
Chasing all our fears, and cheering
  Every poor benighted heart:
Come and manifest thy favor
  To the ransomed, helpless race;
Come, thou glorious God and Saviour!
  Come, and bring the gospel grace.

3 Save us, in thy great compassion,
  O thou mild, pacific Prince!
Give the knowledge of salvation,
  Give the pardon of our sins;
By thine all-sufficient merit,
  Every burdened soul release;
Every weary, wandering spirit,
  Guide into thy perfect peace.
                        Charles Wesley.

192   *"Glorious things."*

GLORIOUS things of thee are spoken,
  Zion, city of our God!
He, whose word cannot be broken,
  Formed thee for his own abode:
On the Rock of Ages founded,
  What can shake thy sure repose?
With salvation's walls surrounded,
  Thou may'st smile at all thy foes.

2 See! the streams of living waters,
  Springing from eternal love,
Well supply thy sons and daughters,
  And all fear of want remove:

Who can faint, while such a river
  Ever flows their thirst to assuage?—
Grace, which, like the Lord, the Giver,
  Never fails from age to age.

3 Round each habitation hovering,
  See the cloud and fire appear
For a glory and a covering,
  Showing that the Lord is near!
Thus deriving from their banner,
  Light by night, and shade by day,
Safe they feed upon the manna
  Which he gives them when they pray.
                        John Newton.

193   *The covenant.*

HEAR what God the Lord hath spoken;
  O my people, faint and few,
Comfortless, afflicted, broken,
  Fair abodes I build for you;
Scenes of heartfelt tribulation
  Shall no more perplex your ways;
You shall name your walls "Salvation,"
  And your gates shall all be "Praise."

2 There, like streams that feed the garden,
  Pleasures without end shall flow;
For the Lord, your faith rewarding,
  All his bounty shall bestow.
Still in undisturbed possession
  Peace and righteousness shall reign;
Never shall you feel oppression,
  Hear the voice of war again.

3 Ye, no more your suns descending,
  Waning moon no more shall see,
But, your griefs for ever ending,
  Find eternal noon in me.
God shall rise, and shining o'er you,
  Change to day the gloom of night;
He, the Lord, shall be your Glory,
  God, your everlasting Light.
                        William Cowper.

THE LORD JESUS CHRIST.

WESLEY. 7s. D.   LOWELL MASON.

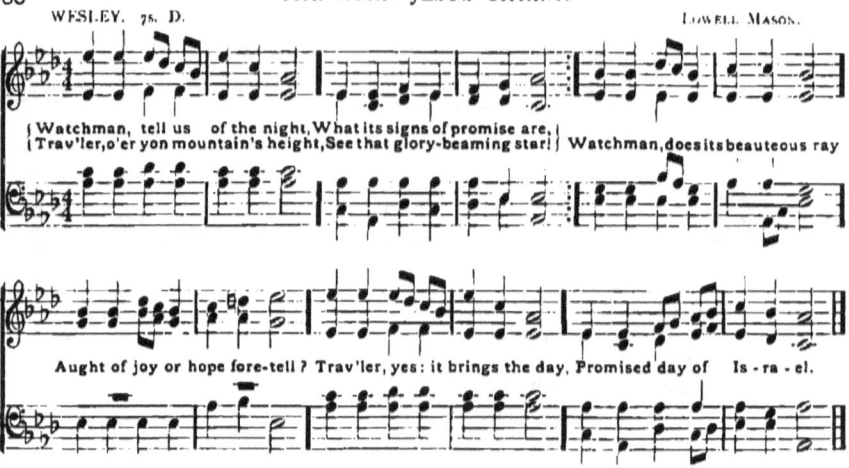

{ Watchman, tell us of the night, What its signs of promise are, }
{ Trav'ler, o'er yon mountain's height, See that glory-beaming star! } Watchman, does its beauteous ray
Aught of joy or hope fore-tell? Trav'ler, yes: it brings the day, Promised day of Is-ra-el.

194   *Isaiah 21: 11.*

WATCHMAN, tell us of the night,
  What its signs of promise are.
Traveler, o'er yon mountain's height,
  See that glory-beaming star!
Watchman, does its beauteous ray
  Aught of joy or hope foretell?
Traveler, yes: it brings the day,
  Promised day of Israel.

2 Watchman, tell us of the night:
  Higher yet that star ascends.
Traveler, blessedness and light,
  Peace and truth, its course portends.
Watchman, will its beams alone
  Gild the spot that gave them birth?
Traveler, ages are its own;
  See! it bursts o'er all the earth!

3 Watchman, tell us of the night,
  For the morning seems to dawn.
Traveler, darkness takes its flight,
  Doubt and terror are withdrawn.
Watchman, let thy wanderings cease;
  Hie thee to thy quiet home.
Traveler, lo! the Prince of Peace,
  Lo! the Son of God is come!
                John Bowring.

195   *Doxology.*

PRAISE our glorious King and Lord,
Angels waiting on his word,
Saints that walk with him in white,
Pilgrims walking in his light:

Glory to the Eternal One,
Glory to his only Son,
Glory to the Spirit be
Now, and through eternity.
                Anon.

196   *"The Lord God reigneth."*

HARK! the song of jubilee,
  Loud as mighty thunders roar,
Or the fullness of the sea,
  When it breaks upon the shore!
Hallelujah! for the Lord
  God omnipotent shall reign!
Hallelujah! let the word
  Echo round the earth and main.

2 Hallelujah! hark, the sound,
  From the depths unto the skies,
Wakes above, beneath, around,
  All creation's harmonies!
See Jehovah's banners furled!
  Sheathed his sword! he speaks—'tis done!
And the kingdoms of this world
  Are the kingdoms of his Son!

3 He shall reign from pole to pole,
  With illimitable sway;
He shall reign, when like a scroll
  Yonder heavens have passed away.
Then the end; beneath his rod
  Man's last enemy shall fall:
Hallelujah! Christ in God,
  God in Christ, is all in all!
                James Montgomery.

COMING AGAIN.

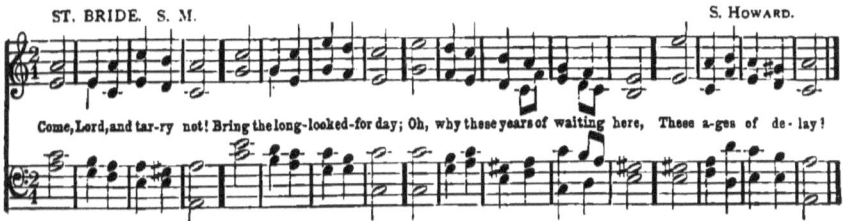

197 *"Come, Lord Jesus."*

Come, Lord, and tarry not!
Bring the long-looked-for day;
Oh, why these years of waiting here,
These ages of delay?

2 Come, for thy saints still wait;
Daily ascends their sigh;
The Spirit and the Bride say, Come!
Dost thou not hear the cry?

3 Come, for creation groans,
Impatient of thy stay,
Worn out with these long years of ill,
These ages of delay.

4 Come, and make all things new,
Build up this ruined earth,
Restore our faded paradise,—
Creation's second birth.

5 Come, and begin thy reign
Of everlasting peace;
Come, take the kingdom to thyself,
Great King of Righteousness!
Horatius Bonar.

198 *The hidden Life.*

Our life is hid with Christ,
With Christ in God above;
Upward our heart would go to him,
Whom, seeing not, we love.

2 When he who is our life
Appears, to take the throne,
We too shall be revealed, and shine
In glory like his own.

3 He liveth, and we live!
His life for us prevails;
His fullness fills our mighty void,
His strength for us avails.

4 Life worketh in us now,
Life is for us in store;
So death is swallowed up of life;
We live for evermore.

5 Like him we then shall be,
Transformed and glorified;
For we shall see him as he is,
And in his light abide.
Horatius Bonar.

199 *The final Judgment.*

And will the Judge descend,
And must the dead arise,
And not a single soul escape
His all-discerning eyes?

2 How will my heart endure
The terrors of that day,
When earth and heaven before his face
Astonished shrink away?

3 But, ere the trumpet shakes
The mansions of the dead,
Hark, from the Gospel's cheering sound
What joyful tidings spread!

4 Ye sinners! seek his grace
Whose wrath ye cannot bear;
Fly to the shelter of his cross,
And find salvation there.
Philip Doddridge.

THE HOLY SPIRIT.

200 *"Inward Teachings."*
Eternal Spirit, we confess
And sing the wonders of thy grace:
Thy power conveys our blessings down
From God the Father and the Son.

2 Enlightened by thy heavenly ray,
Our shades and darkness turn to day;
Thine inward teachings make us know
Our danger and our refuge too.

3 Thy power and glory work within,
And break the chains of reigning sin;
All our imperious lusts subdue,
And form our wretched hearts anew.
Isaac Watts.

201 *"Veni, Creator!"*
Come, O Creator Spirit blest!
And in our souls take up thy rest;
Come, with thy grace, and heavenly aid,
To fill the hearts which thou hast made.

2 Great Comforter! to thee we cry;
O highest gift of God most high!
O fount of life! O fire of love!
Send sweet anointing from above!

3 Kindle our senses from above,
And make our hearts o'erflow with love;
With patience firm, and virtue high,
The weakness of our flesh supply.

4 Far from us drive the foe we dread,
And grant us thy true peace instead;
So shall we not, with thee for guide,
Turn from the path of life aside.
Edward Caswall, tr.

202 *"The book unfold."*
Come, blessèd Spirit! source of light!
Whose power and grace are unconfined,
Dispel the gloomy shades of night—
The thicker darkness of the mind.

2 To mine illumined eyes, display
The glorious truths thy word reveals;
Cause me to run the heavenly way,
Thy book unfold, and loose the seals.

3 Thine inward teachings make me know
The mysteries of redeeming love,
The vanity of things below,
And excellence of things above.

4 While through this dubious maze I stray,
Spread, like the sun, thy beams abroad,
To show the dangers of the way,
And guide my feeble steps to God.
Benjamin Beddome.

203 *Spirit of grace.*
Come, sacred Spirit, from above,
And fill the coldest heart with love:
Oh, turn to flesh the flinty stone,
And let thy sovereign power be known.

2 Speak thou, and from the haughtiest eyes
Shall floods of contrite sorrow rise;
While all their glowing souls are borne
To seek that grace which now they scorn.

3 Oh, let a holy flock await
In crowds around thy temple-gate!
Each pressing on with zeal to be
A living sacrifice to thee.
Philip Doddridge.

THE HOLY SPIRIT.

Holy Ghost! with light divine,
Shine upon this heart of mine;
Chase the shades of night away,
Turn my darkness into day.

204 *All-divine.*
Holy Ghost! with light divine,
Shine upon this heart of mine;
Chase the shades of night away,
Turn my darkness into day.

2 Holy Ghost! with power divine,
Cleanse this guilty heart of mine;
Long hath sin, without control,
Held dominion o'er my soul.

3 Holy Ghost! with joy divine,
Cheer this saddened heart of mine;
Bid my many woes depart,
Heal my wounded, bleeding heart.

4 Holy Spirit! all divine,
Dwell within this heart of mine;
Cast down every idol-throne,
Reign supreme—and reign alone.
Andrew Reed.

205 *"The things of Christ."*
Holy Spirit! gently come,
Raise us from our fallen state;
Fix thy everlasting home
In the hearts thou didst create.

2 Now thy quickening influence bring,
On our spirits sweetly move;
Open every mouth to sing
Jesus' everlasting love.

3 Take the things of Christ, and show
What our Lord for us hath done;
May we God the Father know
Through his well belovéd Son.
William Hammond.

206 *The Gifts bestowed.*
Holy Spirit, in my breast
Grant that lively faith may rest,
And subdue each rebel thought
To believe what thou hast taught.

2 Faith, and hope, and charity,
Comforter, descend from thee;
Thou the anointing Spirit art,
These thy gifts to us impart;—

3 Till our faith be lost in sight,
Hope be swallowed in delight,
Love return to dwell with thee,
In the threefold Deity!
Richard Mant.

207 *"Keep me, Lord!"*
Gracious Spirit, Love divine!
Let thy light within me shine;
All my guilty fears remove,
Fill me with thy heavenly love.

2 Speak thy pardoning grace to me,
Set the burdened sinner free;
Lead me to the Lamb of God;
Wash me in his precious blood.

3 Life and peace to me impart,
Seal salvation on my heart;
Breathe thyself into my breast,—
Earnest of immortal rest.

4 Let me never from thee stray,
Keep me in the narrow way;
Fill my soul with joy divine,
Keep me, Lord! for ever thine.
John Stocker.

THE HOLY SPIRIT.

208 *"Oh, come to-day."*

Come, Holy Ghost! in love,
Shed on us, from above,
 Thine own bright ray:
Divinely good thou art;
Thy sacred gifts impart,
To gladden each sad heart;
 Oh, come to-day!

2 Come, Light serene! and still,
Our inmost bosoms fill;
 Dwell in each breast:
We know no dawn but thine;
Send forth thy beams divine,
On our dark souls to shine,
 And make us blest.

3 Exalt our low desires;
Extinguish passion's fires;
 Heal every wound;
Our stubborn spirits bend;
Our icy coldness end;
Our devious steps attend,
 While heavenward bound.

4 Come, all the faithful bless;
Let all, who Christ confess,
 His praise employ;
Give virtue's rich reward;
Victorious death accord,
And, with our glorious Lord,
 Eternal joy!

Ray Palmer, tr.

209 *"Thy wondrous way."*

Let thy wondrous way be known,
 And let every nation own
Thou art God, and thou alone:
 Spirit, hear our prayer.

2 Let each one thy glorious name
Magnify, and spread thy fame,
And thy love let all proclaim:
 Spirit, hear our prayer.

3 Let the nations join to sing,
 And let hallelujahs ring
To the righteous Judge and King:
 Spirit, hear our prayer.

4 Then shall blessings from thy hand
Fall in showers upon thy land,
And the world in rapture stand:
 Spirit, hear our prayer.

A. Jackson.

THE HOLY SPIRIT.

210 *Heavenly Love.*

GRACIOUS Spirit, Holy Ghost,
Taught by thee, we covet most
Of thy gifts at Pentecost,
   Holy, heavenly love.

2 Faith, that mountains could remove,
Tongues of earth or heaven above,
Knowledge—all things—empty prove,
   Without heavenly love.

3 Love is kind, and suffers long;
Love is meek, and thinks no wrong;
Love, than death itself more strong:
   Give us heavenly love.

4 Prophecy will fade away,
Melting in the light of day;
Love will ever with us stay:
   Give us heavenly love.

5 Faith will vanish into sight;
Hope be emptied in delight;
Love in heaven will shine more bright:
   Give us heavenly love.

6 Faith and hope and love we see
Joining hand in hand agree;
But the greatest of the three,
   And the best, is love.

7 From the overshadowing
Of thy gold and silver wing,
Shed on us, who to thee sing,
   Holy, heavenly love.
                      C. Wordsworth.

211 *"Comforter Divine!"*

HOLY Ghost, the Infinite!
Shine upon our nature's night
With thy blessèd inward light,
   Comforter Divine!

2 We are sinful: cleanse us, Lord;
We are faint: thy strength afford;
Lost,—until by thee restored,
   Comforter Divine!

3 Like the dew, thy peace distill;
Guide, subdue our wayward will,
Things of Christ unfolding still,
   Comforter Divine!

4 In us, for us, intercede,
And with voiceless groanings, plead
Our unutterable need,
   Comforter Divine!

5 In us "Abba, Father," cry,—
Earnest of our bliss on high,
Seal of immortality,—
   Comforter Divine!

6 Search for us the depths of God;
Bear us up the starry road,
To the height of thine abode,
   Comforter Divine!
                      George Rawson.

THE HOLY SPIRIT.

MORNINGTON. S. M.   Arr. by L. MASON.

Lord, bid thy light a-rise On all thy people here, And when we raise our longing eyes, Oh, may we find thee near!

212   *The Light.*

LORD, bid thy light arise
On all thy people here,
And when we raise our longing eyes,
Oh, may we find thee near!

2 Thy Holy Spirit send,
To quicken every soul;
And hearts, the most rebellious, bend
To thy divine control.

3 Let all that own thy name
Thy sacred image bear,
And light in every heart the flame
Of watchfulness and prayer.

4 Since in thy love we see
Our only sure relief,
Oh, raise our earthly minds to thee,
And help our unbelief.
                       W. H. Bathurst.

213   *Teaching Truth.*

COME, Spirit, source of light,
Thy grace is unconfined;
Dispel the gloomy shades of night,
The darkness of the mind.

2 Now to our eyes display
The truth thy words reveal;
Cause us to run the heavenly way,
Delighting in thy will.

3 Thy teachings make us know
The mysteries of thy love,
The vanity of things below,
The joy of things above.

4 While through this maze we stray,
Oh, spread thy beams abroad;
Disclose the dangers of the way,
And guide our steps to God.
                       B. Beddome, alt.

NAOMI. C. M.   LOWELL MASON.

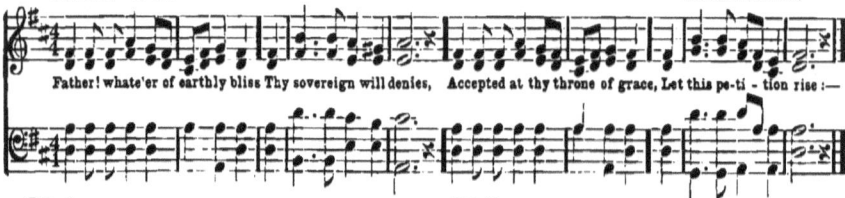

Father! whate'er of earthly bliss Thy sovereign will denies, Accepted at thy throne of grace, Let this peti-tion rise:—

214   *Humble Devotion.*

FATHER! whate'er of earthly bliss
Thy sovereign will denies,
Accepted at thy throne of grace,
Let this petition rise:—

2 "Give me a calm, a thankful heart,
From every murmur free;
The blessings of thy grace impart,
And make me live to thee.

3 "Let the sweet hope that thou art mine
My life and death attend;
Thy presence through my journey shine,
And crown my journey's end."
                       Anne Steele.

215   *Growth in grace.*

COME, Holy Ghost, my soul inspire;
This one great gift impart—
What most I need, and most desire,
An humble, holy heart.

2 Bear witness I am born again,
My many sins forgiven:
Nor let a gloomy doubt remain
To cloud my hope of heaven.

3 More of myself grant I may know,
From sin's deceit be free;
In all the Christian graces grow,
And live alone to thee.
                       Asahel Nettleton.

THE HOLY SPIRIT.

216 *Giver of Grace.*
Come, Holy Spirit, come!
　Let thy bright beams arise;
Dispel the sorrow from our minds,
　The darkness from our eyes.

2 Convince us of our sin;
　Then lead to Jesus' blood,
And to our wondering view reveal
　The mercies of our God.

3 Revive our drooping faith,
　Our doubts and fears remove,

And kindle in our breasts the flame
　Of never-dying love.

4 'Tis thine to cleanse the heart,
　To sanctify the soul,
To pour fresh life in every part,
　And new-create the whole.

5 Come, Holy Spirit, come;
　Our minds from bondage free;
Then shall we know, and praise, and love,
　The Father, Son, and thee.
　　　　　　　　　　Joseph Hart.

217 *"The Spirit searcheth."*
Spirit of the Only Wise,
Thou in whom all knowledge lies,
Reading all with searching eyes—
　Hear us, Holy Spirit.

2 Comforter, to whom we owe
All that we rejoice to know
Of our Saviour's work below,
　Hear us, Holy Spirit.

3 Spirit, whom our failings grieve,
Whom the world will not receive,

Who dost help us to believe,
　Hear us, Holy Spirit.

4 Spirit, guarding us from ill,
Bend aright our stubborn will;
Though we grieve thee, patient still—
　Hear us, Holy Spirit.

5 Thou whose grace the Church doth fill,
Showing her God's perfect will,
Making Jesus present still;
　Hear us, Holy Spirit.
　　　　　　　　Thomas B. Pollock.

THE HOLY SPIRIT.

STEPHENS. C. M.   W. JONES.

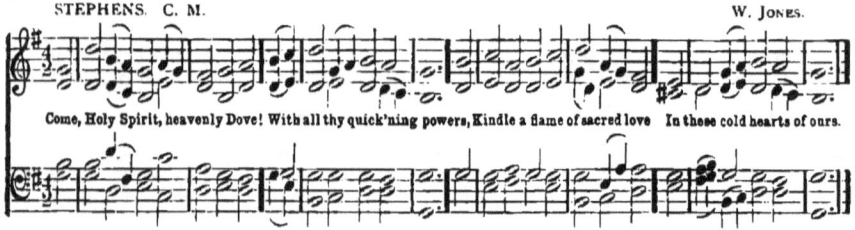

Come, Holy Spirit, heavenly Dove! With all thy quick'ning powers, Kindle a flame of sacred love In these cold hearts of ours.

218   *Invocation.*
COME, Holy Spirit, heavenly Dove!
  With all thy quickening powers,
Kindle a flame of sacred love
  In these cold hearts of ours.

2 Look! how we grovel here below,
  Fond of these trifling toys!
Our souls can neither fly nor go
  To reach eternal joys.

3 In vain we tune our formal songs;
  In vain we strive to rise;
Hosannas languish on our tongues,
  And our devotion dies.

4 Dear Lord, and shall we ever live
  At this poor dying rate—
Our love so faint, so cold to thee,
  And thine to us so great?

5 Come, Holy Spirit, heavenly Dove!
  With all thy quickening powers;
Come, shed abroad a Saviour's love,
  And that shall kindle ours.
                    Isaac Watts.

SUSIMAME. 7s, 6.   Arr. by A. S. SULLIVAN.

Spirit blest, who art a-dored With the Father and the Word, One eternal God and Lord: Hear us, Ho-ly Spir-it.

219   *"Hear us."*
SPIRIT blest, who art adored
With the Father and the Word,
One eternal God and Lord:
  Hear us, Holy Spirit.

2 Holy Spirit, heavenly Dove,
Dew descending from above,
Breath of life, and fire of love;
  Hear us, Holy Spirit.

3 Source of strength and knowledge clear,
Wisdom, godliness sincere,
Understanding, counsel, fear;
  Hear us, Holy Spirit.

4 Source of meekness, love, and peace,
Patience, pureness, faith's increase,
Hope and joy that cannot cease;
  Hear us, Holy Spirit.

5 Spirit guiding us aright,
Spirit making darkness light,
Spirit of resistless might;
  Hear us, Holy Spirit.

6 Thou, whom Jesus from his throne
Gave to cheer and help his own,
That they might not be alone;
  Hear us, Holy Spirit.

7 Come to raise us when we fall,
And, when snares our souls enthrall,
Lead us back with gentle call;
  Hear us, Holy Spirit.

8 Keep us in the narrow way,
Warn us when we go astray,
Plead within us when we pray;
  Hear us, Holy Spirit.

9 Holy, loving, as thou art,
Come, and live within our heart,
Never from us to depart;
  Hear us, Holy Spirit.
                  Thomas B. Pollock.

THE GOSPEL:—ATONEMENT NEEDED.

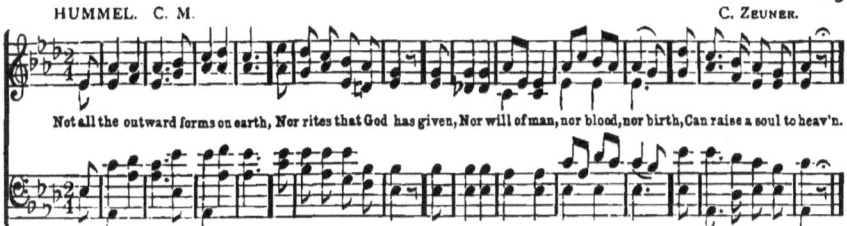

HUMMEL. C. M.   C. ZEUNER.

Not all the outward forms on earth, Nor rites that God has given, Nor will of man, nor blood, nor birth, Can raise a soul to heav'n.

220   *Utter helplessness.*

Not all the outward forms on earth,
  Nor rites that God has given,
Nor will of man, nor blood, nor birth,
  Can raise a soul to heaven.

2 The sovereign will of God alone
  Creates us heirs of grace;
Born in the image of his Son,
  A new, peculiar race.

3 The Spirit, like some heavenly wind,
  Breathes on the sons of flesh,
New-models all the carnal mind,
  And forms the man afresh.

4 Our quickened souls awake and rise
  From the long sleep of death;
On heavenly things we fix our eyes,
  And praise employs our breath.
                                Isaac Watts.

221   *The Soul ruined.*

How sad our state by nature is!
  Our sin—how deep it stains!
And Satan holds our captive minds
  Fast in his slavish chains.

2 But there's a voice of sovereign grace,
  Sounds from the sacred word;
"Ho! ye despairing sinners, come,
  And trust a pardoning Lord."

3 My soul obeys the almighty call,
  And runs to this relief;
I would believe thy promise, Lord:
  Oh, help my unbelief!

4 A guilty, weak, and helpless worm,
  On thy kind arms I fall;
Be thou my Strength and Righteousness,
  My Saviour and my All.
                                Isaac Watts.

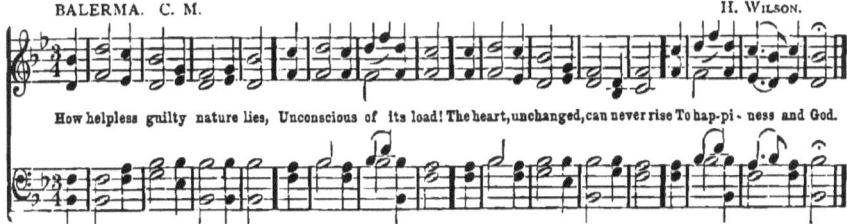

BALERMA. C. M.   H. WILSON.

How helpless guilty nature lies, Unconscious of its load! The heart, unchanged, can never rise To happiness and God.

222   *The load of Sin.*

How helpless guilty nature lies,
  Unconscious of its load!
The heart, unchanged, can never rise
  To happiness and God.

2 Can aught, beneath a power divine,
  The stubborn will subdue?
'Tis thine, almighty Spirit! thine,
  To form the heart anew.

3 'Tis thine, the passions to recall,
  And upward bid them rise;
To make the scales of error fall
  From reason's darkened eyes;—

4 To chase the shades of death away,
  And bid the sinner live;
A beam of heaven, a vital ray,
  'Tis thine alone to give.

5 Oh, change these wretched hearts of ours,
  And give them life divine;
Then shall our passions and our powers,
  Almighty Lord! be thine.
                                Anne Steele.

THE GOSPEL:—ATONEMENT NEEDED.

GORTON. S. M.   Arr. fr. BEETHOVEN.

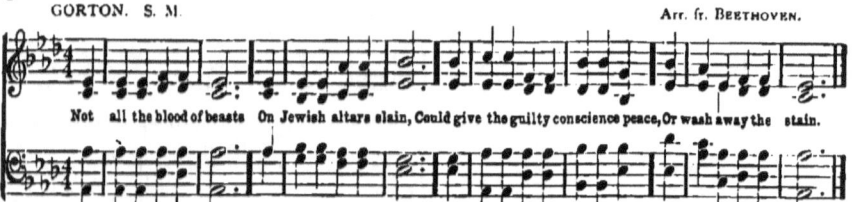

Not all the blood of beasts On Jewish altars slain, Could give the guilty conscience peace, Or wash away the stain.

223   *"No other name."*

Not all the blood of beasts
On Jewish altars slain,
Could give the guilty conscience peace,
Or wash away the stain.

2 But Christ the heavenly Lamb
Takes all our sins away,
A sacrifice of nobler name
And richer blood than they.

3 My faith would lay her hand
On that dear head of thine,
While like a penitent I stand,
And there confess my sin.

4 My soul looks back to see
The burdens thou didst bear,
When hanging on the curséd tree,
And hopes her guilt was there.

5 Believing, we rejoice
To see the curse remove;
We bless the Lamb with cheerful voice,
And sing his dying love.
Isaac Watts.

SHAWMUT. S. M.   LOWELL MASON.

Oh, where shall rest be found—Rest for the wea-ry soul? 'T were vain the ocean's depths to sound, Or pierce to eith-er pole.

224   *Deut. 30: 19.*

Oh, where shall rest be found—
Rest for the weary soul?
'T were vain the ocean's depths to sound,
Or pierce to either pole.

2 The world can never give
The bliss for which we sigh:
'T is not the whole of life to live,
Nor all of death to die.

3 Beyond this vale of tears
There is a life above,
Unmeasured by the flight of years;
And all that life is love.

4 There is a death whose pang
Outlasts the fleeting breath:
Oh, what eternal horrors hang
Around the second death!

5 Lord God of truth and grace!
Teach us that death to shun;
Lest we be banished from thy face,
And evermore undone.
James Montgomery.

225   *A Physician wanted.*

And wilt thou hear, O Lord,
Thy suppliant people's cry?
And pardon, though thy book record
Our crimes of crimson dye?

2 So deep are they engraved,—
So terrible their fear:
The righteous scarcely shall be saved,
And where shall we appear?

3 Let us make all things known
To him who all things sees:
That so his blood may yet atone
For our iniquities.

4 O thou, Physician blest,
Make clean the guilty soul;
And us, by many a sin oppressed,
Restore, and keep us whole!
John M. Neale, tr.

MAN'S LOST CONDITION.

PRAYER. S. M.   L. MARSHALL.

Can sinners hope for heav'n, Who love this world so well? Or dream of future happiness, While on the road to hell?

226 *Pardon and Purity.*
CAN sinners hope for heaven,
  Who love this world so well?
Or dream of future happiness,
  While on the road to hell?

2 Shall they hosannas sing,
  With an unhallowed tongue?
Shall palms adorn the guilty hand
  Which does its neighbor wrong?

3 Thy grace, O God, alone,
  Good hope can e'er afford!
The pardoned and the pure shall see
  The glory of the Lord.
            Benjamin Beddome.

227 *"All downward."*
LIKE sheep we went astray,
  And broke the fold of God—
Each wandering in a different way,
  But all the downward road.

2 How dreadful was the hour,
  When God our wanderings laid,
And did at once his vengeance pour
  Upon the Shepherd's head!

3 How glorious was the grace,
  When Christ sustained the stroke!
His life and blood the Shepherd pays,
  A ransom for the flock.

4 But God shall raise his head,
  O'er all the sons of men,
And make him see a numerous seed,
  To recompense his pain.
            Isaac Watts.

228 *"Jesus only."*
NOT what these hands have done
  Can save this guilty soul:
Not what this toiling flesh has borne
  Can make my spirit whole.

2 Not what I feel or do
  Can give me peace with God;
Not all my prayers, and sighs, and tears,
  Can bear my awful load.

3 Thy work alone, O Christ,
  Can ease this weight of sin;
Thy blood alone, O Lamb of God,
  Can give me peace within.
            Horatius Bonar.

IOWA. S. M.   A. CHAPIN.

A charge to keep I have, A God to glo-ri-fy, A nev-er-dy-ing soul to save, And fit it for the sky.

229 *Probation.*
A CHARGE to keep I have,
  A God to glorify,
A never-dying soul to save,
  And fit it for the sky.

2 To serve the present age,
  My calling to fulfill;
Oh, may it all my powers engage
  To do my Master's will.

3 Arm me with jealous care,
  As in thy sight to live;
And oh, thy servant, Lord, prepare
  A strict account to give.

4 Help me to watch and pray,
  And on thyself rely,
Assured, if I my trust betray,
  I shall for ever die.
            Charles Wesley.

THE GOSPEL:—ATONEMENT PROVIDED.

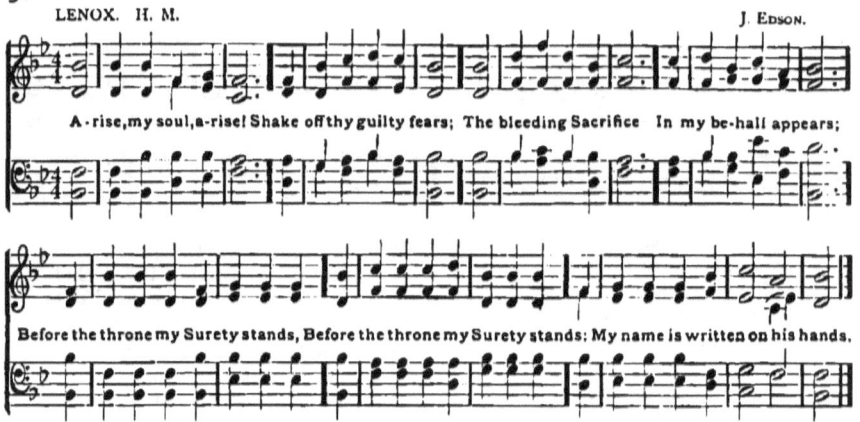

LENOX. H. M.   J. Edson.

A-rise, my soul, a-rise! Shake off thy guilty fears; The bleeding Sacrifice In my be-half appears;
Before the throne my Surety stands, Before the throne my Surety stands: My name is written on his hands.

230   *Our Surety.*
Arise, my soul, arise!
  Shake off thy guilty fears;
The bleeding Sacrifice
  In my behalf appears;
Before the throne my Surety stands:
My name is written on his hands.

2 He ever lives above,
  For me to intercede,
His all-redeeming love,
  His precious blood to plead;
His blood atoned for all our race,
And sprinkles now the throne of grace.

3 My God is reconciled;
  His pardoning voice I hear;
He owns me for his child;
  I can no longer fear;
With confidence I now draw nigh,
And Father, Abba, Father, cry.
                Charles Wesley.

231   *Year of Jubilee.*
Blow ye the trumpet, blow;—
  The gladly solemn sound;—
Let all the nations know,
  To earth's remotest bound,
The year of jubilee is come:
Return, ye ransomed sinners, home.

2 Jesus, our great High Priest,
  Hath full atonement made;
Ye weary spirits, rest;
  Ye mournful souls, be glad:
The year of jubilee is come:
Return, ye ransomed sinners, home.

3 Extol the Lamb of God,
  The all-atoning Lamb;
Redemption in his blood
  Throughout the world proclaim:
The year of jubilee is come;
Return, ye ransomed sinners, home.

4 The gospel trumpet hear,
  The news of heavenly grace;
And, saved from earth, appear
  Before your Saviour's face:
The year of jubilee is come!
Return, ye ransomed sinners, home.
                Charles Wesley.

232   *"The Cross alone."*
Ye saints, your music bring,
  Attuned to sweetest sound,
Strike every trembling string,
  Till earth and heaven resound;
The triumphs of the cross we sing;
Awake, ye saints, each joyful string.

2 The cross, the cross alone,
  Subdued the powers of hell;
Like lightning from his throne
  The prince of darkness fell;
The triumphs of the cross we sing;
Awake, ye saints, each joyful string.

3 The cross hath power to save
  From all the foes that rise;
The cross hath made the grave
  A passage to the skies;
The triumphs of the cross we sing;
Awake, ye saints, each joyful string.
                Andrew Reed.

THE PLAN OF SALVATION.

233 *The seeking love of God.*

God loved the world of sinners lost
  And ruined by the fall;
Salvation full, at highest cost,
  He offers free to all.

Ref.—Oh, 't was love, 't was wondrous love!
  The love of God to me;
  It brought my Saviour from above,
    To die on Calvary.

2 Ev'n now by faith I claim him mine,
  The risen Son of God;
  Redemption by his death I find,
    And cleansing through the blood.—Ref.

3 Love brings the glorious fullness in,
  And to his saints makes known
  The blessèd rest from inbred sin,
    Through faith in Christ alone.—Ref.

4 Believing souls, rejoicing go;
  There shall to you be given
  A glorious foretaste, here below,
    Of endless life in heaven.—Ref.

5 Of victory now o'er Satan's power
  Let all the ransomed sing,
  And triumph in the dying hour
    Through Christ the Lord our King.—Ref.
Mrs. M. M. Stockton.

234 *"Blood of Jesus."*

Precious, precious blood of Jesus,
    Shed on Calvary,
Shed for rebels, shed for sinners,
    Shed for thee!

2 Though thy sins are red like crimson,
    Deep in scarlet glow,
Jesus' precious blood shall wash thee
    White as snow.

3 Precious blood that hath redeemed us!
    All the price is paid!
Perfect pardon now is offered,
    Peace is made.

4 Precious blood! by this we conquer
    In the fiercest fight,
Sin and Satan overcoming
    By its might.
Frances R. Havergal.

THE GOSPEL: —ATONEMENT PROVIDED.

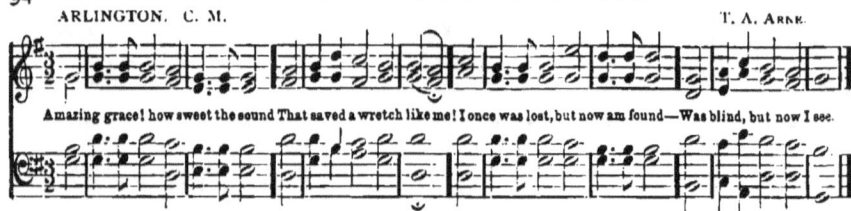

ARLINGTON. C. M.   T. A. Arne.

Amazing grace! how sweet the sound That saved a wretch like me! I once was lost, but now am found—Was blind, but now I see.

235   *"Amazing grace."*
Amazing grace! how sweet the sound
  That saved a wretch like me!
I once was lost, but now am found—
  Was blind, but now I see.

2 'T was grace that taught my heart to fear,
  And grace my fears relieved;
How precious did that grace appear,
  The hour I first believed!

3 Through many dangers, toils, and snares,
  I have already come;
'Tis grace hath brought me safe thus far,
  And grace will lead me home.

4 Yea, when this flesh and heart shall fail
  And mortal life shall cease,
I shall possess within the vail
  A life of joy and peace.

5 The earth shall soon dissolve like snow,
  The sun forbear to shine;
But God, who called me here below,
  Will be for ever mine.
                    John Newton.

236   *Zech. 14: 1.*
There is a fountain filled with blood,
  Drawn from Immanuel's veins;
And sinners, plunged beneath that flood,
  Lose all their guilty stains.

2 The dying thief rejoiced to see
  That fountain in his day;
And there may I, though vile as he,
  Wash all my sins away.

3 Dear dying Lamb, thy precious blood
  Shall never lose its power,
Till all the ransomed church of God
  Be saved to sin no more.

4 E'er since, by faith, I saw the stream
  Thy flowing wounds supply,
Redeeming love has been my theme,
  And shall be, till I die.

5 Then in a nobler, sweeter song,
  I'll sing thy power to save,
When this poor lisping, stammering tongue
  Lies silent in the grave.
                    William Cowper.

FOUNTAIN. C. M.   Western Air.

There is a fountain filled with blood, Drawn from Immanuel's veins; And sinners plunged beneath that flood, Lose all their guilty stains, Lose all their guilty stains, Lose all their guilty stains.

THE PLAN OF SALVATION.

GLASGOW. C. M.   G. F. ROOT.

Great God, when I approach thy throne, And all thy glory see; This is my stay, and this alone, That Jesus died for me.

237   *"Jesus died for me."*

GREAT God, when I approach thy throne,
  And all thy glory see;
This is my stay, and this alone,
  That Jesus died for me.

2 How can a soul condemned to die,
  Escape the just decree?
Helpless, and full of sin am I,
  But Jesus died for me.

3 Burdened with sin's oppressive chain,
  Oh, how can I get free?
No peace can all my efforts gain,
  But Jesus died for me.

4 And, Lord, when I behold thy face,
  This must be all my plea;
Save me by thy almighty grace,
  For Jesus died for me.
                    W. H. Bathurst.

238   *Divine compassion.*

JESUS,—and didst thou leave the sky,
  To bear our griefs and woes?
And didst thou bleed, and groan and die,
  For thy rebellious foes?

2 Well might the heavens with wonder view
  A love so strange as thine!
No thought of angels ever knew
  Compassion so divine!

3 Is there a heart that will not bend
  To thy divine control?
Descend, O sovereign love, descend,
  And melt that stubborn soul.

4 Oh! may our willing hearts confess
  Thy sweet, thy gentle sway;
Glad captives of thy matchless grace,
  Thy righteous rule obey.
                    Anne Steele.

LOVING-KINDNESS. L. M.   Western melody.

A-wake, my soul, to joyful lays, And sing thy great Redeemer's praise; He justly claims a song from me, His lov-ing-kind-ness, oh, how free! Lov-ing-kindness, lov-ing-kindness, His lov-ing-kind-ness, oh, how free!

239   *Loving-kindness.*

AWAKE, my soul, to joyful lays,
And sing thy great Redeemer's praise;
He justly claims a song from me:
His loving-kindness, oh, how free!

2 He saw me ruined in the fall,
Yet loved me, notwithstanding all;
He saved me from my lost estate:
His loving-kindness, oh, how great!

3 Though numerous hosts of mighty foes,
Though earth and hell my way oppose,
He safely leads my soul along:
His loving-kindness, oh, how strong!

4 When trouble, like a gloomy cloud,
Has gathered thick and thundered loud,
He near my soul has always stood:
His loving-kindness, oh, how good!
                    Samuel Medley.

THE GOSPEL:—ATONEMENT PROVIDED.

NAUMANN. C. M. 5 l.   Arr. fr. NAUMANN.

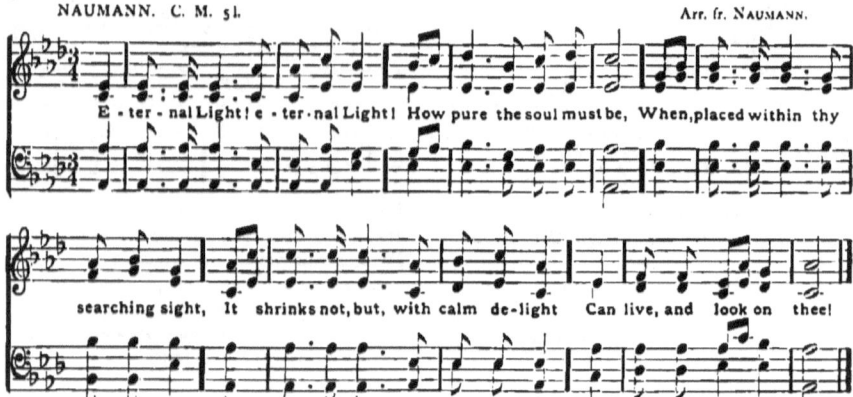

E-ter-nal Light! e-ter-nal Light! How pure the soul must be, When, placed within thy searching sight, It shrinks not, but, with calm de-light Can live, and look on thee!

240   *The Father.*
ETERNAL Light! eternal Light!
  How pure the soul must be,
When, placed within thy searching sight,
  It shrinks not, but, with calm delight
  Can live, and look on thee!

2 The spirits that surround thy throne,
  May bear the burning bliss;
But that is surely theirs alone,
Since they have never, never known
  A fallen world like this.

3 There is a way for man to rise
  To that sublime abode:—
An offering and a sacrifice,
A Holy Spirit's energies,
  An advocate with God.

4 These, these prepare us for the sight
  Of holiness above:
The sons of ignorance and night
May dwell in the eternal Light,
  Through the eternal Love!
                    Thomas Binney.

241   *The Son.*
O SAVIOUR, where shall guilty man
  Find rest except in thee?
Thine was the warfare with his foe,
The cross of pain, the cup of woe,
  And thine the victory.

2 How came the everlasting Son,
  The Lord of life, to die?
Why didst thou meet the tempter's power,
Why, Jesus, in thy dying hour,
  Endure such agony?

3 To save us by thy precious blood,
  To make us one in thee,
That ours might be thy perfect life,
Thy thorny crown, thy cross, thy strife,
  And ours the victory.

4 Oh, make us worthy, gracious Lord,
  Of all thy love to be;
To thy blest will our wills incline,
That unto death we may be thine,
  And ever live in thee.
                    C. E. May.

242   *The Holy Ghost.*
COME, thou who dost the soul endue
  With sevenfold gifts of grace;
Come, thou who dost the world renew,
Author of peace, consoler true,
  Spirit of holiness.

2 Thou didst the gospel-trumpet sound
  O'er all the world afar;
And summon from their sleep profound
The dead, who lay in darkness round,
  To hail the Morning Star.

3 Thine be all praise for evermore,
  From all salvation's heirs;
Thy goodness, truth, and love, and power,
Let all created worlds adore
  In holy hymns and prayers.

4 O thou, who teachest us to place
  In thee our hope and trust,
The stains of former guilt efface,
Confirm the innocent in grace,
  And glorify the just.
                    Edward Caswall, tr.

THE PLAN OF SALVATION.

243   *"None other name."*

I LAY my sins on Jesus,
  The spotless Lamb of God;
He bears them all, and frees us
  From the accurséd load;
I bring my guilt to Jesus,
  To wash my crimson stains
White in his blood most precious,
  Till not a stain remains.

2 I lay my wants on Jesus;
  All fullness dwells in him;
He healeth my diseases,
  He doth my soul redeem:
I lay my griefs on Jesus,
  My burdens and my cares;
He from them all releases,
  He all my sorrows shares.

3 I long to be like Jesus,
  Meek, loving, lowly, mild;
I long to be like Jesus,
  The Father's holy child.
I long to be with Jesus,
  Amid the heavenly throng;
To sing with saints his praises,
  And learn the angels' song.
Horatius Bonar.

244   *"I need thee."*

I NEED thee, precious Jesus!
  For I am full of sin;
My soul is dark and guilty,
  My heart is dead within;
I need the cleansing fountain,
  Where I can always flee,
The blood of Christ most precious,
  The sinner's perfect plea.

2 I need thee, blesséd Jesus!
  For I am very poor;
A stranger and a pilgrim,
  I have no earthly store;
I need the love of Jesus
  To cheer me on my way,
To guide my doubting footsteps,
  To be my strength and stay.

3 I need thee, blesséd Jesus!
  And hope to see thee soon,
Encircled with the rainbow,
  And seated on thy throne:
There, with thy blood-bought children,
  My joy shall ever be
To sing thy praise, Lord Jesus,
  To gaze, my Lord, on thee!
Frederick Whitfield.

7 P

THE GOSPEL:—ATONEMENT OFFERED.

RETURN. C. M.   T. HASTINGS.

Return, O wand'rer, to thy home, Thy Father calls for thee; No longer now an exile roam In guilt and misery: Return, return.

245   *"Return, return!"*

RETURN, O wanderer, to thy home,
Thy Father calls for thee;
No longer now an exile roam
In guilt and misery:
    Return, return.

2 Return, O wanderer, to thy home,
'T is Jesus calls for thee;
The Spirit and the Bride say, "Come,"
Oh, now for refuge flee:
    Return, return.

3 Return, O wanderer, to thy home,
'T is madness to delay;
There are no pardons in the tomb,
And brief is mercy's day:
    Return, return.   *Thomas Hastings.*

MARTYN. 7s. D.   S. B. MARSH.

Sinners, turn, why will ye die? God, your Maker, asks you—Why? God, who did your being give, Made you with himself to live; He the fatal cause demands, Asks the work of his own hands,— Why, ye thankless creatures, why Will ye cross his love, and die?

246   *Ezekiel 33: 11.*

SINNERS, turn, why will ye die?
God, your Maker, asks you—Why?
God, who did your being give,
Made you with himself to live;
He the fatal cause demands,
Asks the work of his own hands,—
Why, ye thankless creatures, why
Will ye cross his love, and die?

2 Sinners, turn, why will ye die?
God, your Saviour, asks you—Why?
He who did your souls retrieve,
Died himself that ye might live.
Will ye let him die in vain?
Crucify your Lord again?
Why, ye ransomed sinners, why
Will ye slight his grace, and die?

3 Sinners, turn, why will ye die?
God, the Spirit, asks you—Why?
He, who all your lives hath strove,
Urged you to embrace his love:
Will ye not his grace receive?
Will ye still refuse to live?
Why, ye long-sought sinners! why,
Will ye grieve your God, and die?
                  Charles Wesley.

INVITATIONS AND WARNINGS.

247 *"Here speaks the Comforter."*

COME, ye disconsolate, where'er ye languish,
  Come to the mercy-seat, fervently kneel,
Here bring your wounded hearts, here tell
    your anguish;
  Earth hath no sorrow that heaven cannot
    heal.

2 Joy of the comfortless, light of the straying,
  Hope of the penitent, fadeless and pure;
Here speaks the Comforter, tenderly saying—
  Earth hath no sorrow that heaven cannot
    cure.

3 Here see the Bread of Life; see waters
    flowing
  Forth from the throne of God, pure from
    above;
Come to the feast of love: come, ever knowing
  Earth hath no sorrow but heaven can
    remove.
Thomas Moore.

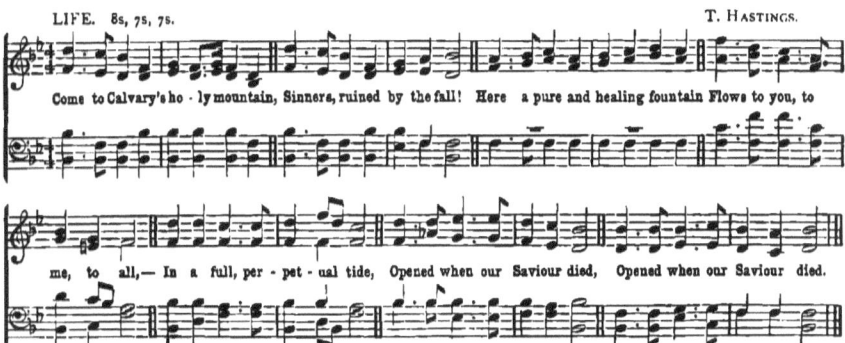

248 *A fountain opened.*

COME to Calvary's holy mountain,
  Sinners, ruined by the fall!
Here a pure and healing fountain
  Flows to you, to me, to all,—
In a full, perpetual tide,
  Opened when our Saviour died.

2 Come, in sorrow and contrition,
  Wounded, impotent, and blind!
Here the guilty, free remission,
  Here the troubled, peace may find;
Health this fountain will restore,
  He that drinks shall thirst no more—

3 He that drinks shall live for ever;
  'Tis a soul-renewing flood:
God is faithful; God will never
  Break his covenant in blood,
Signed when our Redeemer died,
  Sealed when he was glorified.
James Montgomery.

THE GOSPEL:—ATONEMENT OFFERED.

SCOTLAND. 12s.   J. CLARK.

The voice of free grace cries, Escape to the mountain, For Adam's lost race Christ hath opened a fountain; For sin and uncleanness, and every transgression, His blood flows most freely in streams of salvation, His blood flows most freely in streams of salvation. Hallelujah to the Lamb, who hath purchased our pardon, We'll praise him again, when we pass over Jordan, We'll praise him again, when we pass over Jordan.

249   *"Flee for life."*

THE voice of free grace cries, Escape to
    the mountain,
For Adam's lost race Christ hath opened
    a fountain;
For sin and uncleanness, and every transgression,
His blood flows most freely in streams of
    salvation.
    Hallelujah to the Lamb, etc.

2 Ye souls that are wounded! oh, flee to
    the Saviour!
He calls you in mercy, 'tis infinite favor;
Your sins are increasing, escape to the
    mountain—
His blood can remove them, it flows from
    the fountain.
    Hallelujah to the Lamb, etc.

3 With joy shall we stand when escaped
    to the shore;
With harps in our hands we will praise him
    the more!
We'll range the sweet plains on the banks
    of the river,
And sing of salvation for ever and ever!
    Hallelujah to the Lamb, etc.
                        R. Burdsall.

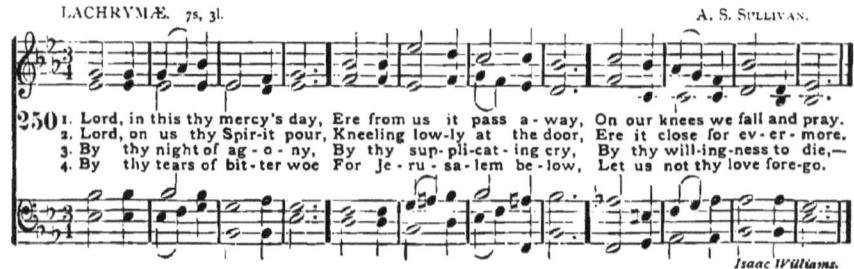

LACHRYMÆ. 7s, 3l.   A. S. SULLIVAN.

250
1. Lord, in this thy mercy's day, Ere from us it pass away, On our knees we fall and pray.
2. Lord, on us thy Spirit pour, Kneeling lowly at the door, Ere it close for evermore.
3. By thy night of agony, By thy supplicating cry, By thy willingness to die,—
4. By thy tears of bitter woe For Jerusalem below, Let us not thy love forego.

Isaac Williams.

INVITATIONS AND WARNINGS.

DETROIT. S. M.   E. P. Hastings.

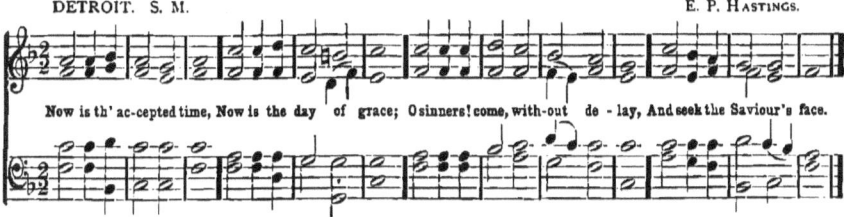

Now is th' ac-cepted time, Now is the day of grace; O sinners! come, with-out de-lay, And seek the Saviour's face.

251 *The accepted time.*

Now is the accepted time,
  Now is the day of grace;
O sinners! come, without delay,
  And seek the Saviour's face.

2 Now is the accepted time,
  The Saviour calls to-day;
To-morrow it may be too late;—
  Then why should you delay?

3 Now is the accepted time,
  The gospel bids you come;
And every promise in his word
  Declares there yet is room.

4 Lord, draw reluctant souls,
  And feast them with thy love;
Then will the angels spread their wings,
  And bear the news above.
                John Dobell.

252 *"Sinner, come!"*

The Spirit, in our hearts,
  Is whispering, "Sinner, come:"
The bride, the Church of Christ, proclaims
  To all his children, "Come!"

2 Let him that heareth say
  To all about him, "Come!"
Let him that thirsts for righteousness,
  To Christ, the fountain, come!

3 Yea, whosoever will,
  Oh, let him freely come,
And freely drink the stream of life;
  'Tis Jesus bids him come.

4 Lo! Jesus, who invites,
  Delares, I "quickly come;"
Lord, even so! we wait thine hour;
  O blest Redeemer, come!
                H. U. Onderdonk.

OWEN. S. M.   J. E. Sweetser.

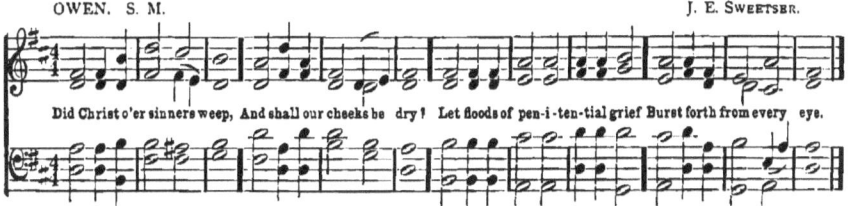

Did Christ o'er sinners weep, And shall our cheeks be dry? Let floods of pen-i-ten-tial grief Burst forth from every eye.

253 *Weeping for sinners.*

Did Christ o'er sinners weep,
  And shall our cheeks be dry?
Let floods of penitential grief
  Burst forth from every eye.

2 The Son of God in tears
  Angels with wonder see;
Be thou astonished, O my soul!
  He shed those tears for thee.

3 He wept that we might weep;
  Each sin demands a tear:
In heaven alone no sin is found,
  And there's no weeping there.
                Benjamin Beddome.

254 *The call of love.*

And canst thou, sinner! slight
  The call of love divine?
Shall God, with tenderness, invite,
  And gain no thought of thine?

2 Wilt thou not cease to grieve
  The Spirit from thy breast,
Till he thy wretched soul shall leave
  With all thy sins oppressed?

3 To-day a pardoning God
  Will hear the suppliant pray;
To-day a Saviour's cleansing blood,
  Will wash thy guilt away.
                Mrs. Abby B. Hyde.

THE GOSPEL:—ATONEMENT OFFERED.

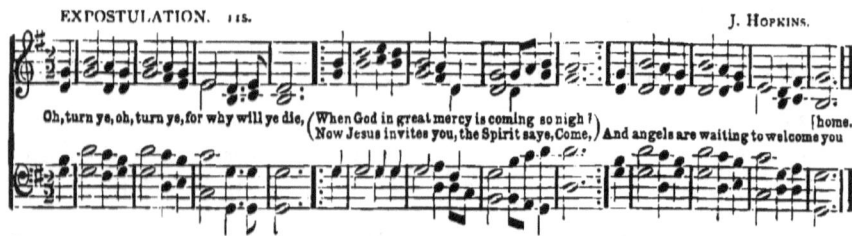

255 *"Why will ye die?"*

Oh, turn ye, oh, turn ye, for why will ye die,
When God in great mercy is coming so nigh?
Now Jesus invites you, the Spirt says, Come,
And angels are waiting to welcome you home.

2 And now Christ is ready your souls to receive,
Oh, how can you question, if you will believe?
If sin is your burden, why will you not come?
'T is you he bids welcome; he bids you come home.
Josiah Hopkins.

256 *Procrastination.*

Delay not, delay not; O sinner, draw near,
The waters of life are now flowing for thee;
No price is demanded; the Saviour is here;
Redemption is purchased, salvation is free.

2 Delay not, delay not, the Spirit of grace,
Long grieved and resisted, may take his sad flight,
And leave thee in darkness to finish thy race,
To sink in the gloom of eternity's night.

3 Delay not, delay not; the hour is at hand;
The earth shall dissolve, and the heavens shall fade,
The dead, small and great, in the judgment shall stand;
What helper, then, sinner, shall lend thee his aid?
Thomas Hastings.

257 *Job 22 : 21.*

Acquaint thyself quickly, O sinner, with God,
And joy, like the sunshine, shall beam on thy road;
And peace, like the dewdrop, shall fall on thy head,
And sleep, like an angel, shall visit thy bed.

2 Acquaint thyself quickly, O sinner, with God,
And he shall be with thee when fears are abroad;
Thy Safeguard in danger that threatens thy path;
Thy Joy in the valley and shadow of death.
William Knox.

REPENTANCE UNTO LIFE.

IRENE. P. M.　　　　　　　　　　　　　　　　　　Arr. fr. Scholefield.

Jesus, heed me, lost and dying, Unto thee for shelter flying, Hear, oh, hear, my heart's sore crying: Heed me, or I die!

258　*The Penitent's Plea.*
Jesus, heed me, lost and dying,
Unto thee for shelter flying,
Hear, oh, hear, my heart's sore crying:
　　Heed me, or I die!

2 All my sin and sorrow feeling,
Come I, as the leper, kneeling;
Come to thee for help and healing,
　　Heal me, or I die!

3 Naught have I to plead of merit,
Naught but curse do I inherit;
By thy gracious, quickening Spirit
　　Save me, or I die!

4 Not my tears of deep contrition
Can secure one sin's remission,
Helpless, hopeless my condition:
　　Help me, or I die!

5 Far away my dead works flinging,
Nothing owning, nothing bringing,
Only to thy mercy clinging:
　　Bless me, or I die!

6 By thy cross, where hope is beaming,
By its crimson fountain streaming,
Flowing for the world's redeeming:
　　Cleanse me, or I die!

7 So my soul shall praise thee ever,
For the love which changes never,
From which not ev'n death can sever:
　　Saved no more to die.
　　　　　　　　　　R. M. Offord.

259　*"The footsteps of the flock."*
Jesus, Shepherd of the sheep,
Who thy Father's flock dost keep,
Safe we wake and safe we sleep,
　　Guarded still by thee.

2 In thy promise firm we stand,
None can pluck us from thy hand,
Speak—we hear—at thy command,
　　We will follow thee.

3 By thy blood our souls were bought,
By thy life salvation wrought,
By thy light our feet are taught,
　　Lord, to follow thee.

4 Father, draw us to thy Son;
We with joy will follow on,
Till the work of grace is done,
　　And from sin set free—

5 We in robes of glory dressed,
Join the assembly of the blest,
Gathered to eternal rest,
　　In the fold with thee.
　　　　　　　　　　Cooke.

260　8s, 7s. D.　*"Take me."*
Take me, O my Father, take me!
　Take me, save me, through thy Son;
That which thou wouldst have me, make me,
　Let thy will in me be done.
Long from thee my footsteps straying,
　Thorny proved the way I trod;
Weary come I now, and praying—
　Take me to thy love, my God!

2 Fruitless years with grief recalling,
　Humbly I confess my sin;
At thy feet, O Father, falling,
　To thy household take me in.
Freely now to thee I proffer
　This relenting heart of mine;
Freely life and soul I offer—
　Gift unworthy love like thine.

3 Once the world's Redeemer, dying,
　Bare our sins upon the tree;
On that sacrifice relying,
　Now I look in hope to thee;
Father, take me! all forgiving,
　Fold me to thy loving breast;
In thy love for ever living,
　I must be for ever blest!
　　　　　　　　　　Ray Palmer.

THE GOSPEL:—ATONEMENT ACCEPTED.

LANGRAN. 10s.   J. LANGRAN.

Weary of earth, and laden with my sin, I look at heaven and long to enter in, But there no evil thing may find a home: And yet I hear a voice that bids me "Come."

261 *"The voice of Jesus."*

WEARY of earth, and laden with my sin,
I look at heaven and long to enter in,
But there no evil thing may find a home:
And yet I hear a voice that bids me "Come."

2 So vile I am, how dare I hope to stand
In the pure glory of that holy land?
Before the whiteness of that throne appear?
Yet there are hands stretched out to draw me near.

3 The while I fain would tread the heavenly way,
Evil is ever with me day by day;
Yet on mine ears the gracious tidings fall,
"Repent, confess, thou shalt be loosed from all."

4 It is the voice of Jesus that I hear,
His are the hands stretched out to draw me near,
And his the blood that can for all atone,
And set me faultless there before the throne.

5 'T was he who found me on the deathly wild,
And made me heir of heaven, the Father's child,
And day by day, whereby my soul may live,
Gives me his grace of pardon, and will give.
Samuel J. Stone.

262 *"Thine all the merit."*

O JESUS Christ the righteous! live in me,
That, when in glory I thy face shall see,
Within the Father's house, my glorious dress
May be the garment of thy righteousness.

2 Then thou wilt welcome me, O righteous Lord,
Thine all the merit, mine the great reward;
Mine the life won, and thine the life laid down,
Thine the thorn-plaited, mine the righteous crown.

3 Naught can I bring, dear Lord, for all I owe;
Yet let my full heart what it can bestow;
Like Mary's gift let my devotion prove,
Forgiven greatly, how I greatly love.
Samuel J. Stone, alt.

263 *"Jesus died."*

LORD, I am come! thy promise is my plea,
Without thy word I durst not venture nigh!
But thou hast called the burdened soul to thee,
A weary, burdened soul, O Lord, am I!

2 Bowed down beneath a heavy load of sin,
By Satan's fierce temptations sorely prest,
Beset without, and full of fears within,
Trembling and faint I come to thee for rest.

3 Be thou my refuge, Lord, my hiding-place;
I know no force can tear me from thy side;
Unmoved, I then may all accusers face,
And answer every charge, with—"Jesus died."
John Newton.

REPENTANCE UNTO LIFE.

ST. HILDA. 7s, 6s. D. E. HUSBAND.

O Je-sus, thou art stand-ing Out-side the fast-closed door, In low-ly pa-tience wait-ing To pass the threshold o'er: We bear the name of Christians, His name and sign we bear: Oh, shame, thrice shame up-on us! To keep him stand-ing there.

264   *At the door.*
O JESUS, thou art standing
  Outside the fast-closed door,
In lowly patience waiting
  To pass the threshold o'er:
We bear the name of Christians,
  His name and sign we bear:
Oh, shame, thrice shame upon us!
  To keep him standing there.

2 O Jesus, thou art knocking:
  And lo! that hand is scarred,
And thorns thy brow encircle,
  And tears thy face have marred:
Oh, love that passeth knowledge,
  So patiently to wait!
Oh, sin that hath no equal,
  So fast to bar the gate!

3 O Jesus, thou art pleading
  In accents meek and low,—
"I died for you, my children,
  And will ye treat me so?"
O Lord, with shame and sorrow
  We open now the door:
Dear Saviour, enter, enter,
  And leave us nevermore!
           William W. How.

265   *"Give us pardon."*
WE stand in deep repentance,
  Before thy throne of love;
O God of grace, forgive us;
  The stain of guilt remove;
Behold us while with weeping
  We lift our eyes to thee;
And all our sins subduing,
  Our Father, set us free!

2 Oh, shouldst thou from us fallen
  Withhold thy grace to guide,
For ever we should wander,
  From thee, and peace, aside;
But thou to spirits contrite
  Dost light and life impart,
That man may learn to serve thee
  With thankful, joyous heart.

3 Our souls—on thee we cast them,
  Our only refuge thou!
Thy cheering words revive us,
  When pressed with grief we bow:
Thou bearest the trusting spirit
  Upon thy loving breast,
And givest all thy ransomed
  A sweet, unending rest.
           Ray Palmer, tr.

THE GOSPEL:—ATONEMENT ACCEPTED.

O Ho-ly Sav-iour! Friend un-seen, Since on thine arm thou bid'st me lean, Help me, throughout life's changing scene, By faith to cling to thee!

266 *Clinging to Christ.*

O Holy Saviour! Friend unseen,
Since on thine arm thou bid'st me lean,
Help me, throughout life's changing scene,
 By faith to cling to thee!

2 Without a murmur I dismiss
My former dreams of earthly bliss;
My joy, my recompense be this,
 Each hour to cling to thee!

3 What though the world deceitful prove,
And earthly friends and hopes remove;
With patient, uncomplaining love,
 Still would I cling to thee.

4 Though oft I seem to tread alone
Life's dreary waste, with thorns o'ergrown,
Thy voice of love, in gentlest tone,
 Still whispers, "Cling to me!"

5 Though faith and hope are often tried,
I ask not, need not, aught beside;
So safe, so calm, so satisfied,
 The soul that clings to thee!
  Charlotte Elliott.

267 *"Plead for me."*

O Thou, the contrite sinner's Friend,
Who loving, lov'st them to the end,
On this alone my hopes depend,
 That thou wilt plead for me.

2 When weary in the Christian race,
Far off appears my resting place,
And, fainting, I mistrust thy grace,
 Then, Saviour, plead for me.

3 When I have erred and gone astray,
Afar from thine and wisdom's way,
And see no glimmering, guiding ray,
 Still, Saviour, plead for me.

4 When Satan, by my sins made bold,
Strives from thy cross to loose my hold,
Then with thy pitying arms enfold,
 And plead, oh, plead for me!

5 And when my dying hour draws near,
Darkened with anguish, guilt and fear,
Then to my fainting sight appear,
 Pleading in heaven for me.
  Charlotte Elliott.

268 *"A will resigned."*

I ask not now for gold to gild,
 With mocking shine, an aching frame;
The yearning of the mind is stilled—
 I ask not now for fame.

2 But, bowed in lowliness of mind,
 I make my humble wishes known;
I only ask a will resigned,
 O Father, to thine own.

3 In vain I task my aching brain,
 In vain the sage's thoughts I scan;
I only feel how weak I am,
 How poor and blind is man.

4 And now my spirit sighs for home,
 And longs for light whereby to see;
And, like a weary child, would come,
 O Father, unto thee.
  John G. Whittier.

REPENTANCE UNTO LIFE.

WOODWORTH. L. M.   W. B. BRADBURY.

Just as I am, with-out one plea, But that thy blood was shed for me, And that thou bid'st me come to thee, O Lamb of God, I come, I come!

269   *"Lamb of God."*

JUST as I am, without one plea,
But that thy blood was shed for me,
And that thou bid'st me come to thee,
   O Lamb of God, I come!

2 Just as I am, and waiting not
To rid my soul of one dark blot,
To thee whose blood can cleanse each spot,
   O Lamb of God, I come!

3 Just as I am, though tossed about
With many a conflict, many a doubt,
Fightings within, and fears without,
   O Lamb of God, I come!

4 Just as I am—thou wilt receive,
Wilt welcome, pardon, cleanse, relieve;
Because thy promise I believe,
   O Lamb of God, I come!

5 Just as I am—thy love unknown
Hath broken every barrier down;
Now, to be thine, yea, thine alone,
   O Lamb of God, I come!
                              Charlotte Elliott.

270   *"Be merciful, O God."*

WITH broken heart and contrite sigh,
A trembling sinner, Lord, I cry:
Thy pardoning grace is rich and free:
O God, be merciful to me!

2 I smite upon my troubled breast,
With deep and conscious guilt oppressed;
Christ and his cross my only plea:
O God, be merciful to me!

3 Nor alms, nor deeds that I have done,
Can for a single sin atone;
To Calvary alone I flee:
O God, be merciful to me!

4 And when, redeemed from sin and hell,
With all the ransomed throng I dwell,
My raptured song shall ever be,
God hath been merciful to me!
                              Cornelius Elven.

271   *Psalm 51.*

SHOW pity, Lord! O Lord! forgive;
Let a repenting rebel live;
Are not thy mercies large and free?
May not a sinner trust in thee?

2 Oh, wash my soul from every sin,
And make my guilty conscience clean;
Here on my heart the burden lies,
And past offences pain mine eyes.

3 My lips with shame my sins confess,
Against thy law, against thy grace:
Lord! should thy judgments grow severe,
I am condemned, but thou art clear.

4 Should sudden vengeance seize my breath,
I must pronounce thee just in death;
And if my soul were sent to hell,
Thy righteous law approves it well.

5 Yet save a trembling sinner, Lord!
Whose hope still hovering round thy word,
Would light on some sweet promise there,
Some sure support against despair.
                                Isaac Watts.

THE GOSPEL:—ATONEMENT ACCEPTED.

HALLE. 7s, 6l.   Arr. by T. Hastings.

272   *"Come and welcome."*

From the cross uplifted high,
Where the Saviour deigns to die,
What melodious sounds we hear,
Bursting on the ravished ear!—
"Love's redeeming work is done—
Come and welcome, sinner, come!

2 "Spread for thee, the festal board
See with richest bounty stored;
To thy Father's bosom pressed,
Thou shalt be a child confessed,
Never from his house to roam;
Come and welcome, sinner, come!

3 "Soon the days of life shall end—
Lo, I come—your Saviour, Friend!
Safe your spirit to convey
To the realms of endless day,
Up to my eternal home—
Come and welcome, sinner, come!"
Thomas Haweis.

SPANISH HYMN. 7s, 6l.   Spanish Melody.

273   *"Only thee."*

Blessed Saviour! thee I love,
All my other joys above;
All my hopes in thee abide,
Thou my hope, and naught beside:
Ever let my glory be,
Only, only, only thee.

2 Once again beside the cross,
All my gain I count but loss;
Earthly pleasures fade away,—
Clouds they are that hide my day:
Hence, vain shadows! let me see
Jesus crucified for me.

3 Blessèd Saviour, thine am I,
Thine to live, and thine to die;
Height, or depth, or earthly power,
Ne'er shall hide my Saviour more:
Ever shall my glory be
Only, only, only thee.
George Duffield.

274   *"I am thine."*

Jesus, Master, whose I am,
Purchased thine alone to be,
By thy blood, O spotless Lamb,
Shed so willingly for me;
Let my heart be all thine own,
Let me live to thee alone.

2 Other lords have long held sway;
Now thy name alone to bear,
Thy dear voice alone obey,
Is my daily, hourly prayer.
Whom have I in heaven but thee?
Nothing else my joy can be.

3 Jesus, Master, I am thine;
Keep me faithful, keep me near;
Let thy presence in me shine
All my homeward way to cheer.
Jesus, at thy feet I fall,
Oh, be thou my All in all.
Frances R. Havergal.

AVON. C. M. HUGH WILSON.

O thou, whose tender mercy hears Contrition's humble sigh; Whose hand indulgent wipes the tears From sorrow's weeping eye;—

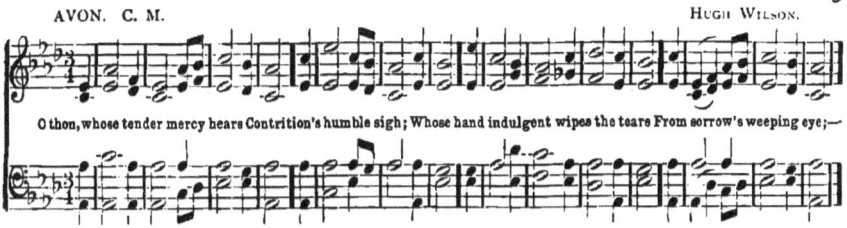

275 "*Return.*"

O THOU, whose tender mercy hears
  Contrition's humble sigh;
Whose hand indulgent wipes the tears
  From sorrow's weeping eye;—

2 See, Lord, before thy throne of grace,
  A wretched wanderer mourn;
Hast thou not bid me seek thy face?
  Hast thou not said—"Return?"

3 And shall my guilty fears prevail
  To drive me from thy feet?
Oh, let not this dear refuge fail,
  This only safe retreat!

4 Oh, shine on this benighted heart,
  With beams of mercy shine!
And let thy healing voice impart
  The sense of joy divine.

Anne Steele.

TELL THE STORY. 7s, 6s. D. W. G. FISCHER.

276

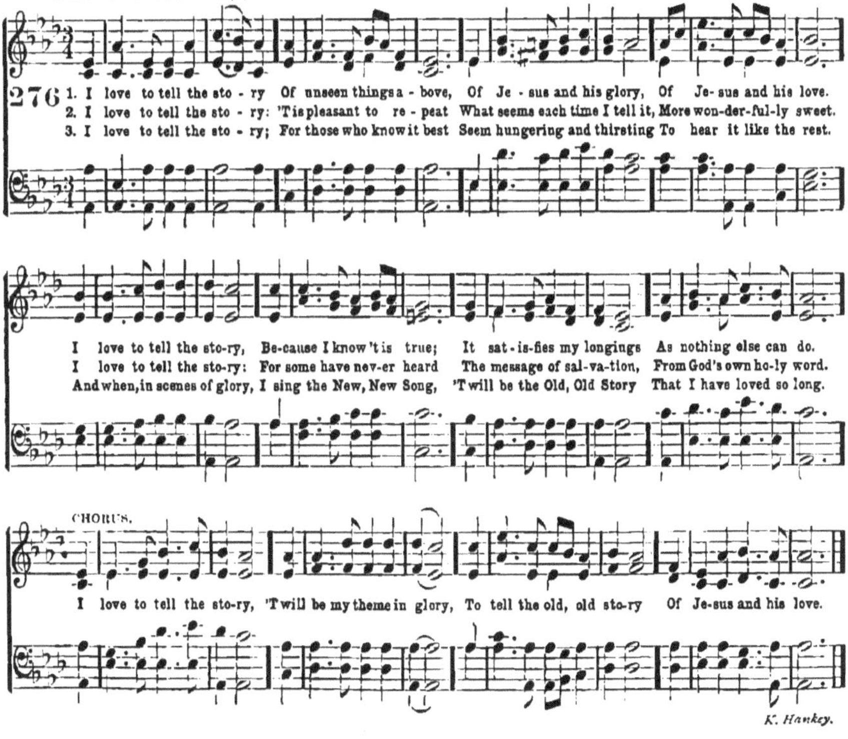
1. I love to tell the sto - ry Of unseen things a - bove, Of Je - sus and his glory, Of Je - sus and his love.
2. I love to tell the sto - ry: 'Tis pleasant to re - peat What seems each time I tell it, More won-der-ful-ly sweet.
3. I love to tell the sto - ry; For those who know it best Seem hungering and thirsting To hear it like the rest.
I love to tell the sto-ry, Be-cause I know 'tis true; It sat - is-fies my longings As nothing else can do.
I love to tell the sto-ry: For some have nev-er heard The message of sal-va-tion, From God's own ho-ly word.
And when, in scenes of glory, I sing the New, New Song, 'T will be the Old, Old Story That I have loved so long.
CHORUS.
I love to tell the sto-ry, 'Twill be my theme in glory, To tell the old, old sto-ry Of Je-sus and his love.

K. Hankey.

THE GOSPEL:—ATONEMENT ACCEPTED.

277 *"At the door."*

BEHOLD a Stranger at the door!
He gently knocks, has knocked before,
Has waited long, is waiting still;
You treat no other friend so ill.

2 Oh, lovely attitude! he stands
With melting heart and laden hands;
Oh, matchless kindness! and he shows
This matchless kindness to his foes.

3 But will he prove a friend indeed?
He will, the very friend you need—
The Friend of sinners; yes, 't is he,
With garments dyed on Calvary.

4 Rise, touched with gratitude divine,
Turn out his enemy and thine,
That soul-destroying monster sin,
And let the heavenly Stranger in.
Joseph Grigg.

278 *One Thing needful.*

WHY will ye waste on trifling cares
That life which God's compassion spares?
While, in the various range of thought,
The one thing needful is forgot?

2 Shall God invite you from above?
Shall Jesus urge his dying love?
Shall troubled conscience give you pain?
And all these pleas unite in vain?

3 Not so your eyes will always view
Those objects which you now pursue;
Not so will heaven and hell appear,
When death's decisive hour is near.

4 Almighty God! thy grace impart;
Fix deep conviction on each heart:
Nor let us waste on trifling cares
That life which thy compassion spares.
Philip Doddridge.

279 *The true Physician.*

HEAL me, O my Saviour, heal;
Heal me, as I suppliant kneel;
Heal me, and my pardon seal.

2 Fresh the wounds that sin hath made;
Hear the prayers I oft have prayed,
And in mercy send me aid.

3 Thou the true Physician art;
Thou, O Christ, canst health impart,
Binding up the bleeding heart.

4 Other comforters are gone;
Thou canst heal, and thou alone,
Thou for all my sin atone.
Godfrey Thring.

REPENTANCE UNTO LIFE.

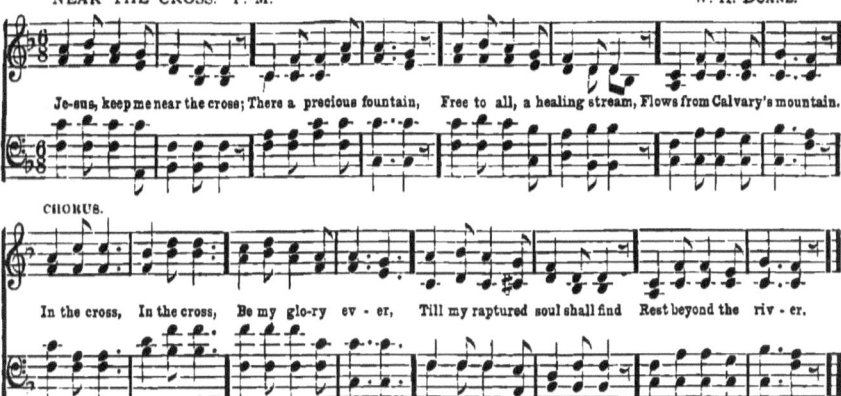

NEAR THE CROSS. P. M. — W. H. Doane.

Je-sus, keep me near the cross; There a precious fountain, Free to all, a healing stream, Flows from Calvary's mountain.

CHORUS.
In the cross, In the cross, Be my glo-ry ev - er, Till my raptured soul shall find Rest beyond the riv - er.

280 *"Near the Cross."*

Jesus, keep me near the cross;
There a precious fountain,
Free to all, a healing stream,
Flows from Calvary's mountain.—Cho.

2 Near the cross, a trembling soul,
Love and mercy found me;
There the bright and morning star
Sheds its beams around me.—Cho.

3 Near the Cross! oh, Lamb of God,
Bring its scenes before me;
Help me walk from day to day,
With its shadow o'er me.—Cho.
Mrs. F. C. Van Alstyne.

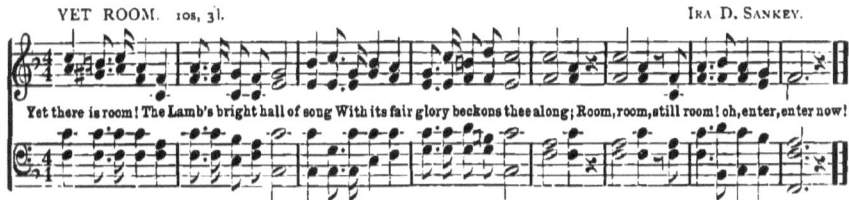

YET ROOM. 10s, 3l. — Ira D. Sankey.

Yet there is room! The Lamb's bright hall of song With its fair glory beckons thee along; Room, room, still room! oh, enter, enter now!

281 *"Yet there is room!"*

Yet there is room! The Lamb's bright
hall of song,
With its fair glory, beckons thee along;
Room, room, still room! oh, enter, enter
now!

2 Day is declining, and the sun is low;
The shadows lengthen, light makes haste
to go:
Room, room, still room! oh, enter, enter
now!

3 The bridal hall is filling for the feast:
Pass in, pass in, and be the Bridegroom's
guest;
Room, room, still room! oh, enter, enter
now!

4 It fills, it fills, that hall of jubilee!
Make haste, make haste; 'tis not too full
for thee:
Room, room, still room! oh, enter, enter
now!

5 Yet there is room! Still open stands the
gate,
The gate of love; it is not yet too late:
Room, room, still room! oh, enter, enter
now!

6 Pass in, pass in! That banquet is for
thee;
That cup of everlasting love is free;
Room, room, still room! oh, enter, enter
now!
Horatius Bonar.

REPENTANCE UNTO LIFE.

283
1. I'm kneeling, Lord, at mercy's gate, With trembling hope and fear; I've wait-ed long, and still I wait Thy gracious word to hear. Thy precious word has bid me seek The joys thou hast in store; O Lord, in mer-cy speak to me, I'm kneeling at the door, I'm kneeling at the door; Kneel-ing at the door; O Lord, in mer-cy speak to me, I'm kneeling at the door.
2. None ev-er emp-ty turned a-way, Who tru-ly sought thy face: And I, my Sav-iour, come to-day, To seek thy pardoning grace. Thy precious blood is all my plea: This can my soul re-store;

Lydia C. Baxter.

284   *"To save the lost."*

There were ninety and nine that safely lay
  In the shelter of the fold,
But one was out on the hills away,
  Far off from the gates of gold—
Away on the mountains wild and bare,
Away from the tender Shepherd's care.

2 "Lord, thou hast here thy ninety and nine;
  Are they not enough for thee?"
But the Shepherd made answer: "This of mine
  Has wandered away from me:
And although the road be rough and steep
I go to the desert to find my sheep."

3 But none of the ransomed ever knew
  How deep were the waters crossed;
Nor how dark was the night that the Lord
  passed through
Ere he found his sheep that was lost;
Out in the desert he heard its cry—
'T was helpless and sick, and ready to die.

4 But all through the mountains, thunder-riven,
  And up from the rocky steep,
There rose a cry to the gate of heaven,
  "Rejoice! I have found my sheep!"
And the angels echoed around the throne,
"Rejoice, for the Lord brings back his own!"

E. C. Clephane.

8 P

THE GOSPEL:—ATONEMENT ACCEPTED.

TIRYUS. P. M.   T. E. PERKINS.

285
1. Come, oh, come with thy broken heart, Wea-ry and worn with care; Come and kneel at the
2. Firmly cling to the bless-ed cross, There shall thy ref-uge be; Wash thee now in the
3. Come and taste of the precious feast, Feast of e - ter - nal love; Think of joys that for -

D.C.—Come, oh, come with thy brok-en heart, Wea-ry and worn with care; Come and kneel at the

o - pen door, Je - sus is wait-ing there: Wait-ing to heal thy wound-ed soul.
crimson fount, Flowing so pure for thee: List to the gen - tle warn - ing voice,
ev - er bloom, Bright in the life a - bove: Come with a trust-ing heart to God,

o - pen door, Je - sus is wait-ing there.

Waiting to give thee rest; Why wilt thou walk where shadows fall? Come to his lov-ing breast.
List to the earn-est call, Leave at thy cross thy bur-den now, Je-sus will bear it all.
Come and be saved by grace; Come, for he loves to clasp thee now, Close in his dear em - brace.

Mrs. F. C. Van Alstyne.

PASS ME NOT. 8s, 5s.   W. H. DOANE.

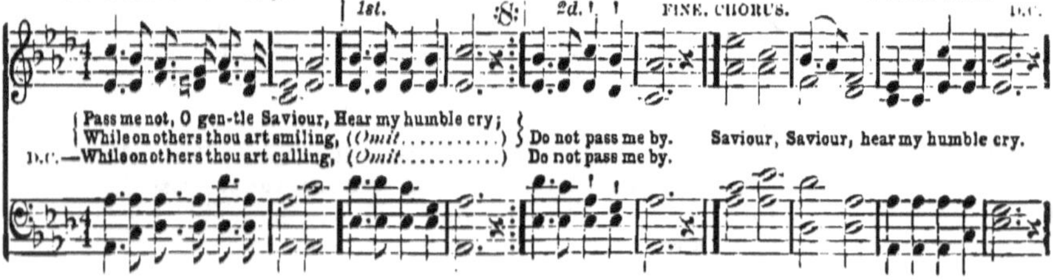

Pass me not, O gen-tle Saviour, Hear my humble cry;
While on others thou art smiling, (Omit............) Do not pass me by. Saviour, Saviour, hear my humble cry.
D.C.—While on others thou art calling, (Omit............) Do not pass me by.

286   *"Do not pass me."*

Pass me not, O gentle Saviour,
   Hear my humble cry;
While on others thou art smiling,
   Do not pass me by.—Cho.

2 Let me at thy throne of mercy
   Find a sweet relief;
Kneeling there in deep contrition,
   Help my unbelief.—Cho.

3 Trusting only in thy merit,
   Would I seek thy face;
Heal my wounded, broken spirit,
   Save me by thy grace.—Cho.

4 Thou the Spring of all my comfort,
   More than life to me,
Whom on earth have I beside thee,
   Whom in heaven but thee!—Cho.

Mrs. F. C. Van Alstyne.

REPENTANCE UNTO LIFE.

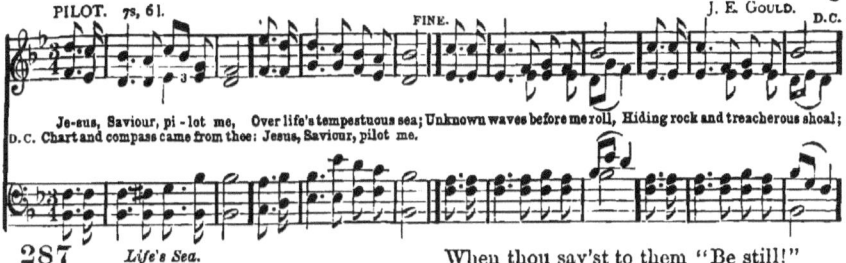

PILOT. 7s, 6 l. J. E. Gould.

Je-sus, Saviour, pi-lot me, Over life's tempestuous sea; Unknown waves before me roll, Hiding rock and treacherous shoal;
D.C. Chart and compass came from thee: Jesus, Saviour, pilot me.

287 *Life's Sea.*
Jesus, Saviour, pilot me,
Over life's tempestuous sea;
Unknown waves before me roll,
Hiding rock and treacherous shoal;
Chart and compass came from thee:
Jesus, Saviour, pilot me.

2 As a mother stills her child,
Thou canst hush the ocean wild;
Boisterous waves obey thy will

When thou say'st to them "Be still!"
Wondrous Sovereign of the sea,
Jesus, Saviour, pilot me.

3 When at last I near the shore,
And the fearful breakers roar
'Twixt me and the peaceful rest,
Then, while leaning on thy breast,
May I hear thee say to me,
"Fear not, I will pilot thee!"
Edward Hopper.

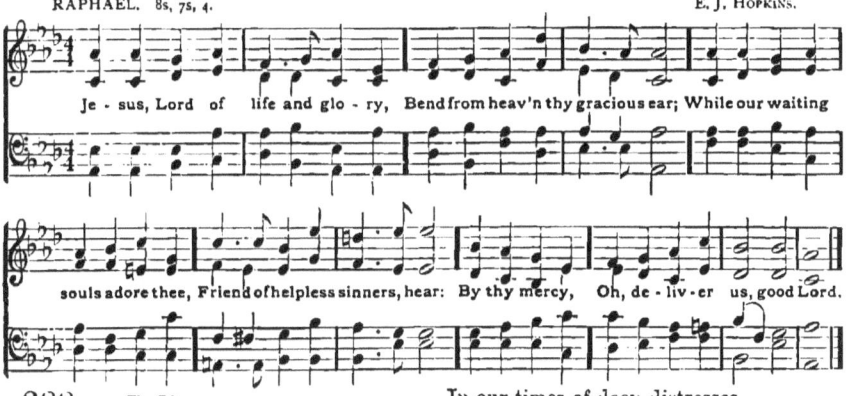

RAPHAEL. 8s, 7s, 4. E. J. Hopkins.

Je - sus, Lord of life and glo - ry, Bend from heav'n thy gracious ear; While our waiting souls adore thee, Friend of helpless sinners, hear: By thy mercy, Oh, de - liv - er us, good Lord.

288 *The Litany.*
Jesus, Lord of life and glory,
Bend from heaven thy gracious ear;
While our waiting souls adore thee,
Friend of helpless sinners, hear:
By thy mercy,
Oh, deliver us, good Lord.

2 From the depths of nature's blindness,
From the hardening power of sin,
From all malice and unkindness,
From the pride that lurks within,
By thy mercy,
Oh, deliver us, good Lord.

3 When temptation sorely presses,
In the day of Satan's power,

In our times of deep distresses,
In each dark and trying hour,
By thy mercy,
Oh, deliver us, good Lord.

4 When the world around is smiling,
In the time of wealth and ease,
Earthly joys our hearts beguiling,
In the day of health and peace,
By thy mercy,
Oh, deliver us, good Lord.

5 In the solemn hour of dying,
In the awful judgment-day,
May our souls, on thee relying,
Find thee still our Hope and Stay:
By thy mercy,
Oh, deliver us, good Lord.
James J. Cummins.

CHRISTIAN EXPERIENCE.

HERMON. C. M. — Lowell Mason.

Oh, for a closer walk with God, A calm and heaven-ly frame,— A light to shine upon the road That leads me to the Lamb!

289 *The closer walk.*

Oh, for a closer walk with God,
A calm and heavenly frame,—
A light to shine upon the road
That leads me to the Lamb!

2 Where is the blessedness I knew
When first I saw the Lord?
Where is the soul-refreshing view
Of Jesus and his word?

3 What peaceful hours I once enjoyed!
How sweet their memory still!
But they have left an aching void
The world can never fill.

4 Return, O holy Dove, return,
Sweet messenger of rest!
I hate the sins that made thee mourn,
And drove thee from my breast.

5 The dearest idol I have known,
Whate'er that idol be,
Help me to tear it from thy throne,
And worship only thee.

6 So shall my walk be close with God,
Calm and serene my frame;
So purer light shall mark the road
That leads me to the Lamb.

William Cowper.

SERENITY. C. M. — Arr. fr. W. V. Wallace.

Oh, not to fill the mouth of fame My longing soul is stirred: Oh, give me a di-viner name! Call me thy servant, Lord!

290 *Greatness in Service.*

Oh, not to fill the mouth of fame
My longing soul is stirred;
Oh, give me a diviner name!
Call me thy servant, Lord!

2 No longer would my soul be known
As uncontrolled and free;
Oh, not mine own, oh, not mine own!
Lord, I belong to thee!

3 Thy servant,—me thy servant choose;
Naught of thy claim abate!
The glorious name I would not lose,
Nor change the sweet estate.

4 In life, in death, on earth, in heaven,
This is the name for me!
The same sweet style and title given
Through all eternity.

Thomas H. Gill.

291 *"Trembleth at my word."*

Oh, for that tenderness of heart,
That bows before the Lord;
That owns how just and good thou art,
And trembles at thy word.

2 Oh, for those humble, contrite tears,
Which from repentance flow;
That sense of guilt which, trembling, fears
The long-suspended blow!

3 Saviour! to me, in pity give,
For sin, the deep distress;
The pledge thou wilt, at last, receive,
And bid me die in peace.

4 Oh, fill my soul with faith and love,
And strength to do thy will;
Raise my desires and hopes above,—
Thyself to me reveal.

Charles Wesley.

CONFLICT WITH SIN.

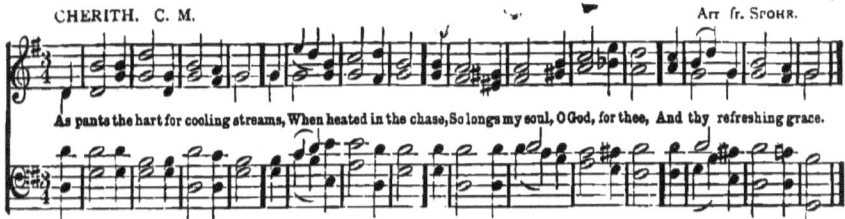

CHERITH. C. M.   Arr fr. Spohr.

As pants the hart for cooling streams, When heated in the chase, So longs my soul, O God, for thee, And thy refreshing grace.

292 *Psalm 42.*

As PANTS the hart for cooling streams,
  When heated in the chase,
So longs my soul, O God, for thee,
  And thy refreshing grace.

2 For thee, my God—the living God,
  My thirsty soul doth pine;
Oh, when shall I behold thy face,
  Thou Majesty divine!

3 Why restless, why cast down, my soul?
  Trust God; who will employ
His aid for thee, and change these sighs
  To thankful hymns of joy.

4 I sigh to think of happier days,
  When thou, O Lord! wast nigh;
When every heart was tuned to praise,
  And none more blest than I.

5 Why restless, why cast down, my soul?
  Hope still; and thou shalt sing
The praise of him who is thy God,
  Thy health's eternal spring.
                    Henry F. Lyte.

293 *"I shall be with Him."*

LORD, it belongs not to my care
  Whether I die or live;
To love and serve thee is my share,
  And this thy grace must give.

2 If life be long, I will be glad
  That I may long obey;
If short, yet why should I be sad
  To soar to endless day?

3 Christ leads me through no darker rooms
  Than he went through before;
No one into his kingdom comes,
  But through his opened door.

4 Come, Lord, when grace has made me meet,
  Thy blesséd face to see;
For if thy work on earth be sweet,
  What will thy glory be!

5 My knowledge of that life is small;
  The eye of faith is dim;
But 'tis enough that Christ knows all,
  And I shall be with him.
                    Richard Baxter.

SEYMOUR. 7s.   Arr. fr. Von Weber.

294 *"My repentings are kindled."*

DEPTH of mercy!—can there be
Mercy still reserved for me?
Can my God his wrath forbear?
Me, the chief of sinners, spare?

2 I have long withstood his grace;
Long provoked him to his face:
Would not hearken to his calls;
Grieved him by a thousand falls.

3 Kindled his relentings are;
Me he now delights to spare;
Cries, How shall I give thee up?—
Lets the lifted thunder drop.

4 There for me the Saviour stands;
Shows his wounds and spreads his hands!
God is love! I know, I feel:
Jesus weeps, and loves me still.
                    Charles Wesley.

CHRISTIAN EXPERIENCE.

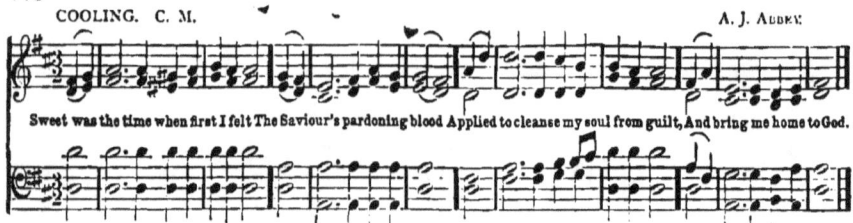

COOLING. C. M.   A. J. Aubry.

Sweet was the time when first I felt The Saviour's pardoning blood Applied to cleanse my soul from guilt, And bring me home to God.

295 *"Where is the blessedness."*

Sweet was the time when first I felt
  The Saviour's pardoning blood
Applied to cleanse my soul from guilt,
  And bring me home to God.

2 Soon as the morn the light revealed,
  His praises tuned my tongue;
And, when the evening shade prevailed,
  His love was all my song.

3 In prayer, my soul drew near the Lord,
  And saw his glory shine;
And when I read his holy word,
  I called each promise mine.

4 Now, when the evening shade prevails,
  My soul in darkness mourns;
And when the morn the light reveals,
  No light to me returns.

5 Rise, Saviour! help me to prevail,
  And make my soul thy care;
I know thy mercy cannot fail,
  Let me that mercy share.
             John Newton.

296 *"What hourly dangers!"*

Alas! what hourly dangers rise!
  What snares beset my way!
To heaven, oh, let me lift mine eyes,
  And hourly watch and pray.

2 How oft my mournful thoughts complain,
  And melt in flowing tears!
My weak resistance, ah, how vain!
  How strong my foes and fears!

3 O gracious God! in whom I live,
  My feeble efforts aid;
Help me to watch, and pray, and strive,
  Though trembling and afraid.

4 Increase my faith, increase my hope,
  When foes and fears prevail;
And bear my fainting spirit up,
  Or soon my strength will fail.

5 Oh, keep me in thy heavenly way,
  And bid the tempter flee!
And let me never, never stray
  From happiness and thee.
             Anne Steele.

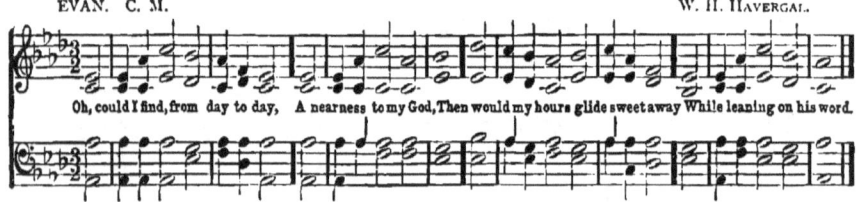

EVAN. C. M.   W. H. Havergal.

Oh, could I find, from day to day, A nearness to my God, Then would my hours glide sweet away While leaning on his word.

297 *"Nearer to thee."*

Oh, could I find, from day to day,
  A nearness to my God,
Then would my hours glide sweet away
  While leaning on his word.

2 Lord, I desire with thee to live
  Anew from day to day,
In joys the world can never give,
  Nor ever take away.

3 Blest Jesus, come and rule my heart,
  And make me wholly thine,
That I may never more depart,
  Nor grieve thy love divine.

4 Thus, till my last, expiring breath,
  Thy goodness I'll adore;
And when my frame dissolves in death,
  My soul shall love thee more.
             Benjamin Cleveland.

CONFLICT WITH SIN.

298   *"I need thee."*

I NEED thee every hour,
  Most gracious Lord;
No tender voice like thine
  Can peace afford.

REF.—I need thee, oh, I need thee;
  Every hour I need thee;
Oh, bless me now, my Saviour!
  I come to thee.

2 I need thee every hour;
  Stay thou near by;
Temptations lose their power
  When thou art nigh.—REF.

3 I need thee every hour,
  In joy or pain;
Come quickly and abide,
  Or life is vain.—REF.

4 I need thee every hour;
  Teach me thy will;
And thy rich promises
  In me fulfill.—REF.

5 I need thee every hour,
  Most Holy One;
Oh, make me thine indeed,
  Thou blessèd Son.—REF.
Mrs. A. S. Hawks.

299   *"Even me."*

LORD, I hear of showers of blessing
  Thou art scattering full and free;
Showers the thirsty soul refreshing;
  Let some droppings fall on me!—REF.

2 Pass me not, O gracious Father!
  Lost and sinful though I be;
Thou might'st curse me, but the rather
  Let thy mercy light on me.—REF.

3 Pass me not, O mighty Spirit!
  Thou canst make the blind to see;
Testify of Jesus' merit,
  Speak the word of peace to me.—REF.

4 Love of God, so pure and changeless;
  Blood of Christ, so rich and free;
Grace of God, so strong and boundless,
  Magnify it all in me.—REF.

5 Pass me not, but, pardon bringing,
  Bind my heart, O Lord, to thee;
Whilst the streams of life are springing,
  Blessing others, oh, bless me.—REF.
Mrs. E. Codner.

CHRISTIAN EXPERIENCE.

300 *The door of mercy.*

The mistakes of my life are many,
  The sins of my heart are more,
And I scarce can see for weeping;
  But I knock at the open door.—Cho.

2 I am lowest of those who love him,
  I am weakest of those who pray:
But I come as he has bidden,
  And he will not say me nay.—Cho.

3 My mistakes his free grace will cover,
  My sins he will wash away,
And the feet that shrink and falter,
  Shall walk through the gate of day.—Cho.
Mrs. O. L. Bailey.

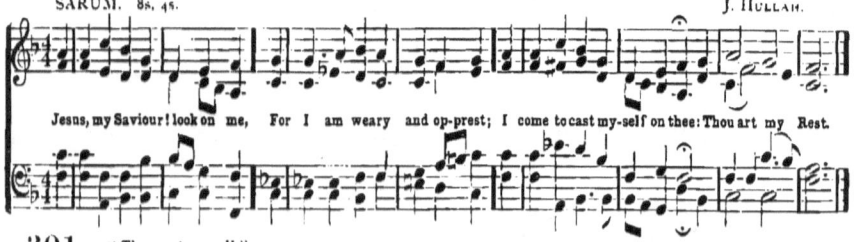

301 *"Thou art my all."*

Jesus, my Saviour! look on me,
  For I am weary and opprest;
I come to cast myself on thee:
    Thou art my Rest.

2 Look down on me, for I am weak,
  I feel the toilsome journey's length;
Thine aid omnipotent I seek:
    Thou art my Strength.

3 I am bewildered on my way,
  Dark and tempestuous is the night;
Oh, send thou forth some cheering ray:
    Thou art my Light.

4 Thou wilt my every want supply,
  Ev'n to the end, whate'er befall;
Through life, in death, eternally,
    Thou art my All.
J. R. Macduff.

CONFLICT WITH SIN.

LYNDE. P. M.   THURINGIAN FOLK-SONG.

Tell me, my Saviour! Where thou dost feed thy flock, Resting be-side the rock, Cool in the shade: Why should I be as one

Turning aside alone, Left, when thy sheep have gone, Where I have strayed?

302   *Cant. 1:7.*

Tell me, my Saviour!
Where thou dost feed thy flock,
Resting beside the rock,
Cool in the shade:
Why should I be as one
Turning aside alone,
Left, when thy sheep have gone,
Where I have strayed?

2 Seek me, my Saviour!
For I have lost the way:
I will thy voice obey;
Speak to me here!
Help me to find the gate
Where all thy chosen wait:
Ere it shall be too late,
Oh, call me near!

3 Show me, my Saviour!
How I can grow like thee;
Make me thy child to be,
Taught from above;
Help me thy smile to win;
Keep me safe folded in,
Lest I should rove in sin,
Far from thy love.
          Charles S. Robinson.

THE HIGH ROCK. P. M.   W. G. FISCHER.

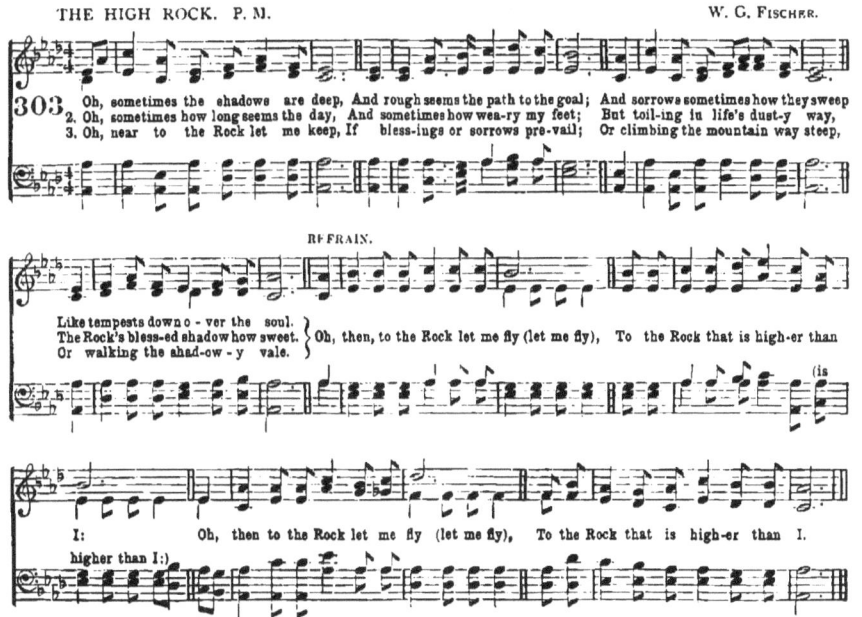

E. Johnson.

CHRISTIAN EXPERIENCE.

SEGUR. 8s, 7s, 4s.   J. P. HOLBROOK.

Guide me, O thou great Jehovah, Pilgrim thro' this barren land; I am weak, but thou art mighty; Hold me with thy powerful hand; Bread of heaven, Bread of heaven, Feed me till I want no more.

304   *Guidance.*
GUIDE me, O thou great Jehovah,
  Pilgrim through this barren land;
I am weak, but thou art mighty;
  Hold me with thy powerful hand;
    Bread of heaven,
  Feed me till I want no more.

2 Open thou the crystal fountain
  Whence the healing streams do flow;
Let the fiery, cloudy pillar
  Lead me all my journey through;
    Strong Deliverer,
  Be thou still my Strength and Shield.

3 When I tread the verge of Jordan,
  Bid my anxious fears subside;
Death of death! and hell's Destruction!
  Land me safe on Canaan's side;
    Songs of praises
  I will ever give to thee.

  William Williams

VENI, LUX. P. M.   A. H. BROWN.

Light, that from the dark abyss Madest all things, none amiss, To share thy beauty, share thy bliss, Come to us: ... come. A-men.

Last verse.

305   *"Come to us: come."*
LIGHT, that from the dark abyss
Madest all things, none amiss,
  To share thy beauty, share thy bliss,
    Come to us: come.

2 Light, that dost o'er all things reign,
Light that dost all life maintain;

O Light, that dost create again,
  Come to us: come.

3 Light of men, that left the skies,
Light that looked thro' human eyes,
And died in darkness as man dies,
  Come to us: come.

4 Light that stooped to rise and raise,
Soared to God above our gaze,
And still art with us all the days,
  Come to us: come.

5 We have done great wrong to thee,
Yet we do belong to thee;
Oh, make our life one song to thee,
  Come to us: come.

E. E. Jirtt.

CONFLICT WITH SIN.

VALLEY OF BLESSING. P. M. — W. G. Fischer.

306
1. I have entered the val-ley of blessing so sweet, And Je-sus a-bides with me there;
2. There is peace in the val-ley of blessing so sweet, And plen-ty the land doth im-part;
3. There is love in the val-ley of blessing so sweet, Such as none but the blood-washed may feel;

And his Spir-it and blood make my cleansing complete, And his per-fect love cast-eth out fear.
There is rest for the wea-ry-worn tra-vel-er's feet, And joy for the sor-row-ing heart.
When heav-en comes down redeemed spirits to greet, And Christ sets his cov-e-nant seal.

CHORUS.
Oh, come to this val-ley of blessing so sweet, Where Je-sus will full-ness be-stow—
And be-lieve, and re-ceive, and con-fess him,...... That all his sal-va-tion may know.

Mrs. A. Wittenmyer.

GUARDIAN. 6s, 4. — H. T. Leslie.

Saviour and Lord of all, Turn every heart to thee; Guard us and guide us safe O-ver life's sea.

307 *Prayer for Help.*
Saviour and Lord of all,
Turn every heart to thee;
Guard us and guide us safe
Over life's sea.

2 When we are full of grief,
Victims of anxious fear,

Give thou our hearts relief,
Jesus, be near.

3 Brighten our darkest hour,
Till the last hour shall come;
Then, in thy love and power,
Oh, take us home!

T. R. Taylor.

308. *All for Jesus.*

TAKE my life, and let it be
Consecrated, Lord, to thee,
Take my hands, and let them move
At the impulse of thy love,
Take my feet, and let them be
Swift and beautiful for thee,
Take my voice, and let me sing
Always, only, for my King.

2 Take my lips, and let them be
Filled with messages from thee,
Take my silver and my gold,
Not a mite would I withhold;
Take my moments and my days,
Let them flow in ceaseless praise,
Take my intellect, and use
Every power as thou shalt choose.

3 Take my will, and make it thine;
It shall be no longer mine.
Take my heart, it is thine own!
It shall be thy royal throne.
Take my love; my Lord, I pour
At thy feet its treasure-store;
Take myself, and I will be,
Ever, only, all, for thee!

Frances R. Havergal.

309. *A hard heart.*

OH, this soul, how dark and blind!
Oh, this foolish, earthly mind!
Oh, this froward, selfish will,
Which refuses to be still!
Oh, these ever-roaming eyes,
Upward that refuse to rise!
Oh, these wayward feet of mine,
Found in every path but thine!

2 Oh, this stubborn, prayerless knee,
Hands so seldom clasped to thee,
Longings of the soul, that go
Like the wild wind, to and fro!
To and fro, without an aim,
Turning idly whence they came,
Bringing in no joy, no bliss,
Only adding weariness!

3 Giver of the heavenly peace!
Bid, oh, bid these tumults cease;
Minister thy holy balm;
Fill me with thy Spirit's calm:
Thou, the Life, the Truth, the Way,
Leave me not in sin to stay;
Bearer of the sinner's guilt,
Lead me, lead me, as thou wilt.

Horatius Bonar.

CONFLICT WITH SIN.

REFUGE. 7s. D.   J. P. HOLBROOK.

310   *Christ, our all.*

Jesus! lover of my soul,
  Let me to thy bosom fly
While the billows near me roll,
  While the tempest still is high;
Hide me, O my Saviour! hide,
  Till the storm of life is past;
Safe into the haven guide;
  Oh, receive my soul at last!

2 Other refuge have I none;
  Hangs my helpless soul on thee;
Leave, ah! leave me not alone,
  Still support and comfort me.
All my trust on thee is stayed;
  All my help from thee I bring;
Cover my defenceless head
  With the shadow of thy wing.

3 Thou, O Christ! art all I want;
  More than all in thee I find;
Raise the fallen, cheer the faint,
  Heal the sick, and lead the blind.
Just and holy is thy name,
  I am all unrighteousness;
Vile and full of sin I am,
  Thou art full of truth and grace.

4 Plenteous grace with thee is found,—
  Grace to pardon all my sin;
Let the healing streams abound,
  Make and keep me pure within;
Thou of life the fountain art,
  Freely let me take of thee;
Spring thou up within my heart,
  Rise to all eternity.

Charles Wesley.

MARTYN. 7s. D.   S. B. MARSH.

CHRISTIAN EXPERIENCE.

OAK. 6s, 4s.   LOWELL MASON.

We are but strangers here, Heaven is our home;
Earth is a desert drear, Heaven is our home.
Danger and sorrow stand
Round us on every hand, Heaven is our Fatherland, Heaven is our home.

311 *"Home at last."*

We are but strangers here,
  Heaven is our home;
Earth is a desert drear,
  Heaven is our home.
Danger and sorrow stand
Round us on every hand,
Heaven is our Fatherland,
  Heaven is our home.

2 What though the tempest rage?
  Heaven is our home;
Short is our pilgrimage,
  Heaven is our home.
And Time's wild wintry blast
Soon shall be overpast,
We shall reach home at last;
  Heaven is our home.

3 There at our Saviour's side,
  Heaven is our home;
May we be glorified;
  Heaven is our home:
There are the good and blest,
Those we love most and best,
Grant us with them to rest;
  Heaven is our home.

4 Grant us to murmur not,
  Heaven is our home,
Whate'er our earthly lot,
  Heaven is our home.
Grant us at last to stand
There at thine own right hand,
Jesus, in Fatherland:
  Heaven is our home!

Thomas R. Taylor, alt.

312 *Jesus is mine.*

Now I have found a Friend;
  Jesus is mine;—
His love shall never end;
  Jesus is mine;
Though earthly joys decrease,
Though earthly friendships cease,
Now I have lasting peace:
  Jesus is mine.

2 Though I grow poor and old,
  Jesus is mine;
Though I grow faint and cold,
  Jesus is mine:
He shall my wants supply;
His precious blood is nigh,
Naught can my hope destroy;
  Jesus is mine.

3 When earth shall pass away,—
  Jesus is mine,—
In the great judgment day,—
  Jesus is mine,—
Oh! what a glorious thing,
Then to behold my King,
On tuneful harp to sing,
  Jesus is mine.

4 Father! thy name I bless;
  Jesus is mine;
Thine was the sovereign grace;
  Praise shall be thine;
Spirit of holiness!
Sealing the Father's grace,
Thou mad'st my soul embrace
  Jesus, as mine.

Henry J. M. Hope.

CONFLICT WITH SIN.

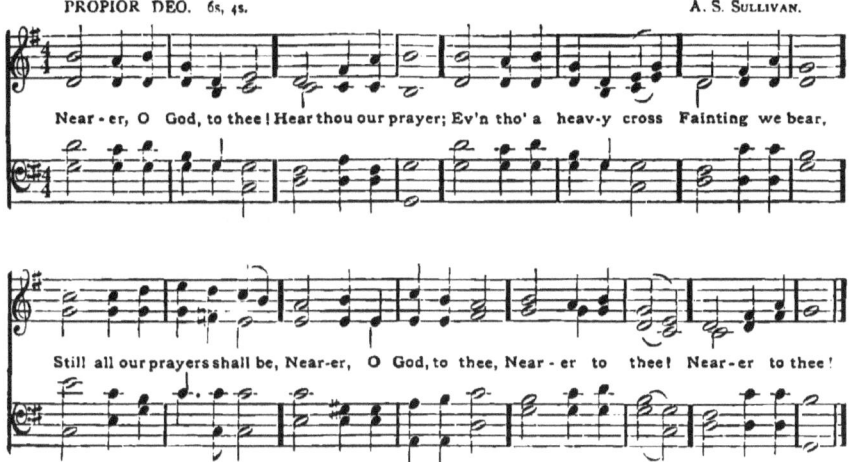

PROPIOR DEO. 6s, 4s. A. S. SULLIVAN.

Near-er, O God, to thee! Hear thou our prayer; Ev'n tho' a heav-y cross Fainting we bear, Still all our prayers shall be, Near-er, O God, to thee, Near-er to thee! Near-er to thee!

313 *Close to God.*

NEARER, O God, to thee!
 Hear thou our prayer;
Ev'n though a heavy cross
 Fainting we bear,
Still all our prayer shall be
 Nearer, O God, to thee,
  Nearer to thee!

2 If, where they led the Lord,
 We too are borne,
Planting our steps in his,
 Weary and worn;
There even let us be
 Nearer, O God, to thee,
  Nearer to thee!

3 If thou the cup of pain
 Givest to drink,
Let not the trembling lip
 From the draught shrink;
So by our woes to be
 Nearer, O God, to thee,
  Nearer to thee!

4 Though the great battle rage
 Hotly around,
Still where our Captain fights
 Let us be found;
Through toils and strife to be
 Nearer, O God, to thee,
  Nearer to thee!

5 And when thou, Lord, once more
 Glorious shalt come,
Oh, for a dwelling-place,
 In thy bright home!
Through all eternity
 Nearer, O God, to thee,
  Nearer to thee!
   William W. How.

314 *The Walk with God.*

WALKING with thee, my God,
 Saviour benign,
Daily confer on me
 Converse divine:
Jesus, in thee restored,
Brother and blessèd Lord,
 Let it be mine.

2 Walking with thee, my God,
 Like as a child
Leans on his father's strength,
 Crossing the wild;
And by the way is taught
Lessons of holy thought,
 Faith undefiled.

3 Walking in reverence
 Humbly with thee,
Yet from all abject fear
 Lovingly free:
Ev'n as a friend with friend,
Cheered to the journey's end,
 Walking with thee.
  George Rawson.

CHRISTIAN EXPERIENCE.

BETHANY. 6s, 4s.   LOWELL MASON.

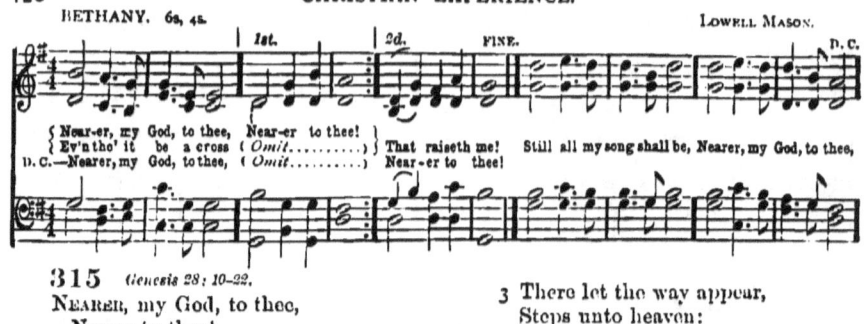

315   *Genesis 28: 10-22.*

NEARER, my God, to thee,
  Nearer to thee!
Ev'n though it be a cross
  That raiseth me!
Still all my song shall be,
Nearer, my God, to thee,
  Nearer to thee!

2 Though, like a wanderer,
  The sun gone down,
Darkness be over me,
  My rest a stone,
Yet in my dreams I'd be
Nearer, my God, to thee,
  Nearer to thee!

3 There let the way appear,
  Steps unto heaven:
All that thou sendest me,
  In mercy given;
Angels to beckon me
Nearer, my God, to thee,
  Nearer to thee!

4 Then, with my waking thoughts
  Bright with thy praise,
Out of my stony griefs
  Bethel I'll raise;
So by my woes to be
Nearer, my God, to thee,
  Nearer to thee!
                Mrs. S. F. Adams.

MORE LOVE. 6s, 4s.   T. E. PERKINS.

316   *"More love."*

MORE love to thee, O Christ,
  More love to thee!
Hear thou the prayer I make
  On bended knee;
This is my earnest plea,—
More love, O Christ, to thee,
  More love to thee!

2 Once earthly joy I craved,
  Sought peace and rest;
Now thee alone I seek,—
  Give what is best;
This all my prayer shall be,—
More love, O Christ, to thee,
  More love to thee!

3 Let sorrow do its work,
  Send grief and pain;
Sweet are thy messengers,
  Sweet their refrain,
When they can sing with me,
More love, O Christ, to thee,
  More love to thee!

4 Then shall my latest breath
  Whisper thy praise,
This be the parting cry
  My heart shall raise;
This still its prayer shall be,—
More love, O Christ, to thee,
  More love to thee!
                Mrs. E. P. Prentiss.

CONFLICT WITH SIN.

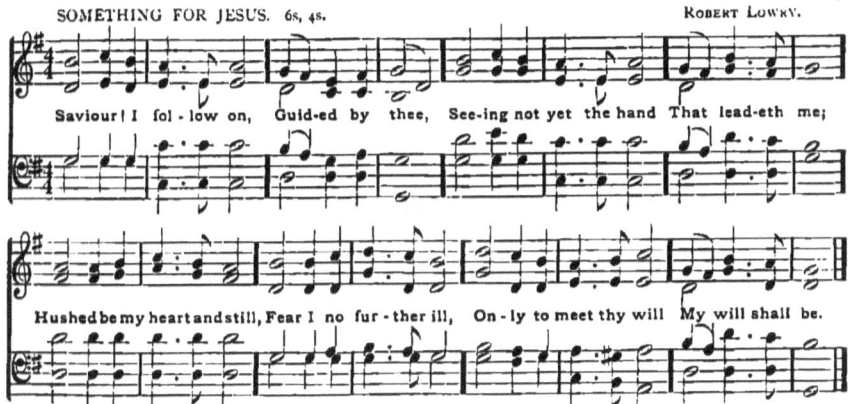

SOMETHING FOR JESUS. 6s, 4s. ROBERT LOWRY.

Saviour! I fol-low on, Guid-ed by thee, See-ing not yet the hand That lead-eth me;
Hushed be my heart and still, Fear I no fur-ther ill, On-ly to meet thy will My will shall be.

317 *"A way they knew not."*

Saviour! I follow on,
  Guided by thee,
Seeing not yet the hand
  That leadeth me;
Hushed be my heart and still,
Fear I no further ill;
Only to meet thy will
  My will shall be.

2 Riven the rock for me
    Thirst to relieve,
  Manna from heaven falls
    Fresh every eve;
  Never a want severe
  Causeth my eye a tear,
  But thou dost whisper near,
    "Only believe!"

3 Often to Marah's brink
    Have I been brought;
  Shrinking the cup to drink,
    Help I have sought;
  And with the prayer's ascent,
  Jesus the branch hath rent—
  Quickly relief hath sent,
    Sweetening the draught.

4 Saviour! I long to walk
    Closer with thee;
  Led by thy guiding hand,
    Ever to be;
  Constantly near thy side,
  Quickened and purified,
  Living for him who died
    Freely for me!
        Charles S. Robinson.

318 *"Something for thee."*

Saviour, thy dying love
  Thou gavest me:
Nor should I aught withhold,
  Dear Lord, from thee:
In love my soul would bow,
My heart fulfill its vow,
Some offering bring thee now,
  Something for thee.

2 O'er the blest mercy-seat,
    Pleading for me,
  My feeble faith looks up,
    Jesus, to thee:
  Help me the cross to bear,
  Thy wondrous love declare,
  Some song to raise, or prayer,
    Something for thee.

3 Give me a faithful heart—
    Likeness to thee,
  That each departing day
    Henceforth may see
  Some work of love begun,
  Some deed of kindness done,
  Some wanderer sought and won,
    Something for thee.

4 All that I am and have—
    Thy gifts so free—
  In joy, in grief, through life,
    Dear Lord, for thee:
  And when thy face I see,
  My ransomed soul shall be,
  Through all eternity,
    Something for thee.
        S. Dryden Phelps.

9 P

CHRISTIAN EXPERIENCE.

MAGDALENE. 6s, 5s. — J. B. Dykes.

In the hour of tri-al, Jesus, plead for me; Lest by base de-ni-al I depart from thee; When thou see'st me waver, With a look re-call, Nor for fear or fa-vor Suf-fer me to fall.

319 *A look from Christ.*

In the hour of trial,
　Jesus, plead for me;
Lest by base denial
　I depart from thee;
When thou see'st me waver,
　With a look recall,
Nor for fear or favor
　Suffer me to fall.

2 With forbidden pleasures
　Would this vain world charm;
Or its sordid treasures
　Spread to work me harm;
Bring to my remembrance
　Sad Gethsemane,
Or, in darker semblance,
　Cross-crowned Calvary.

3 Should thy mercy send me
　Sorrow, toil, and woe;
Or should pain attend me
　On my path below;
Grant that I may never
　Fail thy hand to see;
Grant that I may ever
　Cast my care on thee.

4 When my last hour cometh,
　Fraught with strife and pain,
When my dust returneth
　To the dust again;
On thy truth relying
　Through that mortal strife,
Jesus, take me, dying,
　To eternal life.
　　　　　James Montgomery.

320 *Earnest Longings.*

Purer yet, and purer
　I would be in mind,
Dearer yet and dearer
　Every duty find;
Hoping still and trusting
　God without a fear,
Patiently believing
　He will make all clear.

2 Calmer yet and calmer
　Trial bear and pain,
Surer yet and surer
　Peace at last to gain;
Suffering still and doing,
　To his will resigned,
And to God subduing
　Heart and will and mind.

3 Higher yet and higher
　Out of clouds and night,
Nearer yet and nearer
　Rising to the light—
Oft these earnest longings
　Swell within my breast,
Yet their inner meaning
　Ne'er can be expressed.
　　　　　Anon., 1858.

CONFLICT WITH SIN.

EDINA. 6s, 5s. H. S. OAKLEY.

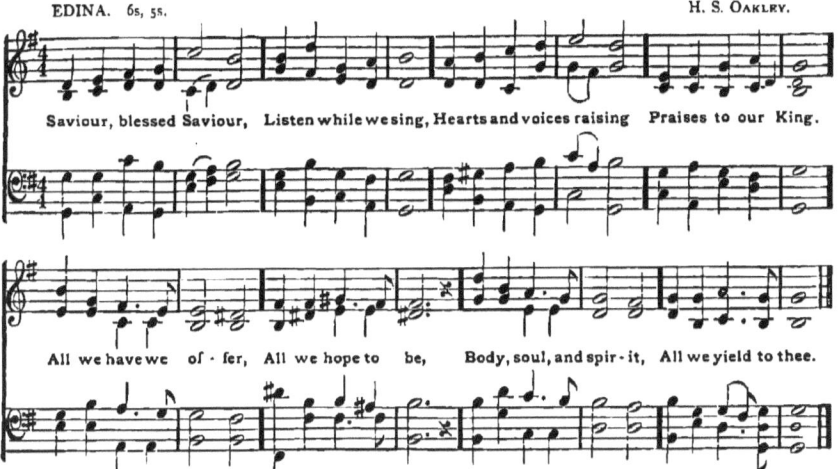

Saviour, blessed Saviour, Listen while we sing, Hearts and voices raising Praises to our King.
All we have we of-fer, All we hope to be, Body, soul, and spir-it, All we yield to thee.

321 *All for Jesus.*

SAVIOUR, blessèd Saviour,
Listen while we sing,
Hearts and voices raising
Praises to our King.
All we have we offer,
All we hope to be,
Body, soul, and spirit,
All we yield to thee.

2 Great and ever greater
Are thy mercies here,
True and everlasting
Are the glories there,
Where no pain, or sorrow,
Toil, or care, is known,
Where the angel-legions
Circle round thy throne.

3 Dark and ever darker
Was the wintry past;
Now a ray of gladness
O'er our path is cast.
Every day that passeth,
Every hour that flies,
Tells of love unfeignèd,
Love that never dies.

4 Clearer still and clearer
Dawns the light from heaven,
In our sadness bringing
News of sin forgiven.

Life has lost its shadows,
Pure the light within;
Thou hast shed thy radiance
On a world of sin.
Godfrey Thring.

322 *"Backward never looking."*

NEARER, ever nearer,
Christ, we draw to thee,
Deep in adoration
Bending low the knee:
Thou for our redemption
Cam'st on earth to die;
Thou, that we might follow,
Hast gone up on high.

2 Onward, ever onward,
Journeying o'er the road
Worn by saints before us,
Journeying on to God;
Leaving all behind us
May we hasten on,
Backward never looking
Till the prize is won.

3 Higher then and higher
Bear the ransomed soul,
Earthly toils forgotten,
Saviour, to its goal;
Where in joys unthought of
Saints with angels sing,
Never weary raising
Praises to their King.
Godfrey Thring.

CHRISTIAN EXPERIENCE.

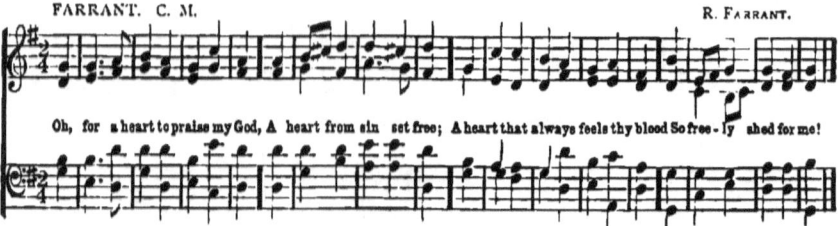

323 *A clean heart.*
Oh, for a heart to praise my God,
　A heart from sin set free;
A heart that always feels thy blood
　So freely shed for me!

2 A heart resigned, submissive, meek,
　My dear Redeemer's throne;
Where only Christ is heard to speak,
　Where Jesus reigns alone!

3 Oh, for a lowly, contrite heart,
　Believing, true, and clean!
Which neither life nor death can part
　From him that dwells within.

4 A heart in every thought renewed,
　And filled with love divine;
Perfect, and right, and pure, and good;
　An image, Lord! of thine.

5 Thy nature, gracious Lord, impart;
　Come quickly from above;
Write thy new name upon my heart,—
　Thy new, best name of Love.
　　　　　　Charles Wesley.

324 *Thanks for victory.*
Oh, for a thousand tongues to sing
　My dear Redeemer's praise!
The glories of my God and King,
　The triumphs of his grace!

2 My gracious Master and my God!
　Assist me to proclaim,
To spread through all the earth abroad,
　The honors of thy name.

3 Jesus—the name that calms my fears,
　That bids my sorrows cease;
'Tis music to my ravished ears;
　'Tis life, and health, and peace.

4 He breaks the power of canceled sin,
　He sets the prisoner free;
His blood can make the foulest clean;
　His blood availed for me.

5 Let us obey, we then shall know,
　Shall feel our sins forgiven;
Anticipate our heaven below,
　And own that love is heaven.
　　　　　　Charles Wesley.

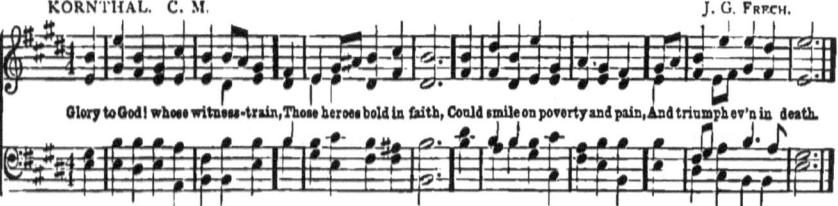

325 *Martyr-faith.*
Glory to God! whose witness-train,
　Those heroes bold in faith,
Could smile on poverty and pain,
　And triumph ev'n in death.

2 Oh, may that faith our hearts sustain,
　Wherein they fearless stood,
When, in the power of cruel men,
　They poured their willing blood.

3 God whom we serve, our God, can save,
　Can damp the scorching flame,
Can build an ark, can smooth the wave,
　For such as love his name.

4 Lord! if thine arm support us still
　With its eternal strength,
We shall o'ercome the mightiest ill,
　And conquerors prove at length.
　　　　　　Moravian, tr.

COURAGE AND CHEER.

326 *The Race.*

Awake, my soul, stretch every nerve,
And press with vigor on;
A heavenly race demands thy zeal,
And an immortal crown.

2 A cloud of witnesses around
Hold thee in full survey;
Forget the steps already trod,
And onward urge thy way.

3 'T is God's all-animating voice,
That calls thee from on high,
'T is his own hand presents the prize
To thine aspiring eye.

4 Blest Saviour, introduced by thee,
Have I my race begun;
And, crowned with victory, at thy feet
I 'll lay my honors down.
Philip Doddridge.

327 *The Warfare.*

Am I a soldier of the cross,
A follower of the Lamb?
And shall I fear to own his cause,
Or blush to speak his name?

2 Must I be carried to the skies
On flowery beds of ease?
While others fought to win the prize,
And sailed through bloody seas?

3 Are there no foes for me to face?
Must I not stem the flood?
Is this vile world a friend to grace,
To help me on to God?

4 Sure I must fight, if I would reign;
Increase my courage, Lord!
I 'll bear the toil, endure the pain,
Supported by thy word.

5 Thy saints, in all this glorious war,
Shall conquer, though they die;
They view the triumph from afar,
And seize it with their eye.

6 When that illustrious day shall rise,
And all thine armies shine
In robes of victory through the skies,
The glory shall be thine.
Isaac Watts.

328 *"I'm not ashamed."*

I 'm not ashamed to own my Lord,
Or to defend his cause;
Maintain the honor of his word,
The glory of his cross.

2 Jesus, my God!—I know his name—
His name is all my trust;
Nor will he put my soul to shame,
Nor let my hope be lost.

3 Firm as his throne his promise stands,
And he can well secure
What I 've committed to his hands,
Till the decisive hour.

4 Then will he own my worthless name
Before his Father's face,
And in the new Jerusalem
Appoint my soul a place.
Isaac Watts.

CHRISTIAN EXPERIENCE.

ALEXANDER. S. M.   CHARLES ZEUNER.

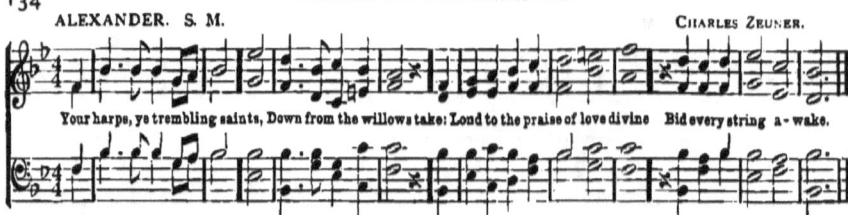

Your harps, ye trembling saints, Down from the willows take: Loud to the praise of love divine Bid every string a-wake.

329 *Our salvation near.*

Your harps, ye trembling saints,
  Down from the willows take:
Loud to the praise of love divine
  Bid every string awake.

2 Though in a foreign land,
  We are not far from home;
And nearer to our house above
  We every moment come.

3 His grace will to the end
  Stronger and brighter shine;
Nor present things, nor things to come,
  Shall quench the spark divine.

4 When we in darkness walk,
  Nor feel the heavenly flame,
Then is the time to trust our God,
  And rest upon his name.

5 Soon shall our doubts and fears
  Subside at his control;
His loving-kindness shall break through
  The midnight of the soul.

6 Blest is the man, O God,
  Who stays himself on thee;
Who waits for thy salvation, Lord,
  Shall thy salvation see.
                A. M. Toplady.

OLMUTZ. S. M.   Arr. by L. MASON.

Give to the winds thy fears; Hope, and be undismayed; God hears thy sighs and counts thy tears; God shall lift up thy head.

330 *"Be of good courage."*

GIVE to the winds thy fears;
  Hope, and be undismayed;
God hears thy sighs and counts thy tears;
  God shall lift up thy head.

2 Through waves, and clouds, and storms,
  He gently clears thy way;
Wait thou his time; so shall this night
  Soon end in joyous day.

3 What though thou rulest not!
  Yet heaven, and earth, and hell
Proclaim, God sitteth on the throne,
  And ruleth all things well.

4 Far, far above thy thought
  His counsel shall appear,
When fully he the work has wrought,
  That caused thy needless fear.
                John Wesley, tr.

331 *"Weigh not thy life."*

My soul, weigh not thy life
  Against thy heavenly crown;
Nor suffer Satan's deadliest strife
  To beat thy courage down.

2 With prayer and crying strong,
  Hold on the fearful fight,
And let the breaking day prolong
  The wrestling of the night.

3 The battle soon will yield,
  If thou thy part fulfill;
For strong as is the hostile shield,
  Thy sword is stronger still.

4 Thine armor is divine,
  Thy feet with victory shod;
And on thy head shall quickly shine
  The diadem of God.
                Leonard Swain.

COURAGE AND CHEER.

LEIGHTON. S. M.   H. W. GREATOREX.

Mine eyes and my desire Are ever to the Lord;
I love to plead his promises, And rest upon his word.

332 *Psalm 25.*
Mine eyes and my desire
Are ever to the Lord;
I love to plead his promises,
And rest upon his word.

2 Lord, turn to thee my soul;
Bring thy salvation near:
When will thy hand release my feet
From sin's destructive snare?

3 When shall the sovereign grace
Of my forgiving God
Restore me from those dangerous ways
My wandering feet have trod?

4 Oh, keep my soul from death,
Nor put my hope to shame!
For I have placed my only trust
In my Redeemer's name.

5 With humble faith I wait
To see thy face again;
Of Israel it shall ne'er be said,
He sought the Lord in vain.
Isaac Watts.

333 *Psalm 60.*
Arise, ye saints, arise!
The Lord our Leader is;
The foe before his banner flies,
And victory is his.

2 We follow thee, our Guide,
Our Saviour, and our King!
We follow thee, through grace supplied
From heaven's eternal spring.

3 We soon shall see the day
When all our toils shall cease;
When we shall cast our arms away,
And dwell in endless peace.

4 This hope supports us here;
It makes our burdens light;
'T will serve our drooping hearts to cheer,
Till faith shall end in sight.

5 Till, of the prize possessed,
We hear of war no more;
And ever with our Leader rest,
On yonder peaceful shore.
Thomas Kelly.

334 *Psalm 31.*
My spirit on thy care,
Blest Saviour, I recline;
Thou wilt not leave me to despair,
For thou art love divine.

2 In thee I place my trust;
On thee I calmly rest:
I know thee good, I know thee just,
And count thy choice the best.

3 Whate'er events betide,
Thy will they all perform;
Safe in thy breast my head I hide,
Nor fear the coming storm.

4 Let good or ill befall,
It must be good for me,—
Secure of having thee in all,
Of having all in thee.
Henry F. Lyte.

CHRISTIAN EXPERIENCE.

PORTUGUESE HYMN. 11s.   M. PORTUGAL.

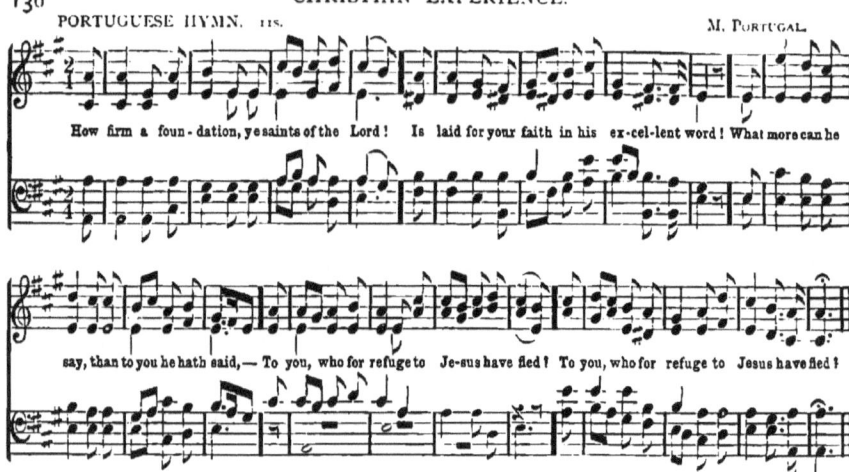

How firm a foun-dation, ye saints of the Lord! Is laid for your faith in his ex-cel-lent word! What more can he say, than to you he hath said,— To you, who for refuge to Je-sus have fled? To you, who for refuge to Jesus have fled?

335   *"Fear Not."*
How FIRM a foundation, ye saints of the Lord!
Is laid for your faith in his excellent word!
What more can he say, than to you he hath said,—
To you, who for refuge to Jesus have fled?

2 "Fear not, I am with thee, oh, be not dismayed,
For I am thy God, I will still give thee aid;
I'll strengthen thee, help thee, and cause thee to stand,
Upheld by my gracious, omnipotent hand.

3 "When through the deep waters I call thee to go,
The rivers of sorrow shall not overflow;
For I will be with thee thy trouble to bless,
And sanctify to thee thy deepest distress.

4 "When through fiery trials thy pathway shall lie,
My grace, all-sufficient, shall be thy supply;
The flame shall not hurt thee; I only design
Thy dross to consume, and thy gold to refine.

5 "Ev'n down to old age all my people Shall prove
My sovereign, eternal, unchangeable love;
And then, when gray hairs shall their temples adorn,
Like lambs they shall still in my bosom be borne.

6 "The soul that on Jesus hath leaned for repose,
I will not—I will not desert to his foes;
That soul—though all hell should endeavor to shake,
I'll never—no never—no never forsake!"
                                    George Keith.

CANA. 11s.   GEO. KINGSLEY.

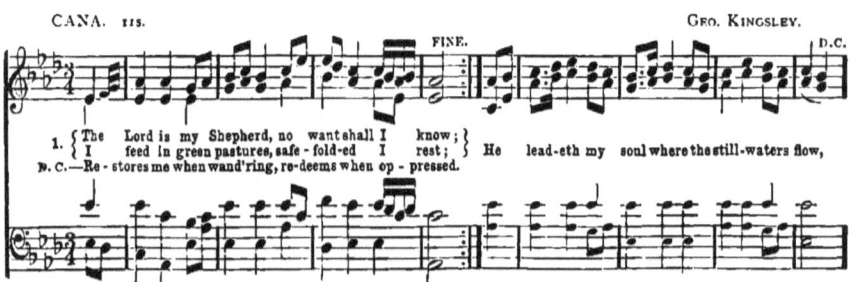

1. { The Lord is my Shepherd, no want shall I know;
     I feed in green pastures, safe-fold-ed I rest; } He lead-eth my soul where the still-waters flow,
D. C.—Re-stores me when wand'ring, re-deems when op-pressed.

COURAGE AND CHEER.

GOSHEN. 11s.   Arr. by T. Hastings.

O eyes that are wea-ry, and hearts that are sore!
Look off un-to Je-sus, now (Omit.........)
D.C.—That here, as in heaven, there (Omit.........)
sor-row no more! The light of his countenance shineth so bright,
need be no night.

336   *"Looking unto Jesus."*

O eyes that are weary, and hearts are sore!
Look off unto Jesus, now sorrow no more!
The light of his countenance shineth so bright,
That here, as in heaven, there need be no night.

2 While looking to Jesus, my heart cannot fear;
I tremble no more when I see Jesus near;
I know that his presence my safeguard will be,
For, "Why are you troubled," he saith unto me.

3 Still looking to Jesus, oh, may I be found,
When Jordan's dark waters encompass me round;
They bear me away in his presence to be:
I see him still nearer whom always I see.

4 Then, then shall I know the full beauty and grace
Of Jesus, my Lord, when I stand face to face;
Shall know how his love went before me each day,
And wonder that ever my eyes turned away.
John N. Darby.

337   *Psalm 23.*

The Lord is my Shepherd, no want shall I know;
I feed in green pastures, safe-folded I rest;
He leadeth my soul where the still waters flow,
Restores me when wandering, redeems when oppressed.

2 Through the valley and shadow of death though I stray,
Since thou art my Guardian, no evil I fear;
Thy rod shall defend me, thy staff be my stay;
No harm can befall, with my Comforter near.

3 In the midst of affliction, my table is spread;
With blessings unmeasured my cup runneth o'er;
With perfume and oil thou anointest my head;
Oh, what shall I ask of thy providence more?

4 Let goodness and mercy, my bountiful God!
Still follow my steps till I meet thee above;
I seek, by the path which my forefathers trod
Through the land of their sojourn, thy kingdom of love.
James Montgomery.

338   *"Faint, yet pursuing."*

Though faint, yet pursuing, we go on our way;
The Lord is our Leader, his word is our stay;
Tho' suffering, and sorrow, and trial be near,
The Lord is our Refuge, and whom can we fear?

2 He raiseth the fallen, he cheereth the faint;
The weak, and oppressed—he will hear their complaint;
The way may be weary, and thorny the road,
But how can we falter?—our help is in God!

3 And to his green pastures our footsteps he leads;
His flock in the desert how kindly he feeds!
The lambs in his bosom he tenderly bears,
And brings back the wanderers all safe from the snares.

4 Though clouds may surround us, our God is our light;
Though storms rage around us, our God is our might;
So, faint yet pursuing, still onward we come;
The Lord is our Leader, and heaven is our home!
John N. Darby.

CHRISTIAN EXPERIENCE.

STEPHANOS. P. M.   W. H. MONK.

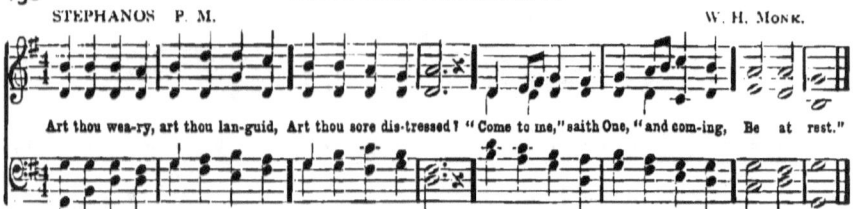

Art thou wea-ry, art thou lan-guid, Art thou sore dis-tressed? "Come to me," saith One, "and com-ing, Be at rest."

339   *Our Master.*

Art thou weary, art thou languid,
   Art thou sore distressed?
"Come to me," saith One, "and coming,
   Be at rest."

2 Hath he marks to lead me to him,
   If he be my Guide?—
"In his feet and hands are wound-prints,
   And his side."

3 Is there diadem, as Monarch,
   That his brow adorns?—
"Yea, a crown, in very surety;
   But of thorns."

4 If I find him, if I follow,
   What his guerdon here?—
"Many a sorrow, many a labor,
   Many a tear."

5 If I still hold closely to him,
   What hath he at last?—
"Sorrow vanquished, labor ended,
   Jordan passed."

6 If I ask him to receive me,
   Will he say me nay?—
"Not till earth, and not till heaven
   Pass away."

7 Finding, following, keeping, struggling,
   Is he sure to bless?—
"Saints, apostles, prophets, martyrs,
   Answer, Yes."

John M. Neale, tr.

LEAD ME ON. P. M.   C. C. CONVERSE.

Trav'ling to the better land, O'er the desert's scorching sand, Father! let me grasp thy hand; Lead me on, lead me on!

340   *"Lead me on."*

Traveling to the better land,
O'er the desert's scorching sand,
Father! let me grasp thy hand;
   Lead me on, lead me on!

2 When at Marah, parched with heat.
I the sparkling fountain greet,
Make the bitter water sweet;
   Lead me on!

3 When the wilderness is drear,
Show me Elim's palm-grove near.
And her wells, as crystal clear:
   Lead me on!

4 Through the water, through the fire.
Never let me fall or tire,

Every step brings Canaan nigher:
   Lead me on!

5 Bid me stand on Nebo's height.
Gaze upon the land of light,
Then, transported with the sight.
   Lead me on!

6 When I stand on Jordan's brink,
Never let me fear or shrink;
Hold me, Father, lest I sink:
   Lead me on!

7 When the victory is won.
And eternal life begun,
Up to glory lead me on!
   Lead me on, lead me on!

Anon.

COURAGE AND CHEER.

MY LIFE FLOWS ON. P. M.   R. LOWRY.

My life flows on in endless song; Above earth's lamentation,
I catch the sweet, though far-off, hymn (Omit........) That hails a new creation;
Through all the tumult and the strife, I hear the music ringing;
It finds an echo in my soul—How can I keep from singing?

341   *"Songs in the night."*

My life flows on in endless song;
  Above earth's lamentation,
I catch the sweet, though far-off, hymn
  That hails a new creation;
Through all the tumult and the strife,
  I hear the music ringing;
It finds an echo in my soul—
  How can I keep from singing?

2 What though my joys and comforts die?
  The Lord my Saviour liveth;
What though the darkness gather round?
  Songs in the night he giveth;
No storm can shake my inmost calm,
  While to that refuge clinging;
Since Christ is Lord of heaven and earth,
  How can I keep from singing?

3 I lift my eyes; the cloud grows thin;
  I see the blue above it;
And day by day this pathway smooths,
  Since first I learned to love it;
The peace of Christ makes fresh my heart,
  A fountain ever springing;
All things are mine since I am his—
  How can I keep from singing?
                 Anon.

LABAN. S. M.   LOWELL MASON.

My soul, be on thy guard, Ten thousand foes arise; And hosts of sin are pressing hard To draw thee from the skies.

342   *"Watch."*

My soul, be on thy guard,
  Ten thousand foes arise;
And hosts of sin are pressing hard
  To draw thee from the skies.

2 Oh, watch, and fight, and pray!
  The battle ne'er give o'er;
Renew it boldly every day,
  And help divine implore.

3 Ne'er think the victory won,
  Nor lay thine armor down;
Thine arduous work will not be done,
  Till thou obtain thy crown.

4 Fight on, my soul, till death
  Shall bring thee to thy God!
He'll take thee at thy parting breath,
  Up to his blest abode.
               George Heath.

CHRISTIAN EXPERIENCE.

ST. ALBAN'S. 6s, 5s. D.   Arr. fr. HAYDN.

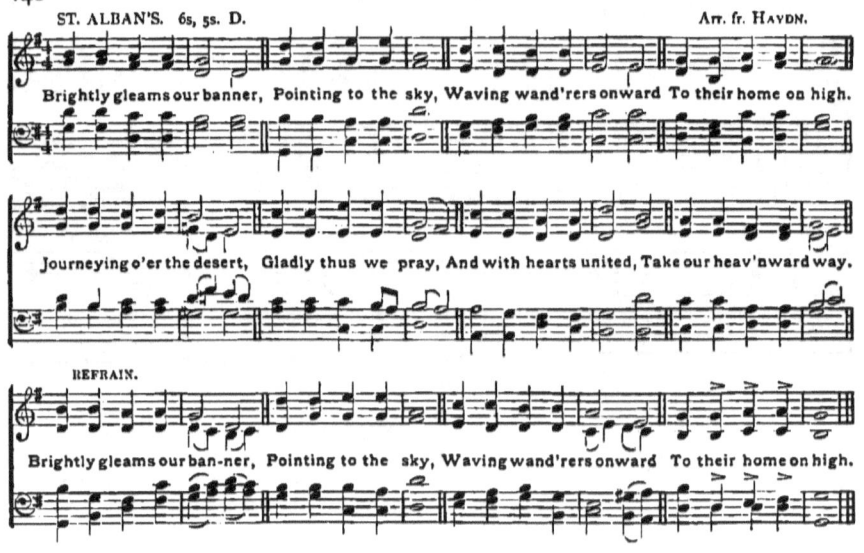

Brightly gleams our banner, Pointing to the sky, Waving wand'rers onward To their home on high.

Journeying o'er the desert, Gladly thus we pray, And with hearts united, Take our heav'nward way.

REFRAIN.

Brightly gleams our ban-ner, Pointing to the sky, Waving wand'rers onward To their home on high.

343   *"Jehovah Nissi."*

BRIGHTLY gleams our banner,
  Pointing to the sky,
Waving wanderers onward
  To their home on high.
Journeying o'er the desert,
  Gladly thus we pray,
And with hearts united,
  Take our heavenward way.—REF.

2 Jesus, Lord and Master,
  At thy sacred feet,
Here with hearts rejoicing
  See thy children meet;

Often have we left thee,
  Often gone astray;
Keep us, mighty Saviour,
  In the narrow way.—REF.

3 All our days direct us
  In the way we go;
Lead us on victorious
  Over every foe:
Bid thine angels shield us
  When the storm-clouds lower;
Pardon thou and save us
  In the last dread hour.—REF.
                      Thomas J. Potter.

WALES. 8s, 4s.   Welsh Melody.

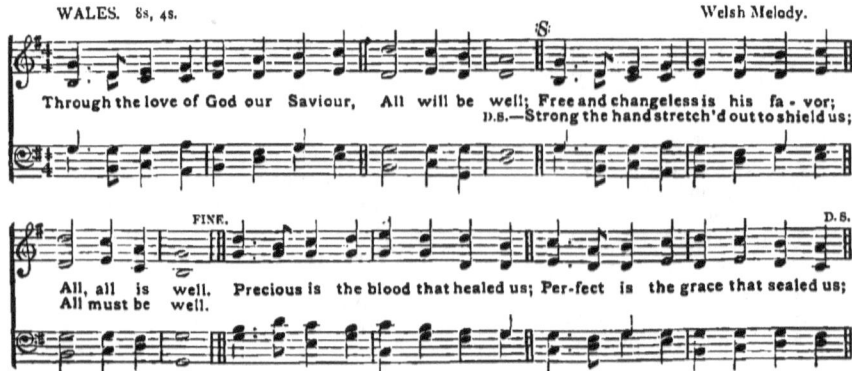

Through the love of God our Saviour, All will be well; Free and changeless is his fa-vor;
D.S.—Strong the hand stretch'd out to shield us;

FINE.   D.S.

All, all is well. Precious is the blood that healed us; Per-fect is the grace that sealed us;
All must be well.

COURAGE AND CHEER.

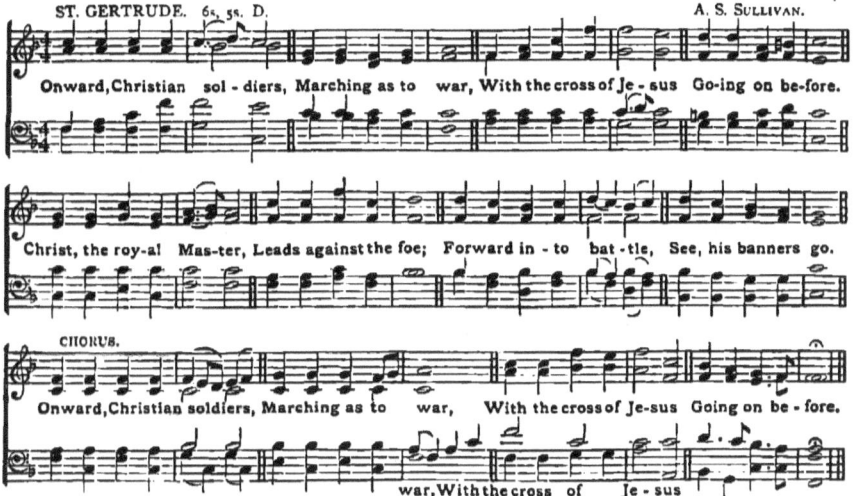

ST. GERTRUDE. 6s, 5s. D.   A. S. SULLIVAN.

344 "*Fight the good fight.*"
ONWARD, Christian soldiers,
  Marching as to war,
With the cross of Jesus
  Going on before.
Christ, the royal Master,
  Leads against the foe;
Forward into battle,
  See, his banners go.—CHO.

2 Like a mighty army,
  Moves the Church of God;
Brothers, we are treading
  Where the saints have trod;
We are not divided,
  All one body we,
One in hope and doctrine,
  One in charity.—CHO.

3 Crowns and thrones may perish,
  Kingdoms rise and wane,
But the Church of Jesus
  Constant will remain;
Gates of hell can never
  'Gainst that Church prevail;
We have Christ's own promise,
  And that cannot fail.—CHO.

4 Onward, then, ye people,
  Join our happy throng;
Blend with ours your voices
  In the triumph-song;
Glory, laud, and honor,
  Unto Christ the King;
This through countless ages,
  Men and angels sing.—CHO.
              S. Baring-Gould.

---

345 8s, 4s. "*All is well.*"
THROUGH the love of God our Saviour,
  All will be well;
Free and changeless is his favor;
  All, all is well.
Precious is the blood that healed us;
Perfect is the grace that sealed us;
Strong the hand stretched out to shield us;
  All must be well.

2 Though we pass through tribulation,
  All will be well:
Ours is such a full salvation;
  All, all is well.
Happy still in God confiding,
Fruitful, if in Christ abiding,
Holy, through the Spirit's guiding,
  All must be well.

3 We expect a bright to-morrow;
  All will be well;
Faith can sing through days of sorrow,
  All, all is well.
On our Father's love relying,
Jesus every need supplying,
Or in living, or in dying,
  All must be well.
              Mrs. Mary B. Peters.

CHRISTIAN EXPERIENCE.

CASKEY. 7s, 6s. D.   T. E. PERKINS.

Sometimes a light sur-pris-es The Christian while he sings; It is the Lord who ris-es
D.S.—A sea-son of clear shin-ing,
With heal-ing in his wings: When comforts are de-clin-ing, He grants the soul a-gain
To cheer it af-ter rain.

346   *Matthew 6: 25–34.*

SOMETIMES a light surprises
  The Christian while he sings;
It is the Lord who rises
  With healing in his wings:
When comforts are declining,
  He grants the soul again
A season of clear shining,
  To cheer it after rain.

2 In holy contemplation,
  We sweetly then pursue
The theme of God's salvation,
  And find it ever new:
Set free from present sorrow,
  We cheerfully can say,
Let the unknown to-morrow
  Bring with it what it may.

3 It can bring with it nothing,
  But he will bring us through;
Who gives the lilies clothing,
  Will clothe his people too:
Beneath the spreading heavens,
  No creature but is fed;
And he who feeds the ravens,
  Will give his children bread.

4 Though vine nor fig-tree neither,
  Their wonted fruit should bear,
Though all the fields should wither,
  Nor flocks, nor herds be there;

Yet God the same abiding,
  His praise shall tune my voice,
For while in him confiding,
  I cannot but rejoice.
William Cowper.

347   *Perfect peace.*

IN heavenly love abiding,
  No change my heart shall fear,
And safe is such confiding,
  For nothing changes here:
The storm may roar without me,
  My heart may low be laid,
But God is round about me,
  And can I be dismayed?

2 Wherever he may guide me,
  No want shall turn me back;
My Shepherd is beside me,
  And nothing can I lack:
His wisdom ever waketh,
  His sight is never dim;
He knows the way he taketh,
  And I will walk with him.

3 Green pastures are before me,
  Which yet I have not seen;
Bright skies will soon be o'er me,
  Where darkest clouds have been:
My hope I cannot measure;
  My path to life is free;
My Saviour has my treasure,
  And he will walk with me.
Anna L. Waring.

COURAGE AND CHEER.

WEBB. 7s, 6s. D.   G. J. WEBB.

Stand up!—stand up for Jesus! Ye soldiers of the cross; Lift high his roy-al ban-ner,
D. S.—Till ev-ery foe is vanquished,
It must not suf-fer loss: From vic-t'ry un-to vic-t'ry His ar-my shall he lead,
And Christ is Lord in-deed.

348 *"Having done all, stand."*

STAND up!—stand up for Jesus!
  Ye soldiers of the cross;
Lift high his royal banner,
  It must not suffer loss:
From victory unto victory
  His army shall he lead,
Till every foe is vanquished,
  And Christ is Lord indeed.

2 Stand up!—stand up for Jesus!
  The trumpet call obey;
Forth to the mighty conflict,
  In this his glorious day:
"Ye that are men, now serve him,"
  Against unnumbered foes;
Let courage rise with danger,
  And strength to strength oppose.

3 Stand up!—stand up for Jesus!
  Stand in his strength alone;
The arm of flesh will fail you—
  Ye dare not trust your own:
Put on the gospel armor,
  And, watching unto prayer,
Where duty calls, or danger,
  Be never wanting there.

4 Stand up!—stand up for Jesus!
  The strife will not be long;
This day, the noise of battle,
  The next, the victor's song;
To him that overcometh,
  A crown of life shall be;
He with the King of glory
  Shall reign eternally!
        George Duffield.

ST. AËLRED. 8s, 3.   J. B. DYKES.

349 *"Peace, be still."*

FIERCE raged the tempest o'er the deep,
Watch did thine anxious servants keep,
But thou wast wrapped in guileless sleep,
  Calm and still.

2 "Save, Lord, we perish," was their cry,
"Oh, save us in our agony!"
Thy word above the storm rose high
  "Peace, be still."

3 The wild winds hushed; the angry deep
Sank, like a little child, to sleep;
The sullen billows ceased to leap,
  At thy will.

4 So, when our life is clouded o'er,
And storm-winds drift us from the shore,
Say, lest we sink to rise no more,
  "Peace, be still."
        Godfrey Thring.

CHRISTIAN EXPERIENCE.

WIMBORNE. L. M. — J. Whitaker.

Stand up, my soul, shake off thy fears, And gird the gos-pel ar-mor on; March to the gates of end-less joy, Where Je-sus, thy great Cap-tain's gone.

350 *Ephesians 6: 14.*

Stand up, my soul, shake off thy fears
  And gird the gospel armor on;
March to the gates of endless joy,
  Where Jesus, thy great Captain's gone.

2 Hell and thy sins resist thy course,
  But hell and sin are vanquished foes;
Thy Saviour nailed them to the cross,
  And sung the triumph when he rose.

3 Then let my soul march boldly on,—
  Press forward to the heavenly gate;
There peace and joy eternal reign,
  And glittering robes for conquerors wait.

4 There shall I wear a starry crown,
  And triumph in almighty grace,
While all the armies of the skies
  Join in my glorious Leader's praise.
                  Isaac Watts.

MISSIONARY CHANT. L. M. — Charles Zeuner.

351 *Isaiah 40: 28–31.*

Awake, our souls! away, our fears!
  Let every trembling thought be gone;
Awake, and run the heavenly race,
  And put a cheerful courage on!

2 True, 't is a strait and thorny road,
  And mortal spirits tire and faint;
But they forget the mighty God,
  Who feeds the strength of every saint—

3 The mighty God, whose matchless power
  Is ever new and ever young,
And firm endures, while endless years
  Their everlasting circles run.

4 From thee, the overflowing spring,
  Our souls shall drink a fresh supply;
While such as trust their native strength
  Shall melt away, and droop, and die.

5 Swift as an eagle cuts the air,
  We 'll mount aloft to thine abode;
On wings of love our souls shall fly,
  Nor tire amid the heavenly road!
                  Isaac Watts.

COURAGE AND CHEER.

PARK STREET. L. M.   F. M. A. VENUA.

Fountain of grace, rich, full, and free, What need I, that is not in thee? Full pardon, strength to meet the day, And peace which none can take away, And peace which none can take away.

352   *"My springs in thee."*
FOUNTAIN of grace, rich, full, and free,
What need I, that is not in thee?
Full pardon, strength to meet the day,
And peace which none can take away.

2 Doth sickness fill my heart with fear,
'T is sweet to know that thou art near;
Am I with dread of justice tried,
'T is sweet to know that Christ hath died.

3 In life, thy promises of aid
Forbid my heart to be afraid;
In death, peace gently vails the eyes,—
Christ rose, and I shall surely rise.
James Edmeston.

353   *Jesus is forever mine.*
WHEN sins and fears, prevailing, rise,
And fainting hope almost expires,
To thee, O Lord, I lift my eyes;
To thee I breathe my soul's desires.

2 Art thou not mine, my living Lord?
And can my hope, my comfort die?
'T is fixed on thine almighty word—
That word which built the earth and sky.

3 If my immortal Saviour lives,
Then my immortal life is sure;
His word a firm foundation gives;
Here may I build and rest secure.

4 Here, O my soul, thy trust repose;
If Jesus is for ever mine,
Not death itself—that last of foes—
Shall break a union so divine.
Anne Steele.

10 P

354   *"Complete in Him."*
MY soul complete in Jesus stands!
It fears no more the law's demands;
The smile of God is sweet within,
Where all before was guilt and sin.

2 My soul at rest in Jesus lives;
Accepts the peace his pardon gives;
Receives the grace his death secured,
And pleads the anguish he endured.

3 My soul its every foe defies,
And cries—'T is God that justifies!
Who charges God's elect with sin?
Shall Christ, who died their peace to win?

4 A song of praise my soul shall sing.
To our eternal, glorious King!
Shall worship humbly at his feet,
In whom alone it stands complete.
Mrs. G. W. Bintliff.

355   *2 Cor. 12:9.*
LET me but hear my Saviour say,
"Strength shall be equal to thy day;"
Then I rejoice in deep distress,
Leaning on all-sufficient grace.

2 I can do all things—or can bear
All suffering, if my Lord be there;
Sweet pleasures mingle with the pains,
While he my sinking head sustains.

3 I glory in infirmity,
That Christ's own power may rest on me;
When I am weak, then am I strong;
Grace is my shield, and Christ my song.
Isaac Watts.

CHRISTIAN EXPERIENCE.

356 "Come home."

BRETHREN, while we sojourn here,
Fight we must, but should not fear;
Foes we have, but we've a Friend,
One that loves us to the end:
Forward, then, with courage go;
Long we shall not dwell below;
Soon the joyful news will come,
"Child, your Father calls—come home!"

2 In the way a thousand snares
Lie, to take us unawares;
Satan, with malicious art,
Watches each unguarded part:
But, from Satan's malice free,
Saints shall soon victorious be;
Soon the joyful news will come,
"Child, your Father calls—come home!"

3 But of all the foes we meet,
None so oft mislead our feet,
None betray us into sin,
Like the foes that dwell within;
Yet let nothing spoil our peace,
Christ shall also conquer these;
Soon the joyful news will come,
"Child, your Father calls—come home!"

Joseph Swain.

357 *Assurance.*

WHEN I can read my title clear
  To mansions in the skies,
I bid farewell to every fear,
  And wipe my weeping eyes.

2 Should earth against my soul engage,
  And fiery darts be hurled,
Then I can smile at Satan's rage,
  And face a frowning world.

3 Let cares like a wild deluge come,
  And storms of sorrow fall,
May I but safely reach my home,
  My God, my heaven, my all!—

4 There shall I bathe my weary soul
  In seas of heavenly rest;
And not a wave of trouble roll
  Across my peaceful breast.

Isaac Watts.

COURAGE AND CHEER.

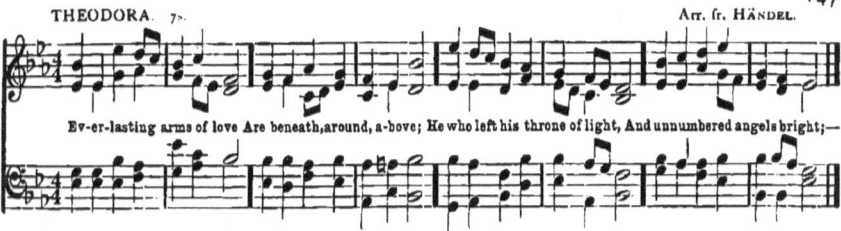

Ev-er-lasting arms of love Are beneath, around, a-bove; He who left his throne of light, And unnumbered angels bright;—

358 *"The everlasting arms."*
EVERLASTING arms of love
Are beneath, around, above;
He who left his throne of light,
And unnumbered angels bright;—

2 He who on the accursèd tree
Gave his precious life for me;
He it is that bears me on,
His the arm I lean upon.

3 All things hasten to decay,
Earth and sea will pass away;
Soon will yonder circling sun
Cease his blazing course to run.

4 Scenes will vary, friends grow strange,
But the Changeless cannot change:
Gladly will I journey on,
With his arm to lean upon.
John R. Macduff.

Children of the heavenly King, As ye journey, sweetly sing; Sing your Saviour's worthy praise, Glorious in his works and ways.

359 *Isaiah 35: 8-10.*
CHILDREN of the heavenly King,
As ye journey, sweetly sing;
Sing your Saviour's worthy praise,
Glorious in his works and ways.

2 Ye are traveling home to God
In the way the fathers trod;
They are happy now, and ye
Soon their happiness shall see.

3 Shout, ye little flock, and blest!
You on Jesus' throne shall rest;
There your seat is now prepared;
There your kingdom and reward.

4 Fear not, brethren; joyful stand
On the borders of your land;
Jesus Christ, your Father's Son,
Bids you undismayed go on.

5 Lord, submissive make us go,
Gladly leaving all below;
Only thou our Leader be,
And we still will follow thee.
John Cennick.

360 *Redeeming Love*
Now BEGIN the heavenly theme,
Sing aloud in Jesus' name;
Ye who Jesus' kindness prove,
Triumph in redeeming love.

2 Ye who see the Father's grace
Beaming in the Saviour's face,
As to Canaan on ye move,
Praise and bless redeeming love.

3 Mourning souls, dry up your tears;
Banish all your guilty fears;
See your guilt and curse remove,
Canceled by redeeming love.

4 Welcome, all by sin opprest,
Welcome to his sacred rest;
Nothing brought him from above,
Nothing but redeeming love.

5 Hither, then, your music bring,
Strike aloud each joyful string;
Mortals, join the host above,
Join to praise redeeming love.
John Langford.

CHRISTIAN EXPERIENCE.

FATHERLAND. 5s, 8s, 5s. Western Melody

Jesus, still lead on, Till our rest be won; And although the way be cheerless, We will follow, calm and fearless; Guide us by thy hand To our Father-land, To our Father-land.

361 *"Still lead on."*
Jesus, still lead on,
Till our rest be won;
And although the way be cheerless,
We will follow, calm and fearless;
Guide us by thy hand
To our Fatherland.

2 If the way be drear,
If the foe be near,
Let not faithless fears o'ertake us,
Let not faith and hope forsake us;
For, through many a foe,
To our home we go.

3 When we seek relief
From a long-felt grief,
When temptations come, alluring.
Make us patient and enduring,
Show us that bright shore,
Where we weep no more.

4 Jesus, still lead on,
Till our rest be won;
Heavenly Leader, still direct us,
Still support, console, protect us,
Till we safely stand
In our Fatherland.

Jane Borthwick, tr.

SARUM. 8s, 4s. J. HULLAH.

Through good report and evil, Lord, Still guided by thy faithful word,—Our staff, our buckler, and our sword,—We follow thee.

362 *"We follow thee."*
Through good report, and evil, Lord,
Still guided by thy faithful word,—
Our staff, our buckler, and our sword,—
We follow thee.

2 With enemies on every side,
We lean on thee, the Crucified;
Forsaking all on earth beside,
We follow thee.

3 Thou hast passed on before our face;
Thy footsteps on the way we trace;
Oh, keep us, aid us by thy grace:
We follow thee.

4 Whom have we in the heaven above,
Whom on this earth, save thee, to love?
Still in thy light we onward move;
We follow thee!

Horatius Bonar.

COURAGE AND CHEER.

363 *"Finish thy new creation."*
Love divine, all love excelling,—
 Joy of heaven, to earth come down!
Fix in us thy humble dwelling,
 All thy faithful mercies crown:
Jesus! thou art all compassion,
 Pure, unbounded love thou art;
Visit us with thy salvation,
 Enter every trembling heart.

2 Breathe, oh, breathe thy loving Spirit,
 Into every troubled breast!
Let us all in thee inherit,
 Let us find the promised rest:
Come, almighty to deliver,
 Let us all thy life receive!
Speedily return, and never,
 Never more thy temples leave!

3 Finish then thy new creation,
 Pure, unspotted may we be:
Let us see our whole salvation
 Perfectly secured by thee!
Changed from glory into glory,
 Till in heaven we take our place;
Till we cast our crowns before thee,
 Lost in wonder, love, and praise.
  Charles Wesley.

364 *The reproach of Christ.*
Cross, reproach, and tribulation!
 Ye to me are welcome guests,
When I have this consolation,
 That my soul in Jesus rests.

The reproach of Christ is glorious!
 Those who here his burden bear,
In the end shall prove victorious,
 And eternal gladness share.
  L. A. Gotter, tr.

365 *Psalm 91.*
Call Jehovah thy salvation,
 Rest beneath the Almighty's shade;
In his secret habitation
 Dwell, and never be dismayed:
There no tumult can alarm thee,
 Thou shalt dread no hidden snare;
Guilt nor violence can harm thee,
 In eternal safeguard there.

2 From the sword, at noon-day wasting,
 From the noisome pestilence;
In the depth of midnight, blasting,
 God shall be thy sure defence:
Fear not thou the deadly quiver,
 When a thousand feel the blow;
Mercy shall thy soul deliver,
 Though ten thousand be laid low.

3 Since, with pure and firm affection,
 Thou on God hast set thy love,
With the wings of his protection
 He will shield thee from above;
Thou shalt call on him in trouble,
 He will hearken, he will save;
Here, for grief reward thee double,
 Crown with life beyond the grave.
  James Montgomery.

CHRISTIAN EXPERIENCE.

ELLESDIE. 8s, 7s. D.   Arr. fr. Mozart.

Je-sus, I my cross have taken, All to leave, and follow thee; Naked, poor, despis'd, for-sak-en,
D. S.—Yet how rich is my con-di-tion,

Thou, from hence, my all shalt be! Perish, every fond ambition, All I've sought, or hoped, or known,
God and heaven are still my own!

366   *Bearing the Cross.*

Jesus, I my cross have taken,
  All to leave, and follow thee;
Naked, poor, despised, forsaken,
  Thou, from hence, my all shalt be!
Perish, every fond ambition,
  All I've sought, or hoped, or known,
Yet how rich is my condition,
  God and heaven are still my own!

2 Let the world despise and leave me,
  They have left my Saviour, too;
Human hearts and looks deceive me—
  Thou art not, like them, untrue;
Oh, while thou dost smile upon me,
  God of wisdom, love, and might,
Foes may hate, and friends disown me,
  Show thy face, and all is bright.

3 Man may trouble and distress me,
  'T will but drive me to thy breast;
Life with trials hard may press me;
  Heaven will bring me sweeter rest!
Oh, 't is not in grief to harm me,
  While thy love is left to me;
Oh, 't were not in joy to charm me,
  Were that joy unmixed with thee.

4 Go then, earthly fame and treasure!
  Come, disaster, scorn, and pain!
In thy service, pain is pleasure,
  With thy favor, loss is gain.
I have called thee—Abba, Father!
  I have stayed my heart on thee!

Storms may howl, and clouds may gather.
  All must work for good to me.
Henry F. Lyte.

367   *The Crown coming.*

Soul, then know thy full salvation,
  Rise o'er sin, and fear, and care;
Joy to find in every station
  Something still to do or bear.
Think what Spirit dwells within thee;
  Think what Father's smiles are thine;
Think that Jesus died to win thee!
  Child of heaven, canst thou repine?

2 Haste thee on from grace to glory,
  Armed by faith and winged by prayer!
Heaven's eternal day's before thee,
  God's own hand shall guide thee there:
Soon shall close thy earthly mission,
  Soon shall pass thy pilgrim days,
Hope shall change to glad fruition,
  Faith to sight, and prayer to praise.
Henry F. Lyte.

368   *A spotless soul.*

Jesus, who on Calvary's mountain
  Poured thy precious blood for me,
Wash me in its flowing fountain,
  That my soul may spotless be.

2 In thy word I hear thee saying,
  Come and I will give you rest;
Now the gracious call obeying,
  See, I hasten to thy breast.
Anon., 1855.

COURAGE AND CHEER.

369
"Abide in me."

Why is thy faith, O child of God, so small?
Why doth thy heart shrink back at duty's call?
Art thou obeying this—"Abide in me,"
And doth the Master's word abide in thee?

2 Oh, blest assurance from our risen Lord!
Oh, precious comfort breathing from the Word!
How great the promise! could there greater be?
"Ask what thou wilt, it shall be done for [thee!"

3 "Ask what thou wilt," but oh, remember this,—
We ask and have not, for we ask amiss
When, weak in faith, we only half believe
That what we ask we really shall receive.

4 Increase our faith, and clear our vision, Lord;
Help us to take thee at thy simple word,
No more with cold distrust to bring thee grief;
Lord, we believe! help thou our unbelief.
W. F. Sherwin.

370
"Eben-ezer."

Come, thou Fount of every blessing,
　Tune my heart to sing thy grace;
Streams of mercy, never ceasing,
　Call for songs of loudest praise;
Teach me some melodious sonnet,
　Sung by flaming tongues above;
Praise the mount—I 'm fixed upon it!—
　Mount of thy redeeming love.

2 Here I 'll raise mine Eben-ezer;
　Hither by thy help I 'm come;
And I hope, by thy good pleasure,
　Safely to arrive at home.

Jesus sought me when a stranger,
　Wandering from the fold of God;
He, to rescue me from danger,
　Interposed his precious blood.

3 Oh, to grace how great a debtor
　Daily I 'm constrained to be!
Let thy goodness, like a fetter,
　Bind my wandering heart to thee;
Prone to wander, Lord, I feel it;
　Prone to leave the God I love;
Here 's my heart; oh, take and seal it:
　Seal it for thy courts above.
Robert Robinson.

CHRISTIAN EXPERIENCE.

CAERSALEM. 8s, 7s, 7. — Welsh melody.

Look to Jesus! till, reviving, Faith and love thy life-springs swell, Strength for all good things deriving; Jesus hath done all things well. Work, while it is called to-day, Works which shall not fade away.

371 *"Looking unto Jesus."*

Look to Jesus! till, reviving,
　Faith and love thy life-springs swell,
Strength for all good things deriving;
　Jesus hath done all things well.
Work, while it is called to-day,
Works which shall not fade away.

2 Look to Jesus, prayerful waking
　Where thy feet on roses tread;
Follow, worldly pomp forsaking,
　With thy cross, where he hath led.
Baffled shall the tempter flee,
And God's angels come to thee.

3 Look to Jesus, when, dark lowering,
　Perils thy horizon dim;
Once from him a band fell cowering;
　Calm in tempests, look on him;
Wind and billow, fire and flood,—
Forward! brave by trusting God.

4 Look to Jesus still to shield thee,
　When no longer thou may'st live;
In that last need, he will yield thee
　Peace the world can never give;
He who finished all for thee
Takes thee, then, with him to be.
　　　　　　　　　Tr. fr. Swedish.

372 *"Tried, Precious, Sure."*—Isa. 28: 16.

Through the yesterday of ages,
　Jesus, thou hast been the same;
Through our own life's checkered pages,
　Still the one dear changeless name;
Well may we in thee confide,
Faithful Saviour, proved and tried.

2 Joyfully we stand and witness
　Thou art still to-day the same;
In thy perfect, glorious fitness,
　Meeting every need and claim;
Chiefest of ten thousand thou!
Saviour, O most precious, now!

3 Gazing down the far forever,
　Brighter glows the one sweet name,
Steadfast radiance paling never,
　Jesus, Jesus! still the same;
Evermore thou shalt endure,
Our own Saviour, strong and pure.
　　　　　　　　Frances R. Havergal.

373 *"Christ, our Head."*

Rise, ye children of salvation,
　All who cleave to Christ the Head:
Wake, arise! O mighty nation,
　Ere the foe on Zion tread—
He draws nigh, and would defy
All the hosts of God most high.

2 Saints and heroes long before us,
　Firmly on this ground have stood:
See their banners waving o'er us—
　"Conquerors through the Saviour's blood!"
Ground we hold, whereon of old
Fought the faithful and the bold.

3 When his servants stand before him
　Each receiving his reward;
When his saints in light adore him,
　Giving glory to the Lord—
Victory! our song shall be,
Like the thunder of the sea!
　　　　　　　　Tr. fr. *Falckner.*

LOVE, AND COMMUNION WITH CHRIST.

GRANGE. 8s, 7s, 7. R. B. BORTHWICK.

Master, speak! thy servant heareth, Longing for thy gracious word, Longing for thy voice that cheereth; Master, let it now be heard. I am listening, Lord, for thee; What hast thou to say to me?

374. *1 Samuel 3 : 10.*

MASTER, speak! thy servant heareth,
  Longing for thy gracious word,
Longing for thy voice that cheereth;
  Master, let it now be heard.
I am listening, Lord, for thee;
What hast thou to say to me?

2 Often through my heart is pealing
  Many another voice than thine;
Many an unwilled echo stealing
  From the walls of this thy shrine.
Let thy longed-for accents fall;
Master, speak! and silence all.

3 Master, speak! I do not doubt thee,
  Though so tearfully I plead;
Saviour, Shepherd! oh, without thee
  Life would be a blank indeed.
But I long for fuller light,
Deeper love and clearer sight.

4 Speak to me by name, O Master,
  Let me know it is to me;
Speak, that I may follow faster,
  With a step more firm and free,
Where the Shepherd leads the flock,
In the shadow of the rock!
  Frances R. Havergal.

375 *"Jesus only!"*

"JESUS only!" In the shadow
  Of the cloud so chill and dim,
We are clinging, loving, trusting,
  He with us, and we with him:
All unseen, though ever nigh,
"Jesus only!"—all our cry.

2 "Jesus only!" in the glory,
  When the shadows all are flown,
Seeing him in all his beauty,
  Satisfied with him alone;
May we join his ransomed throng,
"Jesus only!"—all our song!
  Frances R. Havergal.

376 *"He knoweth our frame."*

YES, he knows the way is dreary,
  Knows the weakness of our frame,
Knows that hand and heart are weary,
  He in all points felt the same.
He is near to help and bless;
Be not weary, onward press.

2 Look to him, who once was willing
  All his glory to resign,
That, for thee the law fulfilling,
  All his merit might be thine.
Strive to follow, day by day,
Where his footsteps mark the way.

3 Look to him, the Lord of Glory,
  Tasting death to win thy life;
Gazing on that wondrous story,
  Canst thou falter in the strife?
Is it not new life to know
That the Lord hath loved thee so?

4 Look to him, and faith shall brighten,
  Hope shall soar, and love shall burn,
Peace once more thy heart shall lighten;
  Rise, he calleth thee, return!
Be not weary on thy way;
Jesus is thy strength and stay.
  Frances R. Havergal.

CHRISTIAN EXPERIENCE.

BARTIMEUS. 8s, 7s.   S. JENKS.

None but Christ: his merit hides me, He was faultless—I am fair; None but Christ, his wisdom guides me, He was out-cast—I'm his care.

377   *None but Jesus.*

None but Christ: his merit hides me,
 He was faultless—I am fair;
None but Christ, his wisdom guides me,
 He was out-cast—I'm his care.

2 None but Christ: his Spirit seals me,
 Gives me freedom with control;
None but Christ, his bruising heals me,
 And his sorrow soothes my soul.

3 None but Christ: his life sustains me,
 Strength and song to me he is;
None but Christ, his love constrains me,
 He is mine and I am his.
 Mrs. Anne R. Cousin.

378   *"Jesus only."*

Jesus only, when the morning
 Beams upon the path I tread;
Jesus only, when the darkness
 Gathers round my weary head.

2 Jesus only, when the billows
 Cold and sullen o'er me roll;
Jesus only, when the trumpet
 Rends the tomb and wakes the soul.

3 Jesus only, when, adoring,
 Saints their crowns before him bring;
Jesus only, I will, joyous,
 Through eternal ages sing.
 Elias Nason.

WILMOT. 8s, 7s.   Arr. by L. MASON.

379   *"With you always."*

Always with us, always with us—
 Words of cheer and words of love;
Thus the risen Saviour whispers,
 From his dwelling-place above.

2 With us when we toil in sadness,
 Sowing much and reaping none;
Telling us that in the future
 Golden harvests shall be won.

3 With us when the storm is sweeping
 O'er our pathway dark and drear;
Waking hope within our bosoms,
 Stilling every anxious fear.

4 With us in the lonely valley,
 When we cross the chilling stream—
Lighting up the steps to glory
 With salvation's radiant beam.
 Edwin H. Nevin.

380   *A Living Christ.*

Now I know the great Redeemer,
 Know he lives and spreads his fame;
Lives—and all the heavens adore him;
 Lives—and earth resounds his name.

2 My Redeemer lives within me,
 Lives—and heavenly life conveys;
Lives—and glory now surrounds me;
 Lives—and I his name shall praise.

3 Pardon, peace, and full salvation
 From my living Saviour flow;
Light, and life, and consolation,—
 All the good I e'er can know.

4 Soon shall I behold my Saviour;
 He who lives and reigns above,
Lives—and I shall live for ever,
 Live and sing redeeming love!
 Richard Burnham.

LOVE, AND COMMUNION WITH CHRIST.

SING FOR JESUS. P. M.   PHILIP PHILLIPS.

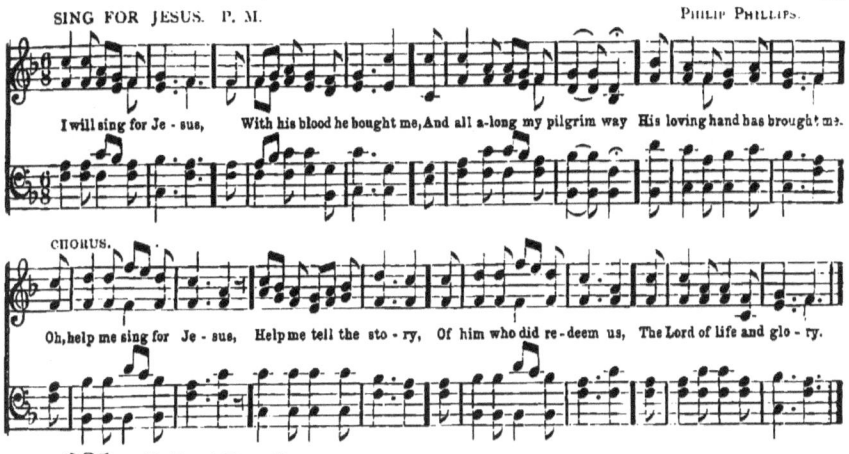

381   "*My blessed Master.*"
I WILL sing for Jesus,
  With his blood he bought me,
  And all along my pilgrim way
  His loving hand has brought me.

CHO.—Oh, help me sing for Jesus,
  Help me tell the story,
  Of him who did redeem us,
  The Lord of life and glory.

2 Can there overtake me
  Any dark disaster
  While I can sing for Jesus,
  My blessèd, blessèd Master?—CHO.

3 I will sing for Jesus,
  His name alone prevailing,
  Shall be my sweetest music,
  When heart and flesh are failing.—CHO.

DOMINUS REGIT. P. M.   J. B. DYKES.

382   *Psalm 23.*
THE King of love my Shepherd is,
  Whose goodness faileth never,
  I nothing lack if I am his,
  And he is mine for ever.

2 Where streams of living water flow
  My ransomed soul he leadeth,
  And where the verdant pastures grow,
  With food celestial feedeth.

3 Perverse and foolish, oft I strayed,
  But yet in love he sought me,
  And on his shoulder gently laid,
  And home, rejoicing, brought me.

4 In death's dark vale I fear no ill
  With thee, dear Lord, beside me,
  Thy rod and staff my comfort still,
  Thy cross before to guide me.

5 Thou spread'st a table in my sight,
  Thy unction grace bestoweth,
  And, oh, what transport of delight
  From thy pure chalice floweth.

6 And so through all the length of days
  Thy goodness faileth never,
  Good Shepherd! may I sing thy praise
  Within thy house for ever.

Henry W. Baker.

CHRISTIAN EXPERIENCE.

LA MONTE. P. M. EMMELAR.

383 *Christ our Rest.*
O LOVE, that wilt not let me go,
　I rest my weary soul in thee;
I give thee back the life I owe,
　That in thine ocean depths its flow
　　May richer, fuller be.

2 O Light, that followest all my way,
　I yield my flickering torch to thee;
My heart restores its borrowed ray,
　That in thy sunshine's blaze its day
　　May brighter, fairer be.

3 O Joy, that seekest me through pain,
　I cannot close my heart to thee;
I trace the sunshine through the rain,
　And feel the promise is not vain
　　That morn shall tearless be.

4 O Cross, that liftest up my head,
　I dare not ask to fly from thee;
I lay in dust life's glory dead,
　And from the ground there blossoms red
　　Life that shall endless be.
　　　　　　　　G. Matheson.

EVERY DAY. P. M. W. H. DOANE.

384 *"Clinging."*
SAVIOUR, more than life to me,
I am clinging, clinging close to thee;
Let thy precious blood applied,
Keep me ever, ever near thy side.

REF.—Every day, every hour,
　Let me feel thy cleansing power:
　May thy tender love to me
　Bind me closer, closer, Lord, to thee.

2 Through this changing world below,
　Lead me gently, gently as I go;
　Trusting thee, I cannot stray,
　I can never, never lose my way.—REF.

3 Let me love thee more and more,
　Till this fleeting, fleeting life is o'er;
　Till my soul is lost in love,
　In a brighter, brighter world above.—REF.
　　　　　　　Mrs. F. C. Van Alstyne.

LOVE, AND COMMUNION WITH CHRIST.

MAGILL. 11s. T. E. PERKINS.

Come, Jesus, Redeemer, abide thou with me; Come, gladden my spirit that waiteth for thee; Thy smile every shadow shall chase from my heart, And soothe every sorrow tho' keen be the smart.

385   "*I will come to you.*"

COME, Jesus, Redeemer, abide thou with me;
Come, gladden my spirit that waiteth for thee;
Thy smile every shadow shall chase from my heart,
And soothe every sorrow though keen be the smart.

2 Without thee but weakness, with thee I am strong;
By day thou shalt lead me, by night be my song;
Though dangers surround me, I still every fear,
Since thou, the Most Mighty, my Helper, art near.

3 Thy love, oh, how faithful! so tender, so pure!
Thy promise, faith's anchor, how steadfast and sure!
That love, like sweet sunshine, my cold heart can warm,
That promise make steady my soul in the storm.

4 Breathe, breathe on my spirit, oft ruffled, thy peace;
From restless, vain wishes, bid thou my heart cease;
In thee all its longings henceforward shall end,
Till, glad, to thy presence my soul shall ascend.

5 Oh, then, blessèd Jesus, who once for me died,
Made clean in the fountain that gushed from thy side,
I shall see thy full glory, thy face shall behold,
And praise thee with raptures for ever untold!   *Ray Palmer.*

386   "*Distresses for Christ's sake.*"

FOR what shall I praise thee, my God and my King,
For what blessings the tribute of gratitude bring?
Shall I praise thee for pleasure, for health, or for ease,
For the sunshine of youth, for the garden of peace?

2 For this I should praise; but if only for this,
I should leave half untold the donation of bliss!
I thank thee for sickness, for sorrow, and care,
For the thorns I have gathered, the anguish I bear;—

3 For nights of anxiety, watching, and tears,
A present of pain, a prospective of fears;
I praise thee, I bless thee, my Lord and my God,
For the good and the evil thy hand hath bestowed!   *Mrs. C. Fry Wilson.*

CHRISTIAN EXPERIENCE.

NOMEN JESU. 7s. — R. REDHEAD.

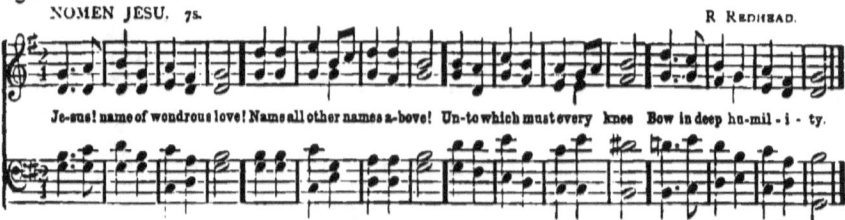

Je-sus! name of wondrous love! Name all other names a-bove! Un-to which must every knee Bow in deep hu-mil-i-ty.

387 *The name "Jesus."*

Jesus! name of wondrous love!
Name all other names above!
Unto which must every knee
Bow in deep humility.

2 Jesus! name decreed of old:
To the maiden mother told,
Kneeling in her lowly cell,
By the angel Gabriel.

3 Jesus! name of priceless worth
To the fallen sons of earth,
For the promise that it gave—
"Jesus shall his people save."—

4 Jesus! only name that's given
Under all the mighty heaven,
Whereby man, to sin enslaved,
Bursts his fetters, and is saved.

5 Jesus! name of wondrous love!
Human name of God above;
Pleading only this we flee,
Helpless, O our God, to thee.
William W. How.

388 *"Immanuel."*

Sweeter sounds than music knows
Charm me in Immanuel's name;
All her hopes my spirt owes
To his birth, and cross, and shame.

2 When he came, the angels sung,
"Glory be to God on high:"
Lord, unloose my stammering tongue;
Who should louder sing than I?

3 Did the Lord a man become,
That he might the law fulfill,
Bleed and suffer in my room,—
And canst thou, my tongue, be still?

4 No; I must my praises bring,
Though they worthless are, and weak;
For should I refuse to sing,
Sure the very stones would speak.

5 O my Saviour! Shield and Sun,
Shepherd, Brother, Lord, and Friend—
Every precious name in one!
I will love thee without end.
John Newton.

ST. BEES. 7s. — J. B. DYKES.

Earth has nothing sweet or fair, Lovely forms or beauties rare, But before my eyes they bring Christ, of beauty Source and Spring.

389 *"Altogether lovely."*

Earth has nothing sweet or fair,
Lovely forms or beauties rare,
But before my eyes they bring
Christ, of beauty Source and Spring.

2 When the morning paints the skies,
When the golden sunbeams rise,
Then my Saviour's form I find
Brightly imaged on my mind.

3 When the star-beams pierce the night,
Oft I think on Jesus' light;
Think how bright that light will be,
Shining through eternity.

4 Come, Lord Jesus! and dispel
This dark cloud in which I dwell,
And to me the power impart
To behold thee as thou art.
Frances E. Cox, tr.

LOVE, AND COMMUNION WITH CHRIST. 159

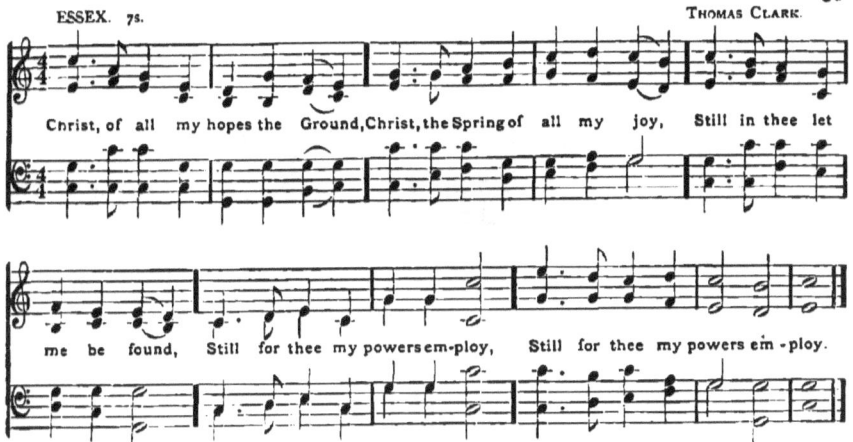

ESSEX. 7s.   THOMAS CLARK.

Christ, of all my hopes the Ground, Christ, the Spring of all my joy, Still in thee let me be found, Still for thee my powers em-ploy, Still for thee my powers em-ploy.

390 *"To live is Christ."*
CHRIST, of all my hopes the Ground,
Christ, the Spring of all my joy,
Still in thee let me be found,
Still for thee my powers employ.

2 Fountain of o'erflowing grace!
Freely from thy fullness give;
Till I close my earthly race,
Be it "Christ for me to live!"

3 Firmly trusting in thy blood,
Nothing shall my heart confound;
Safely I shall pass the flood,
Safely reach Immanuel's ground.

4 When I touch the blessed shore,
Back the closing waves shall roll!
Death's dark stream shall nevermore
Part from thee my ravished soul.

5 Thus—oh, thus an entrance give
To the land of cloudless sky;
Having known it "Christ to live,"
Let me know it "gain to die."
Ralph Wardlaw.

391 *"He first loved us."*
SAVIOUR! teach me, day by day,
Love's sweet lesson to obey;
Sweeter lesson cannot be,
Loving him who first loved me.

2 With a child-like heart of love,
At thy bidding may I move;
Prompt to serve and follow thee,
Loving him who first loved me.

3 Teach me all thy steps to trace,
Strong to follow in thy grace;
Learning how to love from thee,
Loving him who first loved me.

4 Love in loving finds employ—
In obedience all her joy;
Ever new that joy will be,
Loving him who first loved me.

5 Thus may I rejoice to show
That I feel the love I owe;
Singing, till thy face I see,
Of his love who first loved me.
Jane E. Leeson.

392 *"Christ, the Crucified."*
ASK ye what great thing I know
That delights and stirs me so?
What the high reward I win!
Whose the name I glory in?
Jesus Christ, the Crucified.

2 Who is life in life to me?
Who the death of death will be?
Who will place me on his right
With the countless hosts of light?
Jesus Christ, the Crucified.

3 This is that great thing I know;
This delights and stirs me so;
Faith in him who died to save,
Him who triumphed o'er the grave,
Jesus Christ, the Crucified.
Benjamin H. Kennedy.

CHRISTIAN EXPERIENCE.

ARMENIA. C. M.   S. B. POND.

{ Do not I love thee, O my Lord? Be-hold my heart and see; }
{ And turn the dear-est i - dol out (Omit............) } That dares to ri-val thee.

393   *Loving and Beloved.*
Do NOT I love thee, O my Lord?
  Behold my heart, and see;
And turn the dearest idol out
  That dares to rival thee.

2 Is not thy name melodious still
  To mine attentive ear?
Doth not each pulse with pleasure bound,
  My Saviour's voice to hear?

3 Hast thou a lamb in all thy flock
  I would disdain to feed?
Hast thou a foe, before whose face
  I fear thy cause to plead?

4 Would not my heart pour forth its blood
  In honor of thy name?
And challenge the cold hand of death
  To damp the immortal flame?

5 Thou knowest that I love thee, Lord;
  But, oh, I long to soar
Far from the sphere of mortal joys,
  And learn to love thee more.
              Philip Doddridge.

394   *"He is precious."*
BLEST Jesus! when my soaring thoughts
  O'er all thy graces rove,
How is my soul in transport lost,—
  In wonder, joy, and love!

2 Not softest strains can charm my ears,
  Like thy belovéd name;
Nor aught beneath the skies inspire
  My heart with equal flame.

3 Where'er I look, my wondering eyes
  Unnumbered blessings see;
But what is life, with all its bliss,
  If once compared with thee?

4 Hast thou a rival in my breast?
  Search, Lord, for thou canst tell
If aught can raise my passions thus,
  Or please my soul so well.

5 No; thou art precious to my heart,
  My portion and my joy:
For ever let thy boundless grace
  My sweetest thoughts employ.
              O. Heginbotham.

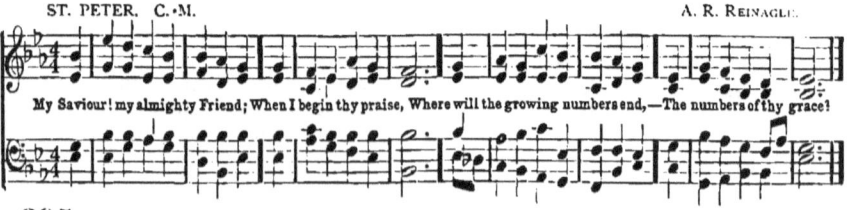

ST. PETER. C. M.   A. R. REINAGLE.

My Saviour! my almighty Friend; When I begin thy praise, Where will the growing numbers end,—The numbers of thy grace!

395   *Psalm 71.*
MY Saviour! my almighty Friend;
  When I begin thy praise,
Where will the growing numbers end,—
  The numbers of thy grace?

2 Thou art my everlasting trust;
  Thy goodness I adore;
And, since I knew thy graces first,
  I speak thy glories more.

3 My feet shall travel all the length
  Of the celestial road;
And march, with courage in thy strength,
  To see my Father God.

4 How will my lips rejoice to tell
  The victories of my King!
My soul, redeemed from sin and hell,
  Shall thy salvation sing.
              Isaac Watts.

LOVE, AND COMMUNION WITH CHRIST.

HOLY CROSS. C. M.   Arr. fr. MENDELSSOHN.

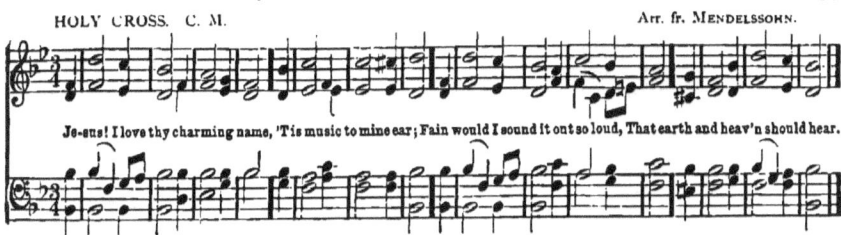

Je-sus! I love thy charming name, 'Tis music to mine ear; Fain would I sound it out so loud, That earth and heav'n should hear.

396   *"His name Jesus."*
JESUS! I love thy charming name,
  'T is music to mine ear;
Fain would I sound it out so loud,
  That earth and heaven should hear.

2 Yes!—thou art precious to my soul,
  My transport and my trust;
Jewels, to thee, are gaudy toys,
  And gold is sordid dust.

3 All my capacious powers can wish,
  In thee doth richly meet;
Not to mine eyes is light so dear,
  Nor friendship half so sweet.

4 Thy grace still dwells upon my heart,
  And sheds its fragrance there;—
The noblest balm of all its wounds,
  The cordial of its care.
                   Philip Doddridge.

HEBER. C. M.   GEO. KINGSLEY.

How sweet the name of Jesus sounds In a be-liev-er's ear! It soothes his sorrows, heals his wounds, And drives away his fear.

397   *"He is precious."*
HOW SWEET the name of Jesus sounds
  In a believer's ear!
It soothes his sorrows, heals his wounds,
  And drives away his fear.

2 It makes the wounded spirit whole,
  And calms the troubled breast;
'T is manna to the hungry soul,
  And to the weary, rest.

3 Jesus! my Shepherd, Guardian, Friend,
  My Prophet, Priest, and King;
My Lord, my Life, my Way, my End,
  Accept the praise I bring.

4 Weak is the effort of my heart,
  And cold my warmest thought;
But when I see thee as thou art,
  I'll praise thee as I ought.

5 Till then I would thy love proclaim,
  With every fleeting breath;
And may the music of thy name,
  Refresh my soul in death.
               John Newton.

398   *"Jesus only."*
JESUS, the very thought of thee,
  With sweetness fill my breast;
But sweeter far thy face to see
  And in thy presence rest.

2 Nor voice can sing, nor heart can frame,
  Nor can the memory find
A sweeter sound than thy blest name,
  O Saviour of mankind!

3 O Hope of every contrite heart!
  O Joy of all the meek!
To those who fall, how kind thou art!
  How good to those who seek!

4 But what to those who find? Ah! this,
  Nor tongue nor pen can show;
The love of Jesus, what it is,
  None but his loved ones know.

5 Jesus, our only joy be thou,
  As thou our prize wilt be;
Jesus, be thou our glory now,
  And through eternity.
              Edward Caswall, tr.

11 P

CHRISTIAN EXPERIENCE.

OLIVET. 6s, 4s. LOWELL MASON.

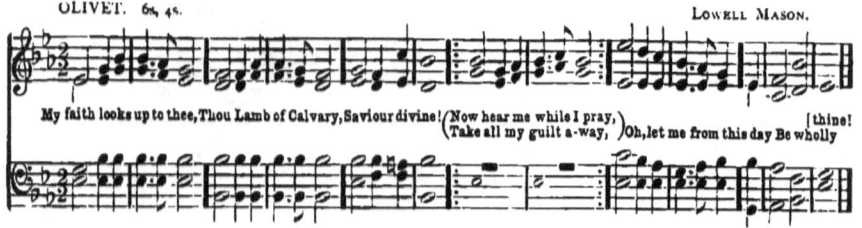

My faith looks up to thee, Thou Lamb of Calvary, Saviour divine! (Now hear me while I pray, Take all my guilt a-way,) Oh, let me from this day Be wholly [thine!

399 *"Look unto Me."*

My faith looks up to thee,
Thou Lamb of Calvary,
  Saviour divine!
Now hear me while I pray,
Take all my guilt away,
Oh, let me from this day
  Be wholly thine!

2 May thy rich grace impart
Strength to my fainting heart;
  My zeal inspire;
As thou hast died for me,
Oh, may my love to thee
Pure, warm, and changeless be,
  A living fire!

3 While life's dark maze I tread,
And griefs around me spread,
  Be thou my guide;
Bid darkness turn to day,
Wipe sorrow's tears away,
Nor let me ever stray
  From thee aside.

4 When ends life's transient dream,
When death's cold, sullen stream
  Shall o'er me roll,
Blest Saviour! then, in love,
Fear and distrust remove;
Oh, bear me safe above,
  A ransomed soul!

Ray Palmer.

PAX TECUM. 10s, 2l. G. T. CALDBECK.

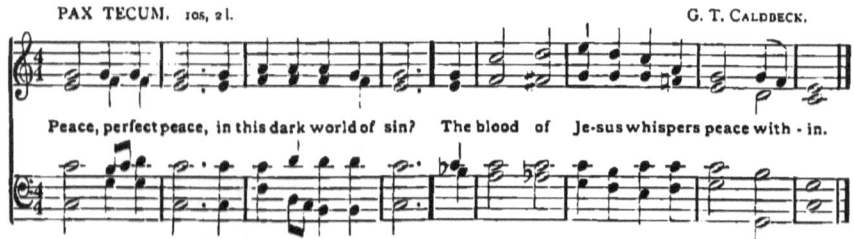

Peace, perfect peace, in this dark world of sin? The blood of Je-sus whispers peace with-in.

400 *"Peace, perfect peace."*

Peace, perfect peace, in this dark world of sin?
The blood of Jesus whispers peace within.

2 Peace, perfect peace, by thronging duties pressed?
To do the will of Jesus, this is rest.

3 Peace, perfect peace, with sorrows surging round?
On Jesus' bosom naught but calm is found.

4 Peace, perfect peace, with loved ones far away?
In Jesus' keeping we are safe and they.

5 Peace, perfect peace, our future all unknown?
Jesus we know, and he is on the throne.

6 Peace, perfect peace, death shadowing us and ours?
Jesus has vanquished death and all its powers.

7 It is enough: earth's struggles soon shall cease,
And Jesus call us to heaven's perfect peace.

E. H. Bickersteth.

LOVE, AND COMMUNION WITH CHRIST.

FEDERAL STREET. L. M.   H. K. OLIVER.

401   *"Ashamed of me."*

JESUS! and shall it ever be,
  A mortal man ashamed of thee?
Ashamed of thee, whom angels praise,
  Whose glories shine through endless days?

2 Ashamed of Jesus! sooner far
  Let evening blush to own a star;
He sheds the beams of light divine
  O'er this benighted soul of mine.

3 Ashamed of Jesus! that dear Friend
  On whom my hopes of heaven depend!
No; when I blush, be this my shame,
  That I no more revere his name.

4 Ashamed of Jesus! yes, I may,
  When I've no guilt to wash away;
No tear to wipe, no good to crave,
  No fears to quell, no soul to save.

5 Till then—nor is my boasting vain—
  Till then, I boast a Saviour slain!
And, oh, may this my glory be
  That Christ is not ashamed of me!
                     Joseph Grigg.

402   *Jesus all in all.*

JESUS, thou Joy of loving hearts,
  Thou Fount of life! thou Light of men!
From the best bliss that earth imparts,
  We turn unfilled to thee again.

2 Thy truth unchanged hath ever stood;
  Thou savest those that on thee call;
To them that seek thee thou art good,
  To them that find thee, All in All.

3 We taste thee, O thou Living Bread,
  And long to feast upon thee still;
We drink of thee, the Fountain Head,
  And thirst our souls from thee to fill!

4 Our restless spirits yearn for thee,
  Where'er our changeful lot is cast;
Glad, when thy gracious smile we see,
  Blest, when our faith can hold thee fast.

5 O Jesus, ever with us stay;
  Make all our moments calm and bright;
Chase the dark night of sin away,
  Shed o'er the world thy holy light!
                     Ray Palmer, tr.

403   *"Not your own."*

OH, not my own these verdant hills,
  And fruits and flowers, and stream, and wood;
But his who all with glory fills,
  Who bought me with his precious blood.

2 Oh, not my own this wondrous frame,
  Its curious work, its living soul;
But his who for my ransom came;
  Slain for my sake, he claims the whole.

3 Oh, not my own the grace that keeps
  My feet from fierce temptations free;
Oh, not my own the thought that leaps,
  Adoring, blessèd Lord, to thee.

4 Oh, not my own; I'll soar and sing,
  When life, with all its toils, is o'er,
And thou thy trembling lamb shalt bring
  Safe home, to wander nevermore.
                     Samuel F. Smith.

CANONBURY. L. M.   Arr. fr SCHUMANN.

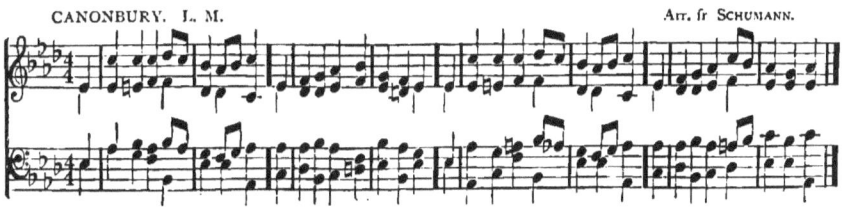

CHRISTIAN EXPERIENCE.

MELODY. C. M.   A. CHAPIN.

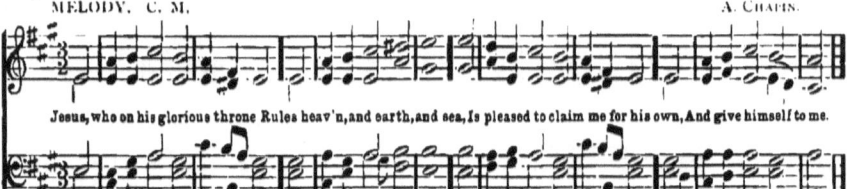

Jesus, who on his glorious throne Rules heav'n, and earth, and sea, Is pleased to claim me for his own, And give himself to me.

404   *"To live is Christ."*
JESUS, who on his glorious throne
  Rules heaven, and earth, and sea,
Is pleased to claim me for his own,
  And give himself to me.

2 His person fixes all my love,
  His blood removes my fear;
And while he pleads for me above,
  His arm preserves me here.

3 His word of promise is my food,
  His Spirit is my guide;
Thus daily is my strength renewed,
  And all my wants supplied.

4 For him I count as gain each loss,
  Disgrace for him renown;
Well may I glory in my cross,
  While he prepares my crown.
                    John Newton.

ST. AGNES. C. M.   J. B. DYKES.

Dear Refuge of my wea-ry soul, On thee, when sorrows rise, On thee, when waves of trouble roll, My fainting hope re-lies.

405   *Strength, Fortress, Refuge.*
DEAR Refuge of my weary soul,
  On thee, when sorrows rise,
On thee, when waves of trouble roll,
  My fainting hope relies.

2 To thee I tell each rising grief,
  For thou alone canst heal;
Thy word can bring a sweet relief
  For every pain I feel.

3 But, oh, when gloomy doubts prevail,
  I fear to call thee mine;
The springs of comfort seem to fail,
  And all my hopes decline.

4 Yet, gracious God, where shall I flee?
  Thou art my only trust;
And still my soul would cleave to thee,
  Though prostrate in the dust.

5 Thy mercy-seat is open still,
  Here let my soul retreat,
With humble hope attend thy will,
  And wait beneath thy feet.
                    Anne Steele.

406   *"Whom unseen, we love."*
JESUS, these eyes have never seen
  That radiant form of thine!
The vail of sense hangs dark between
  Thy blessed face and mine!

2 I see thee not, I hear thee not,
  Yet art thou oft with me;
And earth has ne'er so dear a spot,
  As where I meet with thee.

3 Like some bright dream that comes un-
  When slumbers o'er me roll,   [sought,
Thine image ever fills my thought,
  And charms my ravished soul.

4 Yet though I have not seen, and still
  Must rest in faith alone;
I love thee, dearest Lord!—and will,
  Unseen, but not unknown.

5 When death these mortal eyes shall seal,
  And still this throbbing heart,
The rending vail shall thee reveal,
  All glorious as thou art!
                    Ray Palmer.

LOVE, AND COMMUNION WITH CHRIST.

SPITTA. 7s, 6s. D.   H. P. DANKS.

407 *Never separated.*

I KNOW no life divided,
  O Lord of life, from thee;
In thee is life provided
  For all mankind and me:
I know no death, O Jesus,
  Because I live in thee;
Thy death it is that frees us
  From death eternally.

2 I fear no tribulation,
  Since, whatsoe'er it be,
It makes no separation
  Between my Lord and me.
If thou, my God and Teacher,
  Vouchsafe to be my own,
Though poor, I shall be richer
  Than monarch on his throne.

3 If, while on earth I wander,
  My heart is right and blest,
Ah, what shall I be yonder,
  In perfect peace and rest?
Oh, blessèd thought! in dying
  We go to meet the Lord,
Where there shall be no sighing,
  A kingdom our reward.

Richard Massie, tr.

408 *"The world's true Light."*

O ONE with God the Father
  In majesty and might,
The brightness of his glory,
  Eternal Light of light;
O'er this our home of darkness
  Thy rays are streaming now;
The shadows flee before thee,
  The world's true Light art thou.

2 Yet, Lord, we see but darkly:—
  O heavenly Light, arise,
Dispel these mists that shroud us,
  And hide thee from our eyes!
We long to track the footprints
  That thou thyself hast trod;
We long to see the pathway
  That leads to thee our God.

3 O Jesus, shine around us
  With radiance of thy grace;
O Jesus, turn upon us
  The brightness of thy face.
We need no star to guide us,
  As on our way we press,
If thou thy light vouchsafest,
  O Sun of righteousness!

William H. How.

CHRISTIAN EXPERIENCE.

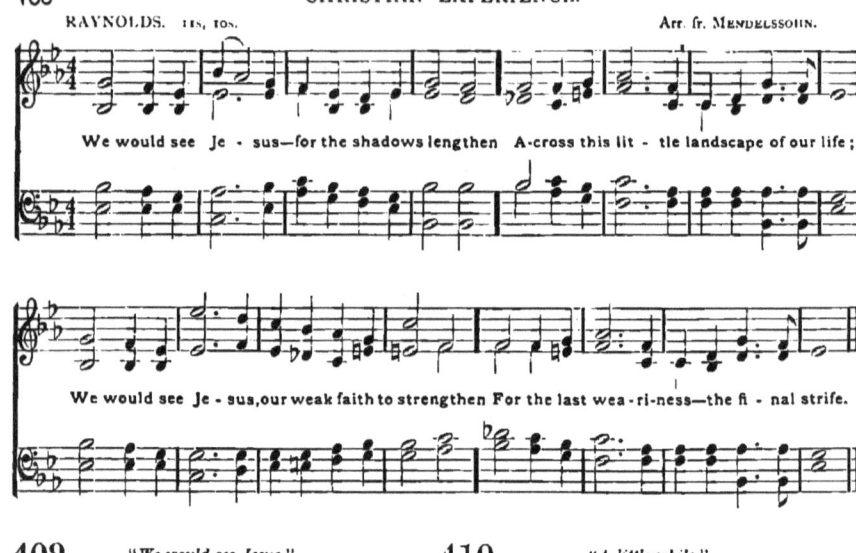

409   *"We would see Jesus."*

WE would see Jesus—for the shadows lengthen
  Across this little landscape of our life;
We would see Jesus, our weak faith to strengthen
  For the last weariness—the final strife.

2 We would see Jesus—the great Rock Foundation,
  Whereon our feet were set with sovereign grace;
Not life, nor death, with all their agitation,
  Can thence remove us, if we see his face.

3 We would see Jesus—other lights are paling,
  Which for long years we have rejoiced to see;
The blessings of our pilgrimage are failing,
  We would not mourn them, for we go to thee.

4 We would see Jesus—this is all we're needing,
  Strength, joy, and willingness come with the sight;
We would see Jesus, dying, risen, pleading,
  Then welcome day, and farewell mortal night!
                                          Anon., 1858.

410   *"A little while."*

Oh, for the peace which floweth like a river,
  Making life's desert places bloom and smile!
Oh, for the faith to grasp heaven's bright "for ever,"
  Amid the shadows of earth's "little while!"

2 A little while for patient vigil-keeping,
  To face the storm, to battle with the strong;
A little while to sow the seed with weeping,
  Then bind the sheaves and sing the harvest song!

3 A little while to keep the oil from failing,
  A little while faith's flickering lamp to trim;
And then, the Bridegroom's coming footsteps hailing,
  To haste to meet him with the bridal hymn!

4 And he who is himself the gift and giver,—
  The future glory and the present smile,—
With the bright promise of the glad "for ever"
  Will light the shadows of the "little while!"
                                Mrs. Jane Crewdson.

LOVE, AND COMMUNION WITH CHRIST.

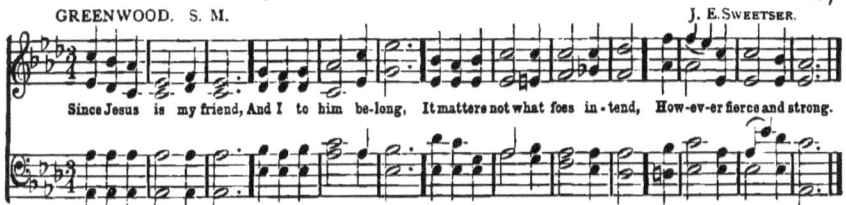

411 *"Jesus is my friend."*
Since Jesus is my friend,
  And I to him belong,
It matters not what foes intend,
  However fierce and strong.

2 He whispers in my breast
  Sweet words of holy cheer,
How they who seek in God their rest
  Shall ever find him near;—

3 How God hath built above
  A city fair and new,
Where eye and heart shall see and prove
  What faith has counted true.

4 My heart for gladness springs;
  It cannot more be sad;
For very joy it smiles and sings,—
  Sees naught but sunshine glad.

5 The sun that lights mine eyes
  Is Christ, the Lord I love;
I sing for joy of that which lies
  Stored up for me above.
C. Winkworth, tr.

412 *Unseen, we love.*
Not with our mortal eyes
  Have we beheld the Lord;
Yet we rejoice to hear his name;
  And love him in his word.

2 On earth we want the sight
  Of our Redeemer's face;
Yet, Lord, our inmost thoughts delight
  To dwell upon thy grace.

3 And when we taste thy love,
  Our joys divinely grow
Unspeakable, like those above,
  And heaven begins below.
Isaac Watts.

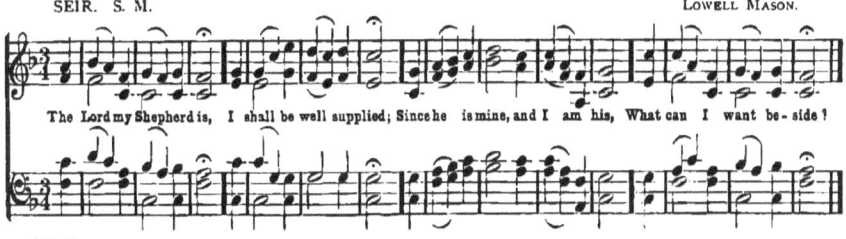

413 *Psalm 23.*
The Lord my Shepherd is,
  I shall be well supplied;
Since he is mine, and I am his,
  What can I want beside?

2 He leads me to the place
  Where heavenly pasture grows,
Where living waters gently pass,
  And full salvation flows.

3 If e'er I go astray,
  He doth my soul reclaim;
And guide me in his own right way,
  For his most holy name.

4 While he affords his aid,
  I cannot yield to fear;
Tho' I should walk thro' death's dark shade,
  My Shepherd's with me there.

5 In spite of all my foes,
  Thou dost my table spread;
My cup with blessings overflows,
  And joy exalts my head.

6 The bounties of thy love
  Shall crown my future days;
Nor from thy house will I remove,
  Nor cease to speak thy praise.
Isaac Watts.

CHRISTIAN EXPERIENCE.

414 *All for Jesus.*
WHAT can I give to Jesus,
Who gave himself for me?
How can I show my love to him
Who died on Calvary?
Myself I give to Jesus,
Who gave himself for me:
Thus will I show my love to him
Who died on Calvary.

2 I give my life to Jesus,
My strength and health and all;
Assured he'll be my constant Friend,
Whatever may befall.
This will I give to Jesus, etc.

3 Thy Spirit give, Lord Jesus,
To strengthen me for this;
That I may have thy loving smile,
And share thine endless bliss.
Then shall I give to Jesus
A song more sweet, more free;
And ever show my love to him
Who died on Calvary. *J. Jacobs.*

415 *"Brother, King!"*
FRIEND of sinners! Lord of glory!
Lowly, mighty! Brother, King!
Musing o'er thy wondrous story,
Fain would I thy praises sing.

2 Friend to help us, comfort, save us,
In whom power and pity blend,
Praise we must the grace which gave us
Jesus Christ, the sinner's Friend.

3 Oh, to love and serve thee better!
From all evil set us free;
Break, Lord, every sinful fetter,
Be each thought conformed to thee.
Newman Hall.

LOVE, AND COMMUNION WITH CHRIST.

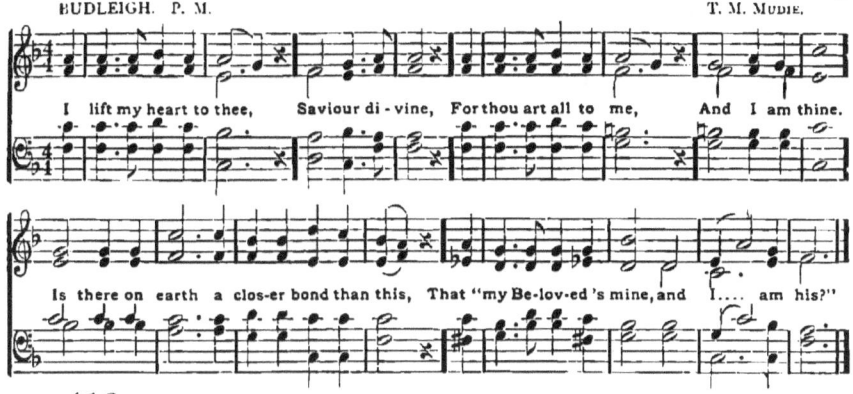

BUDLEIGH. P. M.   T. M. MUDIE.

I lift my heart to thee, Saviour di-vine, For thou art all to me, And I am thine.
Is there on earth a clos-er bond than this, That "my Be-lov-ed's mine, and I.... am his?"

416 "*My Beloved.*"
I LIFT my heart to thee,
  Saviour divine!
For thou art all to me,
  And I am thine.
Is there on earth a closer bond than this,
That "my Beloved's mine, and I am his?"

2 Thine am I by all ties;
  But chiefly thine,
That through thy sacrifice,
  Thou, Lord, art mine.
By thine own cords of love, so sweetly wound
Around me, I to thee am closely bound.

3 To thee, thou bleeding Lamb,
  I all things owe;
All that I have and am,
  And all I know.
All that I have is now no longer mine,
And I am not mine own; Lord, I am thine.

4 How can I, Lord, withhold
  Life's brightest hour
From thee; or gathered gold,
  Or any power?   [thee,
Why should I keep one precious thing from
When thou hast given thine own dear self
  for me?
                                 C. E. Mudie.

PENKIVELL. 6s, 5s.   H. G. TREMBATH.

Christian, work for Jesus, Who on earth for thee Labored, wearied, suffered,—Died up-on the tree.

417 "*Work for Jesus.*"
CHRISTIAN, work for Jesus,
  Who on earth for thee
Labored, wearied, suffered,—
  Died upon the tree.

2 Work with lips so fervid
  That thy words may prove
Thou hast brought a message
  From the God of love.

3 Work with heart that burneth,
  Humbly at his feet

Priceless gems to offer,
  For his crown made meet.

4 Work with prayer unceasing,
  Borne on faith's strong wing,
Earnestly beseeching
  Trophies for the King.

5 Work while strength endureth,
  Until death draw near;
Then thy Lord's sweet welcome
  Thou in heaven shalt hear.
                     M. Haslock.

CHRISTIAN EXPERIENCE.

418 *Faith.*

'T is by the faith of joys to come,
  We walk through deserts dark as night;
Till we arrive at heaven, our home,
  Faith is our guide, and faith our light.

2 The want of sight she well supplies;
  She makes the pearly gates appear;
Far into distant worlds she pries,
  And brings eternal glories near.

3 Cheerful we tread the desert through,
  While faith inspires a heavenly ray;
Though lions roar, and tempests blow,
  And rocks and dangers fill the way.
                              Isaac Watts.

419 *Faith.*

By faith in Christ I walk with God,
  With heaven, my journey's end, in view;
Supported by his staff and rod,
  My road is safe and pleasant too.

2 Though snares and dangers throng my path,
  And earth and hell my course withstand,
I triumph over all by faith,
  Guarded by his almighty hand.

3 The wilderness affords no food,
  But God for my support prepares,
Provides me every needful good,
  And frees my soul from wants and cares.

4 With him sweet converse I maintain;
  Great as he is, I dare be free;
I tell him all my grief and pain,
  And he reveals his love to me.
                              John Newton.

420 *Contentment.*

O LORD, how full of sweet content
  Our years of pilgrimage are spent!
Where'er we dwell, we dwell with thee,
  In heaven, in earth, or on the sea.

2 To us remains nor place nor time:
  Our country is in every clime:
We can be calm and free from care
  On any shore, since God is there.

3 While place we seek, or place we shun,
  The soul finds happiness in none;
But with our God to guide our way,
  'T is equal joy to go or stay.

4 Could we be cast where thou art not,
  That were indeed a dreadful lot;
But regions none remote we call,
  Secure of finding God in all.
                              William Cowper, tr.

421 *Consistency.*

So LET our lips and lives express
  The holy gospel we profess;
So let our works and virtues shine,
  To prove the doctrine all divine.

2 Thus shall we best proclaim abroad
  The honors of our Saviour God;
When his salvation reigns within,
  And grace subdues the power of sin.

3 Religion bears our spirits up,
  While we expect that blessèd hope,—
The bright appearance of the Lord:
  And faith stands leaning on his word.
                              Isaac Watts.

GRACES OF THE SPIRIT.

VALENTIA. C. M.   Arr. by Geo. Kingsley.

Oh, gift of gifts! oh, grace of faith! My God! how can it be
That thou, who hast discerning love, Shouldst give that gift to me?

422   *Faith.*
Oh, gift of gifts! oh, grace of faith!
  My God! how can it be
That thou, who hast descerning love,
  Shouldst give that gift to me?

2 How many hearts thou mightst have had
  More innocent than mine!
How many souls more worthy far
  Of that sweet touch of thine!

3 Ah, grace! into unlikeliest hearts
  It is thy boast to come,
The glory of thy light to find
  In darkest spots a home.

4 The crowd of cares, the weightiest cross,
  Seem trifles less than light—
Earth looks so little and so low
  When faith shines full and bright.

5 Oh, happy, happy that I am!
  If thou canst be, O Faith,
The treasure that thou art in life,
  What wilt thou be in death!
              Frederick W. Faber.

423   *Godly sincerity.*
Walk in the light! so shalt thou know
  That fellowship of love,
His Spirit only can bestow,
  Who reigns in light above.

2 Walk in the light! and thou shalt find
  Thy heart made truly his,
Who dwells in cloudless light enshrined,
  In whom no darkness is.

3 Walk in the light! and ev'n the tomb
  No fearful shade shall wear;
Glory shall chase away its gloom,
  For Christ hath conquered there.

4 Walk in the light! and thou shalt see
  Thy path, though thorny, bright,
For God by grace shall dwell in thee,
  And God himself is light.
              Bernard Barton.

424   *Faith.*
Faith adds new charms to earthly bliss
  And saves me from its snares;
Its aid, in every duty, brings,
  And softens all my cares.

2 The wounded conscience knows its power
  The healing balm to give;
That balm the saddest heart can cheer;
  And make the dying live.

3 Wide it unvails celestial worlds,
  Where deathless pleasures reign;
And bids me seek my portion there,
  Nor bids me seek in vain.

4 It shows the precious promise sealed
  With the Redeemer's blood;
And helps my feeble hope to rest
  Upon a faithful God.

5 There—there unshaken would I rest,
  Till this frail body dies;
And then, on faith's triumphant wings,
  To endless glory rise.
              Daniel Turner.

CHRISTIAN EXPERIENCE.

ROSEFIELD. 7s, 6l.   C. MALAN.

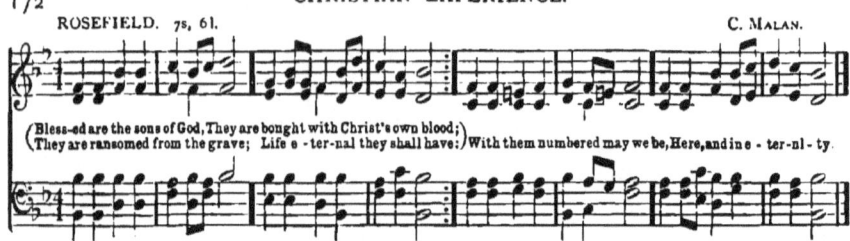

(Bless-ed are the sons of God, They are bought with Christ's own blood;)
(They are ransomed from the grave; Life e-ter-nal they shall have:) With them numbered may we be, Here, and in e-ter-ni-ty.

425   *Brotherly Love.*
BLESSED are the sons of God,
They are bought with Christ's own blood;
They are ransomed from the grave;
Life eternal they shall have:
With them numbered may we be,
Here, and in eternity.

2 They are justified by grace,
They enjoy the Saviour's peace;
All their sins are washed away;
They shall stand in God's great day:
With them numbered may we be,
Here, and in eternity.

3 They are lights upon the earth,
Children of a heavenly birth,—
One with God, with Jesus one:
Glory is in them begun:
With them numbered may we be,
Here, and in eternity.
                       Joseph Humphreys.

426   *Psalm 23.*
SHEPHERD! with thy tenderest love,
Guide me to thy fold above;
Let me hear thy gentle voice;
More and more in thee rejoice;
From thy fullness grace receive,
Ever in thy Spirit live.

2 Filled by thee my cup o'erflows,
For thy love no limit knows:
Guardian angels, ever nigh,
Lead and draw my soul on high;
Constant to my latest end,
Thou my footsteps wilt attend.

3 Jesus, with thy presence blest,
Death is life, and labor rest;
Guide me while I draw my breath,
Guard me through the gate of death;
And at last, oh, let me stand,
With the sheep at thy right hand.
                       Anon., 1805.

GUIDE. 7s, 6l.   M. M. WELLS.

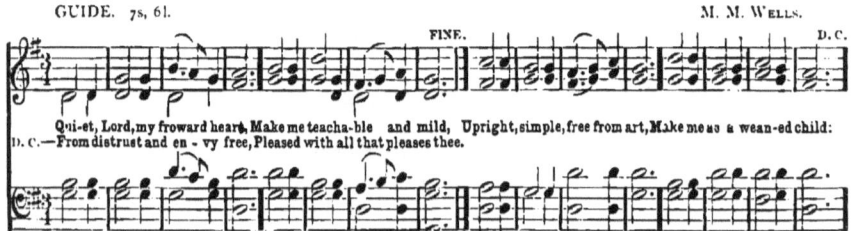

Qui-et, Lord, my froward heart, Make me teacha-ble and mild, Upright, simple, free from art, Make me as a wean-ed child:
D. C.—From distrust and en-vy free, Pleased with all that pleases thee.

427   *Psalm 131.*
QUIET, Lord, my froward heart,
   Make me teachable and mild,
Upright, simple, free from art,
   Make me as a weaned child:
From distrust and envy free,
Pleased with all that pleases thee.

2 What thou shalt to-day provide,
   Let me as a child receive;
What to-morrow may betide,
   Calmly to thy wisdom leave:
'T is enough that thou wilt care;
Why should I the burden bear?

3 As a little child relies
   On a care beyond his own,
Knows he's neither strong nor wise,
   Fears to stir a step alone;—
Let me thus with thee abide,
As my Father, Guard, and Guide.
                       John Newton.

GRACES OF THE SPIRIT.

HERSTMONCEUX. P. M. E. PROUT.

Come thou, oh, come: Sweetest and kindliest, Giver of tranquil rest.. Unto the weary soul; In all anxiety With power from heaven on high Console.

428 *Guidance and Growth.*

Come thou, oh, come:
Sweetest and kindliest,
Giver of tranquil rest
Unto the weary soul;
In all anxiety
With power from heaven on high
   Console.

2 Come thou, oh, come:
Help in the hour of need,
Strength of the broken reed,
Guide of each lonely one;
Orphans' and widows' stay,
Who tread in life's hard way
   Alone.

3 Come thou, oh, come:
Glorious and shadow-free,
Star of the stormy sea,
Light of the tempest-tost;
Harbor our souls to save
When hope upon the wave
   Is lost.

4 Come thou, oh, come:
Joy in life's narrow path,
Hope in the hour of death,
Come, Blessed Spirit, come;
Lead thou us tenderly,
Till we shall find with thee
   Our home.
                G. Moultrie, tr.

HALLE. 7s, 6 l. Arr. by T. HASTINGS.

For the beauty of the earth, For the glory of the skies, For the love which from our birth Over and around us lies: Lord of all, to thee we raise This our grateful psalm of praise.

429 *Gratitude.*

For the beauty of the earth,
  For the glory of the skies,
For the love which from our birth
  Over and around us lies:
Lord of all, to thee we raise
This our grateful psalm of praise.

2 For the joy of human love,
  Brother, sister, parent, child;
Friends on earth, and friends above,
  Pleasures pure and undefiled;
Lord of all, to thee we raise
This our grateful psalm of praise.

3 For thy church that evermore
  Lifts her holy hands above,
Offering up on every shore
  Her pure sacrifice of love;
Lord of all, to thee we raise
This our grateful psalm of praise.
            Folliott S. Pierpoint.

CHRISTIAN EXPERIENCE.

SECURITY. P. M.   English melody.

430   *"The burden rolled away."*

I LEFT it all with Jesus long ago,
All my sins I brought him and my woe;
When by faith I saw him on the tree,
Heard his small, still whisper, "'T is for thee."
From my heart the burden rolled away!
    Happy day.

2 I leave it all with Jesus, for he knows
How to steal the bitter from life's woes;
How to gild the tear-drop with his smile,
Make the desert garden bloom awhile:
When my weakness leaneth on his might,
    All seems light.

3 I leave it all with Jesus day by day;
Faith can firmly trust him, come what may.
Hope has dropped her anchor, found her rest,
In the calm sure haven of his breast;
Love esteems it heaven to abide
    At his side.   *Ellen H. Willis.*

TRUST. P. M.   R. P. STEWART.

431   *"Full Salvation."*

I AM trusting thee, Lord Jesus,
    Trusting only thee!
Trusting thee for full salvation,
    Great and free.

2 I am trusting thee for pardon,
    At thy feet I bow;
For thy grace and tender mercy,
    Trusting now.

3 I am trusting thee for cleansing
    In the crimson flood;
Trusting thee to make me holy
    By thy blood.

4 I am trusting thee to guide me;
    Thou alone shalt lead,
Every day and hour supplying
    All my need.

5 I am trusting thee for power,
    Thine can never fail;
Words which thou thyself shalt give me
    Must prevail.

6 I am trusting thee, Lord Jesus;
    Never let me fall;
I am trusting thee for ever,
    And for all.   *Frances R. Havergal.*

PRIVILEGES OF BELIEVERS.

CYPRUS. 7s.   Arr. fr. MENDELSSOHN.

Day by day the man-na fell: Oh, to learn this les-son well!
Still by con-stant mer-cy fed, Give me, Lord, my dai-ly bread.

432 *"Day by day our daily bread."*
DAY by day the manna fell:
Oh, to learn this lesson well!
Still by constant mercy fed,
Give me, Lord, my daily bread.

2 Lord, my times are in thy hand;
All my sanguine hopes have planned,
To thy wisdom I resign,
And would make thy purpose mine.

3 Thou my daily task shalt give:
Day by day to thee I live:
So shall added years fulfil,
Not mine own—my Father's will.

4 Fond ambition, whisper not;
Happy is my humble lot.
Anxious, busy cares, away!
I'm provided for to-day.

5 Oh, to live exempt from care
By the energy of prayer;
Strong in faith, with mind subdued,
Yet elate with gratitude!
J. Conder.

433 *"The Shadow of a Great Rock."*
SHADOW of a Mighty Rock,
  Stretching o'er a weary land,
Hide me from the tempest's shock,
  Let me in thy shelter stand.

2 When thy Presence, O my God,
  Brighter is than I can see,
Shadow on the heavenward road,
  Let me find my shade in thee.

3 Out of thee are shades of death,
  Weary ways, and hours unblest;
Shadow of the Rock, beneath
  Thee alone are joy and rest.

4 Till the race of life be run,
  Till my soul in rest be laid,
God of gods, thou art my Sun;
  Son of God, be thou my Shade!
J. S. B. Monsell.

434 *"Hallowed be thy name."*
HOLY, holy, holy Lord,
In the highest heavens adored,
Author of all nature's frame,
Father! hallowed be thy name.

2 Though estranged from thee in heart,
Doubtless thou our Father art:
From thy hand our spirits came:
Father! hallowed be thy name.

3 Nor by nature's tie alone
Thou art as our Father known:
Nearer now, in Christ, our claim:
Father! hallowed be thy name.

4 Born anew, oh, may we feel
Filial love, the Spirit's seal;
Cleansed from guilt, redeemed from shame:
Father! hallowed be thy name.

5 Whether, then, in want or wealth,
Joy or sorrow, pain or health,
Still our prayer shall be the same:
Father! hallowed be thy name.
J. Conder.

CHRISTIAN EXPERIENCE.

LUTHER. S. M. — THOMAS HASTINGS.

Grace! 'tis a charming sound! Harmonious to mine ear! Heav'n with the ech-o shall re-sound, And all the earth shall hear, And all the earth shall hear.

435 *Grace.*

GRACE! 'tis a charming sound!
Harmonious to mine ear!
Heaven with the echo shall resound,
And all the earth shall hear.

2 Grace first contrived a way
To save rebellious man;
And all the steps that grace display,
Which drew the wondrous plan.

3 Grace led my roving feet
To tread the heavenly road;
And new supplies each hour I meet
While pressing on to God.

4 Grace all the work shall crown,
Through everlasting days;
It lays in heaven the topmost stone,
And well deserves the praise.
Philip Doddridge.

436 *God our Father.*

HERE I can firmly rest;
I dare to boast of this,
That God, the highest and the best,
My Friend and Father is.

2 Naught have I of my own,
Naught in the life I lead;
What Christ hath given, that alone
I dare in faith to plead.

3 I rest upon the ground
Of Jesus and his blood;
It is through him that I have found
My soul's eternal good.

4 At cost of all I have,
At cost of life and limb,
I cling to God who yet shall save;
I will not turn from him.

5 His Spirit in me dwells,
O'er all my mind he reigns;
My care and sadness he dispels,
And soothes away my pains.

6 He prospers day by day
His work within my heart,
Till I have strength and faith to say,
"Thou, God, my Father art!"
C. Winkworth, tr.

437 *"It is well."*

WHAT cheering words are these;
Their sweetness who can tell?
In time, and to eternal days,
"'Tis with the righteous well!"

2 Well when they see his face,
Or sink amidst the flood;
Well in affliction's thorny maze,
Or on the mount with God.

3 'Tis well when joys arise,
'Tis well when sorrows flow,
'Tis well when darkness vails the skies,
And strong temptations grow.

4 'Tis well when Jesus calls,—
"From earth and sin arise,
To join the hosts of ransomed souls,
Made to salvation wise!"
John Kent.

PRIVILEGES OF BELIEVERS.

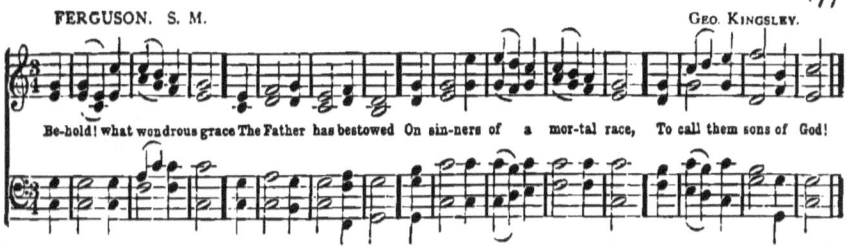

438 *Adoption.*
BEHOLD! what wondrous grace
 The Father has bestowed
On sinners of a mortal race,
 To call them sons of God!

2 Nor doth it yet appear
 How great we must be made;
But when we see our Saviour here,
 We shall be like our Head.

3 A hope so much divine
 May trials well endure,
May purge our souls from sense and sin,
 As Christ the Lord is pure.

4 If in my Father's love
 I share a filial part,
Send down thy Spirit, like a dove,
 To rest upon my heart.

5 We would no longer lie
 Like slaves beneath the throne;
Our faith shall Abba, Father! cry,
 And thou the kindred own.
Isaac Watts.

439 *Peace.*
THOU very present Aid
 In suffering and distress,
The mind which still on thee is stayed,
 Is kept in perfect peace.

2 The soul by faith reclined
 On the Redeemer's breast,
'Mid raging storms, exults to find
 An everlasting rest.

3 Sorrow and fear are gone,
 Whene'er thy face appears;
It stills the sighing orphan's moan,
 And dries the widow's tears.

4 Jesus, to whom I fly,
 Doth all my wishes fill;
What though created streams are dry?
 I have the fountain still.

5 Stripped of each earthly friend,
 I find them all in One,
And peace and joy which never end,
 And heaven, in Christ, alone.
Charles Wesley.

CHRISTIAN EXPERIENCE.

ST. GEORGE'S, BOLTON. 7s, 6s. D.   J. WALCH.

From Sinai's cloud of darkness, The vivid lightnings play, They serve the God of vengeance, The Lord who shall repay. Each fault must bring its penance, Each sin th' avenging blade; For God upholds in justice The laws that he hath made.

440 *Sinai and Calvary.*

FROM Sinai's cloud of darkness
　The vivid lightnings play,
They serve the God of vengeance,
　The Lord who shall repay.
Each fault must bring its penance,
　Each sin the avenging blade;
For God upholds in justice
　The laws that he hath made.

2 But Calvary stands to ransom
　The earth from utter loss,
In shade than light more glorious,
　The shadow of the Cross.
To heal a sick world's trouble,
　To soothe its woe and pain,
On Calvary's sacred summit
　The Paschal Lamb was slain.

3 The boundless might of Heaven
　Its law in mercy furled,
As once the bow of promise
　O'erarched a drowning world.
The law said—As you keep me
　It shall be done to you.
But Calvary prays—Forgive them,
　They know not what they do.

4 Almighty God! direct us
　To keep thy perfect Law!
O blesséd Saviour, help us
　Nearer to thee to draw;
Let Sinai's thunders aid us
　To guard our feet from sin,
And Calvary's light inspire us
　The love of God to win.
　　　　　　　　John Hay.

441 *Security.*

O LAMB of God! still keep me
　Near to thy wounded side;
'T is only there in safety
　And peace I can abide!
What foes and snares surround me,
　What doubts and fears within!
The grace that sought and found me,
　Alone can keep me clean.

2 Soon shall my eyes behold thee,
　With rapture, face to face;
One half hath not been told me
　Of all thy power and grace:
Thy beauty, Lord, and glory,
　The wonders of thy love,
Shall be the endless story
　Of all the saints above.   *James G. Deck.*

PRIVILEGES OF BELIEVERS.

HE LEADETH ME. L. M. D.   W. B. BRADBURY.

He leadeth me! oh, blessed thought, Oh, words with heavenly comfort fraught! Whate'er I do, wher-e'er I be, Still 'tis God's hand that lead-eth me. He lead-eth me! he lead-eth me! By his own hand he leadeth me; His faithful follower I would be, For by his hand he lead-eth me.

442   *"He leadeth me."*
He leadeth me! oh, blesséd thought,
Oh, words with heavenly comfort fraught!
Whate'er I do, where'er I be,
Still 't is God's hand that leadeth me.—REF.

2 Sometimes 'mid scenes of deepest gloom,
Sometimes where Eden's bowers bloom,
By waters still, o'er troubled sea,—
Still 't is his hand that leadeth me!—REF.

3 Lord! I would clasp thy hand in mine,
Nor ever murmur nor repine;
Content whatever lot I see,
Since 't is my God that leadeth me.—REF.

4 And when my task on earth is done,
When by thy grace the victory's won,
Ev'n death's cold wave I will not flee,
Since God through Jordan leadeth me.—
                REF.
           J. H. Gilmore.

443   *Rest at Eventide.*
At even, when the sun was set,
  The sick, O Lord, around thee lay;

Oh, in what divers pains they met!
  Oh, with what joy they went away!
Once more, 't is eventide, and we
  Oppressed with various ills draw near:
What if thy form we cannot see?
  We know and feel that thou art here.

2 O Saviour Christ, our woes dispel;
  For some are sick, and some are sad,
And some have never loved thee well,
  And some have lost the love they had;
And none, O Lord, have perfect rest,
  For none are wholly free from sin;
And they who fain would serve thee best
  Are conscious most of wrong within.

3 O Saviour Christ, thou too art man;
  Thou hast been troubled, tempted, tried;
Thy kind but searching glance can scan
  The very wounds that shame would hide;
Thy touch has still its ancient power;
  No word from thee can fruitless fall;
Hear, in this solemn evening hour,
  And in thy mercy heal us all.
                H. Twells.

CHRISTIAN EXPERIENCE.

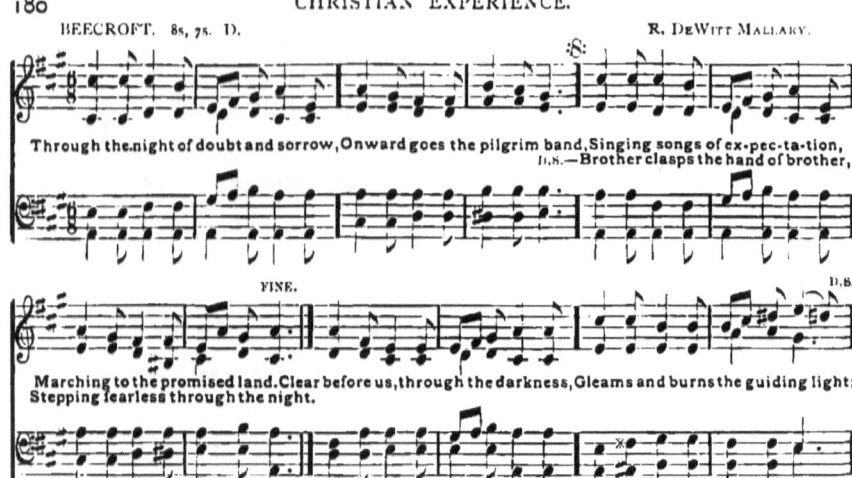

444 *The Church One.*

Through the night of doubt and sorrow,
 Onward goes the pilgrim band,
Singing songs of expectation,
 Marching to the promised land.
Clear before us, through the darkness,
 Gleams and burns the guiding light:
Brother clasps the hand of brother,
 Stepping fearless through the night.

2 One the light of God's own presence,
 O'er his ransomed people shed,
Chasing far the gloom and terror,
 Brightening all the path we tread:
One the object of our journey,
 One the faith which never tires,
One the earnest looking forward,
 One the hope our God inspires.

3 One the strain the lips of thousands
 Lift as from the heart of one;
One the conflict, one the peril,
 One the march in God begun:
One the gladness of rejoicing
 On the far eternal shore,
Where the one Almighty Father,
 Reigns in love for evermore.
                    S. Baring-Gould, tr.

PRIVILEGES OF BELIEVERS.

445 *"All is well!"*

I HEAR a sweet voice ringing clear,
　All is well!
It is my Father's voice I hear;
　All is well!
Where'er I walk that voice is heard:
It is my God, my Father's word,
"Fear not, but trust: I am the Lord:"
　All is well!

2 Clouds cannot long obscure my sight;
　All is well!
I know there is a land of light;
　All is well!
From strength to strength, from day to day,
I tread along the world's highway;
Or often stop to sing or say,
　All is well!

3 In morning hours, serene and bright,
　All is well!
In evening hours or darkening night
　All is well!
And when to Jordan's side I come,
'Midst chilling waves and raging foam,
Oh, let me sing as I go home,
　All is well!
　　　　　　　　E. Paxton Hood.

446 C. M. 6 l. *Tune—"Hallel."*

DISMISS me not thy service, Lord,
　But train me for thy will;
For even I, in fields so broad,
　Some duties may fulfill;
And I will ask for no reward,
　Except to serve thee still.

2 How many serve, how many more
　May to the service come!
To tend the vines, the grapes to store,
　Thou dost appoint for some:
Thou hast thy young men at the war,
　Thy little ones at home.

3 All works are good, and each is best
　As most it pleases thee;
Each worker pleases when the rest
　He serves in charity;
And neither man nor work unblest,
　Wilt thou permit to be.

4 Our Master all the work hath done
　He asks of us to-day;
Sharing his service, every one
　Share too his sonship may;
Lord, I would serve and be a son:
　Dismiss me not, I pray.
　　　　　　　　T. T. Lynch.

447   *"The new life."*

Hark, hark, my soul! angelic songs are swelling
O'er earth's green fields and ocean's wave-beat shore:
How sweet the truth those blessèd strains are telling
Of that new life when sin shall be no more.
Ref.—Angels of Jesus, angels of light,
Singing to welcome the pilgrims of the night.

2 Onward we go, for still we hear them singing,
Come, weary souls, for Jesus bids you come;
And through the dark, its echoes sweetly ringing,
The music of the gospel leads us home.—Ref.

3 Far, far away, like bells at evening pealing,
The voice of Jesus sounds o'er land and sea;
And laden souls, by thousands meekly stealing,
Kind Shepherd, turn their weary steps to thee.—Ref.

4 Angels, sing on, your faithful watches keeping,
Sing us sweet fragments of the songs above;
Till morning's joy shall end the night of weeping,
And life's long shadows break in cloudless love.—Ref.

Frederick W. Faber.

PRIVILEGES OF BELIEVERS.

SOLID ROCK. L. M. 6l.   W. B. Bradbury.

    On Christ the solid rock, I stand;
    All other ground is sinking sand.
2 When darkness seems to veil his face.
I rest on his unchanging grace;
In every high and stormy gale,
My anchor holds within the vail;
    On Christ, the solid rock, I stand;
    All other ground is sinking sand.

3 His oath, his covenant, and blood,
Support me in the whelming flood:
When all around my soul gives way,
He then is all my hope and stay:
    On Christ, the solid rock, I stand;
    All other ground is sinking sand.
                            F. Mote.

448   *In Christ alone.*
My hope is built on nothing less
Than Jesus' blood and righteousness;
I dare not trust the sweetest frame,
But wholly lean on Jesus' name:

PERRIN. C. P. M.   R. De Witt Mallary.

449   *Things working for Good.*
O Lord, how happy should we be,
  If we could cast our care on thee,
    If we from self could rest;
And feel at heart that One above,
In perfect wisdom, perfect love,
  Is working for the best.

2 How far from this our daily life!
Ever disturbed by anxious strife,
  By sudden, wild alarms;

Oh, could we but relinquish all
Our earthly props, and simply fall
  On thine almighty arms.

3 Lord, make these faithless hearts of ours
Thy lessons learn from birds and flowers,
  And from self-torment cease!
Father! we trust; and we lie still;
Leave all things to thy holy will,
  And so find perfect peace.
                         Joseph Anstice.

CHRISTIAN EXPERIENCE.

450 *"Not my will, but thine."*
My Jesus, as thou wilt!
 Oh, may thy will be mine;
Into thy hand of love
 I would my all resign;
Through sorrow, or through joy,
 Conduct me as thine own,
And help me still to say,
 My Lord, thy will be done!

2 My Jesus, as thou wilt!
 Though seen through many a tear,
Let not my star of hope
 Grow dim or disappear;
Since thou on earth hast wept,
 And sorrowed oft alone,
If I must weep with thee,
 My Lord, thy will be done!

3 My Jesus, as thou wilt!
 All shall be well for me;
Each changing future scene
 I gladly trust with thee:
Straight to my home above
 I travel calmly on,
And sing, in life or death,
 My Lord, thy will be done!
Jane Borthwick, tr.

451 *"He knoweth the way."*
Thy way, not mine, O Lord,
 However dark it be!
Lead me by thine own hand;
 Choose out my path for me.
I dare not choose my lot:
 I would not, if I might;
Choose thou for me, my God,
 So shall I walk aright.

2 The kingdom that I seek
 Is thine: so let the way
That leads to it be thine,
 Else I must surely stray.
Take thou my cup, and it
 With joy or sorrow fill,
As best to thee may seem;
 Choose thou my good and ill.

3 Choose thou for me my friends,
 My sickness or my health;
Choose thou my cares for me,
 My poverty or wealth.
Not mine, not mine the choice,
 In things or great or small;
Be thou my Guide, my Strength,
 My Wisdom and my All.
Horatius Bonar.

DISCIPLINE AND SORROW.

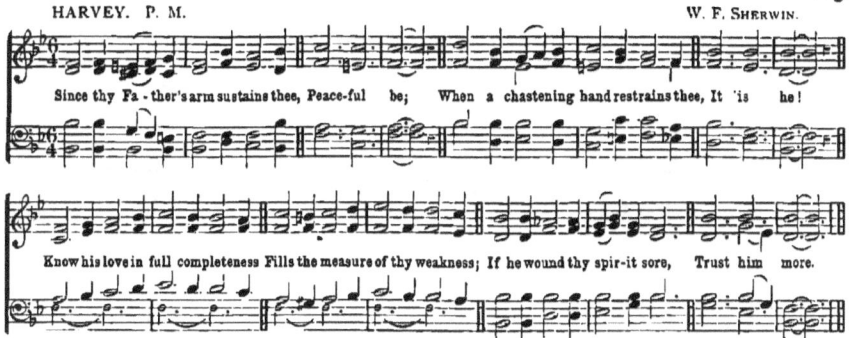

HARVEY. P. M.   W. F. SHERWIN.

Since thy Father's arm sustains thee, Peaceful be; When a chastening hand restrains thee, It is he! Know his love in full completeness Fills the measure of thy weakness; If he wound thy spirit sore, Trust him more.

452 *Resting in God.*

SINCE thy Father's arm sustains thee,
  Peaceful be;
When a chastening hand restrains thee,
  It is he!
Know his love in full completeness
Fills the measure of thy weakness;
If he wound thy spirit sore,
  Trust him more.

2 Without murmur, uncomplaining,
  In his hand
Lay whatever things thou canst not
  Understand:
Though the world thy folly spurneth,
From thy faith in pity turneth,
Peace thy inmost soul shall fill—
  Lying still.

3 Fearest sometimes that thy Father
  Hath forgot?
When the clouds around thee gather,
  Doubt him not!
Always hath the daylight broken—
Always hath he comfort spoken—
Better hath he been for years,
  Than thy fears.

4 To his own thy Saviour giveth
  Daily strength;
To each troubled soul that liveth
  Peace at length:
Weakest lambs have largest sharing
Of this tender Shepherd's caring;
Ask him not, then—when or how—
  Only bow.

                  Tr. fr. K. R. Hagenbach.

TRUST. C. M.   W. F. SHERWIN.

I cannot tell if short or long My earthly journey be; But, all the way, I know thy rod And staff will comfort me.

453 *A Hymn of Trust.*

I CANNOT tell if short or long
  My earthly journey be;
But, all the way, I know thy rod
  And staff will comfort me.

2 Though fierce temptations lie in wait,
  What need have I to care?
Thou wilt not suffer them to hurt
  Beyond my strength to bear.

3 What storms may beat, what burdens fall,
  My soul would not avoid;

Who follows thee, O Lord, may be
  Cast down, but not destroyed.

4 Though over steep and rugged ways
  My weary feet be brought,
Still following where thy footprints lead,
  I take no anxious thought.

5 Oh, perfect peace! oh, endless rest!
  No care, no vain alarms;
Beneath my every cross I find
  The Everlasting Arms.

                  Miss H. O. Knowlton.

CHRISTIAN EXPERIENCE.

454 *"Lead thou me on!"*

Lead, kindly Light! amid the encircling
  Lead thou me on;   [gloom,
The night is dark, and I am far from home,
  Lead thou me on;
Keep thou my feet; I do not ask to see
The distant scene; one step enough for me.

2 I was not ever thus, nor prayed that thou
    Shouldst lead me on;
I loved to choose and see my path; but now
    Lead thou me on:

I loved the garish day, and spite of fears,
Pride ruled my will. Remember not past
  years.

3 So long thy power has blessed me, sure
    Will lead me on   [it still
O'er moor and fen, o'er crag and torrent, till
    The night is gone;
And with the morn those angel faces smile
Which I have loved long since, and lost
    awhile!
                              John H. Newman.

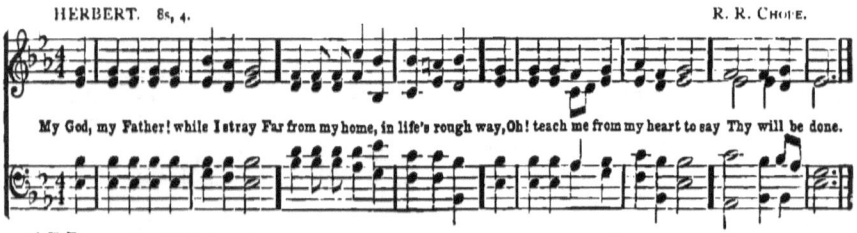

455 *"Thy will be done."*

My God, my Father! while I stray
Far from my home, in life's rough way,
Oh! teach me from my heart to say
    Thy will be done.

2 If thou couldst call me to resign
What most I prize—it ne'er was mine
I only yield thee what was thine;
    Thy will be done.

3 If but my fainting heart be blest
With thy sweet Spirit for its guest,

My God, to thee I leave the rest;—
    Thy will be done.

4 Renew my will from day to day,
Blend it with thine, and take away
All now that makes it hard to say,
    Thy will be done.

5 Then when on earth I breathe no more
The prayer oft mixed with tears before,
I'll sing upon a happier shore,
    Thy will be done.   *Charlotte Elliott.*

DISCIPLINE AND SORROW.

456 *Comfort.*

In the dark and cloudy day,
When earth's riches flee away,
And the last hope will not stay,
 Saviour, comfort me!

2 When the secret idol's gone
That my poor heart yearned upon,—
Desolate, bereft, alone,
 Saviour, comfort me!

3 Thou, who wast so sorely tried,
In the darkness crucified,
Bid me in thy love confide;
 Saviour, comfort me!

4 Comfort me; I am cast down.
'T is my heavenly Father's frown;
I deserve it all, I own:
 Saviour, comfort me!

5 So it shall be good for me
Much afflicted now to be,
If thou wilt but tenderly,
 Saviour, comfort me!
George Rawson.

457 *"For he careth."*

Cast thy burden on the Lord,
Only lean upon his word;
Thou wilt soon have cause to bless
His unchanging faithfulness.

2 He sustains thee by his hand,
He enables thee to stand;
Those, whom Jesus once hath loved,
From his grace are never moved.

3 Heaven and earth may pass away,
God's free grace shall not decay;
He hath promised to fulfill
All the pleasure of his will.

4 Jesus! guardian of thy flock,
Be thyself our constant rock;
Make us by thy powerful hand,
Firm as Zion's mountain stand.
William Hammond.

458 *Love seen in trials.*

'T is my happiness below
 Not to live without the cross,
But the Saviour's power to know,
 Sanctifying every loss.

2 Trials must and will befall;
 But with humble faith to see
Love inscribed upon them all,—
 This is happiness to me.

3 God in Israel sows the seeds
 Of affliction, pain and toil;
These spring up and choke the weeds
 Which would else o'erspread the soil.

4 Did I meet no trials here,
 No chastisement by the way,
Might I not with reason fear
 I should prove a castaway?

5 Trials make the promise sweet;
 Trials give new life to prayer;
Trials bring me to his feet,
 Lay me low, and keep me there.
William Cowper.

CHRISTIAN EXPERIENCE.

WIMBORNE. 8s, 7s.   Arr. fr. WHITAKER.

Like the ea-gle, up-ward, on-ward, Let my soul in faith be borne:
Calm-ly gaz-ing, sky-ward, sun-ward, Let my eye un-shrink-ing turn!

459   *Progress.*
LIKE the eagle, upward, onward,
  Let my soul in faith be borne:
Calmly gazing, skyward, sunward,
  Let my eye unshrinking turn!

2 Where the cross, God's love revealing,
  Sets the fettered spirit free,
Where it sheds its wondrous healing,
  There, my soul, thy rest shall be!

3 Oh, may I no longer, dreaming,
  Idly waste my golden day,
But, each precious hour redeeming,
  Upward, onward, press my way!
                      Horatius Bonar.

460   *"Leaving us an example."*
ONWARD, Christian, though the region
  Where thou art be drear and lone;
God has set a guardian legion
  Very near thee; press thou on.

2 By the thorn-road, and none other,
  Is the mount of vision won;
Tread it without shrinking, brother,
  Jesus trod it; press thou on.

3 Be this world the wiser, stronger,
  For thy life of pain and peace;
While it needs thee, oh, no longer
  Pray thou for thy quick release.

4 Pray thou, Christian, daily rather,
  That thou be a faithful son;
By the prayer of Jesus, "Father,
  Not my will, but thine, be done."
                     Samuel Johnson.

461   *Psalm 127.*
VAINLY, through night's weary hours,
  Keep we watch, lest foes alarm;
Vain our bulwarks, and our towers,
  But for God's protecting arm.

2 Vain were all our toil and labor,
  Did not God that labor bless;
Vain, without his grace and favor,
  Every talent we possess.

3 Vainer still the hope of heaven,
  That on human strength relies;
But to him shall help be given,
  Who in humble faith applies.

4 Seek we, then, the Lord's Anointed;
  He will grant us peace and rest:
Ne'er was suppliant disappointed,
  Who thro' Christ his prayer addressed.
                     Harriet Auber.

462   *Courage and Faith.*
FATHER, hear the prayer we offer!
  Not for ease that prayer shall be,
But for strength that we may ever
  Live our lives courageously.

2 Not for ever by still waters
  Would we idly quiet stay;
But would smite the living fountains
  From the rocks along our way.

3 Be our strength in hours of weakness,
  In our wanderings, be our guide;
Through endeavor, failure, danger,
  Father, be thou at our side!
                     Anon., 1804.

ACTIVITY AND ZEAL.

SOLNEY. 8s, 7s.   Arr. fr. Schulz.

Cast thy bread up-on the wa-ters, Think-ing not 'tis thrown a-way;
God him-self saith, thou shalt gath-er It a-gain some fu-ture day.

463 *Benevolent Efforts.*
Cast thy bread upon the waters,
 Thinking not 't is thrown away;
God himself saith, thou shalt gather
 It again some future day.

2 Cast thy bread upon the waters;
 Wildly though the billows roll,
They but aid thee as thou toilest
 Truth to spread from pole to pole.

3 As the seed, by billows floated,
 To some distant island lone,
So to human souls benighted,
 That thou flingest may be borne.

4 Cast thy bread upon the waters;
 Why wilt thou still doubting stand?
Bounteous shall God send the harvest,
 If thou sow'st with liberal hand.
 Mrs. P. A. Hanaford.

464 *"Not your own."*
Lord of glory! thou hast bought us,
 With thy life-blood as the price,
Never grudging, for the lost ones,
 That tremendous sacrifice.

2 Grant us hearts, dear Lord! to yield thee
 Gladly, freely, of thine own;
With the sunshine of thy goodness,
 Melt our thankless hearts of stone.

3 Wondrous honor hast thou given
 To our humblest charity,
In thine own mysterious sentence,—
 "Ye have done it unto me!"

4 Give us faith, to trust thee boldly,
 Hope, to stay our souls on thee:
But, oh,—best of all thy graces—
 Give us thine own charity.
 Mrs. E. S. Alderson.

STOCKWELL. 8s, 7s.   D. E. Jones.

He that goeth forth with weeping, Bearing precious seed in love, Never tiring, never sleeping, Findeth mercy from a-bove.

465 *Psalm 126: 6.*
He that goeth forth with weeping,
 Bearing precious seed in love,
Never tiring, never sleeping,
 Findeth mercy from above.

2 Soft descend the dews of heaven,
 Bright the rays celestial shine;
Precious fruits will thus be given,
 Through an influence all divine.

3 Sow thy seed, be never weary,
 Let no fears thy soul annoy;
Be the prospect ne'er so dreary,
 Thou shalt reap the fruits of joy.

4 Lo, the scene of verdure brightening!
 See the rising grain appear;
Look again! the fields are whitening,
 For the harvest time is near.
 Thomas Hastings.

CHRISTIAN EXPERIENCE.

REMSEN. C. M.   J. P. HOLBROOK.

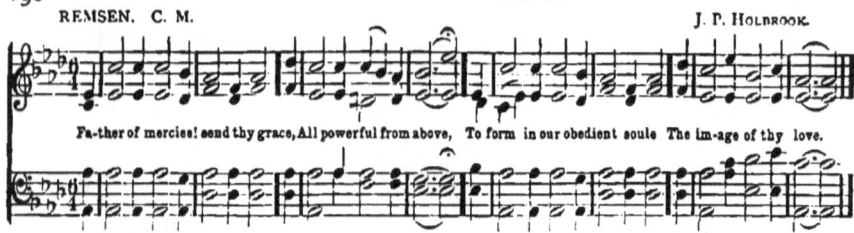

Father of mercies! send thy grace, All powerful from above, To form in our obedient souls The im-age of thy love.

466   *"So Jesus looked."*
FATHER of mercies! send thy grace,
  All powerful from above,
To form in our obedient souls
  The image of thy love.

2 Oh, may our sympathizing breasts
  The generous pleasure know,
Kindly to share in others' joy,
  And weep for others' woe!

3 When the most helpless sons of grief
  In low distress are laid,
Soft be our hearts their pains to feel,
  And swift our hands to aid.

4 So Jesus looked on dying men,
  When throned above the skies;
And 'mid the embraces of his God,
  He felt compassion rise.

5 On wings of love the Saviour flew,
  To raise us from the ground,
And made the richest of his blood
  A balm for every wound.
                          Philip Doddridge.

467   *God's hidden ones.*
LORD, lead the way the Saviour went,
  By lane and cell obscure,
And let love's treasures still be spent,
  Like his, upon the poor.

2 Like him, through scenes of deep distress,
  Who bore the world's sad weight,
We, in their crowded loneliness,
  Would seek the desolate.

3 For thou hast placed us side by side
  In this wide world of ill;
And that thy followers may be tried,
  The poor are with us still.

4 Mean are all offerings we can make;
  Yet thou hast taught us, Lord,
If given for the Saviour's sake,
  They lose not their reward.
                          William Crosswell.

468   *Minute fidelity.*
SCORN not the slightest word or deed,
  Nor deem it void of power;
There's fruit in each wind-wafted seed,
  That waits its natal hour.

2 A whispered word may touch the heart,
  And call it back to life;
A look of love bid sin depart,
  And still unholy strife.

3 No act falls fruitless; none can tell
  How vast its power may be,
Nor what results infolded dwell
  Within it silently.

4 Work on, despair not, bring thy mite,
  Nor care how small it be;
God is with all that serve the right,
  The holy, true, and free.
                          Anon., 1845.

469   *Psalm 41.*
BLEST is the man whose softening heart
  Feels all another's pain;
To whom the supplicating eye
  Was never raised in vain:—

2 Whose breast expands with generous
  A stranger's woes to feel;   [warmth
And bleeds in pity o'er the wound
  He wants the power to heal.

3 He spreads his kind supporting arms
  To every child of grief;
His secret bounty largely flows,
  And brings unasked relief.

4 To gentle offices of love
  His feet are never slow:
He views, through mercy's melting eye,
  A brother in a foe.

5 Peace from the bosom of his God,
  The Saviour's grace shall give;
And, when he kneels before the throne,
  His trembling soul shall live.
                          Mrs. A. L. Barbauld.

ACTIVITY AND ZEAL.

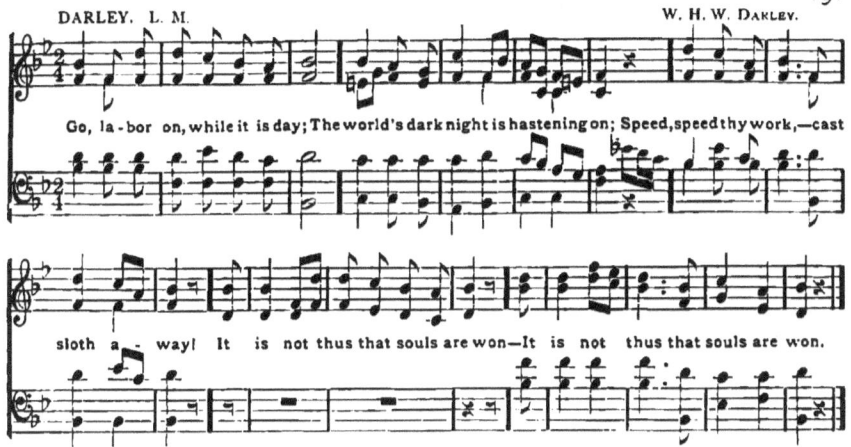

DARLEY. L. M.   W. H. W. Darley.

Go, la-bor on, while it is day; The world's dark night is hastening on; Speed, speed thy work,—cast sloth a-way! It is not thus that souls are won—It is not thus that souls are won.

470   *Zeal.*

Go, LABOR on, while it is day;
  The world's dark night is hastening on;
Speed, speed thy work,—cast sloth away!
  It is not thus that souls are won.

2 Men die in darkness at your side,
  Without a hope to cheer the tomb:
Take up the torch and wave it wide—
  The torch that lights time's thickest gloom.

3 Toil on,—faint not; keep watch and pray!
  Be wise the erring soul to win;
Go forth into the world's highway;
  Compel the wanderer to come in.

4 Go, labor on: your hands are weak;
  Your knees are faint, your soul cast down;
Yet falter not; the prize you seek
  Is near,—a kingdom and a crown!
              Horatius Bonar.

471   *Forbearance.*

OH, what stupendous mercy shines
  Around the majesty of heaven?
Rebels he deigns to call his sons—
  Their souls renewed, their sins forgiven.

2 Go, imitate the grace divine—
  The grace that blazes like the sun;
Hold forth your fair, though feeble light,
  Through all your lives let mercy run.

3 When all is done, renounce your deeds,
  Renounce self-righteousness with scorn:
Thus will you glorify your God,
  And thus the Christian name adorn.
              Thomas Gibbons.

472   *Faith and Works.*

ONE cup of healing oil and wine,
  One offering laid on mercy's shrine,
Is thrice more grateful, Lord, to thee,
  Than lifted eye or bended knee.

2 In true and inward faith we trace
  The source of every outward grace;
Within the pious heart it plays,
  A living fount of joy and praise.

3 Kind deeds of peace and love betray
  Where'er the stream has found its way;
But, where these spring not rich and fair,
  The stream has never wandered there.
              William H. Drummond.

473   *Liberality.*

WHEN Jesus dwelt in mortal clay,
  What were his works from day to day,
But miracles of power and grace,
  That spread salvation through our race?

2 Teach us, O Lord, to keep in view
  Thy pattern, and thy steps pursue;
Let alms bestowed, let kindness done,
  Be witnessed by each rolling sun.

3 That man may last, but never lives,
  Who much receives, but nothing gives;
Whom none can love, whom none can thank,
  Creation's blot, creation's blank!

4 But he who marks, from day to day,
  In generous acts his radiant way,
Treads the same path his Saviour trod,
  The path to glory and to God.
              Thomas Gibbons.

CHRISTIAN EXPERIENCE.

STATE STREET. S. M. — J. C. Woodman.

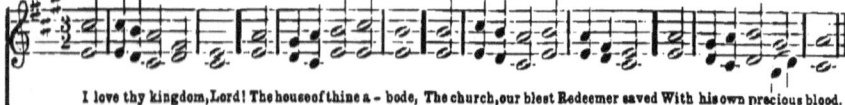

I love thy kingdom, Lord! The house of thine a-bode, The church, our blest Redeemer saved With his own precious blood.

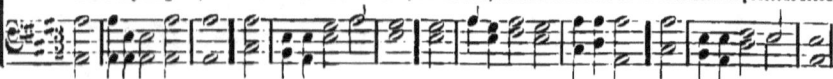

474 *Psalm 137.*
1 LOVE thy kingdom, Lord!
  The house of thine abode,
The church, our blest Redeemer saved
  With his own precious blood.

2 I love thy church, O God!
  Her walls before thee stand,
Dear as the apple of thine eye,
  And graven on thy hand.

3 For her my tears shall fall,
  For her my prayers ascend;
To her my cares and toils be given,
  Till toils and cares shall end.

4 Beyond my highest joy
  I prize her heavenly ways,
Her sweet communion, solemn vows,
  Her hymns of love and praise.

5 Sure as thy truth shall last,
  To Zion shall be given
The brightest glories earth can yield,
  And brighter bliss of heaven.
                              T. Dwight.

475 *"Harvest home."*
Sow IN the morn thy seed,
  At eve hold not thy hand;
To doubt and fear give thou no heed;
  Broad-cast it o'er the land.

2 And duly shall appear
  In verdure, beauty, strength,
The tender blade, the stalk, the ear,
  And the full corn at length.

3 Thou canst not toil in vain;
  Cold, heat, the moist and dry,
Shall foster and mature the grain
  For garners in the sky.

4 Then, when the glorious end,
  The day of God shall come,
The angel-reapers shall descend,
  And heaven sing "Harvest home!"
                        James Montgomery.

476 *Expedition.*
WORK while it is to-day!
  This was our Saviour's rule;
With docile minds let us obey,
  As learners in his school.

2 Lord Christ, we humbly ask
  Of thee the power and will,
With fear and meekness, every task
  Of duty to fulfill.

3 At home, by word and deed,
  Adorn redeeming grace;
And sow abroad the precious seed
  Of truth in every place:—

4 That thus the wilderness
  May blossom like the rose,
And trees spring up of righteousness,
  Where'er life's river flows.
                        James Montgomery.

477 *Contribution.*
WE give thee but thine own,
  Whate'er the gift may be:
All that we have is thine alone,
  A trust, O Lord, from thee.

2 May we thy bounties thus
  As stewards true receive,
And gladly as thou blessest us,
  To thee our first-fruits give.

3 To comfort and to bless,
  To find a balm for woe,
To tend the lone and fatherless—
  Is angel's work below.

4 The captive to release,
  To God the lost to bring,
To teach the way of life and peace—
  It is a Christ-like thing.

5 And we believe thy word,
  Though dim our faith may be;
Whate'er for thine we do, O Lord,
  We do it unto thee.
                        William W. How.

ACTIVITY AND ZEAL.

478 *Days going by.*

There are lonely hearts to cherish
  While the days are going by;
There are weary souls who perish,
  While the days are going by.
If a smile we can renew,
As our journey we pursue,
Oh, the good we all may do,
  While the days are going by.—Cho.

2 There's no time for idle scorning
  While the days are going by;
Let our face be like the morning,
  While the days are going by.

Oh! the world is full of sighs,
Full of sad and weeping eyes;
Help your fallen brothers rise,
  While the days are going by.—Cho.

3 All the loving links that bind us
  While the days are going by,
One by one we leave behind us
  While the days are going by;
But the seeds of good we sow,
Both in shade and shine will grow,
And will keep our hearts aglow
  While the days are going by.—Cho.
Anon.

479 *"Call them in!"*

Call them in!—the poor, the wretched,
  Sin-stained wanderers from the fold;
Peace and pardon freely offer—
  Can you weigh their worth in gold?—
    Ref.

2 Call them in!—the weak, the weary,
  Laden with the doom of sin;

Bid them come and rest in Jesus;
  He is waiting; call them in!—Ref.

3 Call them in!—the Jew, the Gentile,
  Bid the stranger to the feast;
Call them in!—the rich, the noble,
  From the highest to the least.—Ref.

4 Call them in!—the broken-hearted,
  Cowering 'neath the brand of shame;
Speak love's message, low and tender;
  'T was for sinners Jesus came.—Ref.

5 See the shadows lengthen round us,
  Soon the day-dawn will begin:
Can you leave them lost and lonely?
  Christ is coming: call them in!—Ref.
Mrs. T. D. L. Jessup.

13 P

CHRISTIAN EXPERIENCE

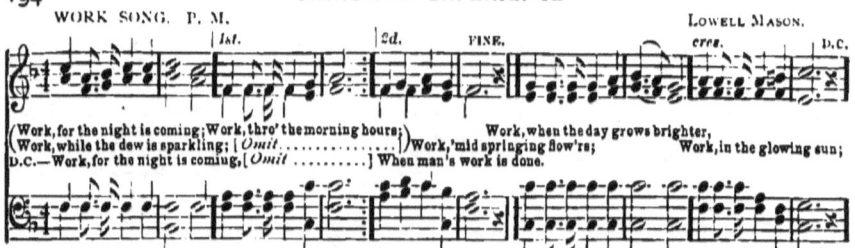

WORK SONG. P. M.   LOWELL MASON.

480   *"The night cometh."*

WORK, for the night is coming;
  Work, through the morning hours;
Work, while the dew is sparkling;
  Work, 'mid springing flowers;
Work, when the day grows brighter,
  Work, in the glowing sun;
Work, for the night is coming,
  When man's work is done.

2 Work, for the night is coming,
  Work through the sunny noon;
Fill brightest hours with labor,
  Rest comes sure and soon,
Give every flying minute
  Something to keep in store;
Work, for the night is coming,
  When man works no more.

3 Work, for the night is coming,
  Under the sunset skies;
While their bright tints are glowing,
  Work, for daylight flies.
Work till the last beam fadeth,
  Fadeth to shine no more;
Work, while the night is darkening,
  When man's work is o'er.
                  Anna L. Walker.

DORNANCE. 8s, 7s.   I. B. WOODBURY.

481   *"Follow me."*

JESUS calls us, o'er the tumult
  Of our life's wild, restless sea;
Day by day his sweet voice soundeth,
  Saying, Christian, follow me!

2 Jesus calls us—from the worship
  Of the vain world's golden store;
From each idol that would keep us,—
  Saying, Christian, love me more!

3 In our joys and in our sorrows,
  Days of toil and hours of ease,
Still he calls, in cares and pleasures,—
  Christian, love me more than these!

4 Jesus calls us! by thy mercies,
  Saviour, may we hear thy call;
Give our hearts to thy obedience,
  Serve and love thee best of all!
                  Mrs. C. F. Alexander.

482   *"Take my heart."*

TAKE my heart, O Father! take it;
  Make and keep it all thine own;
Let thy Spirit melt and break it—
  This proud heart of sin and stone.

2 Father, make me pure and lowly,
  Fond of peace and far from strife;
Turning from the paths unholy
  Of this vain and sinful life.

3 Ever let thy grace surround me,
  Strengthen me with power divine,
Till thy cords of love have bound me:
  Make me to be wholly thine.

5 May the blood of Jesus heal me,
  And my sins be all forgiven;
Holy Spirit, take and seal me,
  Guide me in the path to heaven.
                  Anon. 1840.

ACTIVITY AND ZEAL.

MISSION SONG. 8s, 7s. D.   P. P. Van Arsdale.

Hark! the voice of Jesus calling,—Who will go and work to-day? Fields are white, the harvest waiting,
Who will bear the sheaves away? Loud and long the Master call-eth, Rich reward he of-fers free;
D.S.—Who will answer, glad-ly say-ing, "Here am I, O Lord, send me."

483   *"The Laborers are few."*

Hark! the voice of Jesus calling,—
  Who will go and work to-day?
Fields are white, the harvest waiting,—
  Who will bear the sheaves away?
Loud and long the Master calleth,
  Rich reward he offers free;
Who will answer, gladly saying,
  "Here am I, O Lord, send me."

2 If you cannot cross the ocean
  And the heathen lands explore,
You can find the heathen nearer,
  You can help them at your door;
If you cannot speak like angels,
  If you cannot preach like Paul,
You can tell the love of Jesus,
  You can say he died for all.

3 While the souls of men are dying,
  And the Master calls for you,
Let none hear you idly saying,
  "There is nothing I can do!"
Gladly take the task he gives you,
  Let his work your pleasure be;
Answer quickly when he calleth,
  "Here am I, O Lord, send me."
                  D. March.

484   *"What thy hand findeth."*

If you cannot on the ocean
  Sail among the swiftest fleet,
Rocking on the highest billows,
  Laughing at the storms you meet,
You can stand among the sailors,
  Anchored yet within the bay,
You can lend a hand to help them,
  As they launch their boat away.

2 If you are too weak to journey
  Up the mountain steep and high,
You can stand within the valley,
  While the multitude go by;
You can chant in happy measure,
  As they slowly pass along;
Though they may forget the singer,
  They will not forget the song.

3 If you have not gold and silver
  Ever ready to command;
If you cannot toward the needy
  Reach an ever open hand,
You can visit the afflicted,
  O'er the erring you can weep;
You can be a true disciple
  Sitting at the Saviour's feet.

4 If you cannot in the harvest
  Garner up the richest sheaf,
Many a grain both ripe and golden
  Will the careless reapers leave;
Go and glean among the briers,
  Growing rank against the wall,
For it may be that the shadow
  Hides the heaviest wheat of all.
                  E. H. Gates.

THE CHURCH OF GOD.

GOLDEN HILL. S. M.   A. CHAPIN.

Dear Saviour! we are thine, By ev-er-last-ing bands; Our hearts, our souls, we would resign En-tire-ly to thy hands.

485   *"We are thine."*
Dear Saviour! we are thine,
  By everlasting bands;
Our hearts, our souls, we would resign
  Entirely to thy hands.

2 To thee we still would cleave
  With evergrowing zeal;
If millions tempt us Christ to leave,
  Oh, let them ne'er prevail!

3 Thy Spirit shall unite
  Our souls to thee, our Head;
Shall form in us thine image bright,
  And teach thy paths to tread.

4 Death may our souls divide
  From these abodes of clay;
But love shall keep us near thy side
  Through all the gloomy way.

5 Since Christ and we are one,
  Why should we doubt or fear?
If he in heaven has fixed his throne
  He'll fix his members there.
                Philip Doddridge.

486   *Meeting, after absence.*
And are we yet alive,
  And see each other's face?
Glory and praise to Jesus give,
  For his redeeming grace.

2 What troubles have we seen,
  What conflicts have we passed,
Fightings without, and fears within,
  Since we assembled last!

3 But out of all the Lord
  Hath brought us by his love;
And still he doth his help afford,
  And hides our life above.
                Charles Wesley.

BOYLSTON. S. M.   LOWELL MASON.

Blest be the tie that binds Our hearts in Christian love; The fellowship of kindred minds Is like to that a-bove.

487   *"Christian Love."*
Blest be the tie that binds
  Our hearts in Christian love:
The fellowship of kindred minds
  Is like to that above.

2 Before our Father's throne
  We pour our ardent prayers;
Our fears, our hopes, our aims are one,
  Our comforts and our cares.

3 We share our mutual woes,
  Our mutual burdens bear;
And often for each other flows
  The sympathizing tear.

4 When we asunder part,
  It gives us inward pain;
But we shall still be joined in heart,
  And hope to meet again.

5 This glorious hope revives
  Our courage by the way;
While each in expectation lives,
  And longs to see the day.

6 From sorrow, toil, and pain,
  And sin, we shall be free,
And perfect love and friendship reign
  Through all eternity.
                John Fawcett.

CHRISTIAN FELLOWSHIP.

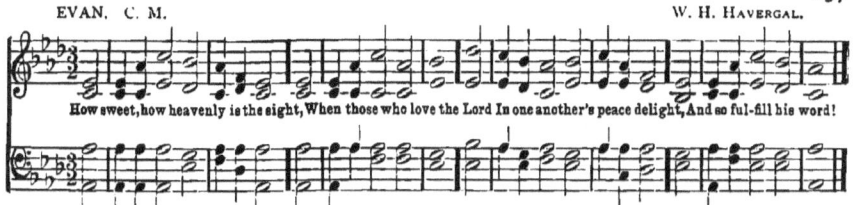
EVAN. C. M. — W. H. HAVERGAL.
How sweet, how heavenly is the sight, When those who love the Lord In one another's peace delight, And so ful-fill his word!

488 *1 John 4 : 21.*
How sweet, how heavenly is the sight,
When those who love the Lord
In one another's peace delight,
And so fulfill his word!

2 When each can feel his brother's sigh,
And with him bear a part!
When sorrow flows from every eye,
And joy from heart to heart!

3 When, free from envy, scorn, and pride,
Our wishes all above,
Each can his brother's failings hide,
And show a brother's love!

4 Let love, in one delightful stream,
Through every bosom flow;
And union sweet, and dear esteem
In every action glow.

5 Love is the golden chain that binds
The happy souls above;
And he's an heir of heaven who finds
His bosom glow with love.
Joseph Swain.

489 *"One Family."*
Let saints below in concert sing
With those to glory gone;
For all the servants of our King
In earth and heaven are one.

2 One family—we dwell in him—
One church above, beneath,
Though now divided by the stream,
The narrow stream of death;—

3 One army of the living God,
To his command we bow;
Part of the host have crossed the flood,
And part are crossing now.

4 Ev'n now by faith, we join our hands,
With those that went before,
And greet the ransomed, blesséd bands
Upon the eternal shore.

5 Lord Jesus! be our constant guide:
And, when the word is given,
Bid death's cold flood its waves divide,
And land us safe in heaven.
Charles Wesley.

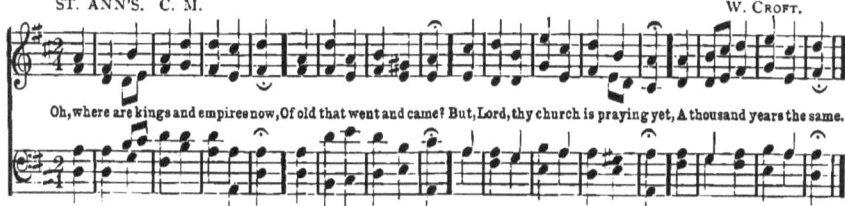
ST. ANN'S. C. M. — W. CROFT.
Oh, where are kings and empires now, Of old that went and came? But, Lord, thy church is praying yet, A thousand years the same.

490 *A growing kingdom.*
Oh, where are kings and empires now,
Of old that went and came?
But, Lord, thy church is praying yet,
A thousand years the same.

2 We mark her goodly battlements,
And her foundations strong;
We hear within the solemn voice
Of her unending song.

3 For not like kingdoms of the world
Thy holy church, O God!
Though earthquake shocks are threatening [her,
And tempests are abroad;—

4 Unshaken as eternal hills,
Immovable she stands,
A mountain that shall fill the earth,
A house not made by hands.
Arthur C. Coxe.

THE CHURCH OF GOD.

AZMON. C. M. Arr. by L. MASON.

O God of Beth-el, by whose hand Thy people still are fed; Who thro' this weary pilgrimage Hast all our fathers led!

491 *Genesis 28: 10–22.*

O God of Bethel, by whose hand
  Thy people still are fed;
Who through this weary pilgrimage
  Hast all our fathers led!

2 Our vows, our prayers, we now present
  Before thy throne of grace;
God of our fathers! be the God
  Of their succeeding race.

3 Through each perplexing path of life
  Our wandering footsteps guide;
Give us, each day, our daily bread,
  And raiment fit provide.

4 Oh, spread thy covering wings around
  Till all our wanderings cease,
And at our Father's loved abode,
  Our souls arrive in peace.

5 Such blessings from thy gracious hand
  Our humble prayers implore;
And thou shalt be our chosen God,
  Our portion evermore.
               Philip Doddridge.

492 *Christ receiving children.*

SEE Israel's gentle Shepherd stands,
  With all engaging charms!
Hark! how he calls the tender lambs,
  And folds them in his arms!

2 "Permit them to approach," he cries,
  "Nor scorn their humble name;
For 't was to bless such souls as these,
  The Lord of angels came."

3 We bring them, Lord, in thankful hands,
  And yield them up to thee;
Joyful that we ourselves are thine,—
  Thine let our offspring be.
               Philip Doddridge.

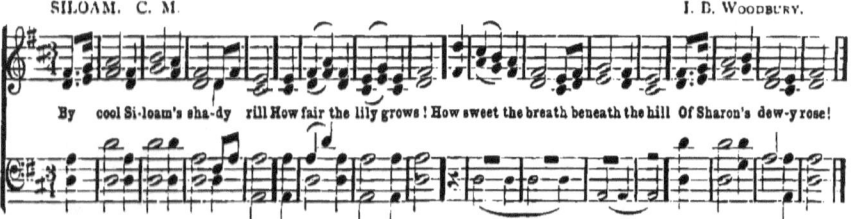

SILOAM. C. M. I. B. WOODBURY.

By cool Si-loam's sha-dy rill How fair the lily grows! How sweet the breath beneath the hill Of Sharon's dew-y rose!

493 *A Christian Child.*

By cool Siloam's shady rill
  How fair the lily grows!
How sweet the breath beneath the hill
  Of Sharon's dewy rose!

2 Lo! such the child whose early feet
  The paths of peace have trod;
Whose secret heart, with influence sweet,
  Is upward drawn to God.

3 By cool Siloam's shady rill
  The lily must decay;
The rose that blooms beneath the hill
  Must shortly fade away.

4 And soon, too soon, the wintry hour
  Of man's maturer age
May shake the soul with sorrow's power
  And stormy passion's rage.

5 O thou, whose infant feet were found
  Within thy Father's shrine,
Whose years, with changeless virtue crowned,
  Were all alike divine!

6 Dependent on thy bounteous breath,
  We seek thy grace alone
In childhood, manhood, age and death,
  To keep us still thine own.
               Reginald Heber.

THE SUNDAY SCHOOL.

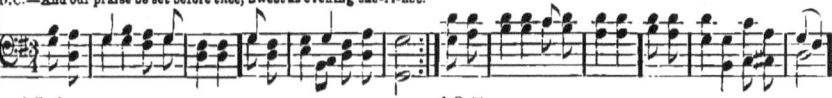

BAVARIA. 8s, 7s. D. — Fr. the German.

Saviour King, in hallowed union, At thy sacred feet we bow; Heart with heart, in blest communion, Join to crave thy favor now! Tho' celestial choirs adore thee, Let our prayer as incense rise; And our praise be set before thee, Sweet as evening sac-ri-fice.

494 *Sabbath School Meeting.*

Saviour King, in hallowed union,
　At thy sacred feet we bow;
Heart with heart, in blest communion,
　Join to crave thy favor now!
Though celestial choirs adore thee,
　Let our prayer as incense rise;
And our praise be set before thee,
　Sweet as evening sacrifice.

2 When we tell the wondrous story
　Of thy rich, exhaustless love,
Send thy Spirit, Lord of glory,
　On the youthful heart to move!
Oh, that he, the ever-living,
　May descend, as fruitful rain;
Till the wilderness, reviving,
　Blossoms as the rose again!
　　　　　　　　Anon., 1805.

495 *"These little ones."*

Saviour! who thy flock art feeding
　With the shepherd's kindest care,
All the feeble gently leading,
　While the lambs thy bosom share;—
Now, these little ones receiving,
　Fold them in thy gracious arm;
There, we know, thy word believing,
　Only there, secure from harm.

2 Never from thy pasture roving,
　Let them be the lion's prey;
Let thy tenderness, so loving,
　Keep them all life's dangerous way:
Then, within thy fold eternal,
　Let them find a resting-place,
Feed in pastures ever vernal,
　Drink the rivers of thy grace.
　　　　　　W. A. Muhlenberg.

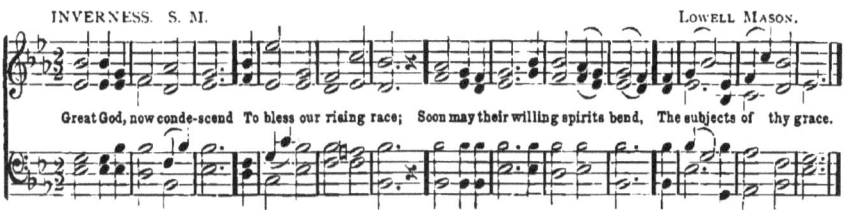

INVERNESS. S. M. — Lowell Mason.

Great God, now conde-scend To bless our rising race; Soon may their willing spirits bend, The subjects of thy grace.

496 *Our children.*

Great God, now condescend
　To bless our rising race;
Soon may their willing spirits bend,
　The subjects of thy grace.

2 Oh, what a pure delight
　Their happiness to see;
Our warmest wishes all unite
　To lead their souls to thee.

3 Now bless, thou God of love,
　The word of truth divine;
Send thy good Spirit from above,
　And make these children thine.
　　　　　　John Fellows.

497 *"Suffer them to come."*

The Saviour kindly calls
　Our children to his breast;
He folds them in his gracious arms,
　Himself declares them blest.

2 "Let them approach," he cries,
　"Nor scorn their humble claim;
The heirs of heaven are such as these,
　For such as these I came."

3 With joy we bring them, Lord,
　Devoting them to thee,
Imploring, that, as we are thine,
　Thine may our offspring be.
　　　　　　H. U. Onderdonk.

THE CHURCH OF GOD.

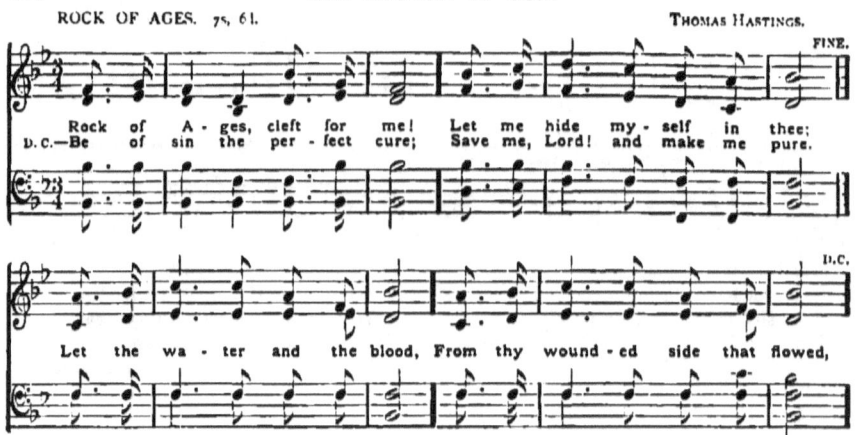

ROCK OF AGES. 7s, 6l.   Thomas Hastings.

Rock of Ages, cleft for me! Let me hide myself in thee;
D.C.—Be of sin the perfect cure; Save me, Lord! and make me pure.

Let the water and the blood, From thy wounded side that flowed,

498   *The Rock of Ages.*
Rock of Ages, cleft for me!
Let me hide myself in thee;
Let the water and the blood,
From thy wounded side that flowed,
Be of sin the perfect cure;
Save me, Lord! and make me pure.

2 Should my tears for ever flow,
Should my zeal no languor know,
This for sin could not atone;
Thou must save and thou alone:
In my hand no price I bring;
Simply to thy cross I cling.

3 While I draw this fleeting breath,
When mine eye-lids close in death,
When I rise to worlds unknown,
And behold thee on thy throne,
Rock of ages, cleft for me!
Let me hide myself in thee.
A. M. Toplady.

499   *"Manifest thyself."*
Son of God! to thee I cry:
By the holy mystery
Of thy dwelling here on earth,
By thy pure and holy birth,
Lord, thy presence let me see,
Manifest thyself to me.

2 Lamb of God! to thee I cry:
By thy bitter agony,
By thy pangs to us unknown,
By thy spirit's parting groan,
Lord, thy presence let me see,
Manifest thyself to me.

3 Prince of Life! to thee I cry:
By thy glorious majesty,
By thy triumph o'er the grave,
Meek to suffer, strong to save,
Lord, thy presence let me see,
Manifest thyself to me.

4 Lord of glory, God most high,
Man exalted to the sky!
With thy love my bosom fill,
Prompt me to perform thy will;
Then thy glory I shall see,
Thou wilt bring me home to thee.
Richard Mant.

500   *"Till he come."*
"Till He come:" oh, let the words
Linger on the trembling chords;
Let the little while between
In their golden light be seen;
Let us think how heaven and home
Lie beyond that—"Till he come."

2 When the weary ones we love
Enter on their rest above,
Seems the earth so poor and vast,
All our life joy overcast?
Hush, be every murmur dumb;
It is only—"Till he come."

3 See, the feast of love is spread,
Drink the wine, and break the bread;
Sweet memorials,—till the Lord
Call us round his heavenly board;
Some from earth, from glory some,
Severed only—"Till he come."
E. H. Bickersteth.

THE LORD'S SUPPER.

FEDERAL STREET. L. M.   H. K. Oliver.

501 *Crucifying the Lord afresh.*

O Jesus! bruised and wounded more
  Than bursted grape, or bread of wheat,
The Life of life within our souls,
  The Cup of our salvation sweet!

2 We come to show thy dying hour,
  Thy streaming vein, thy broken flesh;
And still the blood is warm to save,
  And still the fragrant wounds are fresh.

3 O Heart! that, with a double tide
  Of blood and water, maketh pure;
O Flesh! once offered on the cross,
  The gift that makes our pardon sure;—

4 Let never more our sinful souls
  The anguish of thy cross renew;
Nor forge again the cruel nails,
  That pierced thy victim body through.

5 Come, Bread of heaven, to feed our souls,
  And with thee, Jesus enter in!
Come, Wine of God! and as we drink,
  His precious blood wash out our sin!
                    Mrs. C. F. Alexander.

502 *Feeding on Christ.*

I feed by faith on Christ; my bread,
  His body broken on the tree;
I live in him, my living Head,
  Who died, and rose again for me.

2 This be my joy and comfort here,
  This pledge of future glory mine:
Jesus, in spirit now appear,
  And break the bread, and pour the wine.

3 From thy dear hand, may I receive
  The tokens of thy dying love,
And, while I feast on earth, believe
  That I shall feast with thee above.
                    James Montgomery.

HURSLEY. L. M.   Arr. by W. H. Monk.

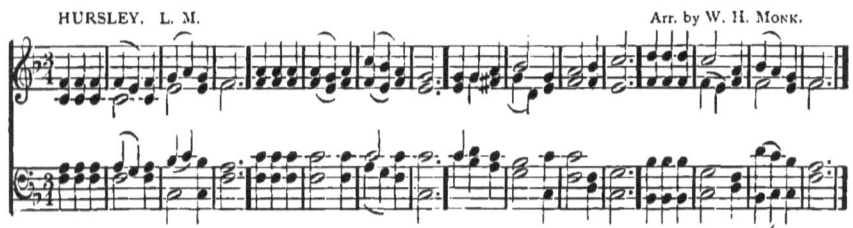

503 *Immanuel.*

Oh, sweetly breathe the lyres above,
  When angels touch the quivering string,
And wake, to chant Immanuel's love,
  Such strains as angel-lips can sing!

2 And sweet, on earth, the choral swell,
  From mortal tongues, of gladsome lays;
When pardoned souls their raptures tell,
  And, grateful, hymn Immanuel's praise.

3 Jesus, thy name our souls adore;
  We own the bond that makes us thine;
And carnal joys that charmed before,
  For thy dear sake we now resign.

4 Our hearts, by dying love subdued,
  Accept thine offered grace to-day;
Beneath the cross, with blood bedewed,
  We bow, and give ourselves away.

5 In thee we trust,—on thee rely;
  Though we are feeble, thou art strong;
Oh, keep us till our spirits fly
  To join the bright, immortal throng!
                    Ray Palmer.

THE CHURCH OF GOD.

DUNDEE. C. M.   G. Franc.

504   *Persistent Love.*

How SWEET and awful is the place,
  With Christ within the doors,
While everlasting love displays
  The choicest of her stores.

2 When all our hearts, and all our songs,
  Join to admire the feast,
Each of us cries with thankful tongue,—
  "Lord, why was I a guest?"

3 "Why was I made to hear thy voice,
  And enter while there's room,
When thousands make a wretched choice,
  And rather starve than come?"

4 'T was the same love that spread the feast,
  That sweetly drew us in;
Else we had still refused to taste,
  And perished in our sin.

5 Pity the nations, O our God!
  Constrain the earth to come;
Send thy victorious word abroad,
  And bring the strangers home.
                            Isaac Watts.

CHERITH. C. M.   Arr. fr. Spohr.

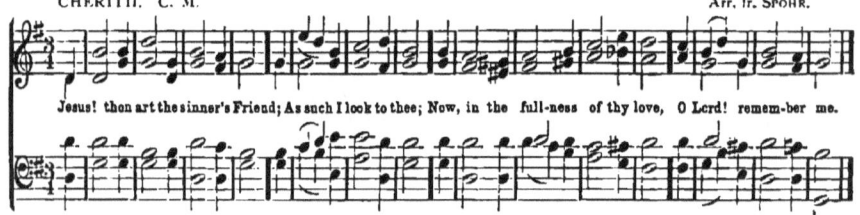

505   *"Friend of Sinners."*

JESUS! thou art the sinner's Friend;
  As such I look to thee;
Now, in the fullness of thy love,
  O Lord! remember me.

2 Remember thy pure word of grace,—
  Remember Calvary;
Remember all thy dying groans,
  And then remember me.

3 Thou wondrous Advocate with God!
  I yield myself to thee;
While thou art sitting on thy throne,
  Dear Lord! remember me.

4 Lord! I am guilty—I am vile,
  But thy salvation's free;
Then, in thine all-abounding grace,
  Dear Lord! remember me.
                           Richard Burnham.

506   *"Prepare us, Lord."*

PREPARE us, Lord, to view thy cross,
  Who all our griefs hast borne;
To look on thee, whom we have pierced—
  To look on thee and mourn.

2 While thus we mourn, we would rejoice,
  And as thy cross we see,
Let each exclaim, in faith and hope,
  "The Saviour died for me!"
                         Thomas Cotterill.

507   *Feeding on Christ.*

TOGETHER with these symbols, Lord,
  Thy blessèd self impart;
And let thy holy flesh and blood
  Feed the believing heart.

2 Come, Holy Ghost, with Jesus' love,
  Prepare us for this feast;
Oh, let us banquet with our Lord,
  And lean upon his breast.
                          John Cennick.

THE LORD'S SUPPER.

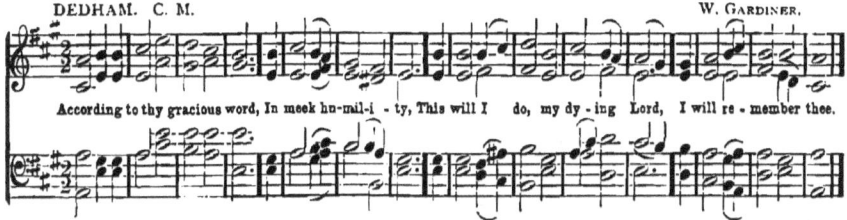

508 *"I will remember thee."*

According to thy gracious word,
  In meek humility,
This will I do, my dying Lord,
  I will remember thee.

2 Thy body, broken for my sake,
  My bread from heaven shall be;
Thy testamental cup I take,
  And thus remember thee.

3 Gethsemane can I forget?
  Or there thy conflict see,
Thine agony and bloody sweat,
  And not remember thee?

4 When to the cross I turn mine eyes,
  And rest on Calvary,
O Lamb of God, my sacrifice!
  I must remember thee:—

5 Remember thee, and all thy pains
  And all thy love to me;
Yea, while a breath, a pulse remains,
  Will I remember thee.

6 And when these failing lips grow dumb,
  And mind and memory flee,
When thou shalt in thy kingdom come,
  Then, Lord, remember me!
                    James Montgomery.

509 *"The cup of blessing."*

Jesus, at whose supreme command,
  We now approach to God,
Before us in thy vesture stand,
  Thy vesture dipped in blood.

2 Now, Saviour, now thyself reveal,
  And make thy nature known;
Affix thy blessèd Spirit's seal,
  And stamp us for thine own.

3 Obedient to thy gracious word,
  We break the hallowed bread,
Commemorate our dying Lord,
  And trust on thee to feed.

4 The cup of blessing, blessed by thee,
  Let it thy blood impart;
The broken bread thy body be,
  To cheer each languid heart.
                    Charles Wesley.

510 *"Greater love hath no man."*

If human kindness meets return,
  And owns the grateful tie;
If tender thoughts within us burn,
  To feel a friend is nigh;—

2 Oh, shall not warmer accents tell
  The gratitude we owe
To him, who died our fears to quell—
  Who bore our guilt and woe!

3 While yet in anguish he surveyed
  Those pangs he would not flee,
What love his latest words displayed,—
  "Meet and remember me!"

4 Remember thee—thy death, thy shame,
  Our sinful hearts to share!—
O memory! leave no other name
  But his recorded there.
                    Gerard T. Noel.

511 *Before the Cross.*

SWEET the moments, rich in blessing,
  Which before the cross we spend;
Life, and health, and peace possessing,
  From the sinner's dying Friend.
Truly blessèd is this station,
  Low before his cross to lie,
While we see divine compassion,
  Beaming in his gracious eye.

2 Love and grief our hearts dividing,
  With our tears his feet we bathe;
Constant still, in faith abiding,
  Life deriving from his death.
For thy sorrows we adore thee,
  For the pains that wrought our peace,
Gracious Saviour! we implore thee
  In our souls thy love increase.

3 Here we feel our sins forgiven,
  While upon the Lamb we gaze,
And our thoughts are all of heaven,
  And our lips o'erflow with praise.
Still in ceaseless contemplation,
  Fix our hearts and eyes on thee,
Till we taste thy full salvation,
  And, unvailed, thy glories see.
      James Allen.

512 *Parting Hymn.*

FROM the table now retiring,
  Which for us the Lord hath spread,
May our souls refreshment finding,
  Grow in all things like our Head!

2 His example while beholding,
  May our lives his image bear;
Him our Lord and Master calling,
  His commands may we revere.

3 Love to God and man displaying,
  Walking steadfast in his way,
Joy attend us in believing,
  Peace from God, through endless day.

4 Praise and honor to the Father,
  Praise and honor to the Son,
Praise and honor to the Spirit,
  Ever Three and ever One.
      John Rowe.

MISSIONS AND GROWTH.

OAKSVILLE. C. M. — C. ZEUNER.

Let Zi-on and her sons re-joice— Be-hold the prom-ised hour! Her God hath heard her mourn-ing voice, And comes t' ex-alt his power.

513   *Psalm 102.*

Let Zion and her sons rejoice—
  Behold the promised hour!
Her God hath heard her mourning voice,
  And comes to exalt his power.

2 Her dust and ruins that remain
  Are precious in our eyes;
Those ruins shall be built again,
  And all that dust shall rise.

3 The Lord will raise Jerusalem,
  And stand in glory there;
Nations shall bow before his name,
  And kings attend with fear.

4 He sits a sovereign on his throne,
  With pity in his eyes,
He hears the dying prisoners' groan,
  And sees their sighs arise.

5 He frees the souls condemned to death;
  Nor, when his saints complain,
Shall it be said that praying breath
  Was ever spent in vain.
  Isaac Watts.

514   *"Can a mother forget?"*

A mother may forgetful be,
  For human love is frail;
But thy Creator's love to thee,
  O Zion, cannot fail.

2 No: thy dear name engraven stands,
  In characters of love,
On thine almighty Father's hands,
  And never shall remove.

3 Before his ever-watchful eye
  Thy mournful state appears,
And every groan, and every sigh,
  Divine compassion hears.

4 O Zion, learn to doubt no more,
  Be every fear suppressed;
Unchanging truth, and love, and power,
  Dwell in thy Saviour's breast.
  Anne Steele.

515   *Psalm 67.*

Shine, mighty God! on Zion shine
  With beams of heavenly grace;
Reveal thy power through all our coasts,
  And show thy smiling face.

2 When shall thy name, from shore to shore,
  Sound all the earth abroad,
And distant nations know and love
  Their Saviour and their God?

3 Sing to the Lord, ye distant lands!
  Sing loud with solemn voice;
Let every tongue exalt his praise,
  And every heart rejoice.

4 Earth shall obey her Maker's will,
  And yield a full increase;
Our God will crown his chosen land
  With fruitfulness and peace.

5 God, the Redeemer, scatters round
  His choicest favors here,
While the creation's utmost bound
  Shall see, adore, and fear.
  Isaac Watts.

THE CHURCH OF GOD.

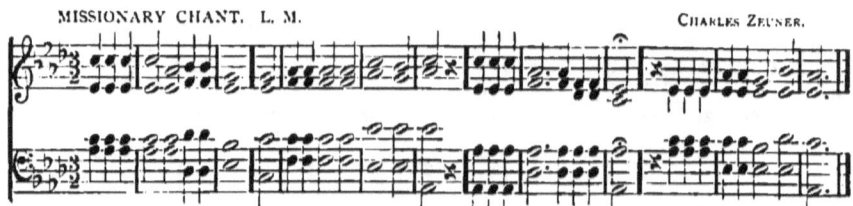

MISSIONARY CHANT. L. M.   Charles Zeuner.

516   *Psalm 72.*
Jesus shall reign where'er the sun
Does his successive journeys run;
His kingdom stretch from shore to shore,
Till moons shall wax and wane no more.

2 For him shall endless prayer be made
And endless praises crown his head;
His name, like sweet perfume, shall rise
With every morning-sacrifice.

3 People and realms of every tongue
Dwell on his love, with sweetest song;
And infant voices shall proclaim
Their early blessings on his name.

4 Blessings abound where'er he reigns;
The prisoner leaps to lose his chains;
The weary find eternal rest,
And all the sons of want are blest.

5 Let every creature rise and bring
Peculiar honors to our King;
Angels descend with songs again,
And earth repeat the loud Amen!
                        Isaac Watts.

517   *Conversion of the World.*
Sovereign of worlds! display thy power;
Be this thy Zion's favored hour;
Bid the bright morning Star arise,
And point the nations to the skies.

2 Set up thy throne where Satan reigns,—
On Afric's shore, on India's plains,
On wilds and continents unknown,—
And make the nations all thine own.

3 Speak! and the world shall hear thy voice;
Speak! and the desert shall rejoice;
Scatter the gloom of heathen night,
And bid all nations hail the light.
                     Bourne Hall Draper.

MENDON. L. M.   Lowell Mason.

518   *"O light of Zion."*
Though now the nations sit beneath
The darkness of o'erspreading death,
God will arise, with light divine
On Zion's holy towers to shine.

2 That light shall shine on distant lands,
And wandering tribes, in joyful bands,
Shall come thy glory, Lord, to see,
And in thy courts to worship thee.

3 O light of Zion, now arise!
Let the glad morning bless our eyes!
Ye nations, catch the kindling ray,
And hail the splendor of the day.
                       Leonard Bacon.

519   *Zion's Glory.*
Zion! awake, thy strength renew;
Put on thy robes of beauteous hue;
And let the admiring world behold
The King's fair daughter clothed in gold.

2 Church of our God! arise and shine,
Bright with the beams of truth divine;
Then shall thy radiance stream afar,
Wide as the heathen nations are.

3 Gentiles and kings thy light shall view,
And shall admire and love thee too:—
They come, like clouds across the sky,
As doves that to their windows fly.
                     William Shrubsole, tr.

MISSIONS AND GROWTH.

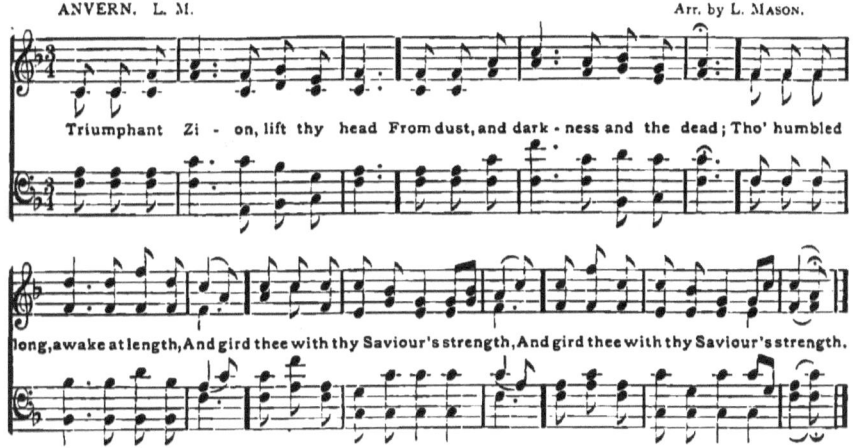

520 *"Triumphant Zion."*

TRIUMPHANT Zion, lift thy head
From dust, and darkness, and the dead;
Though humbled long, awake at length,
And gird thee with thy Saviour's strength.

2 Put all thy beauteous garments on,
And let thy various charms be known:
The world thy glories shall confess,
Decked in the robes of righteousness.

3 No more shall foes unclean invade,
And fill thy hallowed walls with dread;
No more shall hell's insulting host
Their victory and thy sorrows boast.

4 God, from on high, thy groans will hear;
His hand thy ruins shall repair;
Nor will thy watchful Monarch cease
To guard thee in eternal peace.
Philip Doddridge.

521 *Ancient Israel.*

WHY on the bending willows hung,
Israel! still sleeps thy tuneful string?—
Still mute remains thy sullen tongue,
And Zion's song denies to sing?

2 Awake! thy sweetest raptures raise;
Let harp and voice unite their strains:
Thy promised King his sceptre sways:
Jesus, thine own Messiah, reigns!

3 No taunting foes the song require;
No strangers mock thy captive chain;
But friends provoke the silent lyre,
And brethren ask the holy strain.

4 Nor fear thy Salem's hills to wrong,
If other lands thy triumphs share:
A heavenly city claims thy song;
A brighter Salem rises there.

5 By foreign streams no longer roam;
Nor, weeping, think of Jordan's flood:
In every clime behold a home,
In every temple see thy God.
James Joyce.

522 *Home Missions.*

LOOK from thy sphere of endless day,
O God of mercy and of might!
In pity look on those who stray,
Benighted in this land of light.

2 In peopled vale, in lonely glen,
In crowded mart, by stream or sea,
How many of the sons of men
Hear not the message sent from thee!

3 Send forth thy heralds, Lord, to call
The thoughtless young, the hardened old,
A scattered, homeless flock, till all
Be gathered to thy peaceful fold.

4 Send them thy mighty word to speak,
Till faith shall dawn, and doubt depart,
To awe the bold, to stay the weak,
And bind and heal the broken heart.

5 Then all these wastes, a dreary scene,
That makes us sadden as we gaze,
Shall grow with living waters green,
And lift to heaven the voice of praise.
William C. Bryant.

THE CHURCH OF GOD.

MISSIONARY HYMN. 7s, 6s. D. — Lowell Mason.

523 *"Come over, and help us."*

From Greenland's icy mountains,
  From India's coral strand,
Where Afric's sunny fountains
  Roll down their golden sand,—
From many an ancient river,
  From many a palmy plain,
They call us to deliver
  Their land from error's chain.

2 What though the spicy breezes
  Blow soft o'er Ceylon's isle;
Though every prospect pleases,
  And only man is vile;
In vain with lavish kindness
  The gifts of God are strown;
The heathen, in his blindness,
  Bows down to wood and stone!

3 Shall we, whose souls are lighted
  With wisdom from on high,—
Shall we, to men benighted,
  The lamp of life deny?
Salvation, oh, salvation!
  The joyful sound proclaim,
Till earth's remotest nation
  Has learned Messiah's name.

4 Waft, waft, ye winds, his story,
  And you, ye waters, roll,
Till, like a sea of glory,
  It spreads from pole to pole;
Till o'er our ransomed nature
  The Lamb for sinners slain,
Redeemer, King, Creator,
  In bliss returns to reign!
    Reginald Heber.

524 *The day of Jubilee.*

How BEAUTEOUS on the mountains,
  The feet of him that brings,
Like streams from living fountains,
  Good tidings of good things;
That publisheth salvation,
  And jubilee release,
To every tribe and nation,
  God's reign of joy and peace!

2 Lift up thy voice, O watchman!
  And shout, from Zion's towers,
Thy hallelujah chorus,—
  "The victory is ours!"
The Lord shall build up Zion
  In glory and renown,
And Jesus, Judah's lion,
  Shall wear his rightful crown;

3 Break forth in hymns of gladness;
  O waste Jerusalem!
Let songs, instead of sadness,
  Thy jubilee proclaim;
The Lord, in strength victorious,
  Upon thy foes hath trod;
Behold, O earth! the glorious
  Salvation of our God!
    Benjamin Gough.

MISSIONS AND GROWTH.

ORIENS. 7s, 6s. D.   W. F. SHERWIN.

The morning light is breaking; The darkness dis-ap-pears! The sons of earth are wak-ing To pen-i-ten-tial tears;

Each breeze that sweeps the ocean Brings tidings from a-far, Of na-tions in com-mo-tion, Pre-pared for Zion's war.

525   *The morning light.*

THE morning light is breaking;
  The darkness disappears!
The sons of earth are waking
  To penitential tears;
Each breeze that sweeps the ocean
  Brings tidings from afar,
Of nations in commotion,
  Prepared for Zion's war.

2 See heathen nations bending
  Before the God we love,
And thousand hearts ascending
  In gratitude above;
While sinners, now confessing,
  The gospel call obey,
And seek the Saviour's blessing—
  A nation in a day.

3 Blest river of salvation!
  Pursue thine onward way;
Flow thou to every nation,
  Nor in thy richness stay:
Stay not till all the lowly
  Triumphant reach their home:
Stay not till all the holy
  Proclaim—"The Lord is come!"
                  Samuel F. Smith.

526   *Psalm 14.*

OH, that the Lord's salvation
  Were out of Zion come,
To heal his ancient nation,
  To lead his outcasts home!

14 P

How long the holy city
  Shall heathen feet profane?
Return, O Lord, in pity,
  Rebuild her walls again.

2 Let fall thy rod of terror,
  Thy saving grace impart;
Roll back the vail of error,
  Release the fettered heart;
Let Israel, home returning,
  Their lost Messiah see;
Give oil of joy for mourning,
  And bind thy Church to thee.
                  Henry F. Lyte.

527   *Departing Missionaries.*

ROLL on, thou mighty ocean;
  And, as thy billows flow,
Bear messengers of mercy
  To every land below.
Arise, ye gales, and waft them
  Safe to the destined shore;
That man may sit in darkness,
  And death's black shade no more.

2 O thou eternal Ruler,
  Who holdest in thine arm
The tempests of the ocean,
  Protect them from all harm!
Thy presence, Lord, be with them,
  Wherever they may be;
Though far from us, who love them,
  Still let them be with thee.
                  James Edmeston.

THE CHURCH OF GOD.

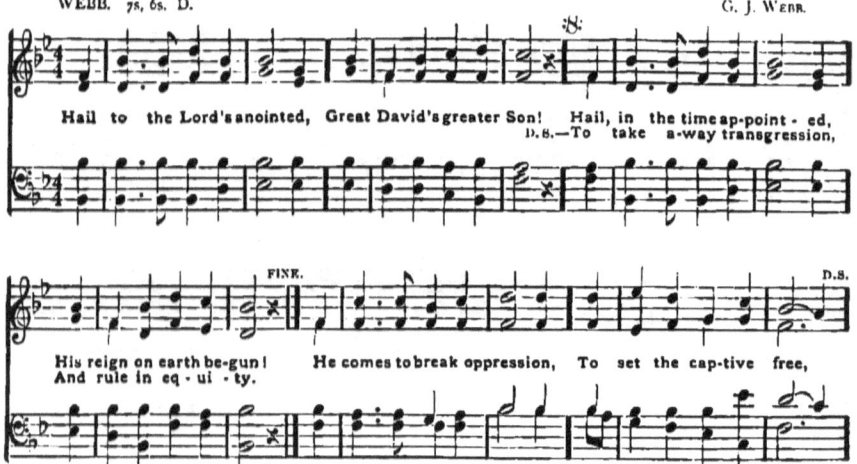

WEBB. 7s, 6s. D. G. J. Webb.

Hail to the Lord's anointed, Great David's greater Son! Hail, in the time ap-point - ed,
D.S.—To take a-way transgression,
His reign on earth be-gun! He comes to break oppression, To set the cap-tive free,
And rule in eq - ui - ty.

528 *Psalm 72.*

Hail to the Lord's anointed,
  Great David's greater Son!
Hail, in the time appointed,
  His reign on earth begun!
He comes to break oppression,
  To set the captive free,
To take away transgression,
  And rule in equity.

2 He comes, with succor speedy,
  To those who suffer wrong;
To help the poor and needy,
  And bid the weak be strong;
To give them songs for sighing,
  Their darkness turn to light,
Whose souls, condemned and dying,
  Were precious in his sight.

3 He shall come down like showers
  Upon the fruitful earth,
And love, and joy, like flowers,
  Spring in his path to birth:
Before him, on the mountains,
  Shall peace the herald go,
And righteousness in fountains
  From hill to valley flow.

4 Arabia's desert-ranger
  To him shall bow the knee;
The Ethiopian stranger
  His glory come to see:
With offerings of devotion,
  Ships from the isles shall meet,
To pour the wealth of ocean
  In tribute at his feet.

5 Kings shall fall down before him,
  And gold and incense bring:
All nations shall adore him;
  His praise all people sing;
For he shall have dominion
  O'er river, sea, and shore,
Far as the eagle's pinion
  Or dove's light wing can soar.

6 For him shall prayer unceasing
  And daily vows ascend;
His kingdom still increasing,
  A kingdom without end.
The heavenly dew shall nourish
  A seed in weakness sown,
Whose fruit shall spread and flourish,
  And shake like Lebanon.

7 O'er every foe victorious,
  He on his throne shall rest;
From age to age more glorious,
  All-blessing and all-blessed.
The tide of time shall never
  His covenant remove;
His name shall stand for ever;
  His great, best name of Love!

James Montgomery.

MISSIONS AND GROWTH.

RATHBUN. 8s, 7s. I. CONKEY.

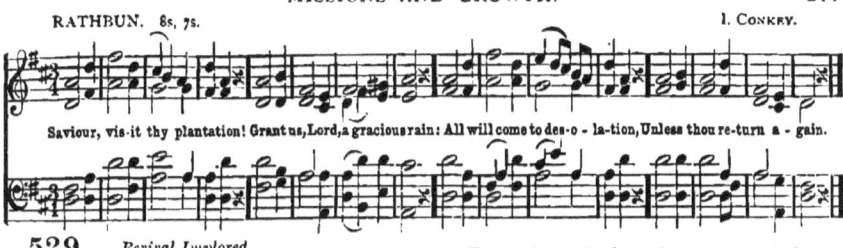

Saviour, vis-it thy plantation! Grant us, Lord, a gracious rain: All will come to des-o-la-tion, Unless thou re-turn a-gain.

529 *Revival Implored.*

SAVIOUR, visit thy plantation!
Grant us, Lord, a gracious rain:
All will come to desolation,
Unless thou return again.

2 Keep no longer at a distance,
Shine upon us from on high,
Lest, for want of thine assistance,
Every plant should droop and die.

3 Once, O Lord, thy garden flourished;
Every part looked gay and green;
Then thy word our spirits nourished:
Happy seasons we have seen.

4 But a drought has since succeeded,
And a sad decline we see:
Lord, thy help is greatly needed:
Help can only come from thee.

5 Let our mutual love be fervent:
Make us prevalent in prayer;
Let each one esteemed thy servant
Shun the world's bewitching snare.

6 Break the tempter's fatal power,
Turn the stony heart to flesh,
And begin from this good hour
To revive thy work afresh.
John Newton.

WESLEY. 11s, 10s. LOWELL MASON.

Hail to the brightness of Zi-on's glad morning! Joy to the lands that in darkness have lain!
Hushed be the accents of sorrow and mourning; Zi-on in tri-umph begins her mild reign.

530 *The Promise.*

HAIL to the brightness of Zion's glad morning!
Joy to the lands that in darkness have lain!
Hushed be the accents of sorrow and mourning;
Zion in triumph begins her mild reign.

2 Hail to the brightness of Zion's glad morning,
Long by the prophets of Israel foretold;
Hail to the millions from bondage returning;
Gentile and Jew the blest vision behold.

3 Lo! in the desert rich flowers are springing,
Streams ever copious are gliding along;
Loud from the mountain-tops echoes are ringing,
Wastes rise in verdure, and mingle in song.

4 See, from all lands—from the isles of the ocean,
Praise to Jehovah ascending on high;
Fallen are the engines of war and commotion,
Shouts of salvation are rending the sky.
Thomas Hastings.

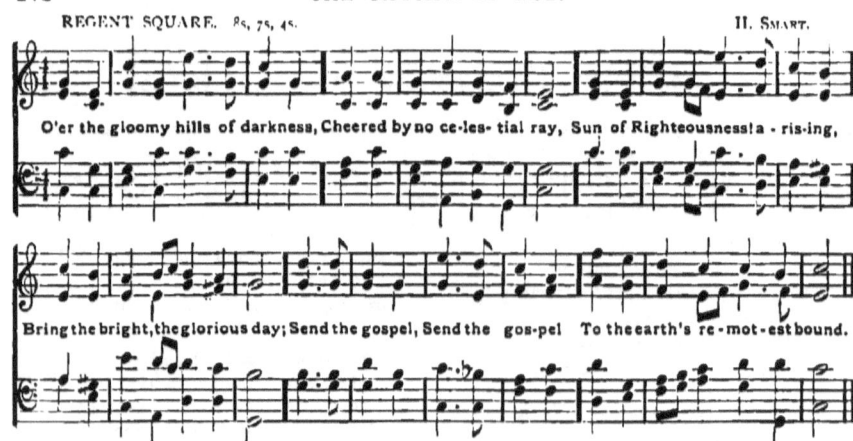

531 *Sun of Righteousness.*

O'er the gloomy hills of darkness,
　Cheered by no celestial ray,
Sun of Righteousness! arising,
　Bring the bright, the glorious day;
　　Send the gospel
　To the earth's remotest bound.

2 Kingdoms wide that sit in darkness,—
　Grant them, Lord! the glorious light:
And, from eastern coast to western,
　May the morning chase the night;
　　And redemption,
　Freely purchased, win the day.

3 Fly abroad, thou mighty gospel!
　Win and conquer, never cease;
May thy lasting, wide dominions
　Multiply and still increase;
　　Sway the sceptre,
　Saviour! all the world around.
　　　　　　William Williams.

532 *Home Missions.*

Saints of God! the dawn is brightening,
　Token of our coming Lord;
O'er the earth the field is whitening;
　Louder rings the Master's word,—
　　"Pray for reapers
　In the harvest of the Lord."

2 Now, O Lord! fulfill thy pleasure,
　Breathe upon thy chosen band,
And, with pentecostal measure,
　Send forth reapers o'er our land, —
　　Faithful reapers,
　Gathering sheaves for thy right hand.

3 Broad the shadow of our nation,
　Eager millions hither roam;
Lo! they wait for thy salvation;
　Come, Lord Jesus! quickly come!
　　By thy Spirit,
　Bring thy ransomed people home.

4 Soon shall end the time of weeping,
　Soon the reaping time will come,—
Heaven and earth together keeping
　God's eternal Harvest Home:
　　Saints and angels!
　Shout the world's great Harvest Home.
　　　　　　Mrs. Mary Maxwell.

533 *The gospel herald.*

On the mountain's top appearing,
　Lo! the sacred herald stands,
Welcome news to Zion bearing—
　Zion long in hostile lands:
　　Mourning captive!
　God himself shall loose thy bands.

2 Has thy night been long and mournful?
　Have thy friends unfaithful proved?
Have thy foes been proud and scornful?
　By thy sighs and tears unmoved?
　　Cease thy mourning,
　Zion still is well beloved.

3 God, thy God, will now restore thee;
　He himself appears thy Friend;
All thy foes shall flee before thee;
　Here their boasts and triumphs end:
　　Great deliverance
　Zion's King will surely send.
　　　　　　Thomas Kelly.

MISSIONS AND GROWTH.

HAMDEN. 8s, 7s, 4s. LOWELL MASON.

534 *"Hallelujah!"*

HALLELUJAH! best and sweetest
 Of the hymns of praise above;
Hallelujah! thou repeatest,
 Angel Host, these notes of love;
  This ye utter,
 While your golden harps ye move.

2 Hallelujah! Church Victorious,
 Join the concert of the sky;
Hallelujah! bright and glorious,
 Lift, ye Saints, this strain on high;
  We, poor exiles,
 Join not yet your melody.

3 Hallelujah! strains of gladness,
 Suit not souls with anguish torn;
Hallelujah! sounds of sadness
 Best become the heart forlorn;
  Our offences
 We with bitter tears must mourn.

4 But our earnest supplication,
 Holy God, we raise to thee;
Visit us with thy salvation,
 Make us all thy joys to see.
  Hallelujah!
 Ours at length this strain shall be.
  John Chandler, tr.

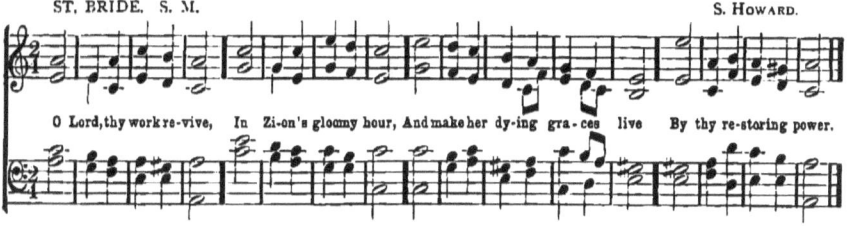

ST. BRIDE. S. M. S. HOWARD.

535 *"Revive thy work."*

O LORD, thy work revive,
 In Zion's gloomy hour,
And make her dying graces live
 By thy restoring power.

2 Awake thy chosen few
 To fervent earnest prayer;
Again may they their vows renew,
 Thy blessèd presence share.

3 Thy Spirit then will speak
 Through lips of feeble clay,
And hearts of adamant will break,
 And rebels will obey.

4 Lord, lend thy gracious ear;
 Oh, listen to our cry;
Oh, come and bring salvation here:
 Our hopes on thee rely.
  Mrs. P. H. Brown, alt.

536 *Declension.*

OH, for the happy hour
 When God will hear our cry,
And send, with a reviving power,
 His Spirit from on high.

2 While many crowd thy house,
 How few, around thy board,
Meet to recount their solemn vows,
 And bless thee as their Lord!

3 Thou, thou alone canst give
 Thy gospel sure success;
Canst bid the dying sinner live
 Anew in holiness.

4 Come, then, with power divine,
 Spirit of life and love!
Then shall this people all be thine.
 This church like that above.
  George W. Bethune.

THE CHURCH OF GOD.

BEAUTEOUS DAY. P. M.
GEO. F. ROOT.

We are watching, we are waiting, For the bright prophetic day: When the shadows, weary shadows, From the world shall roll (Omit..) a-way. We are waiting for the morning, When the beauteous day is dawning; We are wait-ing for the morning, For the golden spires of day. Lo! he comes! see the King draws near; Zi-on, shout! the Lord is here.

537 *We are watching.*

WE are watching, we are waiting,
  For the bright prophetic day:
When the shadows, weary shadows,
  From the world shall roll away.—CHO.

2 We are watching, we are waiting,
  For the star that brings the day:
When the night of sin shall vanish,
  And the shadows melt away.—CHO.

3 We are watching, we are waiting,
  For the beauteous King of day:
For the Chiefest of ten-thousand,
  For the Light, the Truth, the way.—CHO.
                                W. O. Cushing.

---

538 P. M. *"Jordan's Strand."*

MY days are gliding swiftly by,
  And I, a pilgrim stranger.
Would not detain them as they fly,
  Those hours of toil and danger.

REF.—For, oh, we stand on Jordan's strand,
    Our friends are passing over;
    And just before, the Shining Shore
    We may almost discover!

2 We'll gird our loins, my brethren dear,
  Our heavenly home discerning;
Our absent Lord has left us word,
  Let every lamp be burning.—REF.

3 Should coming days be cold and dark,
  We need not cease our singing;
That perfect rest naught can molest,
  Where golden harps are ringing.—REF.

4 Let sorrow's rudest tempest blow,
  Each cord on earth to sever;
Our King says, Come, and there's our home
  For ever, oh, for ever!

REF.—For, oh, we stand on Jordan's strand,
    Our friends are passing over;
    And just before, the Shining Shore
    We may almost discover!
                                D. Nelson.

THE CHRISTIAN'S DEATH.

CHINA. C. M.   T. Swan.

'Tis but the voice that Jesus sends, To call them to his arms.

539   *"We are confident."*

Why do we mourn departing friends,
Or shake at death's alarms?
'Tis but the voice that Jesus sends,
To call them to his arms.

2 Are we not tending upward, too,
As fast as time can move?
Nor would we wish the hours more slow,
To keep us from our love.

3 Why should we tremble to convey
Their bodies to the tomb?
There the dear flesh of Jesus lay,
And scattered all the gloom.

4 The graves of all the saints he blessed,
And softened every bed;
Where should the dying members rest,
But with the dying Head?

5 Thence he arose, ascending high,
And showed our feet the way;
Up to the Lord we, too, shall fly
At the great rising-day.

6 Then let the last loud trumpet sound,
And bid our kindred rise;
Awake! ye nations under ground;
Ye saints! ascend the skies.
                              Isaac Watts.

SHINING SHORE. P. M.   Geo. F. Root.

My days are gliding swiftly by, And I, a pilgrim stranger, Would not detain them as they fly,
D.S.—just before, the Shining Shore
Those hours of toil and danger. For, oh, we stand on Jordan's strand, Our friends are passing over; And
We may al-most dis-cov-er.

THE CHRISTIAN'S DEATH.

NEARER HOME. S. M. D.   I. B. WOODBURY.

540   *"For ever."*

"For ever with the Lord!"
So, Jesus! let it be;
Life from the dead is in that word;
'T is immortality.
Here, in the body pent,
Absent from thee I roam:
Yet nightly pitch my moving tent
A day's march nearer home.

2 My Father's house on high,
Home of my soul! how near,
At times, to faith's aspiring eye,
Thy golden gates appear!
"For ever with the Lord!"
Father, if 't is thy will,
The promise of thy gracious word
Ev'n here to me fulfill.

3 So, when my latest breath
Shall rend the vail in twain,
By death I shall escape from death,
And life eternal gain.
Knowing as I am known,
How shall I love that word,
And oft repeat before the throne,
"For ever with the Lord!"
James Montgomery.

541   *"Nearer."*

One sweetly solemn thought
Comes to me o'er and o'er,—
Nearer my home, to-day, am I
Than e'er I've been before.
Nearer my Father's house,
Where many mansions be;
Nearer to-day the great white throne,
Nearer the crystal sea.

2 Nearer the bound of life,
Where burdens are laid down;
Nearer to leave the heavy cross:
Nearer to gain the crown.
But, lying dark between,
Winding down through the night,
There rolls the deep and unknown stream
That leads at last to light.

3 Ev'n now, perchance, my feet
Are slipping on the brink,
And I, to-day, am nearer home,—
Nearer than now I think.
Father, perfect my trust!
Strengthen my power of faith!
Nor let me stand, at last, alone
Upon the shore of death.
Phoebe Cary.

THE CHRISTIAN'S DEATH.

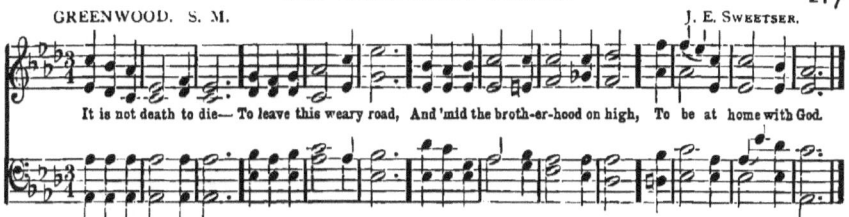

GREENWOOD. S. M.   J. E. SWEETSER.

It is not death to die— To leave this weary road, And 'mid the broth-er-hood on high, To be at home with God.

542   *"Where is thy victory?"*
IT is not death to die—
  To leave this weary road,
And 'mid the brotherhood on high,
  To be at home with God.

2 It is not death to close
  The eye long dimmed by tears,
And wake, in glorious repose
  To spend eternal years.

3 It is not death to bear
  The wrench that sets us free
From dungeon chain,—to breathe the air
  Of boundless liberty.

4 It is not death to fling
  Aside this sinful dust,
And rise, on strong exulting wing,
  To live among the just.

5 Jesus, thou Prince of life!
  Thy chosen cannot die;
Like thee, they conquer in the strife,
  To reign with thee on high.
        Geo. W. Bethune.

543   *Death of a Veteran.*
SERVANT of God, well done!
  Rest from thy loved employ:
The battle fought, the victory won,
  Enter thy Master's joy!

2 The voice at midnight came;
  He started up to hear;
A mortal arrow pierced his frame;
  He fell, but felt no fear.

3 His spirit with a bound
  Left its encumbering clay:
His tent, at sunrise, on the ground
  A darkened ruin lay.

4 The pains of death are past,
  Labor and sorrow cease,
And life's long warfare closed at last,
  His soul is found in peace.

5 Soldier of Christ, well done!
  Praise be thy new employ;
And, while eternal ages run,
  Rest in thy Saviour's joy.
        James Montgomery.

DUNBAR. S. M.   E. W. DUNBAR.

One sweet-ly sol-emn thought Comes to.... me o'er and o'er,—
CHO.—There'll be.... no sor-row there, There'll be.... no sor-row there;

Near-er my home, to-day, am I Than e'er.. I've been be-fore.
In heaven a-bove, where all is love, There'll be.... no sor-row there.

THE CHRISTIAN'S DEATH.

ZEPHYR. L. M.   W. B. BRADBURY.

544   *"His beloved sleep."*
WHY should we start, and fear to die?
  What timorous worms we mortals are!
Death is the gate of endless joy,
  And yet we dread to enter there.

2 The pains, the groans, the dying strife
  Fright our approaching souls away;
We still shrink back again to life,
  Fond of our prison and our clay.

3 Oh, if my Lord would come and meet,
  My soul should stretch her wings in haste,
Fly fearless through death's iron gate,
  Nor feel the terrors as she passed.

4 Jesus can make a dying bed
  Feel soft as downy pillows are,
While on his breast I lean my head,
  And breathe my life out sweetly there!
                         Isaac Watts.

545   *Death of the Righteous.*
How BLEST the righteous when he dies,—
  When sinks a weary soul to rest!
How mildly beam the closing eyes!
  How gently heaves the expiring breast!

2 So fades a summer-cloud away;
  So sinks the gale when storms are o'er;
So gently shuts the eye of day;
  So dies a wave along the shore.

3 A holy quiet reigns around,—
  A calm which life nor death destroys;
And naught disturbs that peace profound,
  Which his unfettered soul enjoys.

4 Life's labor done, as sinks the clay,
  Light from its load the spirit flies;
While heaven and earth combine to say,—
  "How blest the righteous when he dies!"
                      Mrs. Anna L. Barbauld.

REST. L. M.   W. B. BRADBURY.

546   *"Asleep in Jesus."*
ASLEEP in Jesus! blessèd sleep!
From which none ever wake to weep;
A calm and undisturbed repose,
Unbroken by the last of foes.

2 Asleep in Jesus! oh, how sweet
To be for such a slumber meet!
With holy confidence to sing
That death hath lost its venomed sting!

3 Asleep in Jesus! peaceful rest!
Whose waking is supremely blest;
No fear—no woe, shall dim the hour
That manifests the Saviour's power.

4 Asleep in Jesus! oh, for me
May such a blissful refuge be:
Securely shall my ashes lie,
And wait the summons from on high.
                      Mrs. Margaret Mackay.

THE CHRISTIAN'S DEATH.

ST. ASAPH. C. M. D.   J. M. GIORNOVICHI.

Be-hold the west-ern eve-ning light! It melts in deepening gloom; So calmly Christians sink a-way, De-scend-ing to the tomb. The winds breathe low, the withering leaf Scarce whispers from the tree: So gent-ly flows the parting breath, When good men cease to be.

547   *Life's Sunset.*

BEHOLD the western evening light!
  It melts in deepening gloom:
So calmly Christians sink away,
  Descending to the tomb.
The winds breathe low, the withering leaf
  Scarce whispers from the tree:
So gently flows the parting breath,
  When good men cease to be.

2 How beautiful on all the hills
  The crimson light is shed!
'T is like the peace the Christian gives
  To mourners round his bed.
How mildly on the wandering cloud
  The sunset beam is cast!
'T is like the memory left behind
  When loved ones breathe their last.

3 And now above the dews of night
  The rising star appears:
So faith springs in the heart of those
  Whose eyes are bathed in tears.
But soon the morning's happier light
  Its glory shall restore,
And eyelids that are sealed in death
  Shall wake to close no more.
W. H. O. Peabody.

548   *"Number our days."*

BENEATH our feet and o'er our head
  Is equal warning given;
Beneath us lie the countless dead,
  Above us is the heaven!
Death rides on every passing breeze,
  And lurks in every flower;
Each season hath its own disease,
  Its peril every hour!

2 Our eyes have seen the rosy light
  Of youth's soft cheek decay;
And fate descend in sudden night
  On manhood's middle day.
Our eyes have seen the steps of age
  Halt feebly to the tomb;
And yet shall earth our hearts engage,
  And dreams of days to come?

3 Then, mortal, turn! thy danger know;
  Where'er thy foot can tread,
The earth rings hollow from below,
  And warns thee of her dead!
Turn, mortal, turn! thy soul apply
  To truths divinely given:
The dead, who underneath thee lie,
  Shall live for hell or heaven!
Reginald Heber.

THE GENERAL JUDGMENT.

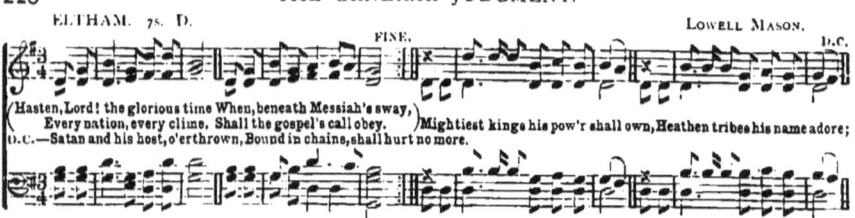

549 *The World's Conversion.*

Hasten, Lord! the glorious time
 When, beneath Messiah's sway,
Every nation, every clime,
 Shall the gospel's call obey.
Mightiest kings his power shall own,
 Heathen tribes his name adore;
Satan and his host, o'erthrown,
 Bound in chains, shall hurt no more.

2 Then shall wars and tumults cease,
 Then be banished grief and pain;
Righteousness and joy and peace
 Undisturbed shall ever reign.
Bless we, then, our gracious Lord;
 Ever praise his glorious name;
All his mighty acts record;
 All his wondrous love proclaim.
    Harriet Auber.

550 *The Day of Judgment.*

Oh, there will be mourning
 Before the judgment-seat,
When this world is burning,
 Beneath Jehovah's feet!

Cho.—Friends and kindred there will part.
 Will part to meet no more;
Wrath will sink the rebel's heart,
 While saints on high adore.
Oh, there will be mourning
 Before the judgment-seat.

2 Oh, there will be mourning
 Before the judgment-seat!
When the trumpet's warning
 The sinner's ear shall greet!—Cho.

3 Oh, there will be mourning
 Before the judgment-seat!
When, from dust returning,
 The lost their doom shall meet.—Cho.

4 Oh, there will be mourning
 Before the judgment-seat;
Justice, ever frowning,
 Shall seal the sinner's fate.—Cho.
    Anon.

THE GENERAL JUDGMENT.

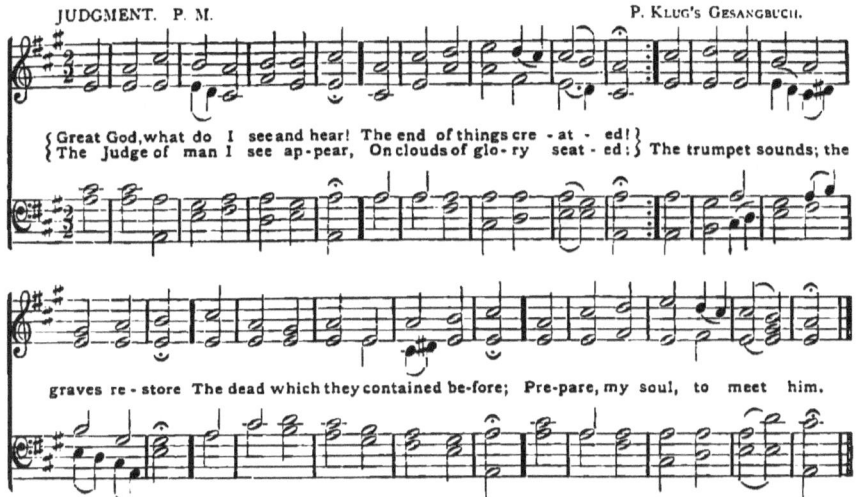

551 *Prepare to meet God.*

GREAT God, what do I see and hear!
  The end of things created!
The Judge of man I see appear,
  On clouds of glory seated:
The trumpet sounds; the graves restore
The dead which they contained before;
  Prepare, my soul, to meet him.

2 The dead in Christ shall first arise,
  At the last trumpet's sounding—
Caught up to meet him in the skies,
  With joy their Lord surrounding;
No gloomy fears their souls dismay,
His presence sheds eternal day
  On those prepared to meet him.

3 But sinners, filled with guilty fears,
  Behold his wrath prevailing;
For they shall rise, and find their tears
  And sighs are unavailing:
The day of grace is past and gone;
Trembling they stand before the throne,
  All unprepared to meet him.

4 Great God! what do I see and hear!
  The end of things created!
The Judge of man I see appear,
  On clouds of glory seated:
Beneath his cross I view the day
When heaven and earth shall pass away,
  And thus prepare to meet him.
                        William B. Collyer.

552 *"Into thine hand."*

WHEN my last hour is close at hand,
  My last sad journey taken,
Do thou, Lord Jesus! by me stand;
  Let me not be forsaken:
O Lord! my spirit I resign
Into thy loving hands divine;
  'Tis safe within thy keeping.

2 Countless as sands upon the shore,
  My sins may then appall me;
Yet, though my conscience vex me sore,
  Despair shall not enthrall me;
For as I draw my latest breath,
I'll think, Lord Christ! upon thy death;
  And there find consolation.

3 I shall not in the grave remain,
  Since thou death's bonds hast severed:
By hope with thee to rise again,
  From fear of death delivered,
I'll come to thee, where'er thou art,—
Live with thee, from thee never part;
  Therefore I die in rapture.

4 And so to Jesus Christ I'll go,
  My longing arms extending;
So fall asleep, in slumber deep,
  Slumber that knows no ending;
Till Jesus Christ, God's only Son,
Opens the gates of bliss, leads on
  To heaven, to life eternal.
                        Edgar A. Bowring, tr.

THE REST OF HEAVEN.

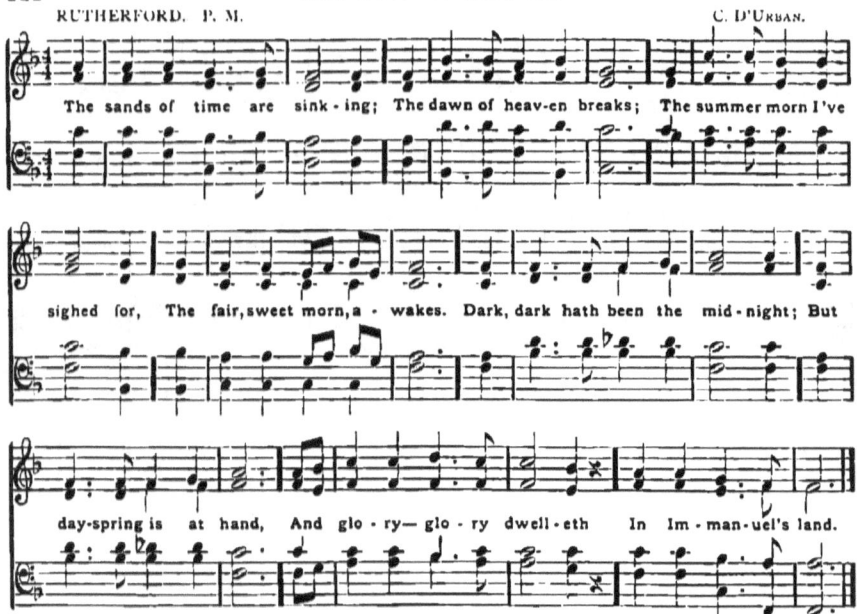

RUTHERFORD. P. M.   C. D'URBAN.

The sands of time are sink-ing; The dawn of heav-en breaks; The summer morn I've sighed for, The fair, sweet morn, a-wakes. Dark, dark hath been the mid-night; But day-spring is at hand, And glo-ry— glo-ry dwell-eth In Im-man-uel's land.

553   *"Immanuel's Land."*

THE sands of time are sinking;
  The dawn of heaven breaks;
The summer morn I've sighed for,
  The fair, sweet morn, awakes.
Dark, dark hath been the midnight;
  But dayspring is at hand,
And glory—glory dwelleth
  In Immanuel's land.

2 Oh, Christ! he is the fountain,
  The deep, sweet well of love;
The streams on earth I've tasted,
  More deep I'll drink above;
There to an ocean fullness
  His mercy doth expand,
And glory—glory dwelleth
  In Immanuel's land.

3 With mercy and with judgment
  My web of time he wove,
And aye the dews of sorrow
  Were lustred by his love;
I'll bless the hand that guided,
  I'll bless the heart that planned,
When throned where glory dwelleth,
  In Immanuel's land.
Mrs. Anne R. Cousin.

554   *"His house of wine."*

OH, Christ, he is the fountain,
  The deep, sweet well of love!
The streams on earth I've tasted,
  More deep I'll drink above:
There to an ocean fullness
  His mercy doth expand,
And glory—glory dwelleth
  In Immanuel's land.

2 Oh, I am my Belovéd's,
  And my Belovéd's mine!
He brings a poor vile sinner
  Into his "house of wine!"
I stand upon his merit,
  I know no other stand,
Not ev'n where glory dwelleth
  In Immanuel's land.

3 The bride eyes not her garment,
  But her dear Bridegroom's face;
I will not gaze at glory,
  But on my King of Grace—
Not at the crown he giveth,
  But on his piercéd hand—
The Lamb is all the glory
  Of Immanuel's land.
Mrs. Anne R. Cousin.

THE REST OF HEAVEN.

WOODLAND. C. M. 5 l. N. G. GOULD.

There is an hour of peaceful rest, To mourning wand'rers giv'n; There is a joy for souls dis-tressed, A balm for ev-ery wounded breast; 'Tis found a-bove—in heav'n.

555 *"No more death."*

THERE is an hour of peaceful rest,
To mourning wanderers given;
There is a joy for souls distressed;
A balm for every wounded breast:
'T is found above—in heaven.

2 There is a home for weary souls,
By sin and sorrow driven,—
When tossed on life's tempestuous shoals,
Where storms arise, and ocean rolls,
And all is drear—but heaven.

3 There faith lifts up her cheerful eye
To brighter prospects given;
And views the tempest passing by,
The evening shadows quickly fly,
And all serene—in heaven.

4 There fragrant flowers immortal bloom,
And joys supreme are given;
There rays divine disperse the gloom:
Beyond the confines of the tomb
Appears the dawn of heaven!
William B. Tappan.

HAPPY LAND. P. M. Telugu Melody.

There is a hap-py land, Far, far a-way, Where saints in glory stand, Bright, bright as day. Oh, how they sweetly sing, "Worthy is our Saviour King," Loud let his praises ring, Praise, praise for aye!

556 *The Happy Land.*

THERE is a happy land,
Far, far away,
Where saints in glory stand
Bright, bright as day.
Oh, how they sweetly sing,
"Worthy is our Saviour King,"
Loud let his praises ring,
Praise, praise for aye!

2 Come to that happy land,
Come, come away,
Why will ye doubting stand,
Why still delay?
Oh, we shall happy be,
When, from sin and sorrow free,
Lord we shall dwell with thee,
Blest, blest for aye.

3 Bright in that happy land,
Beams every eye:
Kept by a Father's hand,
Love cannot die.
Oh, then to glory run;
Be a crown and Kingdom won,
And bright, above the sun,
We'll reign for aye.
Andrew Young.

THE REST OF HEAVEN.

557 *The New Jerusalem.*

JERUSALEM, the golden,
  With milk and honey blest!
Beneath thy contemplation
  Sink heart and voice oppressed:
I know not, oh, I know not,
  What social joys are there,
What radiancy of glory,
  What light beyond compare.

2 They stand, those halls of Zion,
  All jubilant with song,
And bright with many an angel,
  And all the martyr throng;
The Prince is ever in them,
  The daylight is serene;
The pastures of the blessèd
  Are decked in glorious sheen.

3 There is the throne of David;
  And there, from care released,
The song of them that triumph,
  The shout of them that feast:
And they who, with their Leader,
  Have conquered in the fight
For ever and for ever
  Are clad in robes of white.
      John M. Neale, tr.

558 *"Short toil."*

BRIEF life is here our portion;
  Brief sorrow, short-lived care;
The life, that knows no ending,
  The tearless life, is there:
Oh, happy retribution!
  Short toil, eternal rest;
For mortals, and for sinners,
  A mansion with the blest!

2 And there is David's fountain,
  And life in fullest glow;
And there the light is golden,
  And milk and honey flow;
The light, that hath no evening,
  The health, that hath no sore,
The life, that hath no ending,
  But lasteth evermore.

3 There Jesus shall embrace us,
  There Jesus be embraced,—
That spirit's food and sunshine;
  Whence earthly love is chased:
Yes! God my King and Portion,
  In fullness of his grace,
We then shall see for ever,
  And worship face to face.
      John M. Neale, tr.

THE REST OF HEAVEN.

559 *"A City."*

JERUSALEM, the glorious!
 The glory of the elect,—
O dear and future vision
 That eager hearts expect!
Ev'n now by faith I see thee,
 Ev'n here thy walls discern;
To thee my thoughts are kindled,
 And strive, and pant, and yearn!

2 The Cross is all thy splendor,
 The Crucified, thy praise;
His laud and benediction
 Thy ransomed people raise;—
Jerusalem! exulting
 On that securest shore,
I hope thee, wish thee, sing thee,
 And love thee evermore!

3 O sweet and blessèd Country!
 Shall I e'er see thy face?
O sweet and blessèd Country!
 Shall I e'er win thy grace?
Exult, O dust and ashes!
 The Lord shall be thy part;
His only, his for ever,
 Thou shalt be, and thou art!
   John M. Neale, tr.

560 *"The glory that excelleth."*

OH, fair the gleams of glory,
 And bright the scenes of mirth,
That lighten human story
 And cheer this weary earth;
15 P

But richer far our treasure
 With whom the Spirit dwells,
Ours, ours in heavenly measure
 The glory that excels.

2 The lamplight faintly gleameth
 Where shines the noonday ray;
From Jesus' face there beameth
 Light of a sevenfold day;
And earth's pale lights, all faded,
 The Light from heaven dispels;
But shines for aye unshaded
 The glory that excels.

3 No broken cisterns need they
 Who drink from living rills;
No other music heed they
 Whom God's own music thrills.
Earth's precious things are tasteless,
 Its boisterous mirth repels,
Where flows in measure wasteless
 The glory that excels.

4 Since on our life descended
 Those beams of light and love,
Our steps have heavenward tended,
 Our eyes have looked above,
Till through the clouds concealing
 The home where glory dwells,
Our Jesus comes revealing
 The glory that excels.
   Charles I. Cameron.

THE REST OF HEAVEN.

561 *Tune—"Varina."*

On Jordan's rugged banks I stand,
 And cast a wishful eye
To Canaan's fair and happy land,
 Where my possessions lie.
Oh, the transporting, rapturous scene,
 That rises to my sight!
Sweet fields arrayed in living green,
 And rivers of delight!

2 O'er all those wide extended plains
 Shines one eternal day;
There God, the Son, for ever reigns,
 And scatters night away.
No chilling winds, or poisonous breath,
 Can reach that healthful shore;
Sickness and sorrow, pain and death,
 Are felt and feared no more.

3 When shall I reach that happy place,
 And be for ever blest?
When shall I see my Father's face,
 And in his bosom rest?
Filled with delight, my raptured soul
 Can here no longer stay;
Though Jordan's waves around me roll,
 Fearless I'd launch away.
 Samuel Stennett.

CAERSALEM. 8s, 7s, 7. Welsh Melody.

Who are these like stars appearing, These, before God's throne who stand? Each a golden crown is wearing;
Who are all this glorious band? Al-le-lu-ia! hark they sing, Praising loud their heav'nly King.

562 *"Who are these?"*

Who are these like stars appearing,
 These, before God's throne who stand?
Each a golden crown is wearing;
 Who are all this glorious band?
  Alleluia! hark they sing,
  Praising loud their heavenly King.

2 These are they who have contended
 For their Saviour's honor long,
Wrestling on till life was ended,
 Following not the sinful throng:
  These, who well the fight sustained,
  Triumph by the Lamb have gained.

3 These are they whose hearts were riven,
 Sore with woe and anguish tried,
Who in prayer full oft have striven
 With the God they glorified:
  Now, their painful conflict o'er,
  God has bid them weep no more.

4 These, like priests, have watched and waited,
 Offering up to Christ their will,
Soul and body consecrated,
 Day and night they serve him still:
  Now in God's most holy place,
  Blest they stand before his face.

5 Lo, the Lamb himself now feeds them,
 On Mount Sion's pastures fair;
From his central throne he leads them
 By the living fountains there:
  Lamb and Shepherd, Good Supreme,
  Free he gives the cooling stream.
 Frances E. Cox.

THE REST OF HEAVEN. 227

VARINA. C. M. D.   Arr. by G. F. Root.

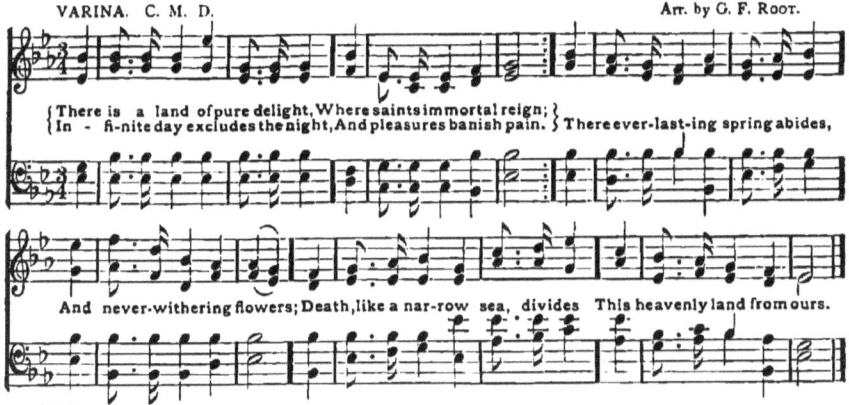

There is a land of pure delight, Where saints immortal reign;
In-fi-nite day excludes the night, And pleasures banish pain. There ever-last-ing spring abides, And never-withering flowers; Death, like a nar-row sea, divides This heavenly land from ours.

563   *"Go over this Jordan."*

THERE is a land of pure delight,
  Where saints immortal reign;
Infinite day excludes the night,
  And pleasures banish pain.
There everlasting spring abides,
  And never-withering flowers;
Death, like a narrow sea, divides
  This heavenly land from ours.

2 Sweet fields beyond the swelling flood
  Stand dressed in living green;
So to the Jews old Canaan stood,
  While Jordan rolled between.

But timorous mortals start and shrink
  To cross this narrow sea;
And linger, shivering on the brink,
  And fear to launch away.

3 Oh, could we make our doubts remove,
  These gloomy doubts that rise,
And see the Canaan that we love
  With unbeclouded eyes:—
Could we but climb where Moses stood,
  And view the landscape o'er,
Not Jordan's stream, nor death's cold flood,
  Should fright us from the shore.
                  Isaac Watts.

JERUSALEM. C. M.   From EPISCOPAL HYMNAL.

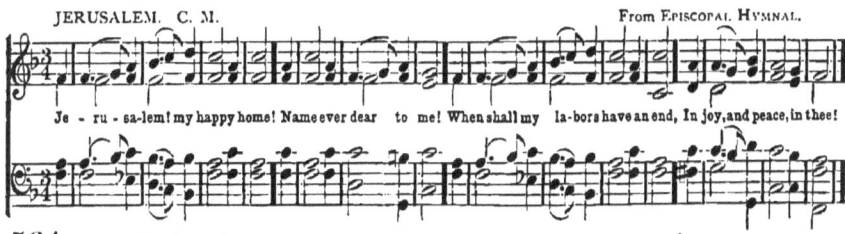

Je-ru-sa-lem! my happy home! Name ever dear to me! When shall my la-bors have an end, In joy, and peace, in thee!

564   *The New Jerusalem.*

JERUSALEM! my happy home!
  Name ever dear to me!
When shall my labors have an end,
  In joy, and peace, in thee!

2 Oh, when, thou city of my God,
  Shall I thy courts ascend,
Where congregations ne'er break up,
  And Sabbaths have no end?

3 There happier bowers than Eden's bloom,
  Nor sin nor sorrow know;
Blest seats! thro' rude and stormy scenes
  I onward press to you.

4 Why should I shrink at pain and woe!
  Or feel, at death, dismay?
I've Canaan's goodly land in view,
  And realms of endless day.

5 Apostles, martyrs, prophets there,
  Around my Saviour stand;
And soon my friends in Christ below,
  Will join the glorious band.

6 Jerusalem! my happy home!
  My soul still pants for thee;
Then shall my labors have an end,
  When I thy joys shall see.
                  "*F. B. P.*" tr. 1616.

THE REST OF HEAVEN.

RHINE. C. M.   German melody.

O mother dear, Je-ru-sa-lem, When shall I come to thee? When shall my sor-rows have an end? Thy joys when shall I see? Thy joys when shall I see?

565   *The New Jerusalem.*

O MOTHER dear, Jerusalem,
  When shall I come to thee?
When shall my sorrows have an end?
  Thy joys when shall I see?

2 O happy harbor of God's saints!
  O sweet and pleasant soil!
In thee no sorrow can be found,
  Nor grief, nor care, nor toil.

3 No dimly cloud o'ershadows thee,
  Nor gloom, nor darksome night;
But every soul shines as the sun,
  For God himself gives light.

4 Thy walls are made of precious stone,
  Thy bulwarks diamond-square,
Thy gates are all of orient pearl—
  O God! if I were there!
                  Anon.

AMSTERDAM. 7s, 6s. D.   J. NARES.

{ Rise, my soul, and stretch thy wings, Thy bet-ter por-tion trace; }
{ Rise from tran-si-to-ry things Tow'rd heav'n, thy native place: } Sun and moon and stars de-cay;
Time shall soon this earth re-move; Rise, my soul, and haste a-way To seats pre-pared a-bove.

566   *The better portion.*

RISE, my soul, and stretch thy wings,
  Thy better portion trace;
Rise from transitory things
  Toward heaven, thy native place:
Sun and moon and stars decay;
  Time shall soon this earth remove;
Rise, my soul, and haste away
  To seats prepared above.

2 Rivers to the ocean run,
  Nor stay in all their course;
Fire ascending seeks the sun;
  Both speed them to their source:
So a soul that's born of God,
  Pants to view his glorious face;
Upward tends to his abode,
  To rest in his embrace.

3 Cease, ye pilgrims, cease to mourn,
  Press onward to the prize;
Soon our Saviour will return
  Triumphant in the skies:
Yet a season,—and you know
  Happy entrance will be given,
All our sorrows left below,
  And earth exchanged for heaven.
                Robert Seagrave.

THE REST OF HEAVEN.

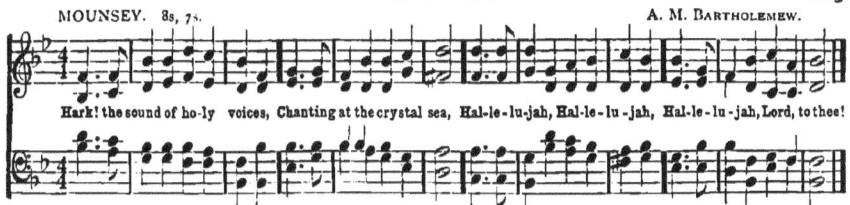

567 *"The sea of glass."*
HARK! the sound of holy voices,
  Chanting at the crystal sea,
Hallelujah, hallelujah,
  Hallelujah, Lord, to thee!

2 Multitudes, which none can number,
  Like the stars in glory stand,
Clothed in white apparel, holding
  Palms of victory in their hands.

3 They have come from tribulation,
  And have washed their robes in blood,
Washed them in the blood of Jesus;
  Tried they were and firm they stood.

4 Mocked, imprisoned, stoned, tormented,
  Sawn asunder, slain with sword,
They have conquered death and Satan
  By the might of Christ the Lord.

5 Love and peace they taste for ever,
  And all truth and knowledge see
In the Beatific Vision
  Of the blessèd Trinity.
C. Wordsworth.

568 *The City.*
DAILY, daily sing the praises
  Of the City God hath made;
In the beauteous fields of Eden
  Its foundation-stones are laid.

2 In the midst of that dear City
  Christ is reigning on his seat,
And the angels swing their censers
  In a ring about his feet.

3 From the throne a river issues,
  Clear as crystal, passing bright,
And it traverses the City
  Like a sudden beam of light.

4 There the wind is sweetly fragrant,
  And is laden with the song
Of the seraphs, and the elders,
  And the great redeemèd throng.

5 Oh, I would my ears were open
  Here to catch that happy strain!
Oh, I would my eyes some vision
  Of that Eden could attain!
S. Baring-Gould.

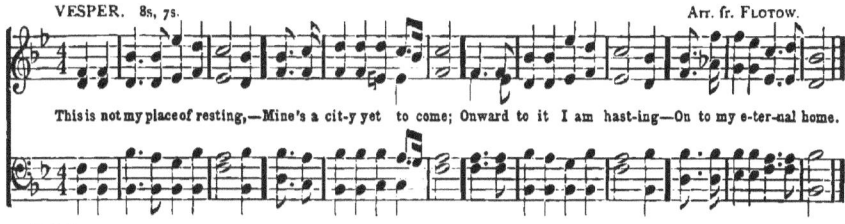

569 *Not our Rest.*
THIS is not my place of resting,—
  Mine's a city yet to come;
Onward to it I am hasting—
  On to my eternal home.

2 In it all is light and glory;
  O'er it shines a nightless day:
Every trace of sin's sad story,
  All the curse, hath passed away.

3 There the Lamb, our Shepherd, leads us
  By the streams of life along,—
On the freshest pastures feeds us,
  Turns our sighing into song.

4 Soon we pass this desert dreary,
  Soon we bid farewell to pain;
Never more are sad or weary,
  Never, never sin again!
Horatius Bonar.

570 *"My Father's House."*

In the house of my Father above,
  There are mansions provided for me,
Where my soul in the fulness of joy shall
    awake
  From its body of sin, to be free.

REFRAIN.

I shall go to that home by and by,
  And my Saviour will welcome me there:
He will crown me with life, he will fill me
    with joy,
  And his garment of love I shall wear.

2 When I weary of labor and toil,
  And with sorrow my heart is oppressed,
Then my Saviour comes near, and I think
    with delight
  Of the beautiful mansions of rest.—REF.

3 I have friends in those mansions above;
  They are waiting me now on the shore;
And I know we shall meet at the portals of
    light,
  When a few fleeting days shall be o'er.—
        REF.
          Mrs. F. C. Van Alstyne.

THE REST OF HEAVEN.

571 *Tune—"Beulah."*

Who are these in bright array,
This innumerable throng
Round the altar, night and day
Hymning one triumphant song?—
"Worthy is the Lamb, once slain,
Blessing, honor, glory, power,
Wisdom, riches, to obtain,
New dominion every hour."

2 These through fiery trials trod;
These from great afflictions came:
Now, before the throne of God,
Sealed with his almighty name,
Clad in raiment pure and white,
Victor-palms in every hand,
Through their dear Redeemer's might,
More than conquerors they stand.

3 Hunger, thirst, disease unknown,
On immortal fruits they feed;
Them the Lamb, amid the throne,
Shall to living fountains lead:
Joy and gladness banish sighs—
Perfect love dispel all fears—
And for ever from their eyes
God shall wipe away the tears.
James Montgomery.

572 *"Beautiful Zion."*

Beautiful Zion, built above,
Beautiful city that I love;
Beautiful gates of pearly white,
Beautiful temple—God its light.
He who was slain on Calvary,
Opens those pearly gates to me.—Ref.

2 Beautiful crowns on every brow,
Beautiful palms the conquerors show;
Beautiful robes the ransomed wear,
Beautiful all who enter there—
Thither I press with eager feet;
There shall my rest be long and sweet.—Ref.

3 Beautiful throne for Christ our King,
Beautiful songs the angels sing;
Beautiful rest—all wanderings cease;
Beautiful home of perfect peace—
There shall my eyes the Saviour see—
Haste to his heavenly home with me.—Ref.
G. Gill.

MISCELLANEOUS.

BENEVENTO. 7s D. S. WEBBE.

573 *New Year.*

WHILE, with ceaseless course, the sun
  Hasted through the former year,
Many souls their race have run,
  Nevermore to meet us here:
Fixed in an eternal state,
  They have done with all below;
We a little longer wait,—
  But how little none can know.

2 As the wingèd arrow flies
  Speedily the mark to find;
As the lightning from the skies
  Darts, and leaves no trace behind,

Swiftly thus our fleeting days
  Bear us down life's rapid stream;
Upward, Lord, our spirits raise,
  All below is but a dream.

3 Thanks for mercies past receive;
  Pardon of our sins renew;
Teach us henceforth how to live,
  With eternity in view:
Bless thy word to young and old;
  Fill us with a Saviour's love;
And, when life's short tale is told,
  May we dwell with thee above!

John Newton.

AMERICA. 6s, 4s. H. CAREY.

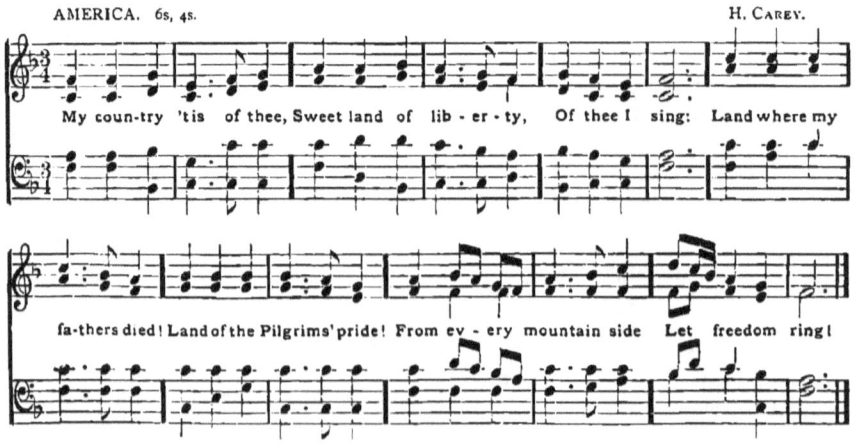

MISCELLANEOUS. 233

ST. GEORGE. 7s. D.   George J. Elvey.

Come, ye thankful people, come, Raise the song of Harvest Home! All is safe-ly gathered in, Ere the winter storms begin;

God our Maker doth provide For our wants to be supplied: Come to God's own temple, come, Raise the song of Harvest Home!

574   *Song for Harvest.*
Come, ye thankful people, come,
Raise the song of Harvest Home!
All is safely gathered in,
Ere the winter storms begin:
God our Maker doth provide
For our wants to be supplied:
Come to God's own temple, come,
Raise the song of Harvest Home!

2 We ourselves are God's own field,
Fruit unto his praise to yield:
Wheat and tares together sown,
Unto joy or sorrow grown:
First the blade, and then the ear,
Then the full corn shall appear:
Grant, O Harvest-Lord, that we
Wholesome grain and pure may be!

3 For the Lord our God shall come,
And shall take his harvest home:
From his field shall in that day
All offences purge away:
Give his angels charge at last
In the fire the tares to cast:
But the fruitful ears to store
In his garner evermore.

4 Then, thou Church Triumphant, come,
Raise the song of Harvest Home!
All are safely gathered in,
Free from sorrow, free from sin:
There, for ever purified,
In God's garner to abide:
Come, ten thousand angels, come,
Raise the glorious Harvest Home!
Henry Alford.

---

575   6s, 4s.   *National Song.*
My country! 't is of thee,
Sweet land of liberty,
  Of thee I sing;
Land where my fathers died!
Land of the Pilgrims' pride!
From every mountain side
  Let freedom ring!

2 My native country, thee—
Land of the noble, free—
  Thy name I love;
I love thy rocks and rills,
Thy woods and templed hills;
My heart with rapture thrills
  Like that above.

3 Let music swell the breeze,
And ring from all the trees
  Sweet freedom's song:
Let mortal tongues awake;
Let all that breathe partake;
Let rocks their silence break,—
  The sound prolong.

4 Our fathers' God! to thee,
Author of liberty,
  To thee we sing:
Long may our land be bright
With freedom's holy light;
Protect us by thy might,
  Great God, our King!
Samuel F. Smith.

GLASGOW. C. M.   G. F. Root.

Lord! while for all mankind we pray, Of every clime and coast, Oh, hear us for our native land, The land we love the most.

576   *National.*
Lord! while for all mankind we pray,
  Of every clime and coast,
Oh, hear us for our native land,
  The land we love the most.

2 Oh, guard our shores from every foe,
  With peace our borders bless,
With prosperous times our cities crown,
  Our fields with plenteousness.

3 Unite us in the sacred love
  Of knowledge, truth, and thee.
And let our hills and valleys shout
  The songs of liberty.

4 Here may religion, pure and mild,
  Smile on our Sabbath hours;
And piety and virtue bless
  The home of us and ours.

5 Lord of the nations, thus to thee
  Our country we commend;
Be thou her refuge and her trust,
  Her everlasting friend.
                John R. Wreford.

577   *Close of the Year.*
Thee we adore, eternal Name!
  And humbly own to thee
How feeble is our mortal frame,
  What dying worms are we!

2 The year rolls round, and steals away
  The breath that first it gave;
Whate'er we do, where'er we be,
  We're traveling to the grave.

3 Great God! on what a slender thread
  Hang everlasting things!
The eternal state of all the dead
  Upon life's feeble strings!

4 Infinite joy, or endless woe,
  Attends on every breath;
And yet, how unconcerned we go
  Upon the brink of death!

5 Waken, O Lord, our drowsy sense,
  To walk this dangerous road!
And if our souls are hurried hence,
  May they be found with God.
                Isaac Watts.

578   *New Year.*
Our Father! through the coming year
  We know not what shall be;
But we would leave without a fear
  Its ordering all to thee.

2 It may be we shall toil in vain
  For what the world holds fair;
And all the good we thought to gain
  Deceive and prove but care.

3 It may be it shall darkly blend
  Our love with anxious fears,
And snatch away the valued friend,
  The tried of many years.

4 It may be it shall bring us days
  And nights of lingering pain;
And bid us take a farewell gaze
  Of those loved haunts of men.

5 But calmly, Lord, on thee we rest;
  No fears our trust shall move;
Thou knowest what for each is best,
  And thou art Perfect Love.
                William Gaskell.

579   *Prayer for Seamen.*
We come, O Lord, before thy throne,
  And, with united plea,
We meet and pray for those who roam
  Far off upon the sea.

2 Oh, may the Holy Spirit bow
  The sailor's heart to thee,
Till tears of deep repentance flow,
  Like rain-drops in the sea!

3 Then may a Saviour's dying love
  Pour peace into his breast,
And waft him to the port above
  Of everlasting rest.
                Mrs. Phoebe H. Brown.

INDEX OF TUNES.

	PAGE
Alexander. S. M	134
Alvan. 8s, 7s, 4	26
America. 6s, 4s	232
Amsterdam. 7s, 6s. D	228
An Open Door. P. M	120
Antioch. C. M	59
Anvern. L. M	207
Ariel. C. P. M	64
Arlington. C. M	94
Armenia. C. M	160
Armstrong. 8s, 7s, D	204
Assurance. 10s	151
Athens. C. M. D	60
Autumn. 8s, 7s, D	73
Avon. C. M	67, 109
Azmon. C. M	74, 198
Balerma. C. M	89
Bartimeus. 8s, 7s	154
Havaria. 8s, 7s, D	199
Beatitude. C. M	203
Beauteous Day. P. M	214
Beecroft. 8s, 7s, D	180
Bemerton. C. M	19
Beminster. 7s	36
Benevento. 7s, D	232
Bera. L. M	110
Bethany. 6s, 4s	128
Beulah. 7s, D	230
Beyrut. P. M	193
Bonar. P. M	15
Boylston. S. M	196
Brattle Street. C. M. D	48
Bread of Life. 6s, 4s	39
Brown. C. M	146
Budleigh. P. M	169
Bullinger. 8s, 3	93
Bycfield. C. M	20
Caersalem. 8s, 7s, 7	152, 226
Cana. 11s	136
Canonbury. L. M	8, 163
Carol. C. M. D	56
Carolyn. 7s, 6s. D	47
Carthage. 8s, 7s	74
Caskey. 7s, 6s, D	142
Chenies. 7s, 6s, D	77
Cherith. C. M	117, 202
Chimes. C. M	43
China. C. M	215
Christmas. C. M	56, 133
Clyde. 8s, 4	44
Come, ye dis. 11s, 10s	99
Communion. C. M. D	67
Concone. C. M. D	68
Cooling. C. M	118
Corinth. C. M	49
Coronation. C. M	75
Corridor Heights. P. M	231
Crux Christi. 7s, 6s, D	69
Culford. 7s, D	124
Cyprus. 7s	175
Darley. L. M	191
Day of Rest. 7s, 6s, D	45
Dedham. C. M	203
Dennis. S. M	32
Detroit. S. M	101
Dijon. M	22
Dix. 7s, 61	29
Dominus Regit. P. M	155
Dornance. 8s, 7s	194
Dover. S. M	61

	PAGE
Downs. C. M	52
Duke Street. L. M	70, 170
Dunbar. S. M	217
Dundee. C. M	53, 202
Edina. 6s, 5s	131
Ellerton. 10s	35
Ellesdie. 8s, 7s, D	150
Eltham. 7s, D	220
Erie. 8s, 7s, D	53
Essex. 7s	159
Evan. C. M	118, 197
Even Me. P. M	119
Evening. S. M	33
Evening Hymn. L. M	30
Evening Praise. P. M	37
Eventide. 10s	34
Every Day. P. M	156
Ewing. 7s, 6s, D	224
Expostulation. 11s	102
Farrant. C. M	20, 132
Fatherland. 5s, 8, 5s	148
Federal Street. L M	163, 201
Ferguson. S. M	177
Flectens. P. M	113
Flemming. 8s, 6s	106
Formosa. 8s, 7s, D	78
Fountain. C. M	94
Gaylord. 8s, 7s, D	102
Gerhardt. 7s, 6s, D	65
Gilton. 7s, 5	84
Glasgow. C. M	95, 234
Glory. S. M	16
God be with you. P. M	41
Golden Hill S. M	196
Gorton. S. M	90
Goshen. 11s	137
Grange. 8s, 7s	153
Grassmere. P. M	181
Gratitude. L. M	31
Greenville. 8s, 7s, 4	39
Greenwood. S. M	167, 217
Grey. 7s, 5	21
Grigg. C. M	63
Guardian. 6s, 4	123
Guide. 7s, 61	172
Hallo. 7s, 61	6, 108, 173
Hallel. C. M. D	180
Hamburg. L. M	69
Hauden. 8s, 7s, 4s	213
Happy Land. P. M	223
Harvey. P. M	185
Harwell. 8s, 7s, D	72
Haydn. C. M	87
He Leadeth Me. L. M. D	179
Heber. C. M	161
Hebron. L. M	31
Helena. C. M	63
Hendon. 7s	23
Henley. 11s, 10s	35
Herald Angels. 7s, D	58
Herbert. P. M	168
Herbert. 8s, 4	186
Hermon. C. M	116
Herstmonceux. P. M	173
Holley. 7s	37
Holy Cross. C. M	161
Holy Trinity. C. M	66
Horton. 7s	28
Hummel. C. M	89

	PAGE
Hursley. L. M	30, 201
Hymn. C. M	19
I Am Coming. P. M	119
I Need Thee. P. M	112
Innocents. 7s	22
Inverness. S. M	199
Iowa. S. M	91
Irby. 8s, 7s, 7s	55
Irene. P. M	103
Italian Hymn. 6s, 4s	51
Jerusalem. C. M	227
Jewett. 6s, D	184
Judgment. P. M	221
Judgment-Seat. P. M	220
Knox. C. M	42
Kornthal. C. M	132
La Monte. P. M	156
Laban. S. M	139
Lachrymae. 7s, 31	100
Langran. 10s	104
Langton. S. M	25
Last Hope. 7s	83, 187
Laud. C. M	55
Laudes Domini. P. M	5
Lead Me On. P. M	138
Leighton. S. M	135
Leila. 10s	14
Lenox. 11. M	92
Life. 8s, 7s, 7s	99
Lisbon. S. M	10
Louvan. L. M	54
Love Divine. 8s, 7s, D	149
Loving kindness. L. M	95
Lowry. L. M	8
Luther. S. M	176
Lux Benigna. 10s, 4s	186
Lux Mundi. 7s, 6s, D	97
Lyndo. P. M	121
Magdalene. 6s, 5s	130
Magill. 11s	157
Manoah. C. M	46, 66
Marlow. C. M	11
Martyn. 7s, D	98, 125
Mayent. 7s, 6	87
Mear. C. M	7
Melody. C. M	164
Mendebras. 7s, 6s, D	11
Mendon. L. M	200
Meribah. C. P. M	76
Messiah. 7s, D	146
Middleton. 8s, 7s, D	79
Migdol. L. M	9
Miriam. 7s, 6s, D	225
Mission Song. 8s, 7s, D	195
Missionary Chant. L. M	144, 206
Missionary Hymn. 7s, 6s, D	208
More Love. 6s, 4s	128
Mornington. S. M	86
Mounsey. 8s, 7s	229
My Life Flows On. P. M	139
Naomi. C. M	86
Naumann. C. M., 51	96
Neale. S. M	32
Near the Cross. P. M	111
Nearer Home. S. M. D	216
Nettleton. 8s, 7s, D	151
New Haven. 6s, 4s	84

235

INDEX OF SUBJECTS.

	PAGE
Newcourt. L. P. M	13
Nicæa. P. M	6
Ninety-and-nine. P. M	112
Noel. C. M. D	50, 57
Nomen Jesu. 7s	154
Oak. 6s, 4s	126
Oaksville. C. M	16, 205
Oberlin. L. M	24
Old Hundred. L. M	12
Olim. P. M	230
Olivet. 6s, 4s	162
Olmutz. S. M	131
Orleus. 7s, 6s, D	209
Ortonville. C. M	61
Owen. S. M	101
Paraclete. 7s, 5	85
Park Street. L. M	145
Pass Me Not. 8s, 5s	114
Pax Tecum. 10s, 21	162
Poukivell. 6s, 5s	109
Perrin. C. P. M	183
Petrox. 6s	45
Philip. 7s, 31	110
Pilot. 7s, 61	115
Pleyel's Hymn. 7s	147
Portuguese Hymn. 11s	136
Prayer. S. M	91
Propior Deo. 6s, 4s	127
Raphael. 8s, 7s, 4	27, 115
Rathbun. 8s, 7s	68, 211
Raynolds. 11s, 10s	166
Refuge. 7s, D	125
Regent Square. 8s, 7s, 4s	212
Remsen. C. M	190
Rest. L. M	218
Retreat. L. M	24
Return. C. M	96
Rhine. C. M	228
Riseholme. S. M	21
Rock of Ages. 7s, 61	200
Rockingham. L. M	61
Rosefield. 7s, 61	172
Rothwell. L. M	71
Rutherford. P. M	222
Sabbath. 7s, D	10
Sarum. 8s, 4s	120, 148
Schumann. S. M	33
Scotland. 12s	100
Security. P. M	174
Segur. 8s, 7s, 4	122
Seir. S. M	167
Serenity. C. M	64, 116
Sessions. L. M	13, 62
Seymour. 7s	36, 117
Shawmut. S. M	90
Shining Shore. P. M	215
Shirland. S. M	25
Sicily. 8s, 7s	204
Siloam. C. M	198
Silver Street. S. M	14
Sing for Jesus. P. M	155
Solid Rock. L. M, 61	183
Solney. 8s, 7s	189
Something for Jes. 6s, 4s	129
Southport. C. M	18
Southwell. C. M	42
Spanish Hymn. 7s, 61	108
Spitta. 7s, 6s, D	165
St. Aelred. 8s, 3	143
St. Agnes. C. M	164
St. Albans. 6s, 5s, D	140
St. Ann's. C. M	46, 197
St. Asaph. C. M. D	219
St. Bees. 7s	158
St. Bride. S. M	81, 213
St. George. 7s, D	233
St. George's, Bolton. 7s, 6s, D	178
St. Gertrude. 6s, 5s, D	141
St. Hilda. 7s, 6s, D	105
St. Peter. C. M	100
St. Sylvester. 8s, 7s	41, 168
St. Thomas. S. M	17
State Street. S. M	192
Stephanos. P. M	138
Stephens. C. M	88
Stockwell. 8s, 7s	33, 186
Susinanne. 7s, 6	88
Sweet Hour. L. M. D	28
Tell the Story. 7s, 6s, D	109
Thatcher. S. M	177
The High Rock. P. M	121
Theodora. 7s	147
Thrnus. P. M	114
Treves. 7s, 5	85
Trust. P. M	174
Trust. C. M	185
Trusting. 7s	65
Uxbridge. L. M	44
Valentia. C. M	171
Valley of Blessing. P. M	123
Varina. C. M, D	227
Veni Lux. P. M	122
Vesper. 8s, 7s	229
Vesper Hymn. 8s, 7s, D	38
Victory. 8s, 7s, 4	75
Vigil. S. M	17
Vox Angelica. P. M	182
Wales. 8s, 4s	140
Warwick. C. M	7
Webb. 7s, 6s, D	143, 210
Wesley. 7s, D	80
Wesley. 11s, 10s	211
Wilmot. 8s, 7s	154
Wimborne. L. M	62, 144
Wimborne. 8s, 7s	148
Wondrous Love. P. M	93
Woodland. C. M, 51	223
Woodstock. C. M	18
Woodworth. L. M	107
Wraysbury. 8s, 7s	40
Yeisley. P. M	193
Yet Room. 10s, 31	111
York. C. M	43
Zephyr. L. M	215

INDEX OF SUBJECTS.

Abide with Me	66, 75, 79, 385
Accepted time	231, 251, 256, 281
Activity	417, 416, 459-484
Adoption	425, 434, 436, 438
Advent of Christ:	
At Birth	137-146
To Judgment	See *Judgment*.
To Kingdom	See *Millennium*.
Advocate	See *Christ*.
Afflictions	450-458
Aged	See *Old Age*.
Almsgiving	See *Charity*.
Angels	139, 255, 365, 447, 460
Ashamed of Jesus	328, 366, 401
Asleep in Jesus	See *Death*.
Assurance:	
Expressed	354, 380, 407, 436, 448
Prayed for	191, 207, 302, 363, 383
Urged	306, 329, 336, 360, 369
Atonement:	
Necessary	220-229
Completed	230-244, 377, 430
Offered	245-257, 339
Accepted	258-288, 341, 416
Backsliding	289-323
Baptism	See *Ordinances*.
Bible	103-114
Calvary	161, 164, 167, 233, 282, 440
Cares	73, 340, 357, 422, 432, 449
Charity	414, 416, 464, 473, 477, 484
Cheerfulness	See *Joy*.
Children	137, 167, 491-497
Childlike Spirit	See *Humility*.
Christ:	
Advent at Birth	137-146
Advocate	50, 174, 240, 267, 505
Ascension of	175, 178, 184
Character of	147-159, 374-417
Crucifixion of	160-170, 272, 240, 511
Divinity of	146, 147, 179, 180, 191
Example of	151, 153, 158, 376, 383
Friend	138, 159, 312, 411, 415
Humanity of	143, 146, 149, 158, 362
Immanuel	143-147, 388, 503, 553
King	173, 177, 181, 190, 196
Lamb	172, 182, 223, 243, 269, 440
Life of	147-159, 376, 383
Love of	147, 157, 164, 167, 169, 170
Mediator	174, 223, 230, 237, 207
Priest	49, 171, 231, 397, 416, 440
Prophet	152, 374, 397, 407
Resurrection of	171-180, 352, 539
Saviour	140, 147, 159, 180, 191
Shepherd	227, 259, 284, 302, 337
Sufferings of	160-170, 241, 511
Way, Truth, and Life	38, 155, 175
Wisdom	111, 146, 155, 451
Christians:	
Afflictions	450-458
Conflicts	289-323
Disciplines	450-458

INDEX OF SUBJECTS.

Duties........................459-484
Encouragements...........324-373
Fellowship..................485-490
Graces......................418-429
Love for Christ.............374-417
Privileges..................430-449
Church:
  Institutions of....192, 193, 474, 490
  Missions of.................513-537
  Ordinances of...............485-512
  Revival of.....190-194, 197, 203, 529
  Triumph of........192, 196, 513-537
  Unity of..........425, 444, 485-490
  Uniting with....See *Ordinances*.
  Work of..........414, 417, 463-484
Close of Worship..............30-102
Confidence.......354, 380, 407, 436, 460
Conflict with Sin............289-323
Conformity......151, 153, 156, 415, 421
Conscience......104, 223, 263, 271, 278
Consecration:
  Of Possessions....416, 464, 473, 477
  Of Self........161, 298, 308, 383, 414
Consistency......151, 153, 156, 415, 421
Consolations........See *Afflictions*.
Contentment....336-341, 346, 420, 449
Conversion......See *Regeneration*.
Conviction.................See *Law*.
Courage..................324-373, 444
Creation......See *God, the Creator*.
Cross:
  Taking........161, 169, 223, 273, 366
  Bearing...156, 280, 313, 383, 453, 458
  Glorying in....168, 232, 234, 328, 364
  Salvation by....See *Atonement*.
Crucifixion.............See *Christ*.

Death........................119, 538-548
Decrees...............115, 133, 135, 136
Delay................245, 250, 251, 256
Dependence:
  On Providence...20, 55, 64, 120-127
  On Grace........45, 156, 208, 217, 298
Depravity...........See *Lost State*.
Despondency.See *Encouragements*.
Devotion...............See *Prayer*.
Diligence.............See *Activity*.
Doubt.........See *Encouragements*.
Doxologies...............17-19, 70, 87

Earnestness.........See *Activity*.
Earnest...........See *Holy Spirit*.
Election..............See *Decrees*.
Encouragements.........324-373, 444
Energy................See *Activity*.
Eternity..........15, 19, 119, 123, 133
Evening..................66-101, 443
Example:
  Of Christ.............See *Christ*.
  Of Christians...See *Consistency*.

Faith...........206, 216-219, 416-424
Fall of Man........See *Lost State*.
Father, God our..........See *God*.
Fellowship..................485-490
Fidelity........121, 308, 318, 362, 421

Forbearance:
  Divine....................See *God*.
  Christian........See *Forgiveness*.
Forgiveness:
  Of Injuries.........153, 156, 362, 469
  Of Sin....See *Atonement* and *Repentance*.
Future Punishment......21, 278, 550

God:
  Attributes.............15-30, 115-136
  Benevolence......20, 64, 69, 73, 429
  Condescension....124, 128, 147, 149
  Creator..........15, 23, 113, 115, 126
  Eternity.........15, 19, 119, 123, 133
  Faithfulness....115-117, 122, 335-339
  Father......125, 130, 427, 434, 436
  Forbearance....49, 98, 122, 124, 132
  Glory.......56, 113, 124, 125, 128, 134
  Goodness.......20, 64, 69, 73, 429
  Grace....128, 235, 370, 425, 435, 440
  Holiness........2, 59, 63, 124, 130, 434
  Justice..........124, 128, 132, 199
  Love........15, 131, 132, 233, 345, 363
  Majesty........2, 15-19, 115, 124, 129
  Mercy......25, 61, 121, 132, 271, 279
  Mystery......115, 116, 125, 135, 433
  Omnipotence...32, 118, 125, 330, 335
  Omnipresence.46, 125, 134, 420, 439
  Omniscience.....55, 84, 121, 208, 217
  Pity.........50, 52, 124, 253, 267, 271
  Providence....91, 115, 120, 330, 335
  Sovereignty......115, 133, 135, 136
  Supremacy..15-23, 373, 419, 433, 444
  Trinity.........2, 25, 40, 56, 63, 129
  Truth..........15, 21, 114, 117, 436
  Unchangeableness......32, 358, 372
  Wisdom............30, 126, 432, 451
Gospel..............See *Atonement*.
Grace....128, 235, 370, 425, 435, 440
Graces, Christian..........418-429, 482
Gratitude......64, 69, 122, 214, 386, 429
Grieving the Spirit.......See *Holy Spirit*.
Growth in Grace....215, 370, 459, 482
Guidance....92, 304, 317, 340, 454, 462

Happiness..................See *Joy*.
Harvest........463, 475, 483, 532, 574
Hearing the Word....57-60, 72, 94-97
Heart:
  Change of......215-222, 240-244, 323
  Deceitfulness of..222, 229, 309, 487
  Searching of...203-208, 217, 269, 393
  Surrender of......260, 306, 370, 482
Heaven................26, 559-572
Hell.........See *Future Punishment*.
Heirship....353, 411, 425, 436, 438, 485
Holiness:
  Of Christians......215, 320, 431, 438
  Of God....................See *God*.
Holy Scriptures...........See *Bible*.
Holy Spirit:
  Divine.........129, 200, 204, 209, 211
  Grieved........217, 246, 254, 256, 294
  Striving........201, 240-242, 246, 255

Witnessing...207, 211, 215, 289, 306
Home........See *Family* or *Heaven*.
Home Missions.....478, 483, 522, 532
Hope:
  In Death......119, 352, 538-548, 552
  Under Afflictions..335-339, 450-458
  Under Conviction.221, 226, 240-244
  Under Despondency...324-373, 444
Humility....53, 214, 215, 268, 291, 300

Immanuel.................See *Christ*.
Importunity............See *Prayer*.
Incarnation..See *Christ.—Advent*.
Ingratitude..........See *Gratitude*.
Inspiration....103, 105, 114, 202, 219
Intercession.49, 171, 231, 397, 416, 440
Invitations..................245-257

Joining the Church............See *Ordinances*.
Joy........1, 27, 208, 306, 341, 392, 411
Judgment Day..185, 189, 199, 549-551
Justice.....................See *God*.
Justification...See *Atonement* and *Faith*.

Kindness........153, 156, 164, 362, 469
Kingdom of Christ....See *Church*.

Labor.................See *Activity*.
Lamb of God............See *Christ*.
Law of God......162, 223, 241, 440, 448
Liberality............See *Charity*.
Little Things..9, 64, 120, 179, 278, 468
Long-suffering..See *Forbearance*.
Lord's Day....................8-14
Lord's Prayer..........130, 432, 434
Lord's Supper................498-512
Lost State of Man...........220-229
Love:
  Of God....................See *God*.
  Of Christ..............See *Christ*.
  Of Holy Spirit..See *Holy Spirit*.
  For God........27, 69, 120-128, 132
  For the Saviour.............374-417
  For Saints.........425, 444, 485-490
  For Souls.....210, 253, 318, 464-479
  For the Church...192, 193, 474, 490
Loving-kindness..............239, 329

Majesty of God............See *God*.
Mediator................See *Christ*.
Mediatorial Reign....See *Church*.
Meditation..........426, 433, 449
Meekness...53, 214, 215, 268, 291, 300
Mercifulness......See *Forgiveness*.
Mercy....................See *God*.
Mercy-seat........29, 33, 48, 61, 230
Millennium..............185-199, 537
Ministry....461, 465, 474, 483, 524, 543
Missions..............459-484, 513-537
Morning Worship..............1-7
Mortality...............See *Death*.
Mysteries of Providence.See *God*.

National................139, 575, 576

Nature........See *God, the Creator.*
Needful, One Thing.....222, 228, 278
New Year..................573, 578

Old Age................80, 335, 541, 553
Omnipotence..............See *God.*
Omnipresence............See *God.*
Omniscience..............See *God.*
Opening of Service...........1-65
Ordinances..................491-512
Orphans............428, 439, 469, 478

Pardon............See *Forgiveness.*
Parting........76, 82, 89, 90, 102, 487
Pastor...................See *Ministry.*
Patience.See *Forbearance*, or *Trust.*
Peace:
 Christian......82, 354, 400, 439, 452
 National..........139, 522, 575, 579
Perseverance...354, 425, 430, 436, 448
Pilgrim-spirit.27, 30, 317, 338, 444, 454
Pity of God..................See *God.*
Pleasures........96, 224, 229, 278, 566
Poor, The........464, 466-469, 472, 479
Praise.........................15-30
Prayer.........................31-65
Preaching............See *Ministry.*
Pride..................See *Humility.*
Procrastination........See *Delay.*
Prodigal Son.........245, 260, 261, 272
Progress......See *Growth in Grace.*
Promises..........21, 117, 335-339, 352

Providence.................See *God.*
Purity..................See *Holiness.*

Race, Christian......326, 351, 392, 433
Redemption........See *Atonement.*
Regeneration............See *Heart.*
Repentance..........258-288, 294, 511
Resignation........See *Afflictions.*
Rest...See *Meditation*, or *Heaven.*
Resurrection:
 Of Christ..............See *Christ.*
 Of Believers.......352, 538-548, 552
Revival................See *Church.*
Rock of Ages....119, 192, 303, 433, 498

Sabbath........................8-14
Sabbath-School......137, 167, 491-497
Sailors......116, 237, 307, 310, 349, 579
Salvation...........See *Growth in Grace.*
Sanctification.......See *Growth in Grace.*
Saviour...................See *Christ.*
Scriptures................See *Bible.*
Self-deception..........See *Heart.*
Self-denial....9, 156, 169, 308, 464, 473
Self-examination........See *Heart.*
Self-righteousness..223, 226, 377, 471
Shepherd.................See *Christ.*
Sickness......92, 121, 352, 355, 451-453
Sin:
 Indwelling..........See *Conflict.*
 Original............See *Lost State.*

Conviction of...........See *Law.*
Sincerity.......9, 35, 215, 320, 421, 423
Soldier, Christian...327, 331, 342, 344
Souls, Love for...........See *Love.*
Sovereignty..............See *God.*
Strength, as Days......319, 355, 452
Submission........See *Afflictions.*
Sunday School.......See *Children.*

Temperance........See *Self-denial.*
Thanksgiving....20, 64, 122, 429, 574
Trials................See *Afflictions.*
Trinity....................See *God.*
Trust........116, 345-347, 353, 431, 449

Union of Believers:
 To Christ.....353, 407, 416, 425, 485
 To each other......425, 444, 485-490

Warfare, Christian....See *Soldier.*
Warnings..........See *Invitations.*
Watchfulness...187, 229, 342, 374, 461
Way of Salvation..See *Atonement.*
Wisdom....................See *God.*
Witness............See *Holy Spirit.*
Word of God............See *Bible.*
Worldliness........See *Pleasures.*

Year, Close of.......119, 123, 573, 577

Zeal.................See *Activity.*
Zion..................See *Church.*

INDEX OF FIRST LINES.

	HYMN		HYMN
A charge to keep I have	229	And wilt thou hear, O Lord	225
A mother may forgetful be	514	Arise, my soul, arise!	230
Abide with me: fast falls the eventide	79	Arise, ye saints, arise!	333
According to thy gracious word	508	Art thou weary, art thou languid	339
Acquaint thyself quickly, O sinner, with	257	As pants the hart for cooling streams	292
Again, as evening's shadow falls	67	As with gladness men of old	65
Alas! and did my Saviour bleed	165	Ask ye what great thing I know	392
Alas! what hourly dangers rise!	296	Asleep in Jesus! blessed sleep!	546
All hail the power of Jesus' name!	183	At even, when the sun was set	443
All people that on earth do dwell	16	Awake, awake, O Zion	186
Almighty Lord, the sun shall fail	112	Awake, my soul, and with the sun	6
Always with us, always with us	379	Awake, my soul, stretch every nerve	326
Amazing grace! how sweet the sound	235	Awake, my soul, to joyful lays	239
Am I a soldier of the cross	327	Awake, our souls! away, our fears!	351
And are we yet alive	486		
And canst thou, sinner! slight	254	Beautiful Zion, built above	572
And will the Judge descend	199	Before Jehovah's awful throne	15

INDEX OF FIRST LINES.

	HYMN
Begin, my tongue, some heavenly	117
Behold a Stranger at the door!	277
Behold the throne of grace!	51
Behold the western evening light	547
Behold! what wondrous grace	438
Beneath our feet and o'er our head	548
Blessed are the sons of God	425
Blessed Saviour! thee I love	273
Blessing, and honor, and glory	22
Blest be the tie that binds	487
Blest is the man whose softening	469
Blest Jesus! when my soaring thoughts	394
Blow ye the trumpet, blow	231
Book of grace, and book of glory!	109
Break thou the bread of life	97
Brethren, while we sojourn here	356
Brief life is here our portion	558
Brightly gleams our banner	343
By cool Siloam's shady rill	493
By faith in Christ I walk with God	419
Call Jehovah thy salvation	365
Call them in! — the poor, the wretched	479
Calm on the listening ear of night	141
Can sinners hope for heaven	226
Cast thy bread upon the waters	463
Cast thy burden on the Lord	457
Children of the heavenly King	359
Christ, above all glory seated!	181
Christ, of all my hopes the Ground	390
Christ, whose glory fills the skies	3
Christian, work for Jesus	417
Come, blessed Spirit! source of light!	202
Come, Holy Ghost! in love	208
Come, Holy Ghost, my soul inspire	215
Come, Holy Spirit, come!	216
Come, Holy Spirit, heavenly Dove!	218
Come, Jesus, Redeemer, abide thou	385
Come, let us join our cheerful songs	182
Come, let us sing the song of songs	172
Come, Lord, and tarry not!	197
Come, my soul, thy suit prepare	47
Come, O Creator Spirit blest!	201
Come, oh, come with thy broken heart	285
Come, pure hearts, in sweetest	24
Come, sacred Spirit, from above	203
Come, sound his praise abroad	23
Come, Spirit, source of light	213
Come, thou almighty King	129
Come, thou Desire of all thy saints	34
Come, thou Fount of every blessing	370
Come, thou long-expected Jesus	190
Come, thou, oh, come	428
Come, thou soul-transforming Spirit	58
Come, thou who dost the soul endue	242
Come to Calvary's holy mountain	248
Come, we who love the Lord	27
Come, ye disconsolate, where'er ye	247
Come, ye thankful people, come	574
Come, ye that know and fear the Lord	131
Cross, reproach, and tribulation!	364
Crown his head with endless blessing	180
Daily, daily sing the praises	568
Day by day the manna fell	432
Day is dying in the West	88
Dear Refuge of my weary soul	405
Dear Saviour! we are thine	485
Delay not, delay not; O sinner, draw	256
Depth of mercy! — can there be	294
Did Christ o'er sinners weep	253
Dismiss me not thy service, Lord	446
Dismiss us with thy blessing, Lord!	72
Do not I love thee, O my Lord?	393
Earth has nothing sweet or fair	389
Eternal Light! eternal Light!	240
Eternal Spirit, we confess	200
Everlasting arms of love	358
Faith adds new charms to earthly	424
Far from the world, O Lord, I flee	37
Father, hear the prayer we offer!	462
Father! how wide thy glory shines!	128
Father, in high heaven dwelling	25
Father! in thy mysterious presence	83
Father of mercies! in thy word	106
Father of mercies! send thy grace	466
Father! whate'er of earthly bliss	214
Fierce raged the tempest o'er the deep	349
For a season called to part	89
For ever with the Lord!	540
For the beauty of the earth	429
For the mercies of the day	85
For what shall I praise thee, my God	386
Fountain of grace, rich, full, and free	352
Friend of sinners! Lord of glory!	415
From all that dwell below the skies	19
From every stormy wind that blows	48
From Greenland's icy mountains	523

INDEX OF FIRST LINES.

	HYMN
From Sinai's cloud of darkness	440
From the cross uplifted high	272
From the table now retiring	512
Gently, Lord, oh, gently lead us	92
Give to the winds thy fears	330
Glorious things of thee are spoken	192
Glory be to God the Father	56
Glory to God! whose witness-train	325
Glory to thee, my God, this night	68
Go, labor on, while it is day	470
God Almighty and All-seeing!	55
God be with you till we meet again	102
God is in his holy temple	59
God loved the world of sinners lost	233
God moves in a mysterious way	116
God of our salvation! hear us	96
God with us! oh, glorious name!	146
Grace! 't is a charming sound!	435
Gracious Saviour, thus before thee	101
Gracious Spirit, Holy Ghost	210
Gracious Spirit, Love divine!	207
Great God! how infinite art thou!	133
Great God, now condescend	496
Great God, what do I see and hear!	551
Great God, when I approach thy throne	237
Great Sun of Righteousness, arise!	111
Guide me, O thou great Jehovah	304
Hail the night, all hail the morn	145
Hail to the brightness of Zion's glad	530
Hail to the Lord's anointed	528
Hallelujah! best and sweetest	534
Hark, hark, my soul! angelic songs are	447
Hark! ten thousand harps and voices	177
Hark! the herald angels sing	142
Hark! the song of jubilee	196
Hark! the sound of holy voices	567
Hark! the voice of Jesus calling	483
Hasten, Lord! the glorious time	549
He has come! the Christ of God	143
He is coming, he is coming	189
He leadeth me! oh, blessed thought	442
He lives! the great Redeemer lives!	174
He that goeth forth with weeping	465
Heal me, O my Saviour, heal	279
Hear my prayer, O heavenly Father	98
Hear what God the Lord hath spoken	193
Heavenly Father, grant thy blessing	99
Here I can firmly rest	436

	HYMN
Holy Ghost, the Infinite!	211
Holy Ghost! with light divine	204
Holy, holy, holy Lord God of	63
Holy, holy, holy Lord, in the	434
Holy, holy, holy, Lord God Almighty	2
Holy Spirit! gently come	205
Holy Spirit, in my breast	206
How beauteous on the mountains	524
How beauteous were the marks divine	153
How blest the righteous when he dies	545
How charming is the place	29
How condescending and how kind	164
How did my heart rejoice to hear	5
How firm a foundation, ye saints of the	335
How gentle God's commands!	73
How helpless guilty nature lies	222
How pleasant, how divinely fair	8
How precious is the book divine	105
How sad our state by nature is!	221
How shall the young secure their	104
How sweet and awful is the place	504
How sweet, how heavenly is the sight	488
How sweet the name of Jesus sounds	397
How sweetly flowed the gospel sound	152
I am coming to the cross	161
I am trusting thee, Lord Jesus	431
I ask not now for gold to gild	268
I cannot tell if short or long	453
I feed by faith on Christ; my bread	502
I have entered the valley of blessing	306
I hear a sweet voice ringing clear	445
I hear thy welcome voice	282
I heard the voice of Jesus say	148
I know no life divided	407
I lay my sins on Jesus	243
I left it all with Jesus long ago	430
I lift my heart to thee	416
I love thy kingdom, Lord!	474
I love to steal awhile away	31
I love to tell the story	276
I'll praise my Maker with my breath	21
I'm kneeling, Lord, at mercy's gate	283
I'm not ashamed to own my Lord	328
I need thee every hour	298
I need thee, precious Jesus	244
I saw One hanging on a tree	102
I sing the almighty power of God	126
I will sing for Jesus	381
If human kindness meets return	510

INDEX OF FIRST LINES.

First Line	HYMN
If you cannot on the ocean	484
In heavenly love abiding	347
In the cross of Christ I glory	168
In the dark and cloudy day	456
In the hour of trial	319
In the house of my Father above	570
In thy name, O Lord! assembling	57
It came upon the midnight clear	139
It is not death to die	542
Jerusalem! my happy home!	546
Jerusalem, the glorious!	559
Jerusalem, the golden	557
Jesus,— and didst thou leave the sky	238
Jesus! and shall it ever be	401
Jesus, at whose supreme command	509
Jesus calls us, o'er the tumult	481
Jesus, heed me, lost and dying	258
Jesus! I love thy charming name	396
Jesus, I my cross have taken	366
Jesus, keep me near the cross	280
Jesus, Lord of life and glory	288
Jesus! lover of my soul	310
Jesus, Master, whose I am	274
Jesus, my All, to heaven is gone	175
Jesus, my Saviour! look on me	301
Jesus! name of wondrous love!	387
"Jesus only!" In the shadow	375
Jesus only, when the morning	378
Jesus, Saviour, pilot me	287
Jesus shall reign where'er the sun	516
Jesus, Shepherd of the sheep	259
Jesus, still lead on	361
Jesus, the very thought of thee	398
Jesus, these eyes have never seen	400
Jesus, thou art the sinner's Friend	505
Jesus, thou Joy of loving hearts	402
Jesus! thy love shall we forget	157
Jesus, who knows full well	52
Jesus, who on Calvary's mountain	368
Jesus, who on his glorious throne	404
Joy to the world; the Lord is come!	144
Just as I am, without one plea	269
Keep silence, all created things!	115
Lead, kindly Light! amid the	454
Let me but hear my Saviour say	355
Let saints below in concert sing	489
Let thy wondrous way be known	209
Let Zion and her sons rejoice	513
Light of those whose dreary dwelling	191
Light, that from the dark abyss	305
Like sheep we went astray	227
Like the eagle, upward, onward	459
Look from thy sphere of endless day	522
Look to Jesus! till reviving	371
Look, ye saints, the sight is glorious	184
Lord, as to thy dear cross we flee	156
Lord, bid thy light arise	212
Lord, dismiss us with thy blessing Bid	94
Lord, dismiss us with thy blessing Fill	95
Lord, how mysterious are thy ways!	135
Lord, I am come! thy promise is my	263
Lord! I cannot let thee go	61
Lord, I hear of showers of blessing	299
Lord! in love and mercy save us	100
Lord! in the morning thou shalt hear	4
Lord, in this thy mercy's day	250
Lord, it belongs not to my care	293
Lord, lead the way the Saviour went	467
Lord, my weak thought in vain would	136
Lord of all being; throned afar	134
Lord of glory! thou hast bought us	464
Lord of mercy and of might	41
Lord, thy word abideth	114
Lord, we come before thee now	45
Lord! when we bend before thy throne	35
Lord! while for all mankind we pray	576
Love divine, all love excelling	363
Majestic sweetness sits enthroned	150
Master, speak! thy servant heareth	374
May the grace of Christ our Saviour	93
Mighty God! while angels bless thee	179
Mine eyes and my desire	332
More love to thee, O Christ	316
My country! 't is of thee	575
My days are gliding swiftly by	538
My dear Redeemer, and my Lord	151
My faith looks up to thee	399
My God, how endless is thy love!	69
My God, how wonderful thou art	124
My God, is any hour so sweet	39
My God, my Father! while I stray	455
My God! permit my tongue	30
My hope is built on nothing less	448
My Jesus, as thou wilt!	450
My life flows on in endless song	341
My Saviour! my almighty Friend	305

16 P

INDEX OF FIRST LINES.

	HYMN
My Shepherd will supply my need	127
My soul, be on thy guard	342
My soul complete in Jesus stands!	354
My soul, weigh not thy life	331
My spirit on thy care	334
Nearer, ever nearer	322
Nearer, my God, to thee	315
Nearer, O God, to thee!	313
New every morning is the love	9
None but Christ; his merit hides me	377
Not all the blood of beasts	223
Not all the outward forms on earth	220
Not what these hands have done	228
Not with our mortal eyes	412
Now begin the heavenly theme	360
Now I have found a friend	312
Now I know the great Redeemer	380
Now is the accepted time	251
Now may he who from the dead	86
Now to the Lord, who makes us know	171
Now to the power of God supreme	170
O Christ, he is the fountain	554
O Christ! our King, Creator, Lord!	173
O, could I find from day to day	297
O, could I speak the matchless worth	159
O day of rest and gladness	13
O eyes that are weary, and hearts that	336
O, fair the gleams of glory	560
O, for a closer walk with God	289
O, for a heart to praise my God	323
O, for a thousand tongues to sing	324
O, for that tenderness of heart	291
O, for the happy hour	536
O, for the peace which floweth like a	410
O, gift of gifts! oh, grace of faith!	422
O, give thanks to him who made	64
O God of Bethel, by whose hand	491
O God, the Rock of Ages	119
O God, thy power is wonderful	125
O God! we praise thee, and confess	130
O Holy Saviour! Friend unseen	266
O, how I love thy holy law!	107
O, if my soul were formed for woe	166
O Jesus! bruised and wounded more	501
O Jesus Christ the righteous! live in	262
O Jesus, "Man of Sorrows"	170
O Jesus, sweet the tears I shed	163
O Jesus, thou art standing	264

	HYMN
O Lamb of God! still keep me	441
O Lord, how full of sweet content	420
O Lord, how happy we should be	449
O Lord, thy work revive	535
O Lord, who by thy presence hast	81
O love, that wilt not let me go	383
O mother dear, Jerusalem	565
O, not my own these verdant hills	403
O, not to fill the mouth of fame	290
O one with God the Father	408
O sacred Head, now wounded	160
O Saviour, where shall guilty man	241
O, see how Jesus trusts himself	149
O, sometimes the shadows are deep	303
O, sweetly breathe the lyres above	503
O, that the Lord's salvation	526
O, that the Lord would guide my ways	108
O, there will be mourning	550
O, this soul, how dark and blind!	309
O thou, the contrite sinner's Friend	267
O thou, whose tender mercy bears	275
O, turn ye, oh, turn ye, for why will ye	255
O, what stupendous mercy shines	471
O, where are kings and empires now	490
O, where shall rest be found	224
O'er the gloomy hills of darkness	531
On Jordan's rugged banks I stand	561
On the mountain's top appearing	533
Once in royal David's city	137
Once more, before we part	76
One cup of healing oil and wine	472
One sweetly solemn thought	541
One there is above all others	138
Onward, Christian soldiers	344
Onward, Christian, though the region	460
Our Father! through the coming year	578
Our God, our help in ages past	123
Our heavenly Father calls	50
Our life is hid with Christ	198
Pass me not, O gentle Saviour	286
Peace, perfect peace, in this dark	400
Praise God, from whom all blessings	17
Praise, Lord, for thee in Zion waits	20
Praise our glorious King and Lord	195
Praise the God of our salvation	87
Prayer is the breath of God in man	36
Prayer is the soul's sincere desire	38
Precious, precious blood of Jesus	234
Prepare us, Lord, to view thy cross	506
Purer yet, and purer	320

INDEX OF FIRST LINES.

First line	HYMN
Quiet, Lord, my froward heart	427
Rejoice, rejoice, believers	187
Return, O wanderer, to thy home	245
Rise, my soul, and stretch thy wings	566
Rise, ye children of salvation	373
Rock of Ages, cleft for me!	498
Roll on, thou mighty ocean	527
Safely through another week	11
Saints of God! the dawn is brightening	532
Saviour, again to thy dear name	82
Saviour and Lord of all	307
Saviour, blessed Saviour	321
Saviour, breathe an evening blessing	91
Saviour! I follow on	317
Saviour King, in hallowed union	404
Saviour, more than life to me	384
Saviour, send a blessing to us	54
Saviour! teach me, day by day	391
Saviour, thy dying love	318
Saviour, visit thy plantation!	529
Saviour! who thy flock art feeding	495
Scorn not the slightest word or deed	468
See Israel's gentle Shepherd stands	492
See, the Conquerer mounts in triumph!	178
Servant of God, well done!	543
Shadow of a Mighty Rock	433
Shepherd! with thy tenderest love	426
Shine, mighty God! on Zion shine	515
Show pity, Lord! O Lord! forgive	271
Since Jesus is my friend	411
Since thy Father's arm sustains thee	452
Sing we the song of those who stand	28
Sinners, turn, why will ye die?	246
So let our lips and lives express	421
Softly now the light of day	84
Sometimes a light surprises	346
Son of God! to thee I cry	499
Soul, then know thy full salvation	367
Sovereign of worlds! display thy	517
Sow in the morn thy seed	475
Spirit blest, who art adored	219
Spirit of the Only Wise	217
Stand up, my soul, shake off thy fears	350
Stand up! — stand up for Jesus	348
Stealing from the world away	43
Still, still with thee, my God	74
Sun of my soul! thou Saviour dear	66
Sweet hour of prayer! sweet hour of	62

First line	HYMN
Sweet is the work, my God, my King!	7
Sweet the moments, rich in blessing	511
Sweet the time, exceeding sweet!	44
Sweet was the time when first I felt	295
Sweeter sounds than music knows	388
Swift to its close ebbs out life's little	80
Take me, O my Father, take me!	260
Take my heart, O Father! take it	482
Take my life, and let it be	308
Tell me, my Saviour!	302
The day is past and gone	78
The day, O Lord, is spent	75
The heavens declare his glory	113
The heavens declare thy glory, Lord!	110
The King of love my Shepherd is	382
The Lord is my Shepherd, no want	337
The Lord my Shepherd is	413
The Lord, our God, is full of might	118
The marriage feast is ready	188
The mistakes of my life are many	300
The morning light is breaking	525
The peace which God alone reveals	70
The sands of time are sinking	553
The Saviour kindly calls	497
The Saviour! oh, what endless charms	147
The Spirit breathes upon the word	103
The Spirit in our hearts	252
The swift declining day	77
The voice of free grace cries	249
Thee we adore, eternal Name!	577
There are lonely hearts to cherish	478
There is a fountain filled with blood	236
There is a green hill far away	167
There is a happy land	556
There is a land of pure delight	563
There is an eye that never sleeps	32
There is an hour of peaceful rest	555
There were ninety and nine that safely	284
There's a wideness in God's mercy	132
They who seek the throne of grace	46
Thine earthly Sabbaths, Lord, we love	10
This is not my place of resting	569
This is the day the Lord hath made	14
Thou art the Way: to thee alone	155
Thou, from whom we never part	90
Thou very present Aid	439
Though faint, yet pursuing, we go on	338
Though now the nations sit beneath	518
Three in One, and One in Three	40

INDEX OF FIRST LINES.

	HYMN		HYMN
Through good report, and evil, Lord	362	What shall I render to my God	121
Through the love of God our Saviour	345	When all thy mercies, O my God!	122
Through the night of doubt and	444	When I can read my title clear	357
Through the yesterday of ages	372	When I survey the wondrous cross	169
Thus far the Lord has led me on	71	When Jesus dwelt in mortal clay	473
Thy way, not mine, O Lord	451	When, like a stranger on our sphere	154
Till He come: oh, let the words	500	When morning gilds the skies	1
'T is by the faith of joys to come	418	When my last hour is close at hand	552
'T is my happiness below	458	When sins and fears, prevailing, rise	353
To God the Father, God the Son	18	When thou, my righteous Judge, shalt	185
To thy pastures fair and large	42	Where high the heavenly temple	49
Together with these symbols, Lord	507	Wherever two or three may meet	33
Traveling to the better land	340	While shepherds watched their flocks	140
Triumphant Zion, lift thy head	520	While thee I seek, protecting Power!	120
		While we lowly bow before thee	53
Upward where the stars are burning	26	While with ceaseless course, the sun	573
		Who are these in bright array	571
Vainly, through night's weary hours	461	Who are these like stars appearing	562
		Why do we mourn departing friends	539
Walk in the light! so shalt thou know	423	Why is thy faith, O child of God, so	369
Walking with thee, my God	314	Why on the bending willows hung	521
Watchman, tell us of the night	194	Why should we start and fear to die?	544
We are but strangers here	311	Why will ye waste on trifling cares	278
We are watching, we are waiting	537	With broken heart and contrite sigh	270
We come, O Lord, before thy throne	579	Work, for the night is coming	480
We give thee but thine own	477	Work while it is to-day!	476
We may not climb the heavenly steeps	158		
We stand in deep repentance	265	Ye saints, your music bring	282
We would see Jesus — for the shadows	409	Yes, he knows the way is dreary	376
Weary of earth, and laden with my sin	261	Yet there is room! The Lamb's bright	281
Welcome, days of solemn meeting	60	Your harps, ye trembling saints	329
Welcome, sweet day of rest	12		
What can I give to Jesus	414	Zion! awake, thy strength renew	519
What cheering words are these	437